ARE
4.0

Programming,
Planning & Practice

Paul Speiregen & Lester Wertheimer
with Contributing Editors Beatriz de Paz & Laura Serebin

KAPLAN) AEC EDUCATION

This publication is designed to provide accurate and authoritative information in regard to the subject matter covered. It is sold with the understanding that the publisher is not engaged in rendering legal, accounting, or other professional service. If legal advice or other expert assistance is required, the services of a competent professional person should be sought.

President: Mehul Patel
Vice President & General Manager: David Dufresne
Vice President of Product Development and Publishing: Evan M. Butterfield
Editorial Project Manager: Jason Mitchell
Director of Production: Daniel Frey
Production Editor: Caitlin Ostrow
Production Artist: Cepheus Edmondson
Creative Director: Lucy Jenkins
Senior Product Manager: Brian O'Connor

Published by Kaplan AEC Education
30 South Wacker Drive, Suite 2500
Chicago, IL 60606-7481
(312) 836-4400
www.kaplanaecarchitecture.com

Printed in the United States of America.

08   09   10   10 9 8 7 6 5 4 3 2

ISBN-13: 978-1-4277-7039-4

ISBN-10:   1-4277-7039-5

CONTENTS

WELCOME

Thank you for choosing Kaplan AEC Education for your ARE study needs. We offer updates annually to keep abreast of code and exam changes and to address any errors discovered since the previous update was published. We wish you the best of luck in your pursuit of licensure.

ARE OVERVIEW

Since the State of Illinois first pioneered the practice of licensing architects in 1897, architectural licensing has been increasingly adopted as a means to protect the public health, safety, and welfare. Today, all U.S. states and Canadian provinces require licensing for individuals practicing architecture. Licensing requirements vary by jurisdiction; however, the minimum requirements are uniform and in all cases include passing the Architect Registration Exam (ARE). This makes the ARE a required rite of passage for all those entering the profession, and you should be congratulated on undertaking this challenging endeavor.

Developed by the National Council of Architectural Registration Boards (NCARB), the ARE is the only exam by which architecture candidates can become registered in the United States or Canada. The ARE assesses candidates' knowledge, skills, and abilities in seven different areas of professional practice, including a candidate's competency in decision making and knowledge of various areas of the profession. The exam also tests competence in fulfilling an architect's responsibilities and in coordinating the activities of others while working with a team of design and construction specialists. In all jurisdictions, candidates must pass the seven divisions of the exam to become registered.

The ARE is designed and prepared by architects, making it a practice-based exam. It is generally not a test of academic knowledge, but rather a means to test decision-making ability as it relates to the responsibilities of the architectural profession. For example, the exam does not expect candidates to memorize specific details of the building code, but requires them to understand a model code's general requirements, scope, and purpose, and to know the architect's responsibilities related to that code. As such, there is no substitute for a well-rounded internship to help prepare for the ARE.

4.0 Exam Format

The seven ARE 4.0 divisions are outlined in the table below.

DIVISION	QUESTIONS	VIGNETTES
Building Design & Construction Systems	85	Accessibility/ Ramp Roof Plan Stair Design
Building Systems	95	Mechanical & Electrical Plan
Construction Documents & Services	100	Building Section
Programming, Planning & Practice	85	Site Zoning
Schematic Design	-	Building Layout Interior Layout
Site Planning & Design	65	Site Design Site Grading
Structural Systems	125	Structural Layout

The exam presents multiple-choice questions individually. Candidates may answer questions, skip questions, or mark questions for further review. Candidates may also move backward or forward within the exam using simple on-

ARCHITECTURAL HISTORY

Questions pertaining to the history of architecture appear throughout the ARE divisions. The prominence of historical questions will vary not only by division but also within different versions of the exam for each division. In general, however, history tends to be lightly tested, with approximately three to seven history questions per division, depending upon the total number of questions within the division. One aspect common to all the divisions is that whatever history questions are presented will be related to that division's subject matter. For example, a question regarding Chicago's John Hancock Center and the purpose of its unique exterior cross bracing may appear on the Structural Systems exam.

Though it is difficult to predict how essential your knowledge of architectural history will be to passing any of the multiple-choice divisions, it is recommended that you refer to a primer in this field—such as Kaplan's *Architectural History*—before taking each exam, and that you keep an eye out for topics relevant to the division for which you are studying. It is always better to be overprepared than taken by surprise at the testing center.

screen icons. The vignettes require candidates to create a graphic solution according to program and code requirements.

Actual appointment times for taking the exam are slightly longer than the actual exam time, allowing candidates to check in and out of the testing center. All ARE candidates are encouraged to review NCARB's *ARE Guidelines* for further detail about the exam format. These guidelines are available via free download at NCARB's Web site (*www.ncarb.org*).

Exam Format

It is important for exam candidates to familiarize themselves not only with exam content, but also with question format. Familiarity with the basic question types found in the ARE will reduce confusion, save time, and help you pass the exam. The ARE contains three basic question types.

The first and most common type is a straightforward multiple-choice question followed by four choices (A, B, C, and D). Candidates are

expected to select the correct answer. This type of question is shown in the following example.

> Which of the following cities is the capital of the United States?
>
> **A.** New York
>
> **B. Washington, DC**
>
> **C.** Chicago
>
> **D.** Los Angeles

The second type of question is a negatively worded question. In questions such as this, the negative wording is usually highlighted using all caps, as shown below.

> Which of the following cities is NOT located on the west coast of the United States?
>
> **A.** Los Angeles
>
> **B.** San Diego
>
> **C.** San Francisco
>
> **D. New York**

THE EXAM TRANSITION

ARE 3.1

In November 2005 NCARB released *ARE Guidelines* Version 3.1, which outlines changes to the exam effective February 2006. These guidelines primarily detailed changes for the Site Planning division, combining the site design and site parking vignettes as well as the site zoning and site analysis vignettes. For more details about these changes, please refer to Kaplan's study guides for the graphic divisions.

The guidelines mean less to those preparing for multiple-choice divisions. Noteworthy points are outlined below.

- All division statements and content area descriptions were unchanged for the multiple-choice divisions.

- The number of questions and time limits for all exams were unchanged.

- The list of codes and standards candidates should familiarize themselves with was reduced to those of the International Code Council (ICC), the National Fire Protection Association (NFPA), and the National Research Council of Canada.

- A statics title has been removed from the reference list for General Structures.

ARE 4.0

In the spring of 2007, NCARB unveiled ARE 4.0, available as of July 2008. According to NCARB, the 4.0 version of the exam will be more subject-oriented than 3.1, and is intended to better assess a candidate's ability to approach projects independently. The format combines the multiple-choice and graphic portions of different divisions, reducing the number of divisions from nine to seven.

The transition will be gradual, with a one-year overlap during which both ARE 3.1 and ARE 4.0 will be administered. Provided you pass at least one ARE 3.1 division prior to May 2008, you can continue to take ARE 3.1 divisions until July 2009.

If you have not passed all ARE 3.1 divisions by June 2009, you will be transitioned to the ARE 4.0 format. You will be given credit for ARE 4.0 divisions according to which 3.1 divisions you have passed. Visit *www. kaplanaecarchitecture.com* for more details.

In order to avoid being retested on subjects you have already passed, you should develop a strategy for which divisions you take in which order. Here are some key points to keep in mind:

- Building Technology is a key division in the transition; its vignettes will be dispersed across four ARE 4.0 divisions. Be sure to pass Building Technology if you have passed and want credit for any of the following ARE 3.1 divisions: Building Design/Materials & Methods; Construction Documents & Services; General Structures; Lateral Forces; or Mechanical & Electrical Systems.

- Pre-Design and Site Planning content will be shuffled in ARE 4.0: If you pass one, pass the other.

- General Structures, Lateral Forces, and the Structural Layout vignette from Building Technology are being merged into the Structural Systems division. If you pass any of these and want to avoid being retested on material you have already seen, pass all three.

The third type of question is a combination question. In a combination question, more than one choice may be correct; candidates must select from combinations of potentially correct choices. An example of a combination question is shown below.

> Which of the following cities are located within the United States?
>
> **I.** New York
> **II.** Toronto
> **III.** Montreal
> **IV.** Los Angeles
> **A.** I only
> **B.** I and II
> **C.** II and III
> **D. I and IV**

The single most important thing candidates can do to prepare themselves for the vignettes is to learn to proficiently navigate NCARB's graphic software. Practice software can be downloaded free of charge from their Web site. Candidates should download it and become thoroughly familiar with its use.

Recommendations on Exam Division Order

NCARB allows candidates to choose the order in which they take the exams, and the choice is an important one. While only you know what works best for you, the following are some general considerations that many have found to be beneficial:

1. The Building Design & Construction Systems and Programming, Planning & Practice divisions are perhaps the broadest of all the divisions. Although this can make them among the most intimidating, taking these divisions early in the process will give a candidate a broad base of knowledge and may prove helpful in preparing for subsequent divisions. An alternative to this approach is to take these two divisions last, since you will already be familiar with much of their content. This latter approach likely is most beneficial when you take the exam divisions in fairly rapid succession so that details learned while studying for earlier divisions will still be fresh in your mind.

2. The Construction Documents & Services exam covers a broad range of subjects, dealing primarily with the architect's role and responsibilities within the building design and construction team. Because these subjects serve as one of the core foundations of the ARE, it may be advisable to take this division early in the process, as knowledge gained preparing for this exam can help in subsequent divisions.

3. Take exams that particularly concern you early in the process. NCARB rules prohibit retaking an exam for six months. Therefore, failing an exam early in the process will allow the candidate to use the waiting period to prepare for and take other exams.

EXAM PREPARATION

Overview

There is little argument that preparation is key to passing the ARE. With this in mind, Kaplan has developed a complete learning system for each exam division, including study guides, question-and-answer handbooks, mock exams, and flash cards. The study guides offer a condensed course of study and will best prepare you for the exam when utilized along with the other tools in the learning system. The system is designed to provide you with the general background necessary to pass the exam and to provide an indication of specific content areas that demand additional attention.

In addition to the Kaplan learning system, materials from industry-standard documents may prove useful for the various divisions. Several of these sources are noted in the "Supplementary Study Materials" section below.

Understanding the Exam

The Programming, Planning & Practice exam is among the most broad of all the ARE divisions. The exam content spans a wide range of topics including city planning, programming, space needs, land development and site planning, codes, financing, geology and soils zoning, project management, interaction among the design team, project delivery methods, practice of architecture, budgeting and cost estimating, accessibility, and building layout. Further, environmental, social, and economic issues as well as sustainability are all subject matters for which the candidate should prepare.

Although the exam content is diverse, the material is all related to the pre-design process and many of the aforementioned topics overlap. Since many of the subjects covered span other exam divisions, this exam is widely considered one of the more difficult for which to prepare. However, the exam tends to focus on general principles of the above issues and avoids detailed calculations and data.

For the Site Zoning vignette, remember not to disturb existing trees, to use the sketch lines, and to align driveways properly. Also be sure to use the zoom, full screen cursor, and background grid to produce more accurate solutions.

Preparation Basics

The first step in preparation should be a review of the exam specifications and reference materials published by NCARB. These statements are available for each of the seven ARE divisions to serve as a guide for preparing for the exam. Download these statements and familiarize yourself with their content. This will help you focus your attention on the subjects on which the exam focuses.

Prior CAD knowledge is not necessary to sucessfully complete vignettes. In fact, it's important for candidates familiar with CAD to realize they will experience significant differences between CAD and the drawing tools used on the exam.

Though no two people will have exactly the same ARE experience, the following are recommended best practices to adopt in your studies and should serve as a guide.

Set aside scheduled study time.
Establish a routine and adopt study strategies that reflect your strengths and mirror your approach in other successful academic pursuits. Most importantly, set aside a definite amount of study time each week, just as if you were taking a lecture course, and carefully read all of the material.

Take—and retake—quizzes.
After studying each lesson in the study guide, take the quiz found at its conclusion. The quiz questions are intended to be straightforward and objective. Answers and explanations can be found at the back of the book. If you answer a question incorrectly, see if you can determine why the correct answer is correct before reading the explanation. Retake the quiz until you answer every question correctly and understand why the correct answers are correct.

Identify areas for improvement.
The quizzes allow you the opportunity to pinpoint areas where you need improvement. Reread and take note of the sections that cover

these areas and seek additional information from other sources. Use the question-and-answer handbook and online test bank as a final tune-up for the exam.

Take the final exam.

A final exam designed to simulate the ARE follows the last lesson of each study guide. Answers and explanations can be found on the pages following the exam. As with the lesson quizzes, retake the final exam until you answer every question correctly and understand why the correct answers are correct.

Use the flash cards.

If you've purchased the flash cards, go through them once and set aside any terms you know at first glance. Take the rest to work, reviewing them on the train, over lunch, or before bed. Remove cards as you become familiar with their terms until you know all the terms. Review all the cards a final time before taking the exam.

Practice using the NCARB software.

Work through the practice vignettes contained within the NCARB software. You should work through each vignette repeatedly until you can solve it easily. As your skills develop, track how long it takes to work through a solution for each vignette.

Supplementary Study Materials

In addition to the Kaplan learning system, materials from industry-standard sources may prove useful in your studies. Candidates should consult the list of exam references in the NCARB guidelines for the council's recommendations and pay particular attention to the following publications, which are essential to successfully completing this exam:

- International Code Council (ICC) *International Building Code*
- *Standard on Accessible and Usable Buildings and Facilities* (ICC/ANSI A117.1-98)
- National Fire Protection Association *Life Safety Code* (NFPA 101)
- American Institute of Architects B141-1997 *Standard Form of Agreement Between Owner and Architect*
- American Institute of Architects A201-1997 *General Conditions of the Contract for Construction*

Test-Taking Advice

Preparation for the exam should include a review of successful test-taking procedures—especially for those who have been out of the classroom for some time. Following is advice to aid in your success.

Pace yourself.

Each division allows candidates at least one minute per question. You should be able to comfortably read and reread each question and fully understand what is being asked before answering. Each vignette allows candidates ample time to complete a solution within the time allotted.

Read carefully.

Begin each question by reading it carefully and fully reviewing the choices, eliminating those that are obviously incorrect. Interpret language literally, and keep an eye out for negatively worded questions. With vignettes, carefully review instructions and requirements. Quickly make a list of program and code requirements to check your work against as you proceed through the vignette.

Guess.

All unanswered questions are considered incorrect, so answer every question. If you are unsure of the correct answer, select your best guess and/or mark the question for later review. If you continue to be unsure of the answer after returning the question a second time, it is usually best to stick with your first guess.

Review difficult questions.

The exam allows candidates to review and change answers within the time limit. Utilize this feature to mark troubling questions for review upon completing the rest of the exam.

Reference material.

Some divisions include reference materials accessible through an on-screen icon. These materials include formulas and other reference content that may prove helpful when answering questions in these divisions. Note that candidates may *not* bring reference material with them to the testing center.

Best answer questions.

Many candidates fall victim to questions seeking the "best" answer. In these cases, it may appear at first glance as though several choices are correct. Remember the importance of reviewing the question carefully and interpreting the language literally. Consider the following example.

> Which of these cities is located on the east coast of the United States?
>
> **A.** Boston
>
> **B.** Philadelphia
>
> **C.** Washington, DC
>
> **D.** Atlanta

At first glance, it may appear that all of the cities could be correct answers. However, if you interpret the question literally, you'll identify the critical phrase as "on the east coast."

Although each of the cities listed is arguably an "eastern" city, only Boston sits on the Atlantic coast. All the other choices are located in the eastern part of the country, but are not coastal cities.

Style doesn't count.

Vignettes are graded on their conformance with program requirements and instructions. Don't waste time creating aesthetically pleasing solutions and adding unnecessary design elements.

ACKNOWLEDGMENTS

This course was written by Paul D. Spreiregen, FAIA. Mr. Spreiregen is an architect, planner, teacher, lecturer, and author who began his career as a Fulbright scholar after graduating from the MIT School of Architecture. He is renowned as an urban designer both in the United States and abroad and is currently in private practice in Washington, DC.

Consulting editor Bea DePaz received her MArch from Tulane University. She currently lives and practices in Orlando, Florida, and specializes in the design of entertainment facilities including zoological parks.

Content discussing the Site Zoning vignette was written and illustrated by Lester Wertheimer, FAIA. Mr. Wertheimer is a licensed architect in private practice in Los Angeles. He has written and lectured on the design aspects of the ARE for many years.

Portions of this edition were revised by Bob J. Wise, AIA. Bob has led ARE review seminars for several years, and is a former member of NCARB's exam writing and scoring committees. He also led ARE review sessions for the Site Planning division at both the 2006 and 2007 AIA national conventions.

This introduction was written by John F. Hardt, AIA. Mr. Hardt is vice president and senior project architect with Karlsberger, an architecture, planning, and design firm based in Columbus, Ohio. He is a graduate of Ohio State University (MArch).

ABOUT KAPLAN

Thank you for choosing Kaplan AEC Education as your source for ARE preparation materials. Whether helping future professors prepare for the GRE or providing tomorrow's doctors the tools they need to pass the MCAT, Kaplan possesses more than 50 years of experience as a global leader in exam prep and educational publishing. It is that experience and history that Kaplan brings to the world of architectural education, pairing unparalleled resources with acknowledged experts in ARE content areas to bring you the very best in licensure study materials.

Only Kaplan AEC offers a complete catalog of individual products and integrated learning systems to help you pass all seven divisions of the ARE. Kaplan's ARE materials include study guides, mock exams, question-and-answer handbooks, video workshops, and flash cards. Products may be purchased individually or in division-specific learning systems to suit your needs. These systems are designed to help you better focus on essential information for each division, provide flexibility in how you study, and save you money.

To order, please visit *www.KaplanAEC.com* or call (800) 420-1429.

Part I

Programming and Analysis

ARCHITECTURAL DESIGN

The Nature of Architectural Design
Considerations in Architectural Design

THE NATURE OF ARCHITECTURAL DESIGN

Architecture is the art and science of designing and constructing buildings. It is the creative process of conceiving and developing physical forms to accommodate human needs and purposes. Architectural forms, while composed of material elements, establish spaces in which human activities take place.

The process of architectural design is extremely complex and demands considerable experience if one is to do it well. It is an exercise in synthesis, of putting together a complex array of disparate parts to form a unified, interdependent composition.

The process of architectural design also requires the collaboration of specialists. No one person can possibly know all that must be known in order to design a building. Thus, one of the chief functions of an architect is to coordinate a team of specialists who, together, create a design. Nevertheless, it is still necessary to have a central design concept: an idea

for a physical design solution which addresses the design problem fully and correctly. It also serves to unite all the separate skills of the contributing specialists around a central theme.

Design is the process of giving form to an idea. It results in a purposeful, physical creation that serves a practical need. Design involves setting forth objectives, analyzing information, planning, and conceiving appropriate spaces and forms. Inspiration, talent, and intuition are invaluable to the process of design. But it is a *process* that occurs, not a mystical activity. Thus, as a process, it can be analyzed and comprehended.

By understanding the specific functional requirements, and with properly developed skills and sufficient experience, one should be able to solve any design problem. Obviously, the degree of skill needed for a simple design exercise is far less than for a highly complex one: a small factory is easier to design than a large hospital.

The difference between the ability to design and the ability to design well is the distinction that elevates mere construction to architecture. When design is particularly well done, we may say that the rare element of art has transcended the rational design solution. In architecture, as in every other kind of design, artful solutions are the goal to be sought.

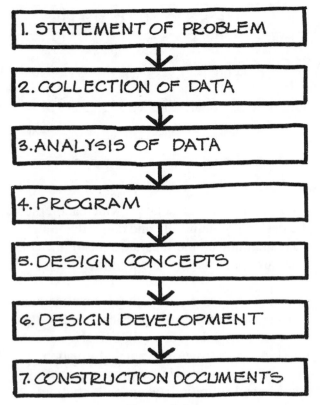

Figure 1.1

The process of design involves the understanding of a functional problem which requires a physical solution. Without an understanding of the problem, no satisfactory solution is ever possible. The more we know about a problem the better our design solutions should be. Functional problems are very complex; each element of a problem may itself be an intricate problem, challenging the designer's ability to deal with it. Thus, the designer must seek expert technical advice, probably in several areas, and assimilate this advice into his or her design solution.

Problems have been increasing in number and complexity, and have also been changing at a rapid pace. Social, cultural, and industrial patterns are in almost constant transition. The designer is constantly challenged to understand

a problem clearly, in order to find an appropriate solution.

During certain architectural periods, designs became so formularized that they constituted a "style." As long as the style answered all the needs of the design problem, it was useful. But when needs changed, those styles became obsolete or even burdensome.

It is more useful in architecture to rely on method than on style. A methodical approach to design examines the problem, the resources and techniques available, and then seeks a physical solution to the design problem.

So-called "traditional design" involves the use of a widely accepted style of design developed in the past. In certain areas where the pace of change has been very slow, and where materials are limited, such design may be called "indigenous architecture." New England and Mediterranean architecture are examples.

TRADITIONAL ARCHITECTURE
Figure 1.2

However, new conditions require new solutions. In any case, there is a rational, methodical process behind both "traditional" and "contemporary" designs. It is well to keep in mind that all traditional design was once called modern, or "contemporary."

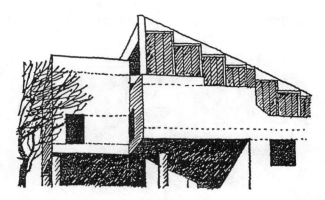

CONTEMPORARY ARCHITECTURE

Figure 1.3

CONSIDERATIONS IN ARCHITECTURAL DESIGN

The process of architectural design involves the simultaneous resolution of a number of considerations, and the combining of a number of elements into a whole. The purposes of architecture are many, but all derive from the basic purpose of accommodating human activities. In pursuit of these many purposes an architect, in undertaking design, should consider the following:

1. Architecture requires an appropriate relationship between the site and the structure it accommodates.

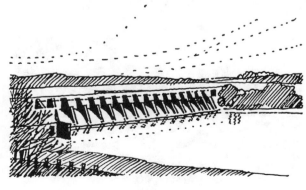

SITE - STRUCTURE RELATIONSHIP

Figure 1.4

2. Architecture should respond to the characteristics of the site: its form, climate, solar position, vegetation, and existing structures.

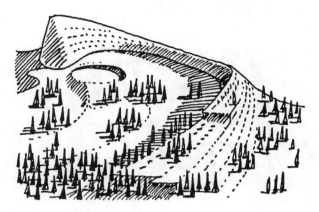

ARCHITECTURE RESPONSIVE TO SITE CHARACTERISTICS

Figure 1.5

3. Architecture should be placed in the landscape so as to be well seen; conversely, views of the surrounding landscape should be visible from the building.

RELATIONSHIP TO LANDSCAPE

Figure 1.6

4. Architecture should serve the purposes it is intended to serve—it should function properly. Function should not be seen narrowly, but as broadly as possible, i.e., beauty is also a function.

ARCHITECTURE RESPONSIVE TO FUNCTION
Figure 1.7

5. Architecture should express the purposes it serves.

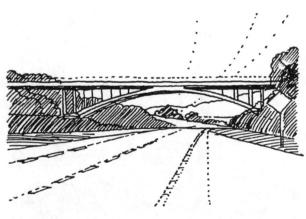

EXPRESSION OF PURPOSE

Figure 1.8

6. Architecture should use economy of means to achieve its purposes.

ECONOMY OF MEANS
Figure 1.9

7. Architecture should utilize available technologies ingeniously.

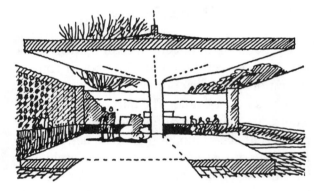

UTILIZATION OF TECHNOLOGY IN DESIGN
Figure 1.10

8. Architecture must have a human scale, in both its material parts and its spaces, and in its interior and its exterior.

HUMAN SCALE — A PLAYGROUND
Figure 1.11

9. Architecture should utilize materials appropriately.

ARCHITECTURE REFLECTING APPROPRIATE USE OF MATERIALS AND METHODS

Figure 1.12

10. Architecture should utilize the familiar and commonplace building techniques of its locale.

ARCHITECTURE UTILIZING INDIGENOUS BUILDING TECHNIQUES

Figure 1.13

11. Architecture should be graceful in silhouette and massing.

ARCHITECTURE —GRACEFUL IN SILHOUETTE AND MASSING

Figure 1.14

12. Architecture should exhibit a degree of exuberance; it is an assertive act.

ARCHITECTURE EXHIBITING EXUBERANCE

Figure 1.15

13. Architecture should exhibit a priority or hierarchy of parts.

A DUAL PURPOSE STRUCTURE

Figure 1.16

14. Architecture should offer the human eye a visually rich and interesting field of view.

VISUAL RICHNESS IN ARCHITECTURE

Figure 1.17

15. Architecture should establish a relationship between interior and exterior spaces.

INTERIOR-EXTERIOR RELATIONSHIP

Figure 1.18

16. Architecture should have integrity—honesty and wholeness throughout.

INTEGRITY AND HONESTY IN ARCHITECTURE

Figure 1.19

17. Architecture should be expressive of human spiritual aspirations.

AN EXPRESSION OF SPIRITUAL ASPIRATIONS
Figure 1.20

18. Every work of architecture should be regarded as an opportunity to demonstrate architecture's basic principles.

A DEMONSTRATION OF BASIC PRINCIPLES
Figure 1.21

19. Architecture should have an all-embracing and encompassing physical design concept.

AN ALL-EMBRACING CONCEPT
Figure 1.22

20. Architecture should be a place, or spatial forum, that encourages human contact. Architectural space is the arena where activity, interaction, and accomplishment take place. Architectural space, therefore, facilitates a broad range of human activities; it does not prescribe or limit them.

A SPATIAL FORUM FOR HUMAN CONTACT
Figure 1.23

The preceding list can be varied or amplified, and in any particular building, some considerations will weigh more heavily than others. But in any case, it is clear that the task of design, of synthesizing 20 or more considerations, is indeed a formidable one.

LESSON 1 QUIZ

1. Which one of the following is NOT part of a methodical approach to design?

   A. Seeking physical solution

   B. Problem examination

   C. Examination of process

   D. Selection of the stylistic approach

2. Which one of the following is a function of architecture?

   A. Facilitates human activities

   B. Exhibits a hierarchy of parts

   C. Establishes relationships between interior and exterior spaces

   D. Expresses the purpose it serves

   E. Utilizes available technologies ingeniously

3. The process of architectural design is

   A. a synthesis of parts that form a unified interdependent composition.

   B. giving form to an idea.

   C. coordination of a team of specialists.

   D. setting objectives, analyzing data, planning space, and form conception.

   E. A and D only

   F. All of the above

FORM PROTOTYPES

INTRODUCTION

All building projects should be organized to fulfill their purposes in an efficient, humane, and responsible manner. To accomplish this, a plan of the project must be developed that sets forth how the work is to be done. An essential element of this plan is the project program. The organization of the program has a fundamental effect on the usefulness, efficiency, and comfort of the project. Program development, therefore, must consider various organizational concepts, together with the factors that may influence the project, such as natural, sustainable, social, cultural, visual, and functional requirements.

A useful approach to programming is to establish the order of importance, or hierarchy, of functions and spaces. Central locations are usually appropriate for spaces that are used frequently by the majority of occupants. Similarly, peripheral locations are appropriate for spaces used by a smaller number of occupants, or for more specialized activities. Thus, on a college campus, the library would occupy a central location, with classrooms nearby, and laboratories and shops located on the periphery.

On a restricted site, the elements may be organized vertically. In that case, heavily used areas would be located on the lower floors, while activities which are less "people-intensive" would take place at higher levels. There are essentially two approaches used to determine the suitability of a particular organizational pattern. The first arranges the major activity in relation to the physical characteristics of the site. A site that is restricted in size, for example, might suggest a multi-level building. Where the site borders a river and the view is particularly attractive, a linear arrangement might be appropriate.

In the second approach, the pattern is based on a logical organization of the activities. Such an organizational pattern may be expressed diagrammatically; however, a diagram should not be regarded as an actual floor plan, but merely a suggested relationship of building functions. In practice, the two approaches are generally combined, that is, the organizational pattern is determined by both the site conditions and the functional requirements.

Designers have available a fairly conventional palette of form prototypes which can be used in single-story or multiple-story configurations. The simplest is the rectangle. Rectangles can be arranged as a star form, an axial form, or a quadrangular form. They can also be linked in series to create a grid. Circular configurations using rectangles are also possible, with angular joints. A particularly useful form is the quadrangle, with activities housed in each of the four comprising sides, and all activities accessible from a central courtyard space.

Each organizational pattern has intrinsic functional implications, such as degree of flexibility, dispersion or concentration, degree of accessibility, and the individuality or repetitiveness of parts. Although using familiar geometric shapes to organize spaces is common practice, it should be done judiciously, to assure that the form is appropriate, i.e., that it satisfies functional needs. Form is best derived from a thorough study of all the functional needs in relation to a specific site. Furthermore, many activities may be organized in any one of several acceptable ways. The determination of an appropriate form must be measured against a building's function, site, cost, and other important aspects of the project. In the end, one form concept, thoroughly analyzed in relation to all the requirements to be served, will be the most satisfactory.

ORGANIZATIONAL VALUES

The physical form of a project has numerous implications. In the interest of creating a successful design, the following general objectives should be considered and satisfied:

Behavioral interests and objectives must be satisfied. One must determine if there is ample space for people to perform their tasks. One must also understand the people using the facility, to determine if the spatial setting facilitates the work.

Circulation aspects refer to the ease with which persons, information, and goods can move within a facility. In certain areas it may be desirable to allow free movement and frequent interpersonal interaction. In other areas it may be necessary to minimize social interaction for reasons of privacy. Circulation and interpersonal communication may be encouraged by providing common corridors, an attractive dining facility, central service facilities, etc. In contrast, impenetrable boundaries, crowded corridors, and remote service points restrict circulation while impeding interpersonal contact.

Health aspects refer to those factors that cause stress and threaten health, such as noise, crowding, glare, unsafe conditions, etc. Environmental form can affect both physical and emotional health.

Adaptive aspects are those that facilitate future change. The organizational functions and operations of a project often change over time. Therefore, the physical form and arrangement of a building must be sufficiently flexible to accommodate future modifications. Adaptability is facilitated by the use of a repetitive basic spatial unit or module, separation of service areas from areas being served, regular layout, wall flexibility, and well-scaled and proportioned basic building spaces.

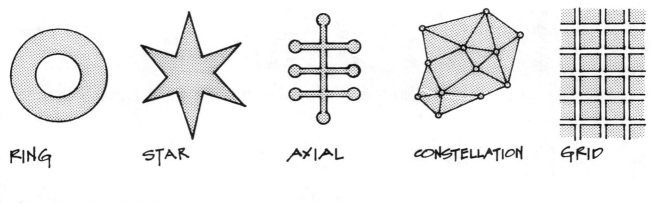

RING   STAR   AXIAL   CONSTELLATION   GRID

PROTOTYPICAL
ORGANIZATION FORMS

Figure 2.1

Cost aspects often determine the organizational pattern of a development. Project costs may be reduced by using regular forms, compact arrangements, and high densities. Lowering design or construction standards is, obviously, another method of reducing costs; however, the initial cost savings may be offset by high maintenance and operating costs over the life of the building.

ORGANIZATION AND DESIGN

Design is the creative act of organizing spaces and forms with the objective of achieving specific programmatic goals. In assessing the suitability of various organizational concepts, some designers employ adaptations of standard solutions that have proven successful over the years. Particularly prevalent are those forms that have become prototypes, including the linear arrangement, the radial plan, the compact layout, the extended layout, and the single- or multi-level floor arrangement. All designers should be aware of these prototypical forms, as well as the type of functions for which they are suited.

In general, the most productive approach to design is one in which the essential functions of a project are identified, and the designer develops a form that satisfies these functions.

In certain situations, the design solution may reflect the unique characteristics of a particular site. Unusually steep terrain or extremely severe weather might make an open or extended design impractical. A mild climate and flat site, on the other hand, are suitable for an extended open layout.

Some projects are difficult to organize because of their numerous parts. In these cases, the total project may be divided into smaller components—modules of spatial forms or social groups. In a large housing development, for example, a group of 10 or 15 units may provide a convenient design module. The designer may then solve each part separately, combine the results, and find a solution to the whole, embodying all aspects of the project.

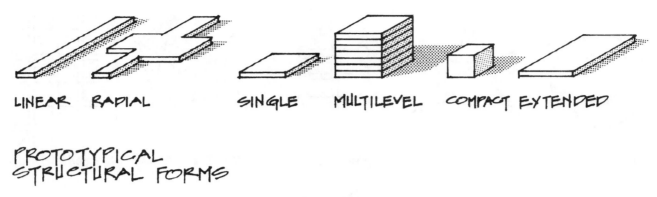

LINEAR   RADIAL   SINGLE   MULTILEVEL   COMPACT EXTENDED

PROTOTYPICAL
STRUCTURAL FORMS

Figure 2.2

ORGANIZATIONAL FACTORS

The architectural program, as a statement of required functions, determines the organization of a project. There are several factors, however, that influence the basic spatial organization, regardless of function. Among these are the form of the site itself, movement patterns, and patterns of growth.

Site factors, such as soil conditions, must be evaluated in order to determine the economic feasibility of a design concept. Adverse subsoil conditions, for example, may require a centralized or compact layout. Certain land forms may also influence the basic organization, for example, extreme topographic variations which limit development or future expansion. The organizational concept may also be influenced by unique site features, natural growth characteristics, and local climate. Severe weather conditions, for example, will reduce acceptable outdoor walking distances and require protection for pedestrian movement.

Movement patterns refer to the accommodation of internal functional systems, as well as the accessibility of the project relative to the larger community. Pedestrian and vehicular access, movement, and control often determine the basic organization of a project. Airports, for example, are organized almost exclusively as a result of these factors.

The distribution and provision of services, too, may determine the shape of a project. Nearly all buildings must be serviced by water, electricity, sewer, telephone, gas, and internal communication. In the majority of cases, compact, centralized schemes are most economical for these services, and multi-level arrangements generally have economic advantages over a single-level, extended arrangement.

Pedestrian movement is often complex and frequently determines the selection of one organizational form over another. The organization of theaters and sports arenas, for example, is based to a large extent on the efficient movement of large groups of people. In situations involving pedestrian movement, it has been found that people are normally willing to walk for about ten minutes. Beyond that, they prefer some type of mechanical transport.

Patterns of future expansion often require that the system of organization be flexible enough to permit change. Changes may include modifications in the number of users, the organization of the project, social or technological developments, and changes to the structure. Since it is difficult to forecast the exact nature of change to be accommodated, the organizational pattern should be sufficiently flexible to allow extensions to the original form.

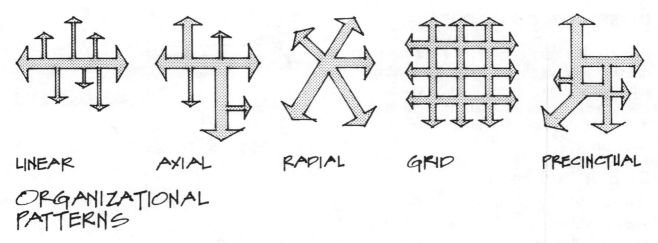

LINEAR   AXIAL   RADIAL   GRID   PRECINCTUAL

ORGANIZATIONAL
PATTERNS

Figure 2.3

ORGANIZATIONAL PATTERNS

Among the conventional systems of organization, the more common patterns in current use are described below:

Linear applies to a pattern consisting of a single spine having one principal direction. Sub-systems or "fingers" can develop along the spine or at right angles to the spine.

Further development may be limited by the availability of land or by the distance between extreme ends. The linear system is useful where major circulation occurs between two points. If lengths are reasonable, it can be an economical form, but it often lacks a focus and may become congested.

Axial is a variation of the linear pattern in which the basic organizing principle is a central axis, spine, or mall around which structures are arranged. Extensions may be developed along secondary paths of growth at right angles to the primary axis. Axial patterns allow for incremental development with relative ease and minor disruption; however, they may become extended.

Radial patterns consist of central cores from which secondary elements radiate in all directions. This pattern is appropriate where the elements have a common origin or destination. Since all paths emanate from a common point, the radial pattern is somewhat inflexible; however, it is compact and allows a maximum of social interaction.

Grid refers to a cellular-type pattern that places the emphasis on flexibility, since it may be extended in several directions. The grid is simple, convenient, compact, and suited for complex distribution flows. It can become monotonous, however, unless it has several points of focus, such as public spaces or buildings.

Precinctual organization consists of dispersed activities, which may or may not have a strong central feature. In this pattern, the composition consists of balanced components, which allow growth to develop in any direction, if the site permits. Precinctual patterns may be flexible, compact, efficient, and often quite economical.

DETERMINANTS OF FORM

Every project has a number of considerations that determine its physical form. Their relative influence as determinants varies depending on the nature of the project itself. The following discussion identifies some of the most important of these.

Site-Structure Relationships

Some sites have a strong visual character, such as a mountainous area. Others are weak, such as a flat, featureless plain. There should be an inverse relationship between a site and the buildings that occupy it: a visually strong site should have visually deferential (passive) structures, while a visually weak site should have visually assertive structures.

Site-Form Relationships

All sites possess certain characteristic forms that are created by their generating lines: the lines of rolling hills, the horizontal lines of cultivated fields, the verticals of clustered skyscrapers, the angles of distant mountains, or the roof lines of houses in an old village. These lines may serve as guides in determining architectural form. Roof slopes can follow the angles of mountain slopes or of ancient rooftops. A high-rise building among other high-rises can reinforce the vertical composition.

Vegetation

A site with characteristic vegetation provides its own clue to an appropriate design form. Northern sites with vertical firs or pines may suggest a contrasting horizontal emphasis. Southern sites with foliage and tree massings, separated by clearings, may suggest a similarly scaled architectural mass.

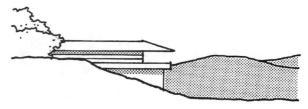

"STRONG" LANDSCAPE...
...DEFERENTIAL ARCHITECTURE

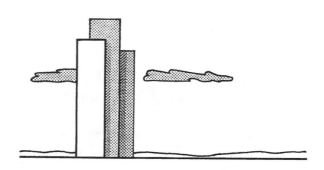

"WEAK" LANDSCAPE...
... STRONG STRUCTURE...

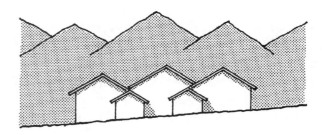

ROOF SLOPES REFLECT THE BACKGROUND MOUNTAINS

Figure 2.4

Climate

Climate, too, can be a powerful form determinant. Extremely cold settings suggest compact buildings with minimum exterior surface. Hot

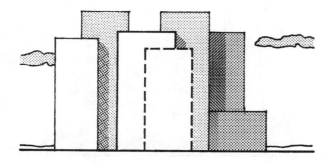

A NEW HIGH-RISE (POTTED)
REINFORCES THE EXISTING
COMPOSITION

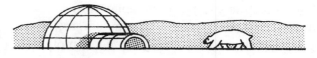

EXTREMELY COLD CLIMATE...
... COMPACT ARCHITECTURAL FORM

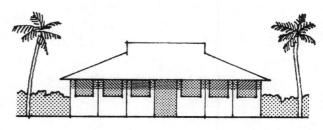

HOT, HUMID CLIMATE...OPEN
PLAN ALLOWS AIR MOVEMENT

VERTICAL TREE FORMS...
HORIZONTAL ARCHITECTURAL
MASSING

RAINY CLIMATE...SLOPED ROOFS

TREE MASSINGS...SIMILARLY
SCALED ARCHITECTURAL MASS

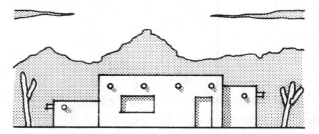

DRY CLIMATE...FLAT ROOFS

Figure 2.5

humid climates suggest open plan forms to allow breezes to penetrate. Rainy climates suggest sloped roofs, while dry climates imply flat roofs.

Sustainable design encourages the architect to explore forms that respond not only to the temperature, but the wind, soil conditions, ground water, native vegetation, and topography. Like much of our indigenous architecture, the result will be forms that are less homogeneous and more responsive to the region and the environment.

Structure

As a general principle, all buildings should have a visible indication of their structural systems. Economy in the structural system often produces the most appropriate expression.

Mechanical Systems

Simple mechanical systems are generally integrated into the architectural forms of a structure. However, there are occasions when they may be visually expressed. The duct system of a simple shell building, for example, may be left exposed, and treated as "ceiling sculpture." Where a building has a complex mechanical system, it may even play a primary visual role.

Materials

The nature of its materials may also suggest a building's form. Brick, for example, which is a material strong in compression, might express compressive forces by the use of arches. Wood or aluminum siding might be expressed by an articulation of joints and by occasional openings, which would indicate that it is an applied surface or an exterior "skin."

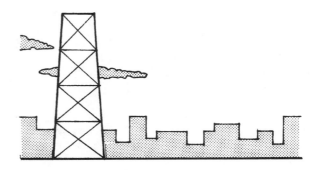

STRUCTURAL EXPRESSION OF A VERY HIGH BUILDING, SHOWING LATERAL BRACING

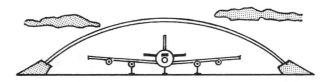

LONG SPAN STRUCTURE TO SHELTER AIRCRAFT

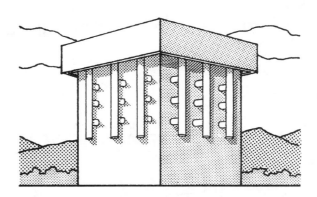

MECHANICAL SYSTEM EXPRESSED --ROOF-TOP AIR HANDLING WITH EXTERIOR VERTICAL DUCTS

Figure 2.6

Traditional Form

All architectural forms convey meanings that result from their traditional use over a long period of time. In these cases, tradition may be the determinant of architectural form. A shed roof, for example, expresses efficiency; a peaked roof, domestic habitat; a dome, government; vertical spires signify aspiration; and horizontal planes convey a sense of repose.

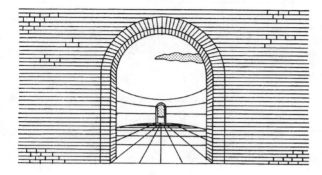

COMPRESSIVE MATERIAL (BRICK) EXPRESSED THROUGH THE USE OF ARCHES

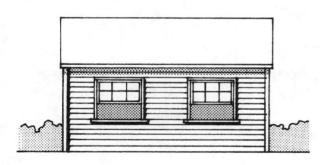

WOOD SIDING EXPRESSED BY LINES OF ARTICULATION AND OPENINGS

Figure 2.7

Function

All building forms should express their functions. The repetitive activities of an office building, for example, can be expressed by the repetitive pattern of the facade. A linear production process suggests a linear massing, and the need for interior flexibility may suggest several similar modules.

Cultural Association

The use of past styles in architecture can be used to express the form of new buildings. This may solve an emotional need, but quite possibly ignore the function and other architectural requirements of the project. The expression of cultural or historic associations, therefore, may be a design determinant, but it takes great skill to unite the past and present successfully.

Scale

The need to establish a human scale, particularly in large structures, may suggest a series of smaller constituent forms.

Proportion

The need for harmonious proportion may determine overall form, or modify it.

Massing and Profile

All building masses are perceived as complete forms in profile. That consideration may modify overall form.

Hierarchy

Architectural form may be influenced by establishing a hierarchy among a building's components. This does not necessarily mean that the focus will be the largest single element, but rather that all other components will be positioned and treated in a subordinate way. The assembly room in a government building or the library on a college campus, while relatively small in size, may still be the hierarchical focal point of the project through positioning and treatment.

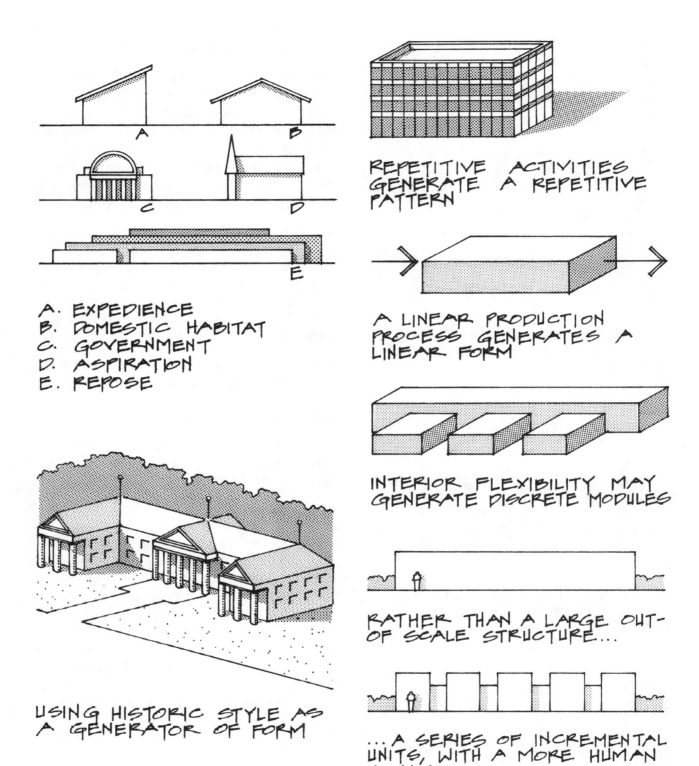

A. EXPEDIENCE
B. DOMESTIC HABITAT
C. GOVERNMENT
D. ASPIRATION
E. REPOSE

REPETITIVE ACTIVITIES GENERATE A REPETITIVE PATTERN

A LINEAR PRODUCTION PROCESS GENERATES A LINEAR FORM

INTERIOR FLEXIBILITY MAY GENERATE DISCRETE MODULES

RATHER THAN A LARGE OUT-OF SCALE STRUCTURE...

...A SERIES OF INCREMENTAL UNITS, WITH A MORE HUMAN SCALE.

USING HISTORIC STYLE AS A GENERATOR OF FORM

Figure 2.8

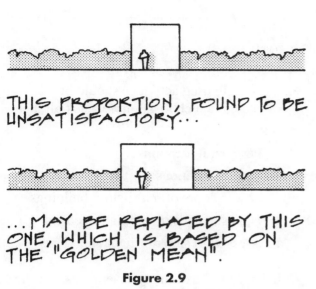

THIS PROPORTION, FOUND TO BE UNSATISFACTORY...

...MAY BE REPLACED BY THIS ONE, WHICH IS BASED ON THE "GOLDEN MEAN".

Figure 2.9

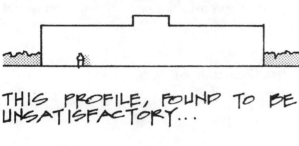

THIS PROFILE, FOUND TO BE UNSATISFACTORY...

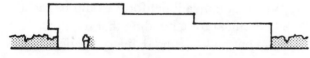

...MAY BE REPLACED WITH THIS MORE RHYTHMIC ONE.

Figure 2.10

THE ROTUNDA OF THE UNIVERSITY OF VIRGINIA, GIVEN A PRIMARY HIERARCHICAL POSITION

Figure 2.11

LESSON 2 QUIZ

1. The most reliable way to determine an appropriate building form is to

    A. use a traditional prototype.

    B. use an innovative solution.

    C. use a compact and efficient layout.

    D. examine the programmatic requirements.

2. The cost of a project is reduced by all of the following, EXCEPT

    A. harmonious proportions.

    B. compact arrangements.

    C. high densities.

    D. regular forms.

3. In which of the following development patterns would utility services generally be least expensive?

    A. Extended

    B. Decentralized

    C. Grid

    D. Linear

4. Compact or centralized patterns of development are generally suited to

    A. mountainous sites.

    B. beach front sites.

    C. rural sites.

    D. forested sites.

5. Frequently used activities should be situated at which locations? Check all that apply.

    A. Peripheral locations

    B. Central locations

    C. Lower floors of multi-story buildings

    D. Opposite ends of circulation corridors

    E. Areas with superior light and views

6. In an area of extremely severe weather, the most appropriate organizational form would be

    A. axial.

    B. decentralized.

    C. linear.

    D. compact.

7. Which organizational form would be most economical for a building that requires frequent pick-up and delivery services?

    A. Centralized

    B. Radial

    C. Linear

    D. Multi-level

8. If one were planning a project for future expansion, which organizational form would be LEAST desirable?

    A. Radial

    B. Grid

    C. Axial

    D. Ring

9. A project's physical form may be determined by all of the following, EXCEPT the

   A. mechanical system.

   B. climate.

   C. length of construction time.

   D. area in which it is built.

10. Social interaction is LEAST encouraged by a building having a(n)

    A. quadrangular plan with major spaces opening onto a central court.

    B. multistory arrangement with lobbies on each floor.

    C. radial plan.

    D. axial plan.

PROGRAMMING AND SPACE NEEDS

INTRODUCTION

Buildings have become increasingly complex and costly, and they must be carefully designed in order to function properly. Occasionally, some building spaces may be underused or even unused, expensive equipment may only be operated intermittently, and expected traffic patterns may not materialize or may have to be altered. A functional building requires skillful design, which must have sensible programming as its foundation.

A building's needs must be described completely and systematically before design can begin. This process, known as building programming, is one of the most significant steps in achieving a successful design.

PROGRAMMING PURPOSE

Architectural programming is the process of identification and systematic organization of the functional, architectural, structural, mechanical, aesthetic, and budget criteria that guide decision making in the design of buildings. Good programming can be achieved through a well-structured process and a comprehensive framework for organizing information. The framework must allow all information and ideas to be expressed, including alternative means for achieving desired objectives. The programming process seeks to illuminate the uniqueness of a particular problem.

All programming techniques are basically similar, regardless of building type, size, or location. Computers can be very useful for programming complex projects in which great amounts of data are collected. An advantage of computer use is its speed in handling information in an orderly and logical way.

A central purpose of programming is to identify and understand the nature of the problems associated with a particular facility. It is essential to obtain a thorough knowledge of the building type being programmed. This can be achieved through research, visits to similar facilities, and interviews. The program writer must concentrate on seeking the problems, not the solutions. It may also be helpful, in this earliest phase of the work, to engage specialized consultants.

It is particularly important that the owner and the architect each designate one responsible representative with complete authority to coordinate communications and make policy decisions. This often leads to the formation of a team consisting of owner, architect, consultants, and those who represent users of the proposed facility. This team effort requires a clear communication system, since all concepts must be thoroughly understood by the concerned parties. Specific space requirements should be considered in the context of the total program. For this purpose, diagrams and other illustrative graphics can be a great aid.

PROGRAMMING PROCESS

Programming is often performed in three phases. In the first phase, broad objectives are stated; in the second phase, functional requirements are described by size and relationships; and in the third phase, detailed requirements are noted. Programming should be done independently of architectural design. One should not attempt to design a building, or anticipate a design solution, while programming. The reason is that the program might become compromised or biased. However, it may be helpful, when a program is completed, to do a "test of concept" of the program. This involves the development of a simple mass and circulation

design in relation to the site, to test the reasonableness of the program within itself and in relation to the site.

An effective format for organizing programmatic information is the division of information into function, form, economy, and time. *Function* considers objectives, methods of achieving them, and human needs. *Form* considers the site, the character of the physical environment, spatial aspects, and pertinent structural aspects. *Economy* considers the construction budget, as well as long-term operating costs. *Time* considers the schedules for design, construction, and occupancy. The final program should conclude with a statement of the problem, which is intended to be solved through the design process.

Effective programming requires facts, the exercise of reason, and objectivity. Each phase in programming can be undertaken through a five-step method, as follows:

1. Establish objectives.
2. Collect, organize, and analyze data.
3. Formulate relationships.
4. Establish priorities.
5. State the problem.

The objective of a programming effort is a full statement of the project requirements. Programming is a process of problem seeking, while design is problem solving.

A further discussion of the five programming steps follows:

1. *Establish objectives.* An owner may often describe project goals in terms of the program, the site, the budget, sustainable design factors, and the element of time. This information should be collected and documented with care. It should be reviewed by the client to prevent

misunderstanding, to clarify ambiguous concepts, and to allow the client an opportunity to confirm, reconsider, or modify his intentions. The program writer must also identify and resolve areas of potential conflict.

2. *Collect, organize, and analyze facts.* Facts must be organized and analyzed before their meaning and relative importance can be determined. It is essential to discriminate between pertinent facts and non-essential details; otherwise, details may become overwhelming and disconcerting. A variety of factual information is necessary; for example, the number of occupants or users and their activities, initially and in the future. In addition, the programmer must determine the characteristics of spaces and their relationships to other spaces. Site data must be collected, organized, and analyzed, since the site influences form by its physical and legal characteristics. Other constraints that affect the project and that must be analyzed include building codes, zoning ordinances, the project budget, construction costs, and all other expenses of the project development.

3. *Formulate relationships.* Functional relationships are established through the use of schematic diagrams, which should not be misconstrued as schematic designs. For example, the organizational concept of a correctional facility may involve an "academy plan" in which individual clusters of facilities are limited to a certain number of inmates. The number of inmates is a fact, whereas the plan of individual clusters is a concept expressing a functional relationship. One depends on and explains the other. At this point it may be helpful to evaluate such concepts. In this example, the idea would be to determine which services should be centralized and which decentralized. Services such as libraries,

administration, dining, and recreation have a marked effect on an institution's social organization, administration, and management. Other concepts that may be tested include integration, compartmentalization, expandability, convertibility, etc. Most important, however, is the investigation of concepts derived from the physical, social, and psychological characteristics of those for whom the facility is to be designed.

4. *Establish priorities.* One of the most important tasks is to balance the programmed spaces with the budget. Unless the programmed space requirements are realistic, relative to the available construction funds, the architect will be burdened with an untenable program. If modifications to the program are found to be necessary because of budget restrictions, they should be made at this time. Construction costs on a square-foot basis should also be established, based on experience and the most recent data available. Allowance should be made for a reasonable building efficiency: the ratio of net usable to gross building areas.

5. *State the problem.* After evaluating all the information derived from the first four steps, the problem should be stated. This statement, concerning the program, the site, the budget, and schedule, all of which are premises for design, should be expressed concisely; otherwise, it may be misinterpreted as detailed design instructions. The statement should be expressed in terms of functions, areas, and relationships. It must also be sufficiently broad so as not to suggest specific architectural designs, or to limit the possible range of those designs.

THE PROGRAMMING PROCESS

1.   ESTABLISH OBJECTIVES
     Primary
     Secondary
     Tertiary, etc.

2.   COLLECT DATA
     Site
     Costs
     Spatial Standards
     Prototypes
     Systems, etc.

3.   FORMULATE RELATIONSHIPS
     Elements
     Components
     Sub-groups
     Interrelationships

4.   ESTABLISH PRIORITIES
     Primary functions
     Secondary (servant) functions
     Locational priorities
     Circulation priorities

5.   PROGRAM STATEMENT
     Review & refine draft statement
     Proof-of-concept analysis of draft
     Final statement

Figure 3.1

These steps outline the basic development of an architectural program. An analytic procedure must be employed throughout each of the five steps, so that the programmer helps the client to reach essential decisions. The architect also helps the owner recognize and analyze the key determinants of design. To repeat, programming, therefore, is a process of problem seeking, whereas design is a process of problem solving. A thorough analysis of specific needs inevitably results in buildings which are more responsive to the requirements of their users.

The value of good programming is manifold. It clarifies the intentions of the owner, user, and architect before design begins. It reduces the necessity for changes during final design, development of construction documents, and construction. It provides a basis for the resolution of differences of opinion, and it also serves as a reference upon which future changes can be based. Finally, good programming minimizes the changes necessitated by wasted space, unnecessary equipment, and poor relationships between component parts.

PROGRAMMING LIMITATIONS

The purpose of this lesson is to describe the programming process. However, no description would be complete without the following precautionary qualification: No building, regardless of how carefully its intended uses may be researched, analyzed, and predicted, will be used precisely as planned. School curricula are often modified, hospital functions are frequently reorganized, and the operations of a company occasionally change.

Thus, in programming and design it is wise to provide for possible change. This may mean designing with a "loose fit," providing spaces that can be reconfigured as needs change; or it may mean planning 10 or 20 percent additional space for expansion. In some cases, those spaces that are likely to require modification should be identified and designed in a way that would facilitate change. A modular layout is among the most useful planning devices for achieving this flexibility. For this reason, its utilization may be suggested as part of a program statement.

The anticipation of change does not invalidate the need for precision in programming; rather it puts the programming process into realistic perspective.

PROGRAM OUTLINE FORMAT

Outline formats are prepared in order to organize programmatic data. These formats help to summarize basic project needs, and the information recorded is subsequently used as a guide during the various design phases.

Depending on the scope and complexity of the project, the criteria are developed in descending order of magnitude, as shown in Figure 3.2.

Total Building Group is concerned with all the buildings that constitute a complex or building group. In the case of a project comprising a number of interrelated facilities, such as a civic center, a college campus, or a new community, the first step should be to develop a master plan for the entire group as an ensemble. Among the primary programming considerations are its shared elements, such as the circulation of vehicles and pedestrians, parking facilities, outdoor areas, and service, maintenance and fire protection. In addition, there are the basic organizational relationships to be accommodated on the site.

A master plan describes the development of a site to be realized over a period of many years. It is important that the planning phases are clearly identified to allow for incremental development.

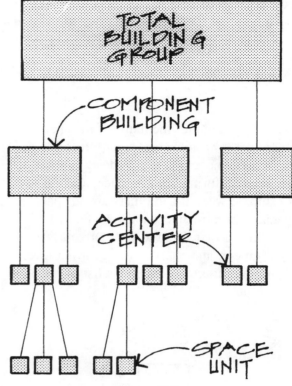

Figure 3.2

Component Building refers to the functions of any single building in the Total Building Group mentioned above. Its program should describe the objectives of the building's activities, the relationship between the major activity centers, the number and types of people to be accommodated, and the amount of space needed to serve the objectives. The program should also describe requirements of access, ingress, egress, internal circulation, and possible expansion.

Activity Center refers to a space or series of spaces related to each other by function. An example is the x-ray suite of a hospital, which is an activity center composed of a number of individual spaces, including x-ray rooms, film storage rooms, viewing rooms, developing rooms, and dressing rooms. As a unit of organization, an activity center's administration and limits of function must be clearly defined. The program should also define the administrative and functional relationships among the various activity centers in a component building. A list of personnel, with their responsibilities, often accompanies the space needs of each activity center.

Space Unit includes the name of the space, its area in net (or assignable) square feet, the number of people occupying it, a description of the activities performed in the space, and the relationship between it and other related spaces. Special requirements can also be described, including those related to structure, utilities, environment, and equipment. A further level of programming may include a list of movable furnishings.

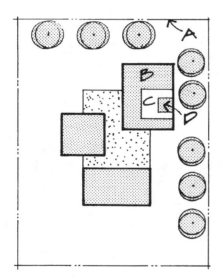

A. CIVIC CENTER
B. CITY HALL
C. PUBLIC WORKS DEPT.
D. ENGINEERING OFFICE

PROGRAM DEVELOPMENT
SEQUENCE OF A
CIVIC CENTER

Figure 3.3

The completed program outline format should be reviewed and approved by owner and archi-

tect, and become a part of the project record for use throughout subsequent phases of development. Technical bulletins and catalog sheets of special equipment to be incorporated can be attached, in order to facilitate the placement of these elements during the design development phase. This practice can also be helpful in preparing cost estimates, when such equipment is not otherwise apparent.

An example of a typical project program is shown at the conclusion of this lesson.

DETERMINING SPACE NEEDS

Effective programming depends on the ability to perceive basic space requirements and conventional standards for different types of uses. It also requires an understanding of the relationship between "assignable" and "gross" building area. The standards of assignable (net) areas for various uses should be established during the programming phase in order to determine the overall size of the project. It should be emphasized that individual spaces are not designed during this phase; therefore, dimensions, configurations, and proportions are deferred, as well, until the design phase.

As an example of employing space standards, the programmer, working with the owner, determines the net area required to seat a certain number of people in an employees' dining room. Normal standards indicate that dining functions can be accommodated in 15 to 17 square feet for each person. This figure is based on the amount of floor area required for one person seated at a table shared by other persons. It also includes that person's share of floor area required for circulation. Therefore, if one were to program the size of an employees' dining room to seat 100 persons, he or she would allocate an area of 1,500 net square feet for the space and its internal circulation needs. This net area, however, does not include the area required to circulate between other spaces of the building or the area needed to service these spaces. Those areas constitute part of the overall building "gross area." Consequently, to calculate gross building area, the employees' dining room may require an additional 25 to even 50 percent of its net area for general service and circulation. The exact amount varies, but it normally includes the circulation, services, toilets, mechanical, electrical, and custodial spaces.

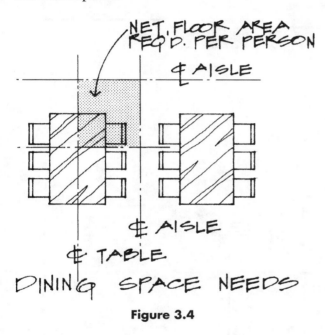

Figure 3.4

The amount of floor area required for service and circulation depends on the type and complexity of the building. For example, a building whose interior is composed of many large open spaces, such as an industrial shop building, requires less circulation space and is therefore more efficient than an administrative office building whose interior is partitioned into numerous small offices, conference rooms, and secretarial spaces. Consequently, the ratio of net to gross area, referred to as *efficiency*, increases as the complexity and number of spaces decrease. In general, the efficiency of

buildings ranges from 60 to 80 percent. Some institutions specify a certain ratio, that is, they prescribe the minimum efficiency to be achieved. Such a constraint then becomes an integral part of the program and exerts a strong influence on the building design.

To calculate the efficiency of a building, the net area is divided by the gross area. The net area is the sum of all usable floor spaces measured to the inside faces of enclosing walls or to the lines of other space separations; but it does not include circulation and general service areas, such as corridors, lobbies, rest rooms, custodial rooms, and mechanical spaces. The gross building area, on the other hand, is the sum of all building areas measured to the exterior face of perimeter walls, including all interior walls, columns, and shafts. The net area divided by the gross area is multiplied by 100 to express the efficiency as a percentage.

To estimate the required gross area of a building, given the net area, one divides the net area by the desired or anticipated efficiency ratio. The result is the gross area of the building expressed in gross square feet. For example, a building containing 100,000 gross square feet, yielding 65,000 net usable square feet, has an efficiency of 65 percent [(65,000 ÷ 100,000) × 100 = 65 percent]. Its ratio of net to gross area is .65. Stated another way, if a building requires 65,000 net square feet and is specified to be 65 percent efficient, the required gross square footage is 100,000 (65,000 divided by .65).

There are several methods used to determine the approximate square-foot floor areas required for various types of buildings. These can be divided into three main categories:

1. Those in which people determine the amount of space required, such as living and working environments.

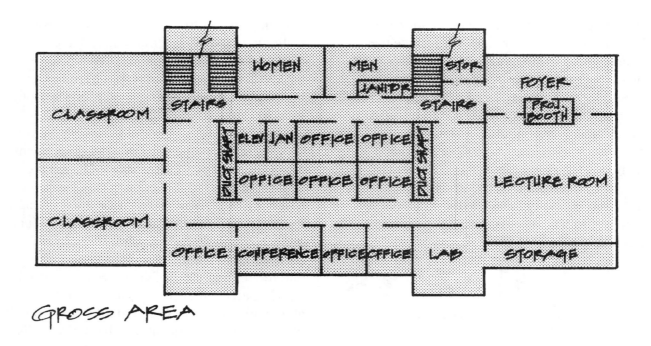

GROSS AREA

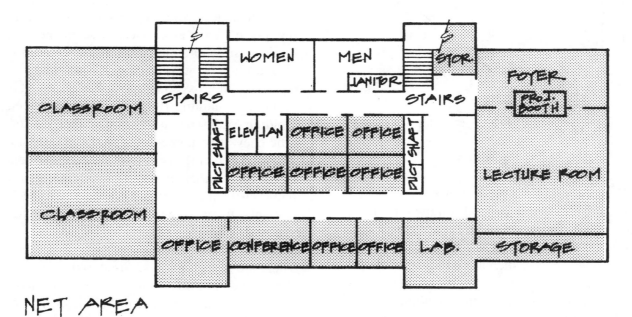

NET AREA
(DOES NOT INCLUDE WALLS, COLUMNS, AND
VERTICAL MECHANICAL SPACES, EXCEPT
IN LEASED COMMERCIAL BUILDINGS)

Figure 3.5

2. Those in which an object determines the amount of space occupied, such as a car in a parking garage.

3. Those in which a specific activity is governed by certain practices or rules, such as the game of handball and its required court.

Criteria have also been developed for various types of occupancies based on a desired level of comfort and/or status. For example, executives and clerks may perform similar physical tasks; however, the executive's office is generally larger, because it is more comfortable and denotes greater status. In addition, minimum standards have been established to assure adequate capacity and safe egress from a space occupied by a number of people. The standards are based on the number of square feet of usable floor area per occupant, and these figures are normally specified in building codes. Space standards not only prescribe the number of occupants that can be safely housed in a space, but also the number and width of exits required to vacate the space during an emergency. Table 3.1 shows the approximate square-foot area per person required for selected uses, and it should offer a general understanding of basic space needs.

ESTIMATING SPACE NEEDS

As previously noted, space requirements derive from the nature of the facility. For example, a parking garage or basketball pavilion requires enough space to accommodate the size of the object (an automobile) or conform to the rules of the game. In the case of living or work spaces, a different method of determining space needs to be employed, commonly known as the *numeric method*. The principle of the numeric method is that physical facilities can be classi-

fied by groups called "use categories," each of which requires a specific amount of space.

In this section, we will look into different building types to better explain the process of determining spatial needs. The candidates need not memorize the specific square footages or areas shown for these building types for the ARE, but rather understand the mathematical equations that lead to the areas studied.

To demonstrate this method of estimating space needs, we will examine some of the major use categories for a college. We assume that the institution's educational objectives are stated in the educational specifications. These establish an *index*, which expresses the amount of space required for each type of use. The amount of space required for each use category depends on enrollment, the educational level of students, and the fields of study offered. Altogether, these form a catchment or tributary area from which the student population is derived. The main purpose of the numeric method, therefore, is to present a logical system for the calculation of space requirements.

The use categories in educational facilities include: classroom, instructional laboratory, office, research laboratory, archive, research storage, library, student services, etc. Some of these categories are analyzed on the following pages.

Use	Net Square Feet per Occupant
Assembly Areas, concentrated use (without fixed seats)	7
Auditoriums	
Churches	
Stadiums	
Assembly Areas, less concentrated use	15
Conference Rooms	
Dining Rooms	
Drinking Establishments	
Exhibit Rooms	
Gymnasiums	
Lounges	
Classrooms	15–20
Dormitories	50
Dwellings	300
Hospitals	80
Hotels and Apartments	200
Kitchens (Commercial)	200
Library Reading Rooms	50
Offices	100
Vocational Shops	50
Shops and Stores	30–50

Table 3.1

Classrooms

In order to program the number and size of instructional classrooms, it is necessary to know:

1. Curriculum uses, to determine size.
2. Instructor-student ratios.
3. Number of students.
4. Number of weekly class-hours of use.
5. Area per student.

The area per weekly student-hour is derived from three sources:

1. The area required for each student.
2. The number of hours per week classrooms are in use.
3. The percentage of time each student-station is occupied when the classroom is in use.

The area required per student varies with the size of the space and type of student accommodation, such as tablet armchairs or fixed seats. In large lecture halls with auditorium-type seating, a standard of nine square feet per student is used, whereas in seminar rooms, 18 to 20 square feet per student is the normal standard. In general, the more students to be accommodated in a classroom, the smaller the assigned area for each student. For conventional classrooms, 15 to 20 square feet is the standard student-station.

The number of hours per week during which classrooms are used is a matter of the educational policy of the school. To assure the maximum utilization of space, some schools use a standard that specifies the number of hours per week classrooms must be used, such as the commonly used standard of 30 hours per week. The percentage of time each student-station is occupied, when the classroom is in use, depends on the educational program; however, a 60 percent station utilization is standard.

The method of computing an *index*, using these factors, which indicates the number of square feet per weekly student-hour is as follows:

Square feet per student-station = 15
Hours per week classroom used = 30
Percent of time each student-station is occupied, when the classroom is in use = 60%
Index = $15 \div (30 \times .60) = .833$

The index of .833 indicates the amount of instructional space, in square feet per weekly student-hour, that is needed for the educational program.

This index can be applied as follows:

Assume that 1,000 sociology students each spend six hours in lecture per week. Therefore, they generate 6,000 weekly student-hours. The result is multiplied by the index, .833, to determine the actual instructional space that must be provided. Thus, the space needed for this program totals 5,000 net square feet (6,000 × .833 = 5,000). This does not consider the number or size of classrooms; these are determined on the basis of class types and number of students per class. The following example illustrates this point.

The school has 1,000 sociology students, and on the basis of each attending six hours of lectures per week, 5,000 net square feet of instructional space is needed. This net area is divided into a number of smaller instructional spaces, determined by the seating arrangements as follows:

5 classrooms for 20 students each at 300 square feet	= 1,500 sf
2 lecture halls for 150 students each at 1,350 square feet	= 2,700 sf
8 seminar rooms for 5 students each at 100 square feet	= 800 sf
Total area	= 5,000 sf

The building area for such an activity has an efficiency of 60 percent. Therefore, to obtain the gross square footage, we divide the net area by 60 percent, or 5,000 ÷ 0.60 = 8,333 gross square feet, which is the total building area required to accommodate the 1,000 sociology students in this particular program.

Laboratories

Estimating the space needs for instructional laboratories illustrates the similarities as well as the differences between the requirements of these more complex spaces and those of the basic lecture rooms. The instructional laboratory space usually contains equipment arranged so that its use is restricted to a particular field of study. Thus, it is a more specialized space, serving a smaller segment of the student population than the general classroom, and having a different relationship to the total space program.

The method for computing the numeric index for instructional laboratory space is the same as for classrooms: weekly student-hours in instructional laboratories and the area per weekly student-hour. However, unlike classrooms, the area required per weekly student-hour in instructional laboratories varies, depending on the field of study. In addition to the area required for the stations occupied by the student in the laboratory, additional space is required for storage rooms, preparation rooms, balance rooms, animal holding quarters, etc. The total area per station, including these auxiliary or support spaces, may vary from 15 to 160 square feet per student.

For example, a student station in the instructional chemistry laboratory may require 50 square feet, but an additional 18 square feet may be required for auxiliary space. In a drafting room, by contrast, only 32 square feet per student may be needed for the teaching space and the auxiliary spaces, combined.

Laboratory and other specialized classrooms are normally used for fewer hours per week than a classroom. Therefore, most schools have adopted standards for instructional laboratories based on 20 to 25 hours per week with 80 percent student-station utilization.

As an illustration, let us suppose that a laboratory is used 20 hours per week and requires 68 square feet per student-station. Thus, the area per weekly student-hour is 4.25 square feet (68 ÷ [20 × .80] = 4.25). Using 24 rather than 20 hours per week, with 80 percent utilization, the square foot area per student-hour is reduced from 4.25 to 3.54. Thus it is evident that space requirements are greatly affected by scheduling and utilization. Furthermore, when the spaces for instructional laboratories and classrooms are compared, it is apparent that the former requires from two to ten times the amount of area per student-station.

Libraries

The programming of space needed for libraries illustrates still another method of calculation. Libraries include space for books, storage, circulation, and the use of books, periodicals, manuscripts, and other reading materials. Library space can be subdivided into three categories: stack space, reader space, and service space.

The amount of stack (book storage) space derives from the number of volumes and periodicals in the collection. The space required is usually planned so that each shelf is filled to about 75 percent capacity. This avoids the relocation of books when the collection increases. Under these conditions, the floor space for the stack collections, including shelving, access aisles, and cross circulation, is calculated on the basis of 0.1 square foot per bound volume; or put another way, one square foot accommodates ten bound volumes. However, as the total collection increases, the need for access aisles and circulation space in the stack area decreases, and the shelves holding some of the least used books can be filled to a greater capacity. Some recommended standards for stack or collection space in a typical library are shown in Table 3.3.

Materials other than books that are stored in libraries also require stack space. Space should be provided for these materials on an equivalent basis; for example, 15 pamphlets are equal in width to one bound volume. The equivalency factors widely used are shown in Table 3.2.

LIBRARY EQUIVALENCY FACTORS		
Type of Material	**Unit**	**Conversion Ratio Unit to Bound Volume**
Roughly Classified Pamphlets	Item	15 to 1
Music Scores and Parts	Item	15 to 1
Sound Recordings	Record	6 to 1
Microfilm Reels	Reel	4 to 1
Maps	Map	9 to 1
Archive Materials	Cubic Feet	1 to 15

Table 3.2

Number of Volumes		Net Square Foot of Floor Space/Volume
1st	150,000	0.1
2nd	150,000	0.09
Next	300,000	0.08
Over	600,000	0.07

Table 3.3

The area of reading room space in institutional libraries is based upon total enrollment. In many instances, such as in community colleges, the standard area is 30 square feet per reading station, with a capacity for 25 percent of the student body. These standards are adequate for undergraduate reading room space; however, in graduate programs, space is needed for study carrels as well as individual stations for both graduate students and faculty. The demand for this type of space varies with the field of study. Those fields of study that do not require laboratory research space generally require more carrel space. Based on these conditions, the following standards are used to determine reading room space:

7.5   square feet per undergraduate student, beginning graduate student, or advanced graduate student in fields of study with low research requirements.

15   square feet per advanced graduate student in fields of study with high research requirements, or teaching and research faculty in departments having low research requirements

30   square feet per teaching and research faculty in departments having high research requirements.

Faculty engaged in administration and counseling do not generate library reading space, nor do nonacademic employees.

Type of Space		Area Required (NSF)
Stack Space	150,000 vols. × .1 NSF/vol.	= 15,000
	150,000 vols. × .09 NSF/vol.	= 13,500
	100,000 vols. × .08 NSF/vol.	= 8,000
		36,500 NSF
Reader Space	4,000 UG. Stu. × 7.5 NSF each	= 30,000
	800 Gr. Stu. × 7.5 NSF each	= 6,000
	250 Faculty × 15 NSF each	= 3,750
		39,750 NSF
Service Space	= 25% × Reader Space	
	= .25 × 39,750	= 9,938 NSF
Total Area Requirement		= 86,188 NSF

Table 3.4

Library service space includes both technical service and public service areas. It also includes office and workroom areas for administration, acquisition, and cataloguing of volumes, which is approximately 25 percent of reader space.

Thus, a school that does not have a research program, and which comprises 4,000 undergraduate students, 800 graduate students, 250 teaching faculty, served by a total collection of 400,000 volumes, generates a total net usable area calculated in Table 3.4.

The area needed for circulation, mechanical, custodial, and general storage space, must be added to the net area to determine the required gross building area. If the building is to be 80 percent efficient, the gross building area would be 86,188 ÷ .80 = 107,735 gross square feet.

On the basis of these standards, a program can be developed which meets the requirements of the institution for the required library space.

The procedures for estimating space needs for classrooms, instructional laboratories, and library space illustrate the numeric method. This methodology can be applied to many other types of facilities, provided that basic standards are available and reliable.

Retail Sales Space

The space needs of retail sales area are directly related to the potential sales expressed in dollars per square foot of leasable area. This yields a profit to those who own and lease the space.

The revenue generated by retail sales is directly related to the number of customers. The greater the number of shoppers, the greater the sales volume will be. There are, of course, certain limiting factors; for example, the optimal travel time for convenience shopping is considerably less than for specialty shopping.

It may be helpful to consider market study research based on population trends, purchasing power, competition, and development costs. These have been used to determine the feasibility of establishing various types of shopping centers, as well as to estimate the amount of retail sales space that can be supported by a community.

Three types of shopping centers will be considered here:

1. The Neighborhood Center
2. The Community Center
3. The Regional Center

Each type of shopping center depends for its support and existence on the population located within a specific radius of the center. This is referred to by several terms: the market area, the trade area, the tributary area, or the catchment area. Each term refers to the population of shoppers who can be expected to use the shopping center.

The Urban Land Institute defines the three basic types of centers as follows:

The *Neighborhood Center* provides convenience goods and personal services for everyday needs, such as foods, pharmaceuticals, automobile service, sundries, etc. It is often built around a supermarket or drugstore and serves 7,500 to 20,000 people within a six-minute driving radius, as well as walk-in shoppers. The building area ranges in size from 30,000 to 75,000 square feet and averages 40,000 square feet. The neighborhood center occupies a site area of four to ten acres.

The *Community Center*, in addition to convenience goods and personal services, provides for the sales of "soft goods" (clothing, towels, etc.) and "hard goods" (hardware, appliances, etc.). It adds depth to the merchandise available in the neighborhood center and adds variety in size, style, color, price, etc., as well. The community center often has as its major tenant a variety store or junior department store, in addition to a supermarket. It serves 20,000 to 100,000 people, and it ranges in size from 100,000 to 300,000 square feet, 150,000 square feet being average. As for its site area, the community center needs 10 to 30 acres, or more.

It is not possible to analyze the market area of this type of center with any degree of certainty, simply because shoppers have such a wide choice of centers available, and they are highly competitive with each other. Additionally, shoppers are not predictable in their selection of clothes or appliances. There is much greater predictability in the habits of shoppers for daily convenience needs.

The *Regional Center* provides general merchandise, apparel, furniture, and home furnishings. It is built around one or more major department stores, which increases shopper attraction. In size, the average building area is 400,000 square feet; the range is 300,000 to 1,000,000 square feet, or more. The regional center requires a tributary population of at least 100,000 to 250,000 people. It offers shopping goods in great depth and variety, and it has a large capacity for comparative shopping within it. Another desirable factor is its accessibility, including the convenience of a large parking area. The regional center has come to replace the facilities once available only in the downtown areas of large cities.

The market area is the primary determinant of the type and size of shopping center that can be supported. This translates into two factors: population and distance. Thus, a high-density

urban area composed of apartment buildings can provide a population of shoppers within a smaller radius than can a single-family suburban area.

Certain other assumptions can be made, based on figures developed by the Urban Land Institute. A neighborhood center can expect a population of 7,500 people to support 30,000 square feet of retail sales area: four square feet per person. The community center can expect 20,000 to 100,000 people to support 100,000 to 300,000 square feet of retail sales area, or three to five square feet per person. The regional center can be supported by 100,000 to 250,000 people generating 300,000 to 1,000,000 square feet, or four to five square feet per person.

Thus, although the total size of each center varies, the amount of sales area that can be supported in each of the three categories is roughly the same: three to five square feet per person.

There are, of course, several additional variables that come into play. Among these are: competing facilities, population change and growth, changes in population characteristics, and changing attitudes towards shopping. However, factors such as these are generally stable in the short run and change only over a long period of time. Therefore, it is possible to use these assumptions to make relevant programming decisions.

The following example demonstrates one method of estimating retail sales space, using the accompanying criteria:

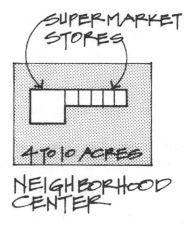

SUPERMARKET STORES

4 TO 10 ACRES

NEIGHBORHOOD CENTER

VARIETY STORE SUPERMARKET STORES

10 TO 30 ACRES

COMMUNITY CENTER

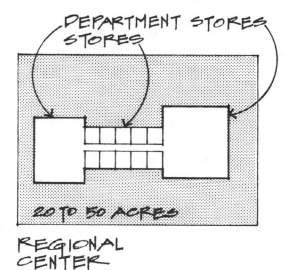

DEPARTMENT STORES STORES

20 TO 50 ACRES

REGIONAL CENTER

Figure 3.6

The catchment area for a proposed shopping center comprises a densely populated urban area of 1,440 acres with a population density of 50 persons per acre. The volume of sales required to produce a profit is determined to be $72 per square foot of leasable area. Assuming that the personal consumption expenditures within the catchment area averages $288 per person, what is the maximum gross leasable area the catchment area can support?

Solution:

1. Total population = 1,440 acres × 50 persons/acre = 72,000 persons.
2. Total sales volume = 72,000 persons × $288/person = $20,736,000.
3. Maximum gross leasable area = $20,736,000 ÷ $72/sf (sales) = 288,000 gross square feet.

The maximum gross leasable area the catchment area can support, therefore, is *288,000 square feet*.

From this example, we can see that the criteria for determining space needs for different building types depend on a building's purpose and function. In the case of a school, the normal and desirable standard for a classroom is 30 students per classroom. However, severe budget constraints may compel a reduction in the number of classrooms in the building program. This might suggest an extension of the teaching schedule, rather than an overcrowding of classrooms.

A commercial enterprise, however, whose purpose is to provide investor income as well as customer service, estimates its space needs on the basis of maximum return on its initial investment and subsequent operating expenses. However, the two building types are similar in that space needs are generated by people, specifically the number of people within the catchment area making up the user population. Furthermore, the criteria for individual space needs are based on accepted standards, whereas the total space needs are related to the total number of users in the geographic area being served.

EXAMPLE PROJECT PROGRAM

Introduction

The following is an example of programming a building project. The purpose is to demonstrate the programming exercise in practice. Although there are alternative methods for developing a program, the basic process is applicable to other types of facilities.

Example Project: A building for a College of Law in a State University

A study prepared by an authority in the field of legal education recommends establishing a law school at a major state university that would serve 300 full-time students. The study recommends a building designed for discussion-type (seminar) teaching with both large and intermediate size spaces. Also included will be a number of small rooms for seminars.

There must be provision for a practice court that can also be used for large public lectures and meetings of the Student Bar Association. Office space should be provided for faculty and staff, in addition to space for the various organizations that characterize an active student body. The Law Building must convey a sense of appropriate purpose, to generate acceptance on the part of the profession and community.

The Law Library will serve the research demands of the law school faculty, the university faculty, and the students. This implies a library of 100,000 volumes at the outset, with a goal within the first decade of a 150,000 volume library.

A faculty-student ratio of 1:15 is contemplated. In addition to the administrative faculty of five deans and directors, and the clerical staff, the total number of professional law staff will range between 19 and 21. Enrollment will commence with an entering class of 70 to 90 students, which should grow by the third year to a total student population of 250 to 300 students.

Subsequent to the preparation of the original feasibility study, a dean is appointed. Additional programmatic ideas are then developed, as follows: The dean stresses that while the building's primary function is to serve as a center for legal education, the legal community must have access to its resources. The "moot court" facilities must be large enough to accommodate half of the entire enrollment, in addition to as many as 30 additional participants or visitors. Research space is not required in the initial increment of development, but expansion for this function, as well as library offices and teaching spaces, must be provided. Students will require common space for a lounge, as well as individual, full-length locker space for books and various other materials. Office and workroom space must be provided for the student publication. An additional amount of space, five percent of the total office and research space, should be provided for archives and research equipment storage.

The dean recommends that since the structure will be adjacent to the existing Education and Life Science Buildings, it should be architecturally harmonious with them. Existing trees and rock outcroppings are to be incorporated in the site design where possible. Service access and parking for 25 cars must also be provided.

The dean also emphasizes that economy denotes architectural simplicity and clarity, which influences not only construction costs, but also the visual harmony of the project.

As for the function of the new Law Building over time, the dean points out that the building, as well as the campus, must be able to accommodate growth. There must be clear visual harmony at each stage of development. At this point in the program development, the essential elements have been established. It is now necessary to identify the space needs, the number and size of spaces, their physical characteristics, and their functional relationships.

The following space needs are identified, based on the recommendations of the feasibility study and the client's additional programmatic ideas:

A. Classrooms: 300 students, each attending classes an average of 17 hours per week, generate 5,100 weekly student-contact-hours. Standards indicate the average student-station size to require 16.5 net usable square feet (NSF). The classroom index is .92 NSF per weekly student-contact-hour (WSCH). Therefore, 5,100 WSCH × .92 NSF = 4,692 NSF.

B. Office Space: Faculty office standards require 150 NSF each, allowing for additional storage and research space. Deans' and directors' offices and adjoining secretarial spaces require 500 NSF each. Therefore, 20 faculty × 150 NSF = 3,000 NSF; five deans and directors at 500 NSF = 2,500 NSF; total office space = 5,500 NSF.

C. Research Space: None at this time.

D. Archive Storage: 5 percent of total office and research space; 5 percent of 5,500 NSF = 275 NSF.

E. Library Space: Current standards for law libraries suggest the following criteria:

1. Collection:

.18 NSF/volume for first 150,000 volumes

.16 NSF/volume for second 150,000 volumes

.14 NSF/volume for next 300,000 volumes

2. Reader Space:

50 percent of enrollment requires 30 NSF each

3. Service Space:

25 percent of total reader space

Therefore, space needs are as follows:

1. 100,000 volumes × .18 NSF/vol.
$$= 18,000 \text{ NSF}$$

2. 50 of 300 students (readers) × 30 NSF
$$= 4,500 \text{ NSF}$$

3. 25% of 4,500 NSF (reader space)
$$\underline{= 1,125 \text{ NSF}}$$

Subtotal   = 23,625 NSF

F. Commons Space:

1. Lounge at 2.5 NSF/student
$$= 750 \text{ NSF}$$

2. Lockers at 4.75 NSF/student
$$= 1,425 \text{ NSF}$$

Subtotal   = 2,175 NSF

G. Moot Courtroom:

(300 students × 50 percent + 30) × 12.5 NSF/student   = 2,250 NSF

H. Law Journal Space:

2 NSF/student   = 600 NSF

I. Support Facilities:

10 percent of classroom space

10 percent × 4,692   = 470 NSF

The space needs are further refined in order to identify space sizes, capacities, and functional relationships. This information is first presented as a tabular summary of spaces, which identifies each space activity, the number of users, and the individual and total square foot areas. The resulting Program Summary for the College of Law Building is shown in Table 3.5.

A summary sheet is prepared for each space contained in the Program Summary to furnish information regarding 1) purposes/functions, 2) activities, 3) spatial relationships, 4) special considerations, and 5) notes. One of these sheets developed for the Lecture Hall is presented in Table 3.5.

Purposes/Functions: To provide an area for lectures and demonstrations for up to 100 students. A secondary function will be for meetings and special events.

Activities: Faculty will lecture and give demonstrations. Frontal projection of films and slides. Students will listen, view projected images, and take notes. Carts and equipment will be moved in and out of the space. General meetings of faculty and/or students.

Spatial Relationships: Easy access from faculty offices, classrooms, and building entrance. Adjacent and with direct access to preparation, storage, and circulation.

Name of Space	Number of Spaces	Capacity Each Space	NSF Each Space	NSF Total Area
Library	—	150	—	24,000
Classrooms	2	40	600	1,200
Seminar Rooms	7	15	300	2,100
Lecture Hall	1	100	1,400	1,400
Preparation Areas	3	—	150	450
Moot Court Room	1	180	2,250	2,250
Faculty Offices	20	1	150	3,000
Deans and Directors	5	2	500	2,500
Archives	1	—	275	275
Lounge	1	50	750	750
Lockers	1	300	1,425	1,425
Law Journal	1	15	600	600
Total Net Area				39,950 NSF
General Service and Circulation (60/40)				26,633 SF
Total Building Area				66,583 GSF

Instructional Areas	Unit Cap.	No. Units	NSF Per Unit	Total Net Area
Lecture Hall	100	1	1,400	1,400

Table 3.5

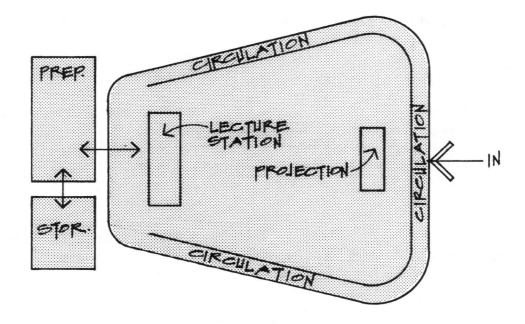

LECTURE HALL - RELATIONSHIP DIAGRAM

Figure 3.7

Special Considerations: Students must be able to enter and be seated without passing the demonstration area. Access must be such that equipment can be moved into the demonstration area from the preparation area. Seating will be upholstered, fixed to the floor, and have tablet arms. Control of audio-visual equipment at lecturer's station and projection area. Provision must be made for three ceiling-mounted viewing screens for simultaneous projection of three images. Illumination must be regulated at lecture station and projection area. Provide enclosed frontal projection area at rear of lecture hall.

Notes:

1. Fenestration undesirable
2. Carpet desirable
3. Sound amplification system with microphones
4. Ceiling mounts for TV monitors

Graphic Representations

Once the individual summary sheets are compiled, the spatial relationship diagrams are prepared for the client/owner's review. These are illustrated in Figures 3.7 and 3.8. The distinction between programmatic diagrams and schematic design studies is intent; the former indicates functions through spatial notation; while the latter explores possible spatial arrangements as the basis for architectural design.

To the extent that the architect can communicate area relationships through the use of these diagrams, and to the extent that the owner can discern their intentions, the project is able to proceed to the design phase. From these diagrams the architect evolves more definitive drawings by delineating spaces, dimensions,

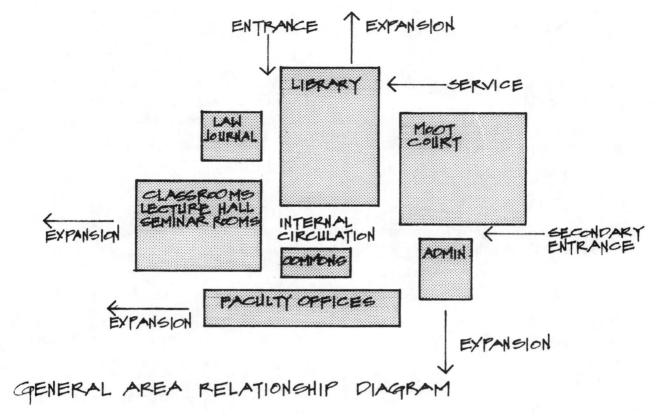

GENERAL AREA RELATIONSHIP DIAGRAM

Figure 3.8

and building openings. The result is a series of schematic design drawings, founded on a realistic building program.

SUMMARY

We have used the preceding examples to illustrate the values and methodology of programming. Every new building must have a program, just as it has plans and specifications. It is an essential step in the creation of a good building; and with a good program, owner/client, user, and architect are better served.

LESSON 3 QUIZ

1. The principal purpose of architectural programming is to

   A. identify the problem.

   B. gather information.

   C. establish project goals.

   D. solve the problem.

2. Which of the following are programmatic factors common to all buildings?

   I.   Circulation

   II.   Fenestration

   III. Site access

   IV.   Structural system

   V.   Efficiency ratio

   A. I and IV   C. I, III, and V

   B. I, II, and III   D. II, IV, and V

3. If the program summary of spaces indicates that a project will exceed the proposed budget by about 10 percent, the architect should

   A. request that the owner obtain additional funds.

   B. maintain the programmed spaces, but reduce the area of each by 10 percent.

   C. maintain the programmed spaces, but reduce the unit building cost by 10 percent.

   D. review the program with the owner and revise it to meet the proposed budget.

4. In an office building, which of the following would be included in the calculations for net square footage?

   A. Vestibule and foyer

   B. Mail room

   C. Electrical closet

   D. Elevator service room

5. During the programming process, goals should be established

   A. after the facts are collected.

   B. after the priorities are established.

   C. after the relationships are formulated.

   D. before the data is analyzed.

6. The final step in the programming process is to

   A. state the problem.

   B. establish objectives.

   C. establish priorities.

   D. solve the problem.

7. If the efficiency ratio for museums is normally 70 percent, and the net square footage for a new art museum is programmed to be 100,000 square feet, the gross square footage of the building would be _____.

8. In which of the following university departments would the greatest amount of space per student-station probably be required?

  A. Architecture

  B. Computer Science

  C. Music

  D. Sociology

9. Functional square foot areas can be determined approximately by considering a variety of criteria, including the

  I. number of people involved.

  II. size of specific objects involved.

  III. proposed project budget.

  IV. established safety standards.

  V. client's arbitrary preferences.

  A. I, III, and IV

  B. I, II, and IV

  C. II, III, and IV

  D. II, III, and V

10. Which of the following would normally receive primary consideration during the programming phase?

  A. Form

  B. Fashion

  C. Function

  D. Financing

BUILDING PROTOTYPES

INTRODUCTION

The objective of a building program is to state the functions and purposes the building must serve. To achieve this, the person writing the program must be aware of the uses to which the building will be put and the functional criteria that apply. During the preliminary design phase this data is evaluated in relation to what the task demands, in addition to what is feasible. In all cases, the individual is the measure of space, since the design of buildings involves solving problems of human function in a physical environment.

In order to consider three-dimensional spaces, we must first consider the size of those who will use the spaces. Shown in Figure 4.2 are the dimensions of a typical adult male. These measurements establish the dimensional standards of all architecture, from the 36-inch wide doorway to the 7-inch high stair riser. Although humans are quite adaptable to varying dimensional standards, excessive deviation from the norm can cause physiological and psychological stress. The needs of people are the chief priority; thus, human dimensions must be considered first, spatial dimensions second, and both of these before the final building dimensions.

Architectural programming involves the process of collecting and organizing information in order to clearly define the building problem. This, in turn, makes it possible to solve the design problem within the limitations imposed by site, budget, and other considerations. To develop the optimal building design, one must know the functional criteria of the common building types that are frequently encountered. Several of these are described below.

HOUSING

Housing is the most fundamental of all building types. It can be found isolated in rural areas, grouped in compact rows, or arranged in vertical high-rise stacks. Its function is to provide an environment in which people live, sleep, eat, bathe, cook, read, entertain themselves, and satisfy a myriad of other needs.

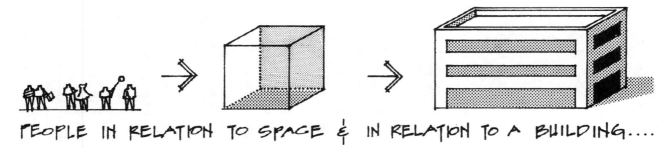

PEOPLE IN RELATION TO SPACE & IN RELATION TO A BUILDING....

Figure 4.1

The outstanding functional problem of housing is that many of these diverse activities occur simultaneously, often in the same space. Residential spaces, therefore, must be designed for flexibility. A child's bedroom, for example, may function for sleeping, as a study, a meeting room for peers, a music room for practicing an instrument, an exercise room, etc. Kitchens and bathrooms, which are generally limited in size and often fixed in arrangement, may also serve functions in addition to those of food preparation and bodily hygiene.

In analyzing the functional aspects of a dwelling, one must first determine which spaces are required; second, how much space is required; and third, how people will circulate from one space to another. Personal tastes aside, all dwellings require certain basic furniture and equipment in order to satisfy basic human functions, and the sizes and arrangements of these have become fairly standard over the years.

The dimensions of spaces, including circulation, have been established by use, habit, and comfort. Dining spaces, for example, require a minimum of two feet of table width per person, as well as three feet from the table to the

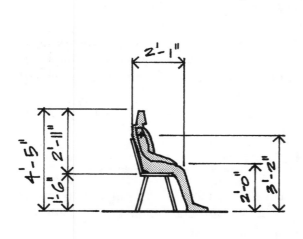

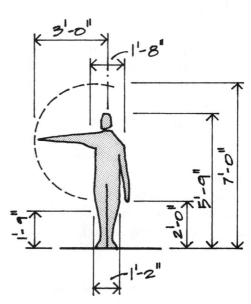

TYPICAL ADULT MALE DIMENSIONS

Figure 4.2

wall, so that one can move the chair back when leaving the table. People are generally unaware of those dimensions when they are correct, but they are very much aware of them when a substandard situation causes discomfort.

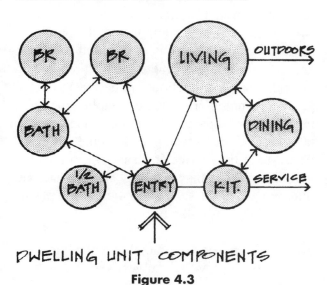

DWELLING UNIT COMPONENTS

Figure 4.3

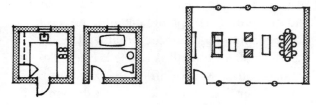

FIXED SPACES CONTRASTED WITH FLEXIBLE SPACE

Figure 4.4

The arrangement of spaces within a dwelling follows a conventional pattern. Bathrooms, for example, are located adjacent to bedrooms, since their functions are closely related. Likewise, a dining area should be next to a kitchen, and in fact, the two areas often occupy the same space. While some functions require close proximity, others may need separation. Noisy home workshops, for example, should be separated from bedrooms.

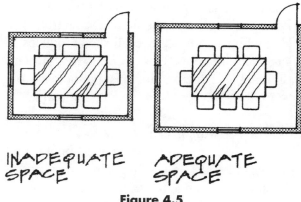

INADEQUATE SPACE   ADEQUATE SPACE

Figure 4.5

Apartment buildings, being groups of dwelling units, must function for the needs of individual families, as well as groups of families. Multifamily living requires lobbies, corridors, and open spaces for access and circulation, as well as shared service elements, such as boiler rooms and refuse disposal areas. The increased density requires special design consideration to maintain privacy between units. It also requires careful design for efficient circulation from public vestibules or garages to individual dwelling units.

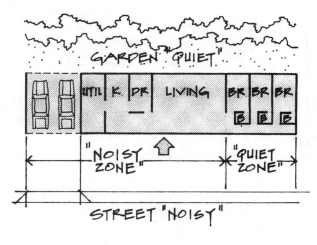

SEPARATION OF QUIET AND NOISY AREAS

Figure 4.6

The shape and size of individual apartment units determine the feasibility of the project.

Standardized or repetitive units with simple shapes help minimize the number of party walls, while a compact overall shape reduces energy requirements. However, the livability of individual apartment units must be the basis of design, if the project is to have lasting value.

Efficiency apartments should be located near elevators, while multibedroom apartments are best located at the ends of building corridors. With such an arrangement, larger apartments can have multiple exterior exposures, and the length of public corridors will be reduced as well. When possible, similar units should be placed back-to-back to economize mechanical servicing and to achieve consistency in construction. Similarly, services are often combined vertically, such as elevators, refuse chutes, flues, standpipes, and stairways.

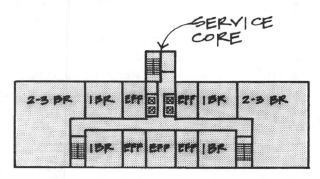

LOCATION OF UNITS IN RELATION TO ELEVATORS IN A HIGH-RISE APARTMENT BUILDING

Figure 4.7

Ground floor spaces require large unobstructed areas to permit convenient circulation to elevators, stairways, garages, mail rooms, storerooms, laundries, and other similar shared spaces. In addition, access areas in apartment buildings should be well illuminated, clearly marked, and secure.

HOTELS

The basic function of a hotel is to provide a comfortable night's rest together with dining, entertainment, and meeting facilities—all in pleasant surroundings. Hotels are divided into two major functional components: the public areas, in which guests enter, dine, and socialize; and the service areas, where food is prepared and other service functions are performed. As a general planning principle, the public circulation areas are separated from the service circulation areas, and in fact, guests should not even be aware of the service areas and operations, vital though they may be. They are separate but interrelated for the sake of efficiency and profitability of the entire facility.

The service portion of a hotel is critical; it must be laid out with the objectives of control and efficiency. It is here that deliveries of services and supplies are made, food is stored and prepared, laundry and cleaning are done, housekeeping facilities are organized, and mechanical equipment is housed. Here also are located administrative offices, locker rooms, banquet services, room service, trash disposal, etc.

The public portion of the hotel comprises all the areas that guests use, such as lobbies, dining spaces, rest rooms, passenger elevators, corridors, guest rooms, etc. Each facility must be planned with the convenience of the guest in mind. In addition, every service, from the registration desk to the coffee shop, must be arranged so that its location is readily apparent to the guest, and confusion is eliminated. From the hotel entry and registration areas, a guest should be able to find the elevators easily, and proceed to his or her individual room. The elevators should be located centrally in order to minimize walking distances. Corridors, usually about six feet wide, should not exceed 100 feet in length.

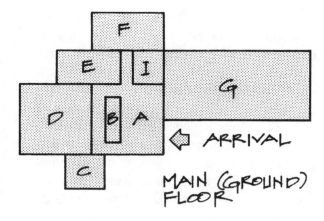

MAIN (GROUND) FLOOR

⬅ ARRIVAL

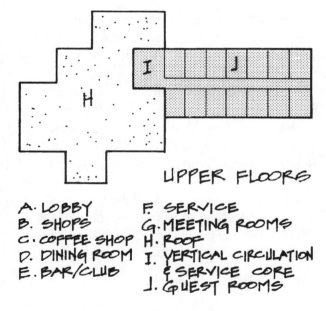

UPPER FLOORS

A. LOBBY
B. SHOPS
C. COFFEE SHOP
D. DINING ROOM
E. BAR/CLUB
F. SERVICE
G. MEETING ROOMS
H. ROOF
I. VERTICAL CIRCULATION & SERVICE CORE
J. GUEST ROOMS

SCHEMATIC ARRANGEMENT OF A MULTI-STORY HOTEL BUILDING

Figure 4.8

Guest rooms should be designed to be comfortable. Room size is determined by the class of the hotel and the degree of comfort being provided. A key unit of measure in a hotel room is the bed size. Its width may range from three and one-half feet for a single bed, to six feet for a king-size bed. Lengths range from six and one-half to seven feet, with the longer dimension fast becoming the standard. Optimal room width is about 12-1/2 feet, while optimal length varies between 14 and 20 feet, depending on room layout.

The guest bathroom should be ample, carefully arranged, and designed to satisfy the needs of the guest, who is generally quite sensitive to the overall quality of accommodations. It is important that the bathroom be designed with guest safety in mind: grab bars, nonskid tubs, properly located and grounded electric fixtures, etc. Closets, too, must be planned with the guests' needs in mind. The longer the duration of the stay, the larger the closet should be. Obviously, closet sizes in a resort hotel and a highway motel would be considerably different.

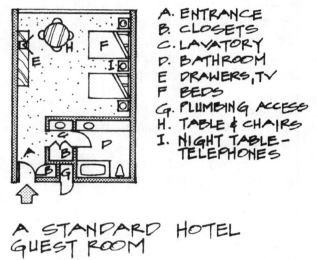

A. ENTRANCE
B. CLOSETS
C. LAVATORY
D. BATHROOM
E. DRAWERS, TV
F. BEDS
G. PLUMBING ACCESS
H. TABLE & CHAIRS
I. NIGHT TABLE - TELEPHONES

A STANDARD HOTEL GUEST ROOM

Figure 4.9

The typical guest room floor also includes a service space designed to serve the entire floor. It is here that towels and linens are stacked, maids' carts are parked, and cleaning supplies are stored. It is desirable to have the service elevator open directly into this area so that the service functions remain out of sight.

SHOPPING CENTERS

The concept of grouping many shops in one place has existed throughout history. The ancient Greek agora has its counterpart in the Arab bazaar, the native markets of Mexico and, indeed, the American shopping center. As a building type, however, the shopping center is entirely a 20th-century development. It may be characterized as a grouping of retail shops, with a limited number of service, recreational, entertainment, and dining establishments, all oriented to access by the automobile. It is a suburban phenomenon. The various types of centers—neighborhood, community, and regional—are similar in spirit and concept, but quite different in overall size, scale, and arrangement. A primary programming objective is the creation of a convenient and attractive project, which offers maximum merchandising potential for constituent tenant stores.

A common feature of the contemporary shopping center is the pedestrian mall or shopping street. The mall may be on one level or on two or more superimposed levels, with the principal access of all stores facing the mall. Some malls are open, with minimum weather protection; however, in most locations they are completely enclosed, and the climate is controlled mechanically. Enclosed malls may be in the form of broad courts or lengthy streets. The street type of mall is 30 to 40 feet wide and a maximum of 800 feet long between department stores or other "anchors"—major retail centers. When planned on two or more levels, malls should have convenient access to all levels from surrounding parking areas, as well as adequate vertical connection between levels, preferably by means of escalators.

A significant planning dimension along the mall is the length of the individual store frontage, which varies from 20 to 30 feet. Store depth may be 120 to 140 feet or more when accommodating very large stores. Shallow depths for smaller shops may result in an L-shaped configuration, with a larger store wrapped around a smaller one. Clear ceiling heights are standardized at about 12 feet.

The term *tenant mix* refers to the variety of store types and facilities in a shopping center. A suitable tenant mix is one that offers the

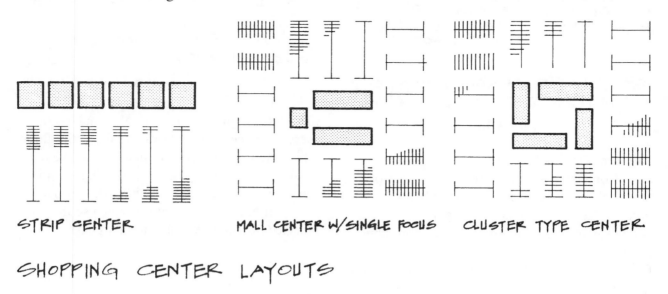

STRIP CENTER   MALL CENTER W/SINGLE FOCUS   CLUSTER TYPE CENTER

SHOPPING CENTER LAYOUTS

Figure 4.10

customer a variety of different but complementary types of merchandise in order to maximize sales volume. The highest sales volume is realized with a well-balanced and complementary pattern of prices, goods, and mix of retail and service facilities. This is true for all shopping centers, whether large or small.

A shopping center must have convenient access. The difficulty of parking in downtown areas was, in fact, one of the original factors that led to the shopping center concept. Adequate and convenient parking, therefore, is an essential requirement for any shopping facility. In suburban areas, where almost all customers come by private automobile, a ratio of five to six car spaces per 1,000 square feet of retail store area is mandatory. This means that for every square foot of retail floor area there must be at least two or more square feet of parking space.

Where there is a good system of regional public transportation, as in some older cities, and where walk-in trade represents a large percentage of customers, the parking ratio can be reduced. Parking may be on one or several levels, either above or below grade. Two-way traffic is more convenient for customers, but may be less safe and more difficult to use than one-way, angled layouts.

Only large downtown department stores are likely to have their own parking garages. Usually, a downtown retail merchants' group will operate a collective parking system, or the municipality or a private parking company will manage this function.

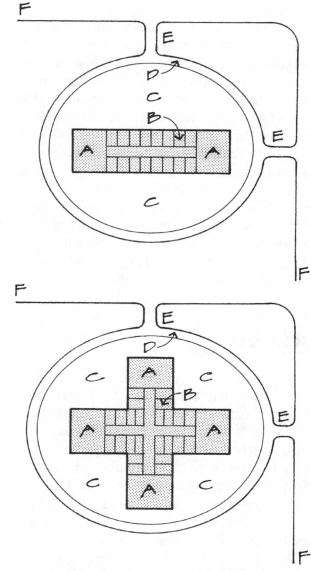

A. MAJOR MAGNET DEPARMENT STORE
B. SMALL SHOPS
C. PARKING
D. LOOP ROAD - A COLLECTOR - DISTRIBUTOR
E. ACCESS ROAD
F. MAJOR TRAFFIC ARTERY

SHOPPING CENTER CONCEPTUAL LAYOUTS

Figure 4.11

The proper planning of shopping centers requires the separation of pedestrian areas from vehicular areas. The movement of vehicles creates danger, fumes, noise, and confusion, which can distract shoppers and diminish shopping enjoyment. Service traffic, too, including delivery vehicles, trash collectors, service vehicles, etc., must be segregated from customer circulation. Such vehicles may be accommodated in special service areas, service roads, or, in some cases, service tunnels. Such systems have a high initial cost, but in a large shopping center they can be cost-effective. Access to public transportation should also be incorporated into the overall planning of a shopping center, so that shoppers are served conveniently.

SCHOOLS

School buildings are places for young people to learn, work, play, communicate, and mature—to develop intellectual, social, and physical skills. An effective learning environment requires a broad range of special qualities that must be considered in the building program. Sensory aspects, such as temperature, visibility, and acoustics, must also be given proper consideration. In addition, school buildings should include environmental qualities such as human scale, warmth, stimulation, and repose, all of which stimulate human development.

The programmatic requirements for schools reflect the combined philosophies of the local board of education, the school administration, and community groups. Their attitudes provide the basis of the architect's design program. Among the criteria to consider are the neighborhood character, the growth rate of the community, the educational program, and the range of probable extracurricular activities. These may include adult evening classes, PTA meetings, public lectures, concerts, and other

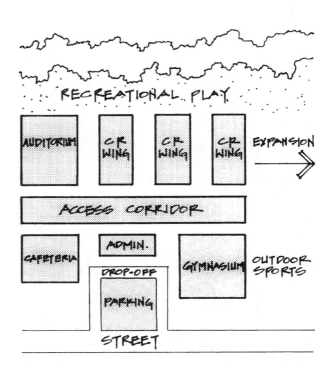

SCHEMATIC
SCHOOL PLAN

Figure 4.12

educational, cultural, social, recreational, or civic functions. All of these influence the program, and hence, the form of the school: its size, teaching staff, scheduling, organizational methods, and special facilities.

The objective of programming a school building is to describe the physical spaces required, the use of these spaces, their functional relationships, and the number of students and equipment needs of each space. To serve these purposes effectively, the architect must be familiar with the teaching methods likely to be employed. This has a critical influence on space needs, room sizes, and building types. Team teaching, for example, requires larger, more open, and more flexible spaces than conventional teaching. Through experience, various spatial standards have been developed in school planning, such as the number of students per teacher, the number of students per teaching station, area per student by type of space, gross square feet per student, and cost per student.

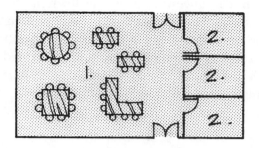

1. OPEN AREAS—NO NOISE OR SOUND PROBLEMS

2. ENCLOSED AREAS—NOISE PRODUCING OR SOUND INSULATED

CLASSROOM LAYOUT W/ SEPARATION OF NOISY AND QUIET AREAS

Figure 4.13

As part of the programming process, an optimum classroom capacity must be established. This may range from 20 pupils in a kindergarten to 40 students in a high school physical education class. Class sizes may vary, but the character of the classroom, the subject being taught, and common practice derived from experience all help determine the desirable capacity.

Classrooms vary in size from 800 to over 1,000 square feet. Academic classrooms, which require quiet locations, should be separated from noisy activity areas such as gymnasiums, playing fields, or band practice rooms. Classroom areas should be flexible and have sufficient space for special projects, teacher demonstrations, equipment storage, etc. Access to classrooms, as well as emergency exits, should be direct. Corridors, stairways, and assembly areas, too, must be efficient, safe, and arranged to encourage social interchange. Due to the nature of their occupancy and use, schools require particularly high standards

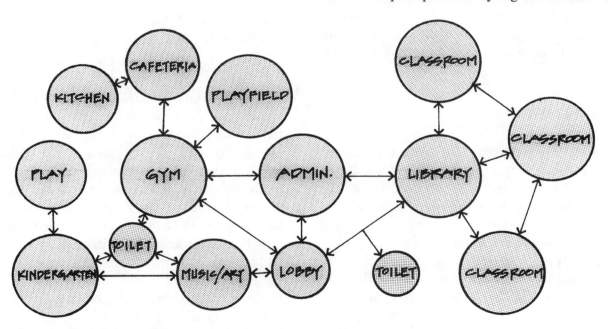

ELEMENTARY SCHOOL DIAGRAM

Figure 4.14

of safety. The high priority of life safety provisions affects the form, organization, and appearance of the school building to a considerable extent.

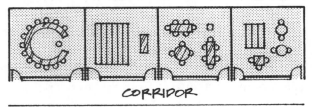

FLEXIBLE CLASSROOM LAYOUT SYSTEM

Figure 4.15

Educational facility planning requires that spaces be flexible, readily adaptable to future uses and arrangements. The open-plan concept, for example, permits groups of various sizes to work together or separately; and when space is shared by several groups simultaneously, it also promotes cooperation. Along with flexibility, educational environments should be designed for comfort, efficiency, and the functional needs of students, teachers, and administrators.

CHURCHES

Church plans are determined by the form of the various rituals which they must accommodate. These vary considerably between faiths, and even within them; however, for most faiths, an altar is the focus of the congregation. Most religions also require visual and aural contact between those who lead the service and the congregation. For this reason, there should be clear sight lines in the sanctuary, as well as good acoustics. Many religious buildings also serve as community or social centers for their members, providing educational, cultural, sports, and other activities.

Seating design is partially determined by elements of the service that require periods of standing or kneeling, as well as the nonreligious uses that the church must accommodate. The conventional pew normally serves for both. Multi-use requirements may suggest individual folding or stacking chairs, which necessitates storage space, but generally allows more seating space per person.

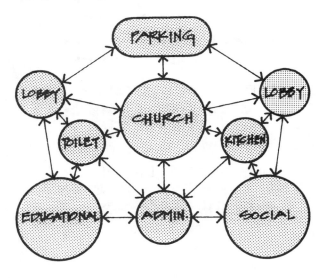

DIAGRAM OF CHURCH ELEMENTS

Figure 4.16

The most common Christian church plan form is the rectangle, with the altar at one end and the seating in rows oriented toward the principal focal point. A single central aisle, together with side aisles, is customary in churches of moderate size. When the congregation exceeds 500 people, the rectangular plan arrangement may require modification, such as an elevated pulpit or a mezzanine, in order to maintain contact between congregants and the service.

Cruciform plans have a long historical precedent and continue to serve effectively today. The altar may be located at the crossing of nave and transept, or at the head of the cross. The seating arrangement, however, must be such

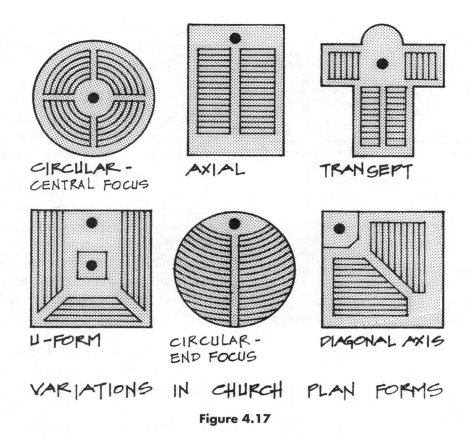

CIRCULAR - CENTRAL FOCUS   AXIAL   TRANSEPT

U-FORM   CIRCULAR - END FOCUS   DIAGONAL AXIS

VARIATIONS IN CHURCH PLAN FORMS

Figure 4.17

as to engender a sense of congregational unity. Another type of plan is the circular form, based on the concept of an encircling congregation, similar to a theater-in-the-round. This shape has a sense of intimacy and unity, but it has several shortcomings. Seating layouts and sight lines may be awkward. Some ceremonial functions, such as those utilizing processions, may be difficult to conduct. However, a circular form can be useful for social activities.

For all religious buildings, space must be provided for a multitude of support activities, in addition to the major area for worship. Such spaces as an entry or vestibule, sacristy, choir room, meeting room, storage room, classrooms, offices, lounge, toilets, mechanical space, etc., must also be provided.

Religious schools consist of classrooms, which also function as multi-use areas to accom-

modate activities such as crafts, hobbies, recreation, drama, and musical programs. The number of pupils and the type of school determine the number of classrooms required. Classrooms are generally similar in size and teacher-student ratios to those in conventional public schools.

Churches generally include facilities for community and social functions, such as a social hall with a stage. The social hall should be planned as a multi-use space with removable seating and facilities for showing films, and be of sufficient size and shape to accommodate large groups.

Finally, the conscientious designer must be sensitive to the many different religions in our society. These different religions have very different practices, which require varying architectural expressions.

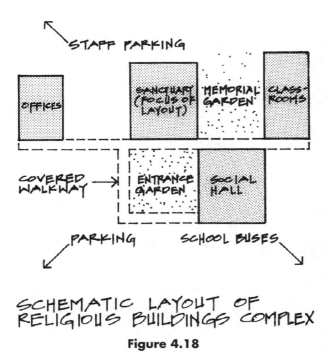

SCHEMATIC LAYOUT OF
RELIGIOUS BUILDINGS COMPLEX

Figure 4.18

THEATERS

A theater is a space in which people may view various performances, including plays, operas, concerts, movies, recitals, lectures, etc. It is not generally practical to use one type of theater to accommodate all the performing arts. Desirable music reverberation time, for example, demands a greater spatial volume than that needed for the spoken word. Appropriate stage dimensions, seating arrangements, and sight lines all vary with the type of performance. Therefore, the so-called multi-use auditorium is limited in its ability to accommodate all types of performances.

In order for the audience to see and hear satisfactorily, the dimensions and geometry of the seating area and stage must be carefully coordinated. A common practice is to curve the rows of seats so that the center of curvature is located on the center line of the auditorium. This establishes a good viewing relation

between audience and stage. It is also common practice to stagger seats in adjacent rows so that no person sits directly in front of another person.

Aisles are necessary for access to seats, for egress, and for emergency evacuation. A center aisle wastes the most desirable seating area in the theater, but it may be unavoidable because of the available theater space. "Continental seating," which is permitted in some localities, provides widely-spaced continuous rows. This makes it possible to have transverse circulation and eliminates the need for longitudinal aisles which cut through the seating area. The optimal layout is generally determined by testing several alternative layouts.

The size of the theater, including the relationship between width and depth of house and width of proscenium, is determined by several empirical formulas, which are variable. Typical standards indicate that the optimum house depth equals four to five times the stage width. Depth also equals about twice the house width when the house width is about three times the stage width. In legitimate theater, that is, in live performances, the maximum house depth, based upon visibility, is 75 feet. In contrast, for certain types of performances, such as those where large spectacles are presented, the maximum viewing distance, or house depth, can be far greater. Spectators at the Radio City Music Hall in New York, for example, may be seated up to 200 feet from the stage.

Sight lines determine proscenium splay and house width; visibility limits and house capacity determine depth; and minimum distance from the stage to the first row is determined by a vertical angle of 30 degrees. Floor slope is determined in a variety of ways, with the objective that all patrons have an unobstructed view.

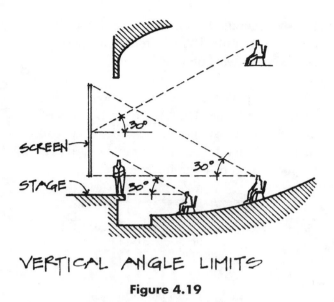

VERTICAL ANGLE LIMITS

Figure 4.19

The stage proper is composed of the acting area in which the actors perform; the scenery space, where the scenery, props, and control rooms are located; and the working and storage space, which includes dressing rooms, costume and rehearsal rooms, shops, loading docks, etc. All of these spaces have a functional relationship that must be logically arranged.

PARKING FACILITIES

Automobile parking is a major consideration in all site development, including central city areas which are also served by public transportation. In some cases, a ground-level parking lot may provide sufficient capacity, but where

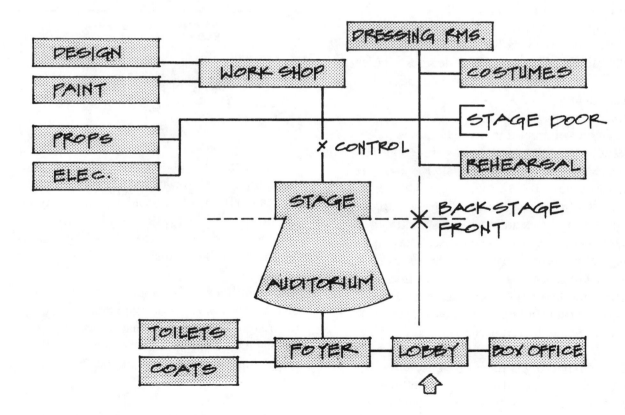

ORGANIZATION OF THEATER

Figure 4.20

land cost is high and parking demand intense, a multi-level garage structure may be required. In some central urban areas, the high construction cost of an underground facility may be justified. Examples are found in all major cities.

As a general rule, a surface parking space costs approximately one-fifth as much as an average automobile, a parking structure space costs about the same as an average automobile, and an underground parking structure car space costs twice that.

After many years, it has been found that for multifloor garage structures, whether above ground or below, a gradually sloped or ramped floor system is most desirable. However, it may also be necessary to use spiral or straight circulation ramps with steep slopes and tight turns, or double-spiral systems, which segregate up and down traffic flow. Ramp grades are a maximum of 8 percent (4.5 degrees), which is the steepest angle that can be negotiated conveniently.

The layout of a parking area should be designed to minimize traveling time. One hundred feet of extra travel distance to or from a parking stall adds seven and one-half seconds to driving time, and 20 seconds to walking time. This reduces an attendant's parking rate by one car per hour. It also causes increased congestion during normal rush hours. For self-parking lots, walking distance should not exceed 300 feet from the parked car to the entrance point. In larger garages, elevators or escalators may be required.

90-degree parking is most often used for efficiency and to permit two-way traffic flow. Parking stalls are laid out to accommodate large cars. Some projects provide smaller spaces for compact cars, but it is often difficult to regulate stall usage according to automobile size. Park-

ing stalls should be a minimum of 8'-4" wide, and are generally 18 to 20 feet long. End stalls should be at least one foot wider.

90-degree parking aisles should be no less than 24 feet wide. Thus, the overall width of an aisle, with a stall on either side, is approximately 62 feet. It is also desirable that the 62-foot width be column-free.

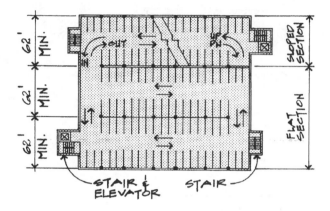

AN EFFICIENT
SELF-PARKING GARAGE

Figure 4.21

Ramp approach and departure angles, turning radii, and driveway specifications are all critical, and must be considered in the layout of parking garages. If the facility is difficult or dangerous to use, people will avoid it, and its usefulness will diminish.

The sight lines within a garage structure should also be given special design attention. Long clear sight lines make it easier for a driver to locate an empty parking space, as well as improving safety. No less important, they facilitate internal security.

Control areas, as well, must be located with regard to efficiency and safety. There must be space to drop off cars, stack waiting automobiles off the street, collect fees, and maintain a safe separation between moving cars and pedestrians.

HOSPITALS

Programming a hospital is enormously complex, since this type of facility consists of many highly specialized components. The extent of services, the kind of equipment necessary, and the optimum space requirements vary from one hospital to another. However, certain facilities and equipment requirements are common to all hospitals and determine the critical organization of space. Another common characteristic of hospitals is the need to expand in large increments. The average American hospital, in fact, is triple its original size due to periodic expansion.

The basic hospital bedroom unit, including toilet facilities, varies in net floor area from 150 square feet for a single room to 200 square feet for a double room, and as much as 400 square feet for a four-bed room. The depth of rooms varies from 15 to 22 feet, depending on the number of beds, mechanical services, and fenestration. Single rooms may be a minimum of 10 feet in width, while double rooms measure at least 12 feet in width. Four-bed rooms are generally twice this width, since their layout is approximately the same as that for two double rooms, but without a dividing partition. All rooms must include individual wardrobes for storage of patients' clothing.

The next most important architectural consideration is the provision and arrangement of mechanical services. Although some older hospitals may lack individual patient facilities, a toilet measuring about three by five feet, and connected to each room, is now regarded as a necessity. Toilet rooms that are shared by adjoining bedrooms may conserve space and reduce initial construction costs; however, this arrangement usually disturbs patients, lacks privacy, and requires segregation of room assignment by sex.

Standard hospital bedroom doors are four feet wide in order to allow the passage of beds. Windows, however, may vary considerably in size, depending on climate, orientation, aesthetics, and economics. Room finishes may vary, but in all cases should be designed for ease of maintenance, durability, and initial cost. The most common preference is for gypsum board walls that are either painted or covered with a vinyl fabric. It is particularly important that interior detailing be as smooth as possible, and free of crevices, which create ideal breeding places for germs.

One of the more conventional floor plans for a typical patient care floor is the double-corridor nursing unit. In this layout, patient rooms are arranged along the length of both sides of the floor, and are separated by a central service core composed of nursing stations, storage and supply rooms, equipment rooms, toilets, and other related spaces. This common plan type permits a close relationship between patients' rooms and service areas, while staff activity is localized, thereby reducing both movement and noise in patient corridors. This layout also permits flexibility in the segregation of patients according to medical condition. The number of beds per nursing station ranges between 25 and 35.

The circulation within a hospital is complex and continuous. Its efficiency can very often determine the difference between life and death. In this regard, the architect must consider corridor width, location of intensive care facilities, placement of elevators and stairways, and the integration of various support areas.

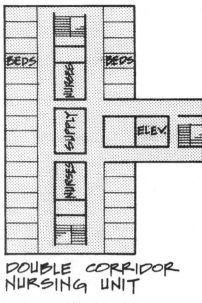

DOUBLE CORRIDOR NURSING UNIT

Figure 4.22

In addition to patient rooms, hospital programming involves the complex functions of surgical suites, pediatric units, diagnostic and x-ray suites, therapy rooms, laboratories, examination and treatment rooms, etc. Other considerations include administrative offices, staff facilities, parking areas, access, circulation, and control.

SUMMARY

The buildings described in this lesson represent a range of types that an examination candidate might encounter. While it is obviously not possible to include every building type or each specific functional requirement, the programming process in each case is similar. One must collect all pertinent functional data, qualitative as well as quantitative, organize them, and finally, determine their relationships. From this exercise, a sound, realistic program may be developed and defined.

LESSON 4 QUIZ

1. The principal objective of a building program is to

   A. discover the building's function and purpose.

   B. define the essential building problem.

   C. determine the schematic building solution.

   D. decide on the prototypical building form.

2. Which of the following criteria demands the highest priority during the programming phase?

   A. Function

   B. Security

   C. Structural factors

   D. Access and egress

3. The success of a suburban shopping mall is most affected by which factors? Check all that apply.

   A. Variety of store types

   B. Prevailing climate

   C. Convenient access

   D. Adequate parking

   E. Public transportation

4. The 36-inch-wide doorway commonly used in many building types is generally established by

   A. code requirements.

   B. traditional use.

   C. building industry standards.

   D. typical human dimensions.

5. Which of the following would have a relatively small influence on the architectural program for a new theater?

   A. The type of performance for which it is used.

   B. The maximum seating capacity.

   C. The proposed cost of an admission ticket.

   D. The size and shape of the site.

6. Compared to a single-family detached residence, the normal activity spaces in a unit of a high-rise apartment building are generally

   A. less flexible.

   B. less spacious.

   C. more compact.

   D. quite similar.

7. Separating residential functions into quiet and noisy zones generally implies that

   A. utility rooms will be in a quiet zone.

   B. dining spaces will be in a quiet zone.

   C. entry halls will be in a noisy zone.

   D. bathrooms will be in a noisy zone.

8. Which of the following statements regarding the planning of multi-level apartments is generally FALSE?

  A. Elements common to all floors, such as refuse chutes, standpipes, and flues should be aligned vertically.

  B. The increased density requires special planning in order to maintain privacy.

  C. The larger apartments should be located closest to the elevators.

  D. It is generally desirable to standardize units by using simple shapes.

9. 90-degree parking is often preferred because it

  I.   is easiest to use.

  II.   is easiest to lay out.

  III. minimizes parking time.

  IV.   allows two-way traffic.

  V.   uses space most efficiently.

  A. I and III   C. II, III, and IV

  B. IV and V   D. I, IV, and V

10. The principal priority in programming is to consider

  A. human dimensions.

  B. spatial dimensions.

  C. unit dimensions.

  D. functional dimensions.

Lesson One

1. D

2. A

3. F

Lesson Two

1. D The physical form of a building is largely determined by the uniqueness of the project and its program.

2. A Harmonious proportions are visually desirable, but they have no effect on project costs. See page 13.

3. C Developments that are extended or decentralized require longer, and hence, more expensive utility services. Those that are more compact, such as grid systems, are generally efficient and more suited for complex distribution flows.

4. A Compact or centralized developments are best suited to sites that are steep or irregular, such as in the mountains. Extended or open layouts are more suited to the other site choices listed.

5. B and C

6. D Severe weather suggests compact organizational forms.

7. A Access is always more efficient and economical in buildings having compact forms. Although multilevel buildings are often more compact than single-level structures, an extended two-story building would not necessarily be more centralized.

8. D A ring form, which is closed and complete in itself, does not lend itself to future expansion.

9. C The length of construction time is irrelevant in determining a project's physical form.

10. B Social interaction is encouraged by the use of elements that bring people together. See page 12.

Lesson Three

1. A See page 25.

2. C Fenestration and structural systems are design considerations, not programmatic factors.

3. D Each of the first three choices is a possibility, however, any decision to revise the scope, quality, or cost of a project should be made by the owner.

4. B Net areas include all usable floor spaces, but exclude circulation and general service areas. Thus, a mail room is considered usable space, whereas an electrical closet is considered a service space.

5. D Project goals are always established first, before any other considerations. See page 26.

6. A The statement of a problem is always the final step in the programming process. See pages 26–28.

7. 142,857 square feet Establish the following ratio: 100,000 (net square feet) = .70 × G (gross square feet). Thus, G = 142,857 square feet.

8. A It is probable that student stations in the architecture department would require the greatest amount of space because of the size of equipment—such as drawing boards—that is used.

9. B The project budget and clients' preferences have no direct effect on the way in which spaces function, or consequently, on their areas.

10. C   Function is always the primary consideration in determining the statement of a program.

Lesson Four

1. B   See page 49.

2. A   Programming is primarily a process used to define a building's function.

3. A, C, and D

4. D   Typical space dimensions were first established by human need. These dimensions then became confirmed by traditional habit, industry standards, and finally, code requirements.

5. C   See pages 60–61.

6. D   Regardless of the type of residence, normal activity spaces generally accommodate required human functions in much the same manner.

7. C   Residential functions may be generally divided as follows: Sleeping spaces, studies, and adjacent baths are in a quiet zone, while all other residential functions fall into a noisy zone.

8. C   The smallest apartments should be located near elevators, while larger apartments should be located at the end of corridors. With this arrangement, large apartments will have multiple exterior exposures and corridor lengths will be minimized.

9. B   Angled parking is actually easier and takes less time to use than 90-degree parking. See page 62.

10. A   Because programming relates primarily to function, it follows that the principal programming priority is to consider the human dimensions of those who will use the spaces.

Part II

Environmental, Social, and Economic Issues

DESIGN RELATIONSHIP TO THE HUMAN BODY

INTRODUCTION

A design is composed of several basic elements, which may be combined in a number of ways. Depending on how the parts are combined, one may produce an adequate design or a great work of art. Design is a reflection of the society that produces it, and, even more, it is a reflection of the whole of human nature. Sustainable design is concerned with a holistic approach that understands the coexistence between the inhabitants and the natural environment in which the architecture is placed. As a practical art, design concerns itself with things that are to be used by people. Therefore, there is a connection between the human body and designed objects. We often judge the success of a design by how well it responds to or recalls the form of human features. For

example, just as gracefully proportioned legs on a person are judged to be attractive, similarly proportioned legs on a chair or table are similarly regarded.

Anthropomorphic design relationships have existed since the beginning of design. They establish associations between human characteristics and manmade objects. Inanimate objects are frequently described as though they were alive. An example of this is found in classical architecture, where a supporting column was given a human form, such as a Caryatid or an Atlantid. The same concept is expressed in Greek columns by a slight outward curve, entasis, that gives an impression of vertical strength, as in a leg. Similarly, the echinus curve of a Doric capital approximates the shape of an upraised hand supporting the entablature above.

In both cases these subtleties of form reflect the eye's and mind's dependence on an association with forms found in nature, particularly the human body. In the design of objects, we often refer to various elements with the same names that are applied to parts of the human body. The component parts of a chair are called legs, arms, seat, and back. In architecture, too, we refer to a supporting leg of a structure, the head of a door, and the face (facade) of a building. Design may be viewed, therefore, from a perspective of human associations.

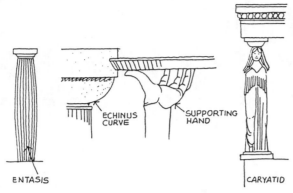

ANTHROPOMORPHISM IN ARCHITECTURE

Figure 5.1

Human awareness of design and its derivations is acquired during the earliest years of life. Through a variety of early physical experiences, one learns about the distances and heights of space, the force of gravity, and various rhythmic patterns. The forces that act on all things— whether to pull them down, overturn them, or blow them away—also operate on human beings. Thus, everyone develops an intuitive awareness for judging the appropriateness of a design, based on personal experience.

HUMAN AWARENESS OF DESIGN

Figure 5.2

There is a direct relationship between the human body and units of measurement used to describe objects. Originally, all measurements derived from parts of the body. The smallest measurement was the breadth of the thumb, from which came the inch; the human foot became the foot, or 12 inches; from the center of the body to the arm extended was a yard; and the spread of the arms was a fathom.

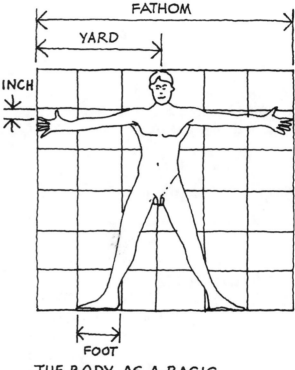

THE BODY AS A BASIS
OF MEASUREMENT

Figure 5.3

By the 18th century, in Europe, most other systems of measurement had been replaced by the metric system, in which the meter was calculated as one-ten millionth part of the length of a meridian from the earth's pole to the equator. The meter also approximates the yard. The adoption of the meter established a measurement system for the globe, as it was then known. The point is that the systems of measurement in architecture are generally derived from, and must be related to, familiar human dimensions as well as the dimensions of the world we inhabit.

NATURE AS A SOURCE OF INSPIRATION

A story is told regarding the Crystal Palace, which in 1851 was considered to be one of the greatest engineering achievements of its time. Its designer, Joseph Paxton, the English horticulturist and engineer, was contemplating a water lily, when the idea occurred to him to adopt the structural system of the lily as the basis of his design for an enormous exhibition hall. In the lily's structure he recognized a regular, precise, and delicate skeletal pattern. Its constituent veins enabled the stalk to support a very large area of leaf surface.

While the truth of this story cannot be confirmed, the point is that we all carry in our memories our experiences of nature. We continue to bear within ourselves a sense of structure in nature, since so much of our experience derives from that.

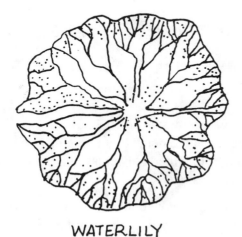

WATERLILY

Figure 5.4

Children discover the qualities of objects by playing with pebbles, sea shells, twigs, and the variety of natural objects with which they are surrounded. The range of lessons learned from these early experiences depends on one's particular environment, as well as his or her powers of observation. A person who is brought up among fruit orchards will understand the deformation of tree branches when loaded with ripe fruit. Children raised in a desert area, on the other hand, learn to appreciate the value of a deep shading overhang, and the natural ventilation of trees.

PRINCIPLES OF NATURE IN ARCHITECTURE

Figure 5.5

Objects found in nature, being the products of evolution, of the natural response to particular forces, are well-suited to their purposes. Otherwise they would not survive. Because natural things are so appropriate to their purposes, and so expressive of them, designers have always found creative inspiration in the realm of nature. Houses have been designed that are inspired by the form of seashells. Airline terminals have been designed that are inspired by symbols of flight, such as the wings of a bird. Commercial structures have been designed as tree-like forms, in which the floors are cantilevered like branches.

It is one thing, however, to find inspiration in nature, and quite another to know how to make use of it. What we appreciate in nature cannot be transformed literally into a manmade product. The rugged configuration of a piece of driftwood along the beach loses its character when transformed into a table lamp, because the relationship between it and the forces that created it originally are no longer its reason for being. To learn from nature, therefore, one must understand the principles underlying natural forms and their evolution, transposing those processes into our own. We should not imitate form, but rather emulate process.

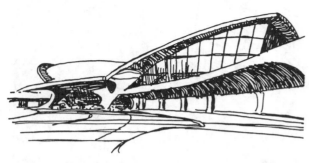

TWA TERMINAL, NEW YORK

Figure 5.6

A VOCABULARY OF FORM

Basic System of Geometry

Design concepts are described by a visual language that can be learned, just as one learns a verbal language. There is a vocabulary of design, and of concepts of visual organization. An understanding of this vocabulary enhances proficiency in design.

The component elements of design are inextricably related to each other, and should not be separated. However, they can be identified and discussed. When we look at an object, we do not see individual lines or planes. Rather, we see the whole object. Individually, these elements constitute the factors contributing to the

overall appearance of a design. Consider the geometry which generates three-dimensional form:

1. A *point* indicates position. It has no dimension nor does it occupy any space. It can represent the beginning or end of a line; it is the place where two lines intersect.

2. A *line* is the path described when a point moves. It has position, direction, and length, but no thickness. A line is bounded by points and forms the border of a plane.

3. A *plane* is the path described by a line in motion, in a direction other than its own direction. A plane has position, direction, length, and breadth, but no thickness. It is bounded by lines and defines the external limits of a volume.

4. A *volume* is the three-dimensional space described by a plane in motion, in a direction other than parallel to itself. It has position in space and is bounded by planes.

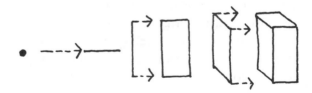

POINT   LINE   PLANE   VOLUME

THREE DIMENSIONAL FORM

Figure 5.7

When one draws on paper, the drawn lines represent elements of an imagined concept. These imagined concepts have the following attributes:

1. *Shape* is the outline or configuration of a thing. Anything that can be seen has shape.

2. *Size* is the physical dimension, magnitude, or extent of something. All shapes have size.

3. *Color* is the appearance of something caused by the quality of light reflected by it. Shapes are distinguished from their surroundings in part due to color. White is the absence of color; black is the absence of light.

4. *Texture* is the surface characteristic of an object.

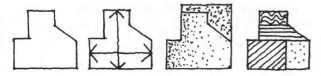

SHAPE   SIZE   COLOR   TEXTURE

ASPECTS OF FORMS
Figure 5.8

With lines, planes, and volumes, which are the structure of objects, and shape, size, color, and texture, which are an object's characteristics, a designer has the basic tools or "language" necessary to represent almost any design. In addition, a designer thinks about circulation, such as the movement of people through designed spaces, which influences his or her spatial design.

The geometric shapes that are particularly useful include the square, the circle, and the triangle. The corresponding three-dimensional shapes are the cube, sphere, pyramid, cone, and cylinder.

Their usefulness for designers lies in the fact that they are usually the basic organizing forms for structures. By thinking in terms of these basic shapes, the designer has a simple and quick design "shorthand" at his or her disposal.

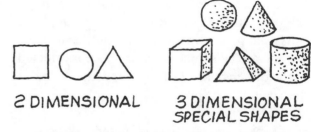

2 DIMENSIONAL   3 DIMENSIONAL SPECIAL SHAPES

FORM IN TWO AND THREE DIMENSIONS
Figure 5.9

Characteristics of Architectural Designs

The characteristics of an architectural design can be isolated, described, and analyzed. Among these characteristics are space, form, scale, proportion, rhythm, balance, symmetry, light, and color. A design may emphasize one characteristic more than another; for example, formal symmetry, intense use of color, the artful manipulation of space, or a persisting rhythm. The characteristics of architectural design include the following:

1. *Space*

Space is the interval between points or objects. Architectural space is the three-dimensional volume enclosed by building elements, which is limited, where the movement and activities of people take place.

SPACE - A THEATER LOBBY
Figure 5.10

Space is perceived by all our senses, which interpret what they experience. For example, our visual perception interprets light and shade into form. The sound within a space is affected by the dimensions of the space, which helps to characterize the space.

Every space has an effect on people, depending on its size, height, scale, light, color, and details. Some spaces may feel awkward, restrictive, or uncomfortable, while others seem pleasant and inviting. There are some general principles that establish desirable dimensions and proportions of spaces.

Severely restricted spaces can produce claustrophobia, the fear caused by the feeling of confinement. Even though a person may have sufficient space, light, and air to function, he or she may feel threatened or uncomfortable. Good design of interior space must provide the proper balance of openness and sheltering containment if one is to feel comfortable.

A room with a very low ceiling may feel overly confining and oppressive. A similarly unpleasant feeling can be created by a windowless room, or one with rough textured walls that a person is compelled to rub against when walking. A narrow room with a high ceiling can arouse the fear of being trapped or of being under surveillance. A room with twisted or curved walls may tend to disorient its users in much the same way that oddly placed mirrors do. The aim of all design should be to create spaces in which one will feel secure, sheltered, oriented, and therefore at ease.

Since space also exists to accommodate movement, the shape of spaces can indicate how one is expected to move. Movement is governed by the amount of spatial freedom, or access, provided. A long narrow space suggests efficient axial movement; a perfectly square or round room, with no specific orientation, implies repose—that one may pause or remain at rest. In the case of a stairway, movement is governed by width, tread and riser dimensions, and the location of landings. A stairway may abet graceful movement or prevent it, depending on the stair's design.

When we speak of "manipulating space" we are describing the relationship between spatial design and the feeling of people in that space, achieved through design.

2. *Form*

The perception of form is based on memory associations developed in childhood, which involve the tactile as well as visual sense. For example, we are aware of how a jagged rock will feel even before touching it. Smooth, rounded forms tend to be inviting, encouraging touching. Sharp-edged objects issue a visual warning that they should not be touched, or touched with caution, An object that is soft and lightweight poses little threat. A designer wishing to create an object that is comfortable to touch, such as a doorknob, would use curved forms, which encourage grasping. To convey a sense of stability, or rigidity, one might utilize straight lines and right angles. These imply that the forces they are controlling are clearly directed. They convey a sense of orderliness and repose.

Form can also imply movement, such as a church spire that thrusts toward heaven. Similar effects can be created by the use of spiral forms or shapes that are accentuated by long parallel lines, especially when they are vertical. The twisted columns of a Baroque interior suggest perpetual motion.

FORM

Figure 5.11

SCALE

Figure 5.12

3. *Scale*

Scale in design is the relative size of a structure or space with reference to the human body. For example, a stair riser is six to seven inches high because that is the distance one raises one's foot comfortably when climbing a stairway. Similarly, a handrail is about waist high; the top of a door is above head height; seat height is approximately the length of the lower leg. All are said to be "in scale."

In moving about in space, our eyes constantly scan the scenery and gauge the size of objects through perspective distance, or by clues from nearby objects, such as a car or tree.

When something does not conform to its expected size, when it is found to be too large or too small, it is said to be "out of scale."

When we ask how big something is, we are inquiring about its size relative to ourselves. When it is exaggerated or distorted, scale can be used for dramatic effect, just as superhuman scale is used to create monumental effects. These types of contrived scale also depend on visual reference to the human body, but in ways that dramatize the relationship. Monumental scale utilizes the limit of scale relationships.

Extra-human scale derives from allowing functions to determine size. A large factory, for example, derives its size from its production processes. The length of a runway at an airport is determined by the laws of aerodynamics that govern flight.

PROPORTIONED HIERARCHY OF SCALE
Figure 5.13

Objects whose size derives from such extra-human functions may, nevertheless, contain clues of scalar reference—for example, a window in a factory or a sign on a runway.

4. *Proportion*

Proportion is the relationship between the constituent parts of a structure. It expresses the order of importance of the parts, casting some into "primary" roles, others into "secondary" or "supporting" roles. Proportion suggests the role played by a component part in a structure. For example, a very slender column suggests a light load. A "fat" column suggests a heavy load. Sensitivity to proportion may suggest changing the number of columns so that they will be neither too slender (and thus, possibly, too many in number) or too squat (and thus, possibly, too far apart).

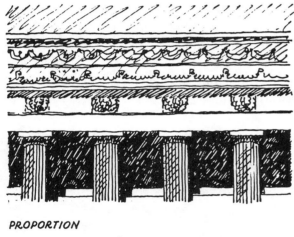

PROPORTION

Figure 5.14

Since ancient times designers have sought the key to beauty through systems of mathematical proportion. Consistency in the proportional relationship between a structure's parts made the aesthetic intent easier to comprehend. From Pythagoras to Leonardo to Le Corbusier, proportioning systems have been devised whose purpose was to provide harmonious order.

The most ancient system in Western architecture and art is the so-called "Golden Section," which is based on proportions found in nature, as well as the human body. (It is the basis of the "modulor" system devised by Le Corbusier.)

The "Golden Section" was a Renaissance concept of proportion in which a whole is divided so that the smaller part is to the larger as the larger is to the whole. The mathematical expression of the Golden Section is A:B = B:C.

With reference to the sketch of the human body shown in Figure 5.15, we can see that the full height of the body (A), is to the distance from the feet to the navel (B), as (B) is to the distance from the navel to the top of the head (C).

The so-called intuitive systems of proportion usually confirm the "Golden Section."

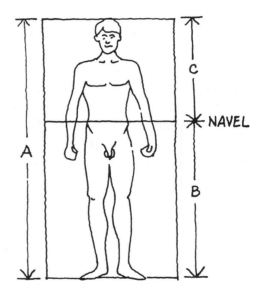

THE GOLDEN SECTION
Figure 5.15

5. *Rhythm*

Rhythm is another design device for establishing order. Rhythm is the regular occurrence of elements, in time or in space. We are all familiar with the basic rhythms of nature, such as a beating heart or the changing seasons. The essence of sonic rhythm is timing, such as the sound of a drum beat. The essence of visual rhythm is spacing, which is conveyed by a recurring design element.

The rhythmic spacing of elements can have an emotional impact. Historical examples of this can be seen in an Egyptian "Avenue of Sphinxes" or the nave of an Early Christian church. In the latter the regular recurrence of the same elements accentuates the formality of the design. Other rhythmic systems commonly found in architecture include exposed structural elements, the placement of windows, and the repetition of material patterns. A texture can be thought of as a fine-scale rhythm.

RHYTHM

Figure 5.16

Rhythm can be experienced on a large as well as small scale, such as a block of row houses or an entire section of a city.

6. *Balance*

Balance is equilibrium among the constituent parts of a structure. It is also a visual quality.

There are two types of balance, static and dynamic. In static balance the parts are equal in size, and located equally about a reference axis. In dynamic balance the parts are of unequal size, and arranged about a reference axis so as to compensate for their differences. For example, a large window close to a centerline can be balanced by a smaller one at a greater distance on the other side.

If the furniture in a room is arranged in a corner, the room may seem to be unbalanced. Pictures hung on a wall in a downhill pattern will appear to be falling. These phenomena can be disconcerting, since we expect stationary objects to have balanced compositions.

BALANCE

Figure 5.17

7. *Symmetry*

Symmetry is a balanced arrangement of elements, equally deployed on either side of a central axis. Symmetrical designs are found throughout nature.

From the Temple of Amon, to the Parthenon, to the Pitti Palace, the principle of symmetry has been utilized. It has come to be associated with formality and authority, as well as certainty.

SYMMETRY

Figure 5.18

Symmetry also requires a relatively uncomplicated building program. Modern times are less authoritarian, building programs are complex, and building sites may have irregular shapes. Hence, symmetry may not be practical for many structures.

8. *Light*

Light is radiant energy that is perceived by the human eye. Among design elements, daylight is one that a designer is particularly able to control. Not only does the quality of light change during the day and from one day to another, but its intensity and color vary considerably in different regions. These variations must be recognized in architectural design.

Traditional architecture has recognized and made use of prevailing light conditions. For example, the light intensity of the hot, dry plains of India led to perforated screens that shielded as they ventilated. In a different climate, that of France, the stained glass of medieval cathedrals converted the often overcast northern light into a warm radiant glow. In strong sunlight the slightest break in a surface produces a strong, crisp shadow. This was recognized by the ancient Egyptians, who employed incised surface decoration. It was also recognized by the Greeks, who developed classic mouldings to create strong lines of visual emphasis in their architectural designs. Designers must always be concerned with light for the aesthetic contribution it can make to designs.

The designer can determine how daylight falls on a building, how it enters a building, and how its quality and intensity may be utilized. Light within a building is essential in experiencing space. By relocating an opening from the middle to the top of a wall, for example, a space can be transformed into an environment of diffused light, thus emphasizing the unity of the space.

Light also possesses psychological connotations. We associate light with clarity and darkness with the obscure, mysterious, and unknown. Dim light is associated with meditation or rest, such as in a church or hospital. Bright spots of light are used to draw attention or create a focus, as on a stage. To create the effect of openness, we use a dispersed, even light. A concentration of light, on the other hand, gives a sense of closure, the darkness outside of the light acting as a container.

9. *Color*

Light and color are inseparable; when we see a color, we are experiencing a sensation caused by radiation of a particular wave length of light. In very dim light all colors appear as shades of gray, almost colorless. Color in design is not experienced independently, but rather as one of several characteristics of an object or place. Color is useful for articulating form and space. We respond emotionally to color. Colors have associations such as warmth, coolness, weight, size, distance, and even sound. For example, red is considered a "warm" color as well as a "loud" one.

Colors also have psychological effects. Red, for example, is exciting. Green is soothing. Leathery browns are masculine. Pink is feminine. Black is solid but mysterious. Color can also affect the perception of time. In a green environment, time seems to pass more slowly than in a red one. Color can express the character of design and emphasize the spirit intended.

There are many theories on the effects of color, but there is general agreement only on the most fundamental issues. A blue environment is relaxing; a red one is stimulating, even exciting. A totally white environment leads to boredom and restlessness. This does not mean that one should paint a room red, white, or blue to achieve particular results, but rather that a designer should be aware of colors as they affect behavior.

Color has been used in architecture to accentuate form, establish physical divisions or zones, direct traffic, and emphasize architectural elements. Color can also be used, as a paint, to unify a surface where finish possesses blemishes or discordant elements.

Human Elements

Design is a human activity; it is performed by people for people. Therefore, a designer must develop a sensitivity to people—to their senses, habits, and feelings.

1. *The Senses*

Environmental "messages" are continuously communicated to our sense organs, and we respond to these messages constantly. For example, upon entering a restaurant we are immediately presented with "messages," which are received through our senses. We notice the table arrangement, color scheme, and ceiling height; we sense the carpet underfoot; we see and smell the food being served; we hear the sound of dishes and the murmur of conversation. All in all, our senses comprehend the experience of this restaurant. Of all the senses, vision is of greatest concern to the designer. However, the other senses—hearing, smell, and touch—are also significant.

When we speak of "hearing" architecture, what we experience is the reflection or reverberation of sound that gives us an impression of size, shape, and material. Every space possesses unique acoustical qualities, absorbing or reflecting the sound with a variety of reverberation times. Gothic churches have a long reverberation time. Therefore, the sound of religious chanting is prolonged, and produces a dramatic musical experience. Opera houses, in contrast, have shorter reverberation times, since projected sounds would otherwise be muffled.

The sense of smell also aids our perception of spaces. There is a characteristic smell of new construction and a characteristic smell of age. There is a distinctive hospital scent, and a distinctive scent in an incense-filled church. These spaces communicate a message of place through aroma.

The sense of touch and the associations it engenders are also relevant in design. Certain materials, such as smooth wood or marble, are conducive, even attractive, to touch. Surfaces of rough stone or bush hammered concrete, on the other hand, discourage touching. Texture is somewhat similar to color; some combinations are harmonious while others are not. Smooth, shiny surfaces, like strong colors, tend to divert attention away from shape to surface. The extreme example is a mirror, which looks like what it reflects. Buildings covered by mirror glass become "non-buildings," since they appear as reflections of their surroundings.

2. *Style*

All societies develop a general consensus about what is acceptable. This applies to social behavior as well as to aesthetic judgment. The general range of possibilities as to what is right or wrong constitutes the limits of a style, which is a system of accepted order. Although we are all individuals, we are also members of a society, and, therefore, we conform in most respects to socially accepted norms.

Some societies developed highly formularized systems of building, which can be referred to as styles. Thus, the appearance of ancient monuments is clearly associated with the culture that produced them. These civilizations established aesthetic codes, which dealt with the form of the entire building, as well as its component details. For example, the Roman Doric column was considered "correct" if the ratio of its diameter to height was 1:7.

Today, our less rigid society permits great design freedom. Designers are not, however, totally autonomous. They are limited by available materials, the skill of construction workers, the discretion of lenders, public opinion, and—not least of all—the sensibilities of clients.

Preoccupation with style in design is both good and bad. On the positive side, style enables designers to produce buildings that are functional and attractive. In such cases, conforming to a style—that is, relying on conventionally acceptable solutions—helps produce buildings that conform to accepted design standards. The use of an accepted style maintains consistency and harmony, at the very least.

On the other hand, the rigid acceptance of a standardized style of design is overly restrictive, and may prevent innovation where it is needed, as in a new type of building serving a new type of function.

3. Culture

Architectural design is a practical art concerned with buildings used by people. We should therefore be aware of some of the differences that exist among peoples of varying cultures.

With the dramatic advances in modern communications, many of these differences have lessened in recent years. Nevertheless, some of these differences, compared to American customs, are as follows:

The English are raised with a higher degree of sociability than Americans. Therefore, when they need privacy, they set up some internalized barriers and cease talking. Americans may interpret this as rejection, when, in fact, it is not.

The French arrange their offices, homes, and cities so as to be in close contact with each other. This can be seen in the way they crowd together in cafes. Counterbalancing this living pattern are their generous, open parks, boulevards, and sidewalks.

Germans are relatively sensitive to intrusion. An American may talk through a screen door from outside a house, or from the corridor outside an office, and still consider that to be suitable behavior. A German person, in contrast, would feel that to be an intrusion into his or her personal space.

The Japanese language does not have a word for privacy, although the concept does exist. Another interesting practice is that of naming intersections rather than the streets leading to them. The meeting place, or center, is considered more important than the route leading to it.

Conversation between Arabs involves intense eye contact and very close head-to-head proximity. When they desire privacy, like the English, they simply cease talking.

These random examples illustrate the point that people who are raised in different cultures have different ideas of personal conduct, manners, and conversational methods.

In the United States, we design not only for the dominant culture, but also for a great diversity of subcultures, such as those of American Indians, blacks, and Latinos. In every case, members of these cultural groups have distinctive communication systems, institutions, habits, and values. Responsible designers, therefore, must consider cultural diversity in solving design problems.

On the other hand, it is also true that people from different cultures can and do mix. An American raised in comfortable 20th-century American buildings can be perfectly comfortable, possibly even more comfortable, in an 18th-century cottage or rudimentary tropical hut. There are universal qualities in architecture that transcend cultural differences and artifacts.

4. *Beauty*

Designers make many decisions during the design process, many of which concern aesthetics. One effect of these decisions is to produce a characterizing identity for a building. A good design is not an accident; it is a purposeful and imaginative use of the elements of design.

Beauty is infinite in its variety. Throughout history, attempts have been made to formulate rules that lead to a beautiful design. But these rules have often been transgressed in the search for something new. Nevertheless, there are certain enduring design principles that inform and guide us.

A beautiful design must express order. It must also possess quality. It must be skillfully made from appropriate materials. It must also be useful and practical, based on the function it serves. Beauty confirms our ideas of what is right, proper, and fit for the use of human beings.

The human sense of beauty has prevailed through the generations. A Greek temple, a Michelangelo sculpture, a Renoir painting— all are testimony to the existence of a common basis of the quality of beauty. The purpose of beauty in a design is to enrich the viewer, who

is enlarged by the experience. Beauty is thus a vital function of architecture.

BEAUTY IN DETAIL

Figure 5.19

A beautiful design alone, as George Nelson has said, cannot transform a dark, unhappy life into a joyful one; only the person living the life can do that. The purpose of a beautiful design is to enrich life.

5. *Architectural Design*

Architectural design is the creative organization of forms that are developed to serve certain functional needs. Architecture combines external form, internal space, materials, and structure into a unified whole.

Materials and structure represent the science of architecture; form and space represent the art. Materials can be analyzed and structure can be calculated, but the form and space of architecture must be experienced or sensed.

6. *Organizational Concepts*

Architectural designs satisfy people's needs in an efficient and comfortable way. The designer can determine the proper system of organization when he or she has determined what people want to do in a building, and how they will do it.

The organizational arrangement in any project is the key to successful function. Central locations are provided for activities used by the majority of people. The activities used by fewer people, or for specialized purposes, are placed toward the periphery. On a college campus, therefore, the library should occupy a central location, while the shops and labs should be located at the outer edge of the campus. Similarly, in a bookstore the most important books would be displayed near the entrance, while the texts and reference works would be located toward the rear of the store.

Architects generally refer to a variety of archetypal forms that have become part of the vocabulary of design. These forms include the ring, the radial star, the axis, the constellation, and the grid. (Note the similarities to urban design.) Each of these forms has particular functional implications. They continue to be valid under certain circumstances. For example, a large office may be designed using a grid layout, which is regular and flexible and lends itself to planning. The constellation form might also be appropriate. It might consist of a series of independent zones, each laid out in a grid.

The use of established patterns is helpful because it facilitates organization. Some problems, however, may develop from the use of patterns. One may "force" a plan into the predetermined form, when the form is not appropriate. No one form will solve every problem, since most activities can be organized in a number of ways.

No system guarantees good design, even if that system is based on traditional forms.

SUMMARY

Design is a highly complex process. Many factors must be considered simultaneously. When an architect designs, he or she considers all factors, some of them possibly on a subconscious level.

An experienced designer may do a very quick sketch of a house plan in just a few minutes. This is possible because the designer is fully aware of the program; he or she knows what the client wants and how to arrange the building's component spaces. In addition, the designer knows the size of the major rooms, how much space people need, how much light is desirable, and what kind of structural system is possible. All this is learned through experience, and recalled when needed. It is all part of the design process. This rapid sketch becomes the basis of more careful study, the development of the design into a buildable scheme.

Such a sketch concept embraces the three cornerstones of architectural design: "firmness, commodity, and delight." (This expression has been incorrectly attributed to the Roman architect, Vitruvius. It was, in fact, authored by a British writer in the 18th century.) The triad is a valid guide, nevertheless. Using the language of our own time, the expression might be restated as "structural soundness, economy, and beauty."

LESSON 5 QUIZ

1. The system of architectural measurement in use in the United States (the "English System") is generally related to the

   A. natural world.

   B. metaphysical world.

   C. primitive world.

   D. ancient European world.

2. All of the following represent anthropomorphic design elements in classical architecture with the exception of

   A. architraves.

   B. caryatids.

   C. dentils.

   D. pedestals.

3. The regular occurrence of elements is known as _____.

4. All visible things have which of the following qualities? Check all that apply.

   A. Shape

   B. Scale

   C. Symmetry

   D. Texture

5. A structure that has equilibrium among its constituent parts is considered to be

   A. symmetrical.

   B. in scale.

   C. in proportion.

   D. in balance.

6. The major goal in architectural design should be to produce a solution that is

   A. traditional.

   B. stylized.

   C. functional as well as beautiful.

   D. indigenous.

7. Which of the following arrangements best illustrates a regular and repetitive rhythm?

   A.

   B.

   C.

   D.

8. The "Golden Section" is based on

   A. the proportioning system devised by Pythagoras.

   B. the "modulor" system devised by LeCorbusier.

   C. proportions described during the Golden Age of Greece.

   D. proportions found in nature and the human form.

9. Which of the following statements are true concerning the use of color in architecture?

   I. The perception of form is unaffected by color.

   II. Color cannot be distinguished in dim light as readily as in bright.

   III. Color affects human emotions.

   IV. Defects can be hidden with color.

   A. I only

   B. II and IV

   C. III and IV

   D. II, III, and IV

10. Architectural scale refers to

    A. the absolute size of a structure.

    B. the size of a structure relative to human dimensions.

    C. the proportion of a structure's facade.

    D. an abstract system of measure.

URBAN DESIGN

URBAN DESIGN IN HISTORY

The physical design forms utilized in planning cities and towns, like those used in agriculture, are less a matter of invention than they are of discovery. Workable forms, obtained by trial and error, eventually become the physical design models for planning.

Two patterns have characterized town form in history: the rectilinear and the circular. The *rectilinear* pattern originated in agricultural societies. Derived from the logic of parallel furrow plowing, it also suited the logic of ordered land planning, property ownership, and building construction. The *circular* pattern was derived from practices of herding societies: the

necessity of enclosing the maximum amount of land with the minimum amount of fence, as for a cattle pen, also suited the logic of economical fortification construction. In the case of a fort, the circular pattern enclosed a maximum area with a minimum amount of defensive wall.

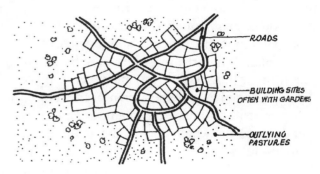

RECTILINEAR LAND PATTERN
IN AN AGRICULTURAL LANDSCAPE

Figure 6.1

CIRCULAR LAND PATTERN
IN A MIGRATORY HERDSMEN TERRAIN

Figure 6.2

Both rectilinear and circular forms have been used for planning towns, throughout history and throughout mankind's numerous societies. Both systems were used by colonists: the rectilinear usually but not exclusively for agricultural settlements, the circular usually but not exclusively for military installations.

Another significant form has been the radiocentric, which is a consequence of incremental urban growth, radiating from a center and expanding outward to an urban periphery. Radiocentric growth can be guided by an overall plan that recognizes that phenomenon; it can also be guided by smaller-scale plans for incremental growth.

To think in terms of "planned" vs. "unplanned" human settlements is erroneous. Though growth and development, especially when rapid, may seem to be spontaneous, they are in fact the result of a combination of forces or events—a collective intention. A plan may be good or bad in quality, narrow or broad in concept, mundane or overly ambitious. But it is still a plan. Similarly, most plans are based on the form of previous growth and recent experience projected as an expectation of the future. The constant challenge of urban design is to set down forms which aid and expand future opportunities.

One early and influential theory of town planning evolved in classical Greece. Formulated by Hippodamus, Greek town planning utilized the rectilinear pattern of blocks, forming a town, and terminating in an irregular enclosing wall. Topography determined the enclosing wall's shape and position. Such towns were limited in size, contained a harbor, a central market place, a theater, a temple, and other public buildings, including a stadium for sports. The size of such towns was limited by the food supply obtainable from the surrounding region.

Roman town planning, derived from Greek experience, also utilized the rectilinear form, but with a significant difference. As prescribed by Vitruvius, and unlike Greek towns, Roman towns had *regular* rectilinear enclosing walls and two main intersecting streets, the *cardo* and *decumanus*, as well as sites for markets, business, government, sport, and worship. Roman towns were of two types: the commercial town or *oppidum* and the military camp or *castrum*. All were connected by a transport network— overland routes, navigable rivers, the ocean, and the sea—to form a regional system, the

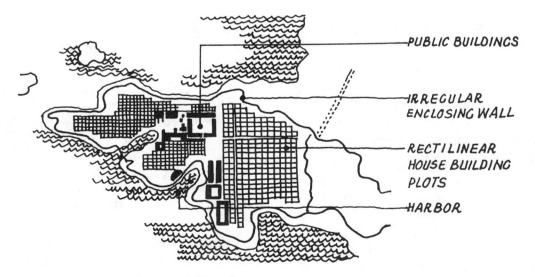

A GREEK COLONIAL TOWN — MILETOS
ADAPTATION OF GEOMETRY TO THE IRREGULARITIES OF SITE

Figure 6.3

Roman Empire. As with Greek towns, the size of Roman towns was limited by the productive capabilities of the surrounding region. In fact, the productivity of the surrounding region was often a reason for selecting a particular town site. Territorial control was another reason: Roman military towns were often sited to command strategic land areas.

Medieval towns, often built on the foundations of pre-existing Roman outpost towns, may upon casual observation seem to lack geometric order. (Florence, Paris, and London were originally Roman towns.) But the absence of precise geometry is not an indication of a lack of order, i.e., a lack of plan. It is, rather, an indication of a sensitive on-the-site adjustment to particular conditions. Furthermore, medieval towns were often founded and planned with the use of orderly geometry: rectilinear, circular, and radiocentric. Medieval towns were usually walled, for defense, and depended on hygienic practices such as waste removal, the use of public bath facilities, providing hospitals for the sick, and proper burial of the dead.

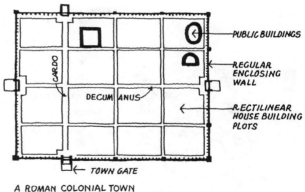

A ROMAN COLONIAL TOWN
NOTE THE RECTANGULAR ENCLOSING WALL AND TWO MAIN STREETS

Figure 6.5

The Renaissance Era recalled the tenets and forms of the classical world, including those of architecture and town planning. It also made use of the classical forum, or town square. As in the towns of antiquity, it served as a public gathering place (most frequently a market), as well as a setting for principal public buildings. Several plazas might be connected in a careful composition. Examples are found in Italy, France, England, and throughout Europe. Indeed, plazas or squares are found in all cul-

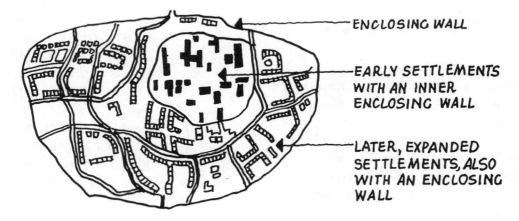

A MEDIEVAL TOWN – ESSEN, GERMANY
NOTE THE GEOMETRY OF THE HOUSES AND THE QUASI-GEOMETRY OF THE STREET PATTERN

Figure 6.4

tures, worldwide, and for the same utilitarian reasons.

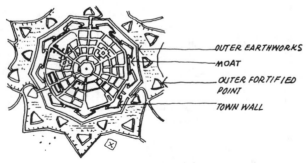

A RENAISSANCE "IDEAL CITY" – PALMANOVA
THE STARLIKE PATTERN IS DERIVED FROM THE PRINCIPLES OF MILITARY FORTIFICATION DESIGN

Figure 6.6

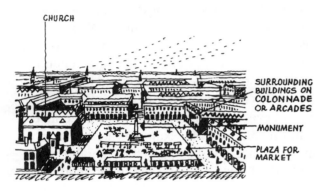

A RENAISSANCE URBAN SQUARE
COVENT GARDEN, LONDON
SHOWING A STALL MARKET OPERATING IN THE SQUARE

Figure 6.7

Where Renaissance town planning made much use of the plaza as a design device, Baroque town planning, its outgrowth, made much use of the boulevard. The plaza served as a convening public forum in a town of succinct size. The boulevard, on the other hand, served to unite the various parts of a larger, often expanding, city. One was a focus, the other a connector.

The "ideal" city of the Renaissance—a star shaped configuration—was an idealization of a military town, with encircling defensive walls, subdivided into a star pattern of streets and blocks. Few were built in pure form.

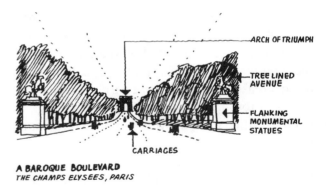

A BAROQUE BOULEVARD
THE CHAMPS ELYSEES, PARIS

Figure 6.8

The precepts of Baroque planning developed in the practices of French landscape architecture, as at Versailles. Long straight "vista avenues" served to make large expanses of terrain visible, thus comprehensible. The principle was developed first for forest landscapes, and later applied to towns. A landmark plan, using these principles, was that of London, which was drafted in 1666 as a proposal to rebuild the city after its great plagues and fire. The idea was to connect the city with long broad boulevards, to create new building quarters, and to create sites for key public buildings. The plans of London and of the town and gardens of Versailles were approximately contemporary, indicating that these design principles were quite well known. The plan of Washington, D.C., (1792) was based on these same concepts, as was modern Paris, rebuilt in the late 19th century. The "city beautiful" plans for remaking Chicago and San Francisco, around the turn of the century, also illustrate these planning concepts. Canberra, Australia, and New Delhi, India, were the last major city plans to be so formulated. Even modern Brasilia, the capital of Brazil, bears that influence.

American colonial planning merits understanding and often admiration. The Spanish colonists were ambitious regionalists and town planners, working in the arid American Southwest. The French also had a regionalist view, establishing a system of outpost towns on the continent's major rivers. The English, as colonists, established numerous harbor- or water transport-oriented towns, utilized numerous planning forms, and gave us the basis of our land ownership system. They also practiced regional settlement planning, as in Philadelphia and Savannah.

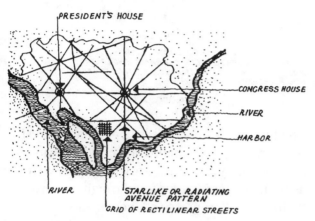

WASHINGTON, D.C.
PLANNED IN THE 1790's; COMBINATION OF RECTILINEAR GRID PATTERN AND DIAGONAL BOULEVARD PATTERN

Figure 6.9

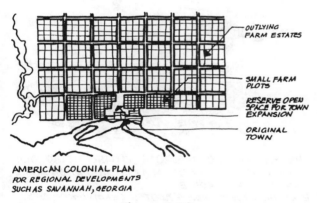

AMERICAN COLONIAL PLAN
FOR REGIONAL DEVELOPMENTS SUCH AS SAVANNAH, GEORGIA

Figure 6.10

Independence and nationhood provided major opportunities for national, regional, and urban planning. Largely under Jefferson's leadership, over a period of approximately 25 years, the United States established the ubiquitous system of rectilinear land division, territorial settlements that led to the creation of states, a national overland and waterway route system, and westward land exploration. All of this ush-

ered in a great era of new town creation, which dominated the 19th century. While new towns were being built almost overnight, older eastern cities were being rebuilt.

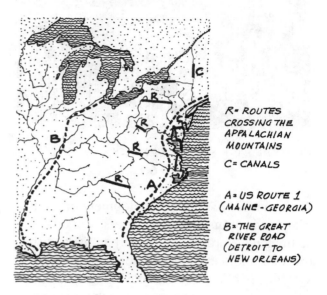

FIRST NATIONAL TRANSPORTATION PLAN
(PREPARED DURING THOMAS JEFFERSON'S PRESIDENCY)

Figure 6.11

With the evolution of industrial technology, and because of our abundant natural resources, our agricultural and trade-based cities grew into great industrial cities, a trend that accelerated after the Civil War. Even before that, the United States had established water-powered manufacturing "worker towns" (Lowell, Mass.) as well as residential "garden suburb" towns (Llewellyn Park, N.J.). At mid-century, Frederick Law Olmsted, the father of American landscape architecture, introduced the concept of the urban park to American cities. Our national park system, exemplifying a consciousness of land and resource conservation, also dates from this period.

CENTRAL PARK – NEW YORK CITY
Figure 6.12

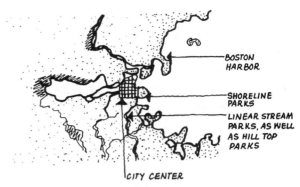

BOSTON REGIONAL PARK SYSTEM
*A PLAN TO PRESERVE HILLS, STREAMS, SHORELINES
AND OTHER NATURAL FEATURES BY INTERCONNECTION
INTO A REGIONAL PATTERN*
Figure 6.13

After the Civil War, the development of industrial towns, transportation centers, workers' settlements, garden suburbs, urban parks, urban transportation, urban sanitation and utility systems, public services, housing, and municipal management became vital to the operability and productivity of our cities. Thus began the relative decline of the so-called "primary population" (farmers, miners, raw materials extractors), the growth of "secondary" (factory workers), and the still increasing "tertiary" (service workers). Altogether, the shift represented a betterment of the conditions of life for most Americans, the growth of the American "standard of living." However, these changes were often accompanied by painful dislocations—abrupt changes in the lives and fortunes of great segments of the population. As these sociological transformations took place, our national pattern of landscape and cities emerged.

A significant exchange of information and technique regarding town planning and urban design occurred between the United States and Europe. One of the most popular concepts in this regard was that of the late 19th-century "Garden City."

The turn of the century saw a popular interest in improving urban habitability and appearance (the City Beautiful Movement), as well as social betterment for all, through numerous "reform" or "progressive" movements.

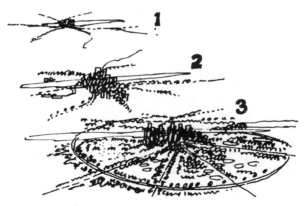

THE EVOLUTION OF THE 20TH CENTURY METROPOLIS
1. *THE BEGINNING OF A CITY AT AN INTERRUPTION ALONG AN OVERLAND ROUTE.*
2. *RADIAL GROWTH ALONG ROUTES LEADING INTO CITY. CONGESTION IN THE CENTER INCREASES WITH GROWTH. RESIDENCES AND SOME INDUSTRIES MOVE AWAY FROM CENTER AS AFFLUENCE INCREASES.*
3. *A BELTWAY ROUTE CONNECTS RADIALS OUTSIDE THE DEVELOPED AREA LEADING TO AUTO-ORIENTED DEVELOPMENT AROUND PERIMETER.*
Figure 6.14

The 1920s saw the maturation of a number of environmental design concepts geared to industrial technology, under the leadership of such luminaries as Henry Wright and Clarence

Stein. Their works, largely in the New York City area, embodied well-designed housing and residential communities. The culmination of their efforts was the town of Radburn, N.J., a satellite commuter suburb for Manhattan, but with its own work places, commercial center, schools, parks, etc. Radburn introduced a circulation network that included a separate pedestrian system and a street pattern that prevented through automobile traffic.

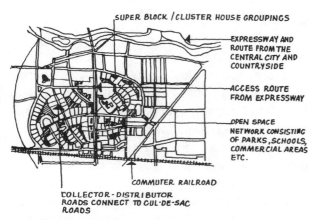

COLLECTOR - DISTRIBUTOR
ROADS CONNECT TO CUL-DE-SAC
ROADS

RADBURN, NEW JERSEY
A LANDMARK PLAN BASED ON THE
"GARDEN CITY" IDEA ADJUSTED FOR
THE AUTOMOBILE

Figure 6.15

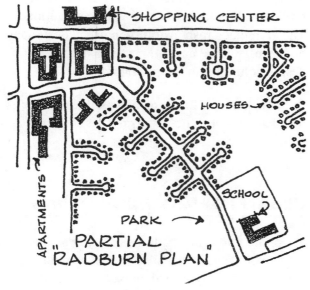

Figure 6.16

An equally important accomplishment of Stein and Wright was the replanning of the entire state of New York—wilderness, rural, and urban—with the objectives of utilizing land resources rationally and distributing urban and rural population workably. This plan provided for conserving natural resources, restoring damaged landscapes, rebuilding obsolete cities or towns, and accommodating future growth. Today, we would call such a plan an ecologically-determined regional management program.

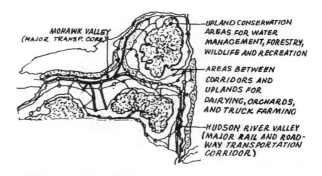

REGIONAL PLAN FOR NEW YORK STATE
Figure 6.17

The 1920s emphasized the importance of natural resource conservation and management, an attitude traceable to the early 19th century, and never absent from American environmental consciousness.

Another landmark accomplishment of the 1920s, also in New York, was the development of the techniques of metropolitan planning, through the work of the Regional Planning Association of New York.

These environmental concepts of the 1920s were extended and applied to the 1930s, through federal agencies such as the NRPB (National Resources Planning Board), the WPA (Work Projects Administration), and the PWA (Public Works Administration). Among the results are the Tennessee Valley Authority, the Columbia River development, and many projects in land reclamation, forestry, wildlife husbandry, national park development, and river and harbor improvements.

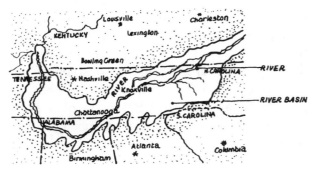

TENNESSEE VALLEY AUTHORITY PLAN
TENNESSEE RIVER VALLEY, A POOR, FLOOD-PRONE RURAL AREA REMADE INTO HIGHLY PRODUCTIVE AND LIVABLE REGION

Figure 6.18

The post-World War II era witnessed the acceleration of metropolitan trends that had long been in existence. This included the decline of small and mid-size towns and the growth of the large city. Here emerged, in full form, the 20th-century city—the regional metropolis. With it appeared the extensive and low density residential suburb. American cities all but abandoned their public transit systems, or failed to extend their systems into the growing suburbs. As a result, the suburban auto-dependent shopping center largely replaced the old downtown public transit-dependent shopping areas, leaving the latter principally as commercial office centers. European cities, on the other hand, with less land to develop and stronger traditions in urban planning and public transit, have succeeded in creating quite livable and economical environments. We can also look to our neighboring Canadian cities as examples of the successful application of urban design concepts long espoused here. Among the keys are: ecologically-based regional land planning, a proper balance of public (collective) and private (individual) transit, adequate tax financing for public improvements, and tax policies that encourage proper development.

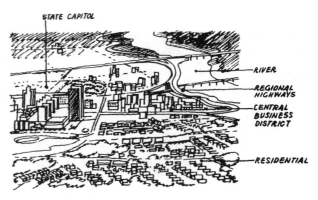

A MODERN AMERICAN METROPOLIS
ALBANY, NEW YORK

Figure 6.19

The form of cities has always been a reflection of how a society lives and operates. The challenge in effective urban design is to understand how our society functions, and how government policy, taxation, production, and distribution are the forces that shape cities. The test is to be able to create urban forms that aid social and urban evolution. If we understand the shaping forces, and have workable design ideas, we can build habitable and even beautiful cities.

We have not done badly, but neither have we done as well as we might. We are not without problems, but neither are we without solutions. The architect's responsibility in urban design, as both professional and citizen, is to help develop design solutions and to promote their use.

In the balance of this lesson we will examine the characteristics of city form that are pertinent to urban design.

URBAN FORMS AND PATTERNS

There are numerous patterns of land use that have evolved as urban areas have developed. Three particularly prevalent patterns are: the concentric zone pattern, the sector pattern, and the multiple nuclei pattern.

CONCENTRIC ZONE PATTERN

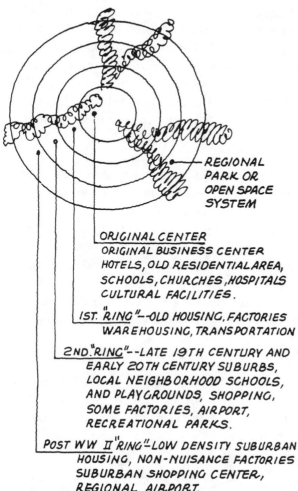

REGIONAL PARK OR OPEN SPACE SYSTEM

ORIGINAL CENTER
ORIGINAL BUSINESS CENTER
HOTELS, OLD RESIDENTIAL AREA,
SCHOOLS, CHURCHES, HOSPITALS
CULTURAL FACILITIES.

1ST. "RING"--OLD HOUSING, FACTORIES
WAREHOUSING, TRANSPORTATION

2ND. "RING"--LATE 19TH CENTURY AND
EARLY 20TH CENTURY SUBURBS,
LOCAL NEIGHBORHOOD SCHOOLS,
AND PLAYGROUNDS, SHOPPING,
SOME FACTORIES, AIRPORT,
RECREATIONAL PARKS.

POST WW II "RING"-LOW DENSITY SUBURBAN
HOUSING, NON-NUISANCE FACTORIES
SUBURBAN SHOPPING CENTER,
REGIONAL AIRPORT.

EXAMPLES: CHICAGO, ST LOUIS, DETROIT,
HOUSTON, BOSTON, ALBANY
BALTIMORE DALLAS, ETC.

Figure 6.20

Concentric Zone Pattern

The concentric zone pattern portrays the modern American city as a series of concentric rings around an original central business district. These rings, beginning with that closest to the core, are the results of progressive phases of growth, contain various mixtures of use, and may have places of obsolescence, depending on the type and age of the city. The pattern within each ring is largely determined by the type of

urban transportation in predominant use during the zone's development. The rings do not have precise boundaries, but blend one into the other.

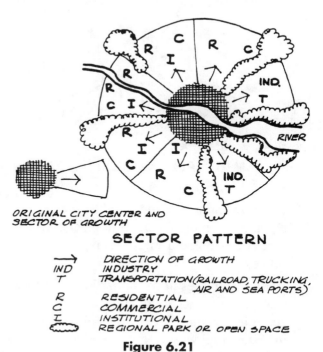

ORIGINAL CITY CENTER AND
SECTOR OF GROWTH

SECTOR PATTERN

IND	DIRECTION OF GROWTH
T	INDUSTRY
	TRANSPORTATION (RAILROAD, TRUCKING, AIR AND SEA PORTS)
R	RESIDENTIAL
C	COMMERCIAL
I	INSTITUTIONAL
	REGIONAL PARK OR OPEN SPACE

Figure 6.21

Sector Pattern

The sector pattern portrays various land uses in pie-shaped wedges, radiating from the center of the city. The composition of the sectors varies from city to city. Land values and housing costs are related to the pattern of sectors.

Multiple Nuclei Pattern

The multiple nuclei pattern describes a city composed of several distinct nuclei. Some of these nuclei, or sub-centers, are old, while others developed as urbanization progressed.

The establishment of multiple nuclei reflects some or all of these factors:

1. In a large metropolitan area, many of the nuclei are similar in purpose, as well as form (e.g., shopping centers).

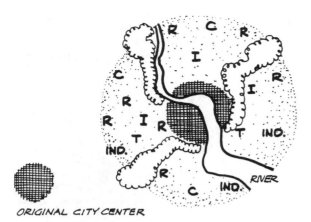

ORIGINAL CITY CENTER

MULTIPLE NUCLEI PATTERN
Figure 6.22

2. Certain similar activities tend to group together for mutual benefit (e.g., certain types of manufacturing, shipping, or offices).

3. Certain activities have similar long distance transportation access requirements (e.g., activities needing access to an airport or interstate highway system).

4. Activities and land values are interrelated, that is, one influences the other.

The number of nuclei in an urban area varies considerably, depending on the particular city. The larger the population and area of the city, the more numerous and specialized are the nuclei.

Other forms within urban areas illustrate the influence of high speed expressways and public transit systems. These circulation systems determine the patterns of growth and development in and around an urban area. The characteristic forms are: the finger, the cluster, and the satellite configuration.

In the *finger plan* or form, development occurs along corridors of public transit and automobile expressway routes.

The *cluster* form consists of varying centers or clusters of activity, which may include new

towns, whose populations may range from 10,000 to 100,000 inhabitants, or more. Each cluster is served by an interconnected system of expressways and other arterial roads, providing multidirectional travel throughout the region. Ideally, public transit systems connect the cluster centers with each other and with the urban core. This system supplements the vehicular route.

The *satellite* pattern is a variant of the cluster. The difference is that the satellite system has a dominating center, usually the original city. Each satellite is a regional civic, cultural, and commercial center. It may be surrounded by extensive undeveloped agricultural lands or other low density land usage. Both expressways and rapid transit systems connect the satellites to each other and to the central urban core.

Other Descriptions

Other ways of describing the various forms or pattern systems of the modern city and urbanized regions, which relates form to transportation, are as follows:

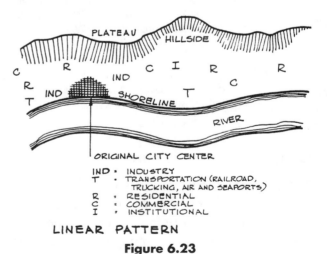

ORIGINAL CITY CENTER

IND : INDUSTRY
T : TRANSPORTATION (RAILROAD, TRUCKING, AIR AND SEAPORTS)
R : RESIDENTIAL
C : COMMERCIAL
I : INSTITUTIONAL

LINEAR PATTERN
Figure 6.23

Linear describes the shape formed by a city or several cities strung out in a continuous line, and connected by a transportation spine. The continuum of the eastern seaboard cities, from Portland, Maine, to Richmond, Virginia, forms a large-scale linear configuration. The urbanized area along the St. Lawrence River is another. The term "megalopolis" was coined to describe extensive linear arrangements of cities, as from Portland to Richmond. That term might also suggest that such arrays of cities are interdependent, which is not the case. They function separately; physically, however, they have continuity.

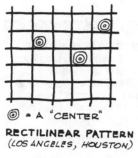

⊚ = A "CENTER"

RECTILINEAR PATTERN
(LOS ANGELES, HOUSTON)

Figure 6.24

Rectilinear patterns are formed by systems of streets and blocks at right angles. Usually two or more corridors of intense development intersect at a central core. This is the typical pattern of development for most smaller cities and towns, as well as some larger ones.

Radiocentric describes a large circular urban form with a series of radial bands of intense development emanating from the central core. This is the most typical form of urban development, and of cities that grew over time.

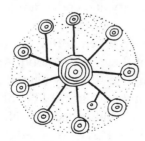

RADIOCENTRIC PATTERN
(WASHINGTON DC; BOSTON)

Figure 6.25

Star or *finger* describes a radiocentric form with open spaces or low density agricultural bands or fingers of development. Automobile usage makes it difficult to conserve the hoped-for open space wedges.

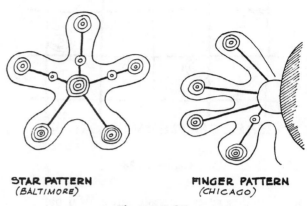

STAR PATTERN
(BALTIMORE)

FINGER PATTERN
(CHICAGO)

Figure 6.26

Ring shaped development describes a linear form encircling an open undeveloped area, such as a body of water or a reserve. With the construction of loop roads skirting the edges of an expanding metropolis, the ring is modified to combine with the star or finger configuration. The cities around San Francisco Bay form a ring.

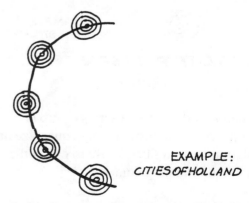

EXAMPLE:
CITIES OF HOLLAND

RING OF CITIES DEVELOPMENT
Figure 6.27

Sheet describes the shape of an extensive urban area without specific focal points, well defined routes, or articulated form. It describes low-density development (urban or suburban "sprawl"), as exemplified by the greater Los Angeles and Tampa-St. Petersburg areas.

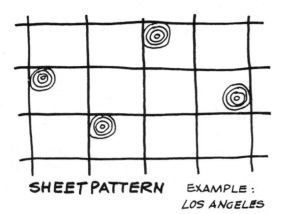

SHEET PATTERN   EXAMPLE: LOS ANGELES

Figure 6.28

Satellite describes a constellation of urban developments, each with its own central core, located around a major urban center.

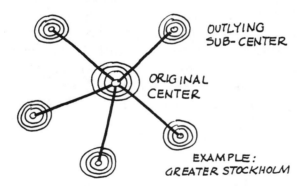

OUTLYING SUB-CENTER

ORIGINAL CENTER

EXAMPLE: GREATER STOCKHOLM

SATELLITE PATTERN

Figure 6.29

Constellation describes a series of urban developments of approximately equal size and population located fairly close to each other but without a dominating center.

Most American cities can be described in one of the ways outlined above, in whole or part. More often, a city may be described as a combination of more than one of these forms or patterns.

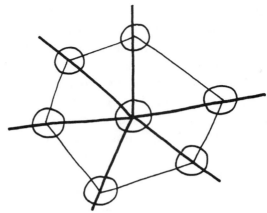

A CONSTELLATION OF CITIES

THIS PATTERN IS FOUND IN LARGE AGRICULTURAL AREAS, AS IN THE U.S. MIDWEST. THE CITIES ARE ALL SMALL IN SIZE — — — "COLLECTOR-DISTRIBUTOR" CITIES FOR FARMING.

Figure 6.30

THE NEIGHBORHOOD CONCEPT

Since the greatest use of land in a city is residential, the concept of the neighborhood has been a major influence in 20th-century planning.

The neighborhood can be defined as a number of families (dwelling units) living in close proximity and having common needs. The concept of the neighborhood is very old. All through history, people formed villages and towns for security and cooperation.

There have been several efforts to formulate the concept of the neighborhood. Among them is that of Clarence A. Perry who, through the Committee on the Regional Plan of New York and its Environs, published the "Neighborhood Theory" in 1929. Perry proposed that all neighborhood planning should reflect the following six principles:

1. No major traffic arterials or through routes should pass through residential neighborhoods. Instead, these roads should form the boundaries of each neighborhood.

2. Interior street patterns should use cul-de-sacs, curvilinear layouts, and low volume roadway systems, in order to limit traffic and thereby preserve a quite, safe, residential atmosphere.

3. The population of each neighborhood unit should be determined by the number of people necessary to support one elementary school. When Perry developed this theory, the neighborhood population by this standard would be around 5,000. (Busing and extended urban access, because of the automobile, have rendered this concept all but meaningless. So has the change in the composition of the American family.)

4. The neighborhood focal point would be the elementary school, centrally situated on a common green space. (The elementary school is not the only element that can form a neighborhood center. Indeed, it is possible for a neighborhood to exist without a clearly distinguishable center at all.)

5. The neighborhood would occupy approximately 160 acres of land, at a density of roughly ten families per acre. It would be shaped so that no child would have to walk more than one-half mile to school. (Busing obviously makes this concept obsolete.)

6. The unit would be served by shopping facilities, churches, a library, and a community center located in conjunction with the school. About 10 percent of the total area would be allocated to recreation.

Perry's theories have influenced many community plans, but have also drawn criticism. The most questionable points have been the strict interpretation of the distance from the farthest point of the neighborhood to the elementary school and the size and population of the hypothetical neighborhood unit.

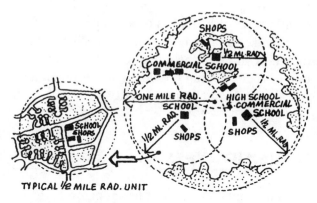

CONCEPT OF A "NEIGHBORHOOD UNIT" IN THE 1920's – 1930's

Figure 6.31

In 1942, Clarence Stein suggested similar theories concerning the elements a typical neighborhood should include. The diagram above shows the grouping of three neighborhood units served by a high school and one or two major commercial centers. The maximum walking distance to these facilities is one mile. The same diagram shows one of the three units in more detail, and locates the elementary school in the center within one-half mile of all residents. Near the school is a small convenience shopping center.

The neighborhood unit has been defined in various ways by a number of theorists, but its essential character is fairly consistent: it comprises a group of people with common needs and goals for living, education, work, recreation, and other activities.

The concept of "neighborhood" can be expanded to the "community," a group of several neighborhoods, having a total population of between 20,000 and 100,000 people. The quality of a community can be measured by the degree to which its population shares and participates in mutual interests.

As urban areas have grown, the sense of community has become weaker. To counteract this tendency, public and private development should be coordinated in order to produce efficient and habitable new urban areas. Thus we may now think of the neighborhood as a basic unit of metropolitan growth: a developmental, social, fiscal, and physical entity.

HOUSING TYPES

A fundamental element of urban planning is housing. The planner should be familiar with the common residential building types and the various patterns of arranging them into an integrated community. The most common residential building types are described below:

The single-family house has all but dominated the new housing market in America since World War II. It enjoys a number of advantages over the other types of housing: it provides a considerable amount of natural light and air, space for cultivating a garden, to play, and to enjoy the outdoors. The detached house affords direct access to its own ground and the street; it can be screened from view and shielded from noise. For several decades it has been possible to build the single-family house at a reasonable cost as a salable unit for single family ownership. However, there are negative aspects to the detached house, such as the relatively large land area required, potential urban sprawl, and loss of communal open space. Where land costs are high, the single-family house becomes uneconomical, affordable only by the affluent. When densities begin to exceed five to six units per acre, the advantages of space, privacy, and noise control begin to diminish considerably for the single-family house. Row or town houses then become a possible alternative.

The arrangement of single-family houses into a well-integrated visual composition is considerably more difficult than grouping larger multi-family complexes.

No less significant, the American family has been changing. The traditional nuclear family is no longer the predominant form of household. More people live alone and more couples are without children. These changes require a different form of housing than that which characterized the post-World War II suburb.

The two-family house (*duplex*) comprises two attached living units, either side-by-side or one above the other. It is somewhat less costly than the single-family house due to more efficient land use. It can be sited to create higher densities, and retains most of the advantages of natural light, air, access, and privacy enjoyed by the single-family house. It requires as much design coordination to organize into a cohesive visual scene as the single-family house. Otherwise its usage can result in a monotonous series of geometric forms separated by more or less uniform setbacks.

The row house consists of three or more attached units, with a maximum of eight in most municipalities. It can provide greater privacy on sites of limited area and makes more efficient use of available land than single or duplex houses, because it does away with side yards. Row houses are usually two stories high, may have basements, and are between 20 and 35 feet wide. The higher densities that can be achieved provide opportunities for more visually cohesive effects, and its physical continuity can be shaped to follow curvilinear patterns of contours and streets.

Its disadvantages include the problems of sound control between adjacent units and some loss of individuality, despite the separate access to each unit.

The walk-up apartment, normally limited to three stories in height, combines efficient land use with a comfortable human scale. Such units have gained popularity in recent times because they offer apartment living at relatively low densities and provide housing at a comparatively attractive residential scale. Furthermore, they provide considerable freedom and flexibility to small families and single persons in both the inner city and the suburbs. The more imaginatively designed units often achieve an urban atmosphere and sense of place. At times they are combined with high-rise buildings, giving them a human scale. They also allow a broad range of tenant mix, and are frequently operated as rental units.

The high-rise apartment accommodates a large number of people conveniently in relatively small areas of land. The problems of fire safety in such buildings are obviously more complex; hence, the necessity for more stringent code requirements. Elevators, greater security, etc., all contribute to higher costs. Nevertheless, the potential for privacy, air, light, and social freedom make this type of housing attractive to many people.

Potential traffic congestion, parking, and recreation spaces at ground level are some of the problems inherent in this building type.

Private balconies providing outdoor space can be a part of every unit. Passenger loads, elevator speeds, means of egress in case of fire, alarm systems, etc., are some of the considerations in the design of high-rise apartments. Properly sited, high-rise apartments can make a considerable contribution to the cityscape, provide a relatively large number of housing units in relation to land coverage, while conserving valuable open space.

HOUSING PATTERNS

Residential "density" is a measure of the number of people accommodated in a given area of land. Densities may be expressed in two basic ways: net or gross. Net density is the ratio of inhabitants to housing land, and excludes streets, which may represent approximately 25 percent of the total site. Gross density is the ratio of inhabitants to total land, including streets, local facilities, and open spaces. It is therefore a more useful measurement.

Much has been written about population density, including "optimal" population density. The fact is that it is possible to design perfectly livable communities at a great range of densities. The difficulty arises from trying to build communities with only one type of building, such as too many single-family houses with very low densities, or too many high-rise buildings with very high densities. Housing types should be mixed in carefully designed blends, with adequate communal open spaces and access to shopping, work, recreation, schools, etc.

Density determinations are important for planning public services and for calculating traffic volumes. Lower densities mean expensive public utility distribution costs. Roads, sewer, water, power, and other distribution networks are greater in length in relation to population served. Dependence on automobile circulation favors low densities. Effective and efficient public transit requires moderate densities, the threshold being an average of 30 persons per acre.

Thirty persons per acre is a relatively high density for American residential suburbs, which are generally about a third of that. However, it is an entirely livable density—often more livable than low suburban densities. Many

European new towns, as well as some older American ones, are built to this density. To be livable, careful design of the site and all buildings is essential. The detached-house suburb, or even the so-called "PUD," is not sufficient. Only skilled physical design can achieve it.

Housing patterns are determined by the layout and configuration of streets, open spaces, and the apportionment of land into building lots. The individual buildings are arranged to form repeatable units or design modules. Although these modules of housing provide a workable reference for preliminary design, they should not be repeated monotonously. The most common housing patterns are described below.

The "street-front" pattern, one of the most common, is developed in a linear fashion, with houses and apartments lining both sides of the street. The pattern provides easy access to units, uniformity of orientation, and a clearly defined plan. Although the linear design may result in monotony, a strong axial feeling can be softened with varying setbacks and landscaped areas, particularly trees. At best it produces neighborly blocks of residences.

The "end-on" pattern consists of rows of units located at right angles to the street. This pattern reduces the total street frontage considerably, but increases lot depth. There can be a real saving in street length, however. Units are more remote from traffic noise and hazards. Parking must be handled in grouped rather than individual arrangements. Units may face each other on pleasant common pathways, or they may be placed front to back to enjoy a favorable orientation.

The "court" pattern groups units to face into a common open space. The result is a visually pleasant enclosed space encouraging sociability. Vehicles may penetrate the open space or

be excluded entirely. Since this pattern also reduces street frontage, the land costs per unit are reduced considerably, allowing for generous landscaped areas at reasonable cost.

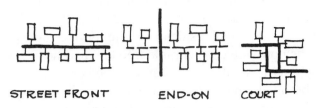

STREET FRONT   END-ON   COURT

HOUSING PATTERNS
Figure 6.32

These patterns may be used in planning residential areas containing single-family residences, mobile homes, row houses, large scale apartment buildings, or combinations. Building masses, heights, etc., will, of course, produce varying effects in human scale, function, views, open spaces, circulation, and visual quality.

None of these patterns should be adopted without careful consideration of their full impact. A thorough examination of all of the aesthetic and social influences is the basis of designing livable neighborhoods.

Cluster developments are so named because the dwelling units are grouped, and more densely sited, than in conventional developments. The remaining land serves as common open space. Although the overall density may remain the same as that of conventional development, common space can be artfully developed into parks, playfields, lakes, and recreation areas. Development costs are less because the length of utility runs and streets is reduced.

Because the open spaces may be concentrated into one or more large areas, rather than a series of isolated small spaces, the site planner is able to make better use of this space. Because the primary purpose of open space is to serve the residents within the development, it

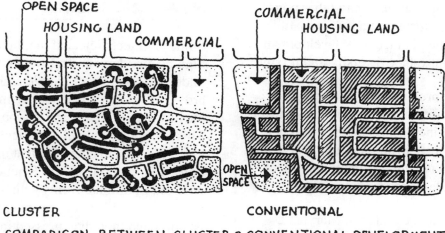

OPEN SPACE
HOUSING LAND
COMMERCIAL
COMMERCIAL
HOUSING LAND
OPEN SPACE
CLUSTER
CONVENTIONAL
COMPARISON BETWEEN CLUSTER & CONVENTIONAL DEVELOPMENT
Figure 6.33

should not be considered a substitute for public parks, schools, and other improvements.

The common space may be deeded to the public, and thus maintained as a public space; or owned and operated cooperatively by the residents through an association; or maintained through the formation of a special tax and use district.

The planned unit development (PUD) is the legally recognized zoning designation used to achieve the cluster concept. It seeks a flexible approach to permit the development of larger areas as unified concepts. The planned unit development may apply to commercial and industrial as well as residential types of development. It is therefore broader in concept than the purely residential cluster pattern.

The three major characteristics of the planned unit development are:

1. It normally involves large developments, ranging from an entire neighborhood to a new town.
2. It usually involves a mixture of uses and types, in contrast to the conventional subdivision, which is generally limited to a single use or type.
3. It requires phased development extended over a long period of time, during which arrangements and uses may be replanned to respond to later concepts or changes in requirements or financing.

Urban redevelopment and its successor, *urban renewal* (names for federally funded programs) are forms of "planned unit developments" for central city areas. Urban renewal refers to rebuilding, in whole or in part. Planned unit development refers to new development, as in the developing suburbs.

Historically, the city brought together a wide variety of people and activities into limited areas; people came there to be a part of this mixture and its opportunities. However, the proliferation of poorly planned developments resulted in the adoption of zoning ordinances, one effect of which was to segregate the urban areas into separate use districts. Zoning prevents discordant or harmful uses while protecting property values, but it does so at the cost of monotony and uniformity. Increasingly, uses and types are mixed; single-family, town house, and high-rise apartment units are joined by commercial, institutional, and other non-residential uses to form mutually compatible environments. The planned unit development is an attempt to reintroduce diversity and mixture.

Variable density provisions in zoning ordinances permit different size lots within a development, without increasing the total number of units. This flexibility in subdividing a large area permits the PUD to dedicate the unbuilt open space to the residents for common use.

Reston, Virginia, and Columbia, Maryland, both developed in the 1960s, as well as Irvine, California, are examples of residential planned communities. The RPC zoning permits the developers to integrate residential, commercial, and industrial uses, and to divide the land into different density areas. The plans for these communities are based on a village-neighborhood-town concept.

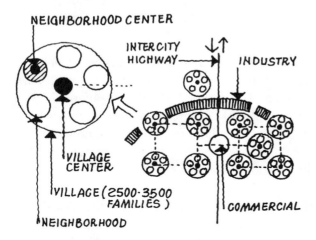

CONCEPT FOR A RESIDENTIAL PLANNED COMMUNITY. (COLUMBIA, MARYLAND)

Figure 6.34

The strong desire for ownership of land and real property somewhat discourages PUD and RPC developments. Nevertheless, the increasing scarcity of land in and around urban centers, as well as rising building costs and environmental controls, fosters future developments of this kind.

NEW URBANISM

Some architects rejected the flip allusions of high postmodernism and sought to embrace the underlying themes of classic architecture. Richard A. M. Stern called classicism "the fulcrum about which architectural discourse balances." This neotraditionalism is evident in projects that dutifully emulate classical orders, proportions, and materials. Leon Krier and Aldo Rossi engaged traditional forms with a real interest in the possibilities of a rigorous traditionalist approach though expressed in a relatively abstract manner.

New Urbanism marked a neotraditionalist return to early models of city planning and was a rebuttal to roadside strip architecture celebrated most famously in Learning from Las Vegas. In the broadest sense, New Urbanist planning provided a humanist approach to landscape planning. It embraced smaller-scale development based on pedestrian use patterns rather than on the culture of the automobile. The movement also tended to embrace traditional over modern building aesthetics. Architect Leon Krier was involved with Poundsbury Village in Dorchester, England, a new town development founded in 1996 but modeled as an ideal village featuring the traditional buildings favored by Prince Charles. A similar project, Celebration, Florida, Disney's ideal planned community, was meant to evoke the simple joys of small town America and its associated values. Robert A. M. Stern, Philip Johnson, and Aldo Rossi are among the architects who collaborated with Disney's "Imagineering" to design housing and faux civic buildings for the new town that broke ground in 1994.

Seaside (1984–1991), in Seaside, Florida, designed by Andres Duany and Elizabeth Plater-Zyberk, followed the principles of traditional neighborhood design and is evocative of the City Beautiful and Garden City movements.

It is one of the most successful and influential New Urbanist projects. Seaside was conceived as a diminutive resort town featuring higher density living. Ample space is granted to pedestrian ways and garden paths, while cars and garages are relegated to alleys. Neighborhood interaction is encouraged by small lots and zoning restrictions that mandate generous porches on each house and prescribe each home's massing, materials, and design vocabulary. All shops and services are arranged according to the five-minute walk principle, wherein services and shops are located just a short walk from each home. While Seaside was planned as a moderately priced, 2,000-resident vacation community, it has morphed into a larger, higher-priced enclave. It has also spawned several other communities of similar design across the country.

THE FUTURE OF THE CITY

Effective city planning must deal with the larger physical scale in which the city exists; at the same time, it must also deal with the small scale of the "neighborhood," however that term may be defined or understood.

To deal with the larger or contextual scale, we must use the techniques of ecological planning to determine where we should and should not build, always discerning the inherent possibilities or limitations of buildable areas.

At the smaller, neighborhood scale, we must be sure that we provide for the full range of needs of all segments of the population, and for a variety of lifestyles.

To accomplish this, we need competent professionals in all areas of technical expertise. We also need effective governmental agencies and methods. And we need equitable tax policies to pay the costs of the city and its operations.

Simply said, the task is to preserve the good things we have, to repair the inadvertent damage of the past, and to provide for further growth and change.

All this requires technical knowledge, design skill, social sensitivity, and the right tools. It is a never ending task. It is one of the most challenging, and hence interesting, tasks for the architect, whose role is primarily physical design, but can be much more.

SUMMARY

The forms of cities are derived from long historical experience and reflect their utilitarian origins. These forms, in the hands of skilled designers, have sometimes evolved into a high form of social art. Always, they must be based on a respect and understanding of both natural and human social needs.

Urban forms, and their consequent planning configurations, must be suitable for change and growth. That has been the outstanding characteristic of American urban design. Moreover, we must be able to work effectively at the scale of the regional metropolis as well as the neighborhood.

We must also understand and be able to design the various elements of our cities: town centers, residential neighborhoods, manufacturing and industrial areas, educational campuses, etc. All have characteristic forms, some ancient, some quite new, which should be in the purview of competent architects.

LESSON 6 QUIZ

1. Which of the following statements about medieval towns is correct? Check all that apply.

    A. They were usually walled for defense.

    B. They were often built on earlier Roman foundations.

    C. They generally had a rectilinear layout.

    D. Their plans were often adjusted to meet particular conditions.

2. During the early 19th century, Thomas Jefferson influenced territorial development throughout the country by proposing land division based on

    A. rectilinear patterns.

    B. concentric patterns.

    C. linear patterns.

    D. organic patterns.

3. Compared to conventional residential developments, cluster developments have

    A. greater density.

    B. less open area.

    C. units more densely sited.

    D. lower development costs.

4. In a sprawling metropolitan growth pattern, the edges of individual urban areas blend into each other to create a new form known as a

    A. cluster.

    B. megalopolis.

    C. metropolis.

    D. municipality.

5. Long-term real estate investments are stabilized and property values are protected by means of

    A. residential developments.

    B. local tax policies.

    C. zoning ordinances.

    D. local street patterns.

6. The pattern of a city that contains a number of commercial centers of equal size is known as

    A. multi-nuclei.

    B. multi-use.

    C. multi-core.

    D. megalopolis.

7. Older downtown shopping areas were replaced by the suburban shopping center largely because

    A. of the inability of cities to control the increase in crime.

    B. high property taxes forced retailers to abandon properties.

    C. of the lack of accessibility by private auto as well as the decline in public transit service.

    D. people prefer to drive to shopping areas.

8. In planning residential communities, population density is a major influence on

    A. traffic volumes.

    B. the design of utility systems.

    C. public services such as education, law enforcement, and fire protection.

    D. all of the above.

9. A population density of 30 persons per acre

    A. is average in most American single-family residential suburbs.

    B. is typical in many European "new towns."

    C. results in overcrowded living conditions.

    D. requires uneconomical layouts of utility distribution systems.

10. Clarence A. Perry proposed that

    A. no major traffic through routes should pass through residential neighborhoods.

    B. the population of a typical neighborhood should be around 50,000.

    C. the neighborhood focal point should be the regional shopping center.

    D. the neighborhood should be designed for a density of roughly 30 families per acre.

THE HUMAN DIMENSION

INTRODUCTION

One of society's most important tasks is to create and maintain an environment that fosters physical and social well-being. In this lesson, we will examine the relationship between the urban environment and the physical and psychological well-being of society.

For over 200 years, the increasingly predominant form of human settlement in Western society has been the city. Urban life and civilization have become, for most people, virtually synonymous. The great majority of our population lives in urbanized areas. The question is to what extent cities promote the development of physical and social well-being.

Much of the popular discussion of cities deals with the problems of crime, air and noise pollution, transportation, congestion, deteriorating services, and the impersonality of urban life. Yet most of us still live in or close to cities. The simple reason for this is opportunity, primarily the opportunity to earn a living. Most of us seem to feel that the disadvantages of city life are outweighed by the opportunities it offers. Furthermore, the compensations include convenience, privacy, and proximity to cultural institutions. Therefore, we are willing to tolerate the imperfections of urban life.

There are psychological aspects of city life that have not always been adequately understood. Low-income residents, for example, may prefer to live in older housing, at least from a sociability standpoint, rather than in new high-rise "superblocks." The change from the setting of an older neighborhood to a new institutionalized housing project can be a highly disruptive and traumatic experience. Such change may destroy the delicate social structure of an older neighborhood without providing a suitable replacement. The sterile public housing project offers no substitute for this vital fabric, which is essential to a healthful environment. Thus is may be far wiser, when possible, to seek effective ways to rehabilitate older neighborhoods.

CONTRAST OF OLDER URBAN NEIGBORHOODS
WITH STERILE, INSTITUTIONALIZED "HOUSING"

Figure 7.1

The task of creating environments, urban and rural, which are sociable, healthful, and physically beautiful is indeed formidable. But it can be accomplished, given the will to do so and sufficient financial resources, applied consistently over long periods of time.

The purpose of planning is to create an optimum environment for the widest range of human activity. To accomplish this it is necessary to understand the relationship between people and their environments. It has been demonstrated that two human beings, presented with identical sensory stimuli, may have substantially different responses. Therefore, no single environment can satisfy all people.

Where, then, does this place us as designers? What are we to design? Since no one design can satisfy all needs, our objective ought to be to create designs that permit, even encourage, the widest diversity of human activities, designs that offer opportunity for social contact as well as individual privacy, sensory stimulation as well as restfulness. Our designs should not prescribe, but rather allow. A proper design is one that is broadly inclusive of opportunity, rather than narrowly exclusive.

BIOLOGICAL CONSIDERATIONS

Cro-Magnon man, named after the area of France where the first remains were found, lived approximately 100,000 years ago. He stood upright, had the same body shape, and

his cranium was as large as that of modern man. The tools, instruments, and utensils he devised still fit our hands. The urges and needs that shaped his personal activities as well as his organizations still operate within us. His artistic efforts still move us, symbolically·and aesthetically.

CRO-MAGNON MAN ···A CAVE MOUTH
SERVED AS A SHELTER --- FOOD
WATER AND GAME WERE NEARBY
MAN'S EARLY SOCIAL STRUCTURE
EVOLVED.

Figure 7.2

Cro-Magnon man differed from modern man only culturally. Our biological and physical endowments were fully developed by 100,000 years ago; however, our cultural systems— our physical, environmental, and institutional systems—were not. That is the difference.

These facts are important because they indicate that modern man's mental and biological characteristics are constants. Our physiological needs and drives, our responses to environmental stimuli, and our potentialities and limitations are largely determined by the same innate characteristics that governed human life when ancient man was a paleolithic hunter or a neolithic farmer.

The relationship between our environment, its cycles, and human behavior is readily seen. Ancient man lived in intimate contact with nature, and his activities were shaped by the natural rhythms of day and night, as well as the change of seasons. Man's psychological functions and rhythms were a response to and in harmony with natural cycles. Today, these biological cycles persist, even when modern technology makes the physical environment uniform. The phenomenon of "jet lag" is a familiar example of our biological "time clocks" at work. It has also been found, through experiment, that simulating the conditions of daytime, at night, through the use of artificial illumination, and maintaining a constant temperature and a uniform food supply for a sustained period can be physiologically harmful, if not destructive. The body is denied the opportunity to function according to its natural rhythms.

The fact that man is able to exist in diverse environments does not mean that man has enlarged his range of biological adaptability without limitation. Whether orbiting in space or traveling under water, man can survive only when the environmental conditions are similar to those under which he evolved. Man does not "master" his environment. Rather, he creates environments in which the physical and social factors in the natural environment are replicated.

Man's potential range of social adaptations is considerably greater than his biological or physiological adaptations. Our biological, psychological, and social evolution has made the human species the least specialized on earth. Man can hunt or farm, eat a variety of foods, live in forests or by the sea, work alone or in teams, and live under various forms of government. Mankind has invented more languages than can be known and identified.

Societies that are highly specialized, and therefore very efficient, are highly vulnerable and even liable to collapse when conditions change—if they are not able to adapt. Even when a social system collapses, resourceful and adaptable individuals are able to survive in rather unfamiliar cultures. Uniformity of environment is as potentially dangerous as narrow

conformity in social behavior. Both are prone to breakdown. The richness of human nature requires a corresponding richness of diversified physical and social environments.

The sustainable design approach leads the architect to design the site and building in sympathy with the ecology or natural conditions of the area in which the building is placed.

Environmental factors influence many aspects of human life. Biological cycles, for example, are often disturbed by environmental forces not encountered in man's evolutionary past. He may develop temporary tolerances for environmental pollution, severe crowding, excessive noise, and the regimentation of modern mechanized life. But this tolerance has a deleterious effect in the long run. A child who grows up in a biologically or socially unhealthful environment will differ, as an adult, from one who has spent his early life in a healthful environment. Early influences condition growth, longevity, behavior, learning ability, and resistance to stress.

However, neither a rural nor an urban environment is necessarily superior in this regard. There are both healthful and unhealthful rural environments, as well as healthful and unhealthful urban ones. Children raised in either setting may become either well developed or unhealthy human beings.

A CHILD'S EARLY ENVIROMENTAL EXPERIENCES CAN BE STRESSFUL ···· OR HARMONIOUS

Figure 7.3

When we refer to "environment," we mean everything that surrounds us: physical, visual, social, etc. As designers, we deal with the physical environment, and in so doing influence all the other aspects of the environment as well.

The genetic endowment of man has not changed materially for the past half million years, nor is there much likelihood that it will in the future. What changes constantly are man's choices in creating his environment, including his lifestyle. Within his physiological limits, man can determine how he and his descendants will live. As technology advances, so does the range of choices we can make within our physiological limitations.

PERCEPTUAL CONSIDERATIONS

There is a quality required of our physical environment that goes beyond function. That quality may be described as sensory stimulation. Just as our bodies need food and exercise, our brain needs adequate sensory stimulation. The measure is not how much we perceive, but the variety of the significantly different images we perceive. Diversity of sensory and perceptual experiences is vital to our well-being.

More varied early environments produce adults who are perceptually and behaviorally more alert, flexible, and better able to deal with change. Perceptual deprivation in infancy hinders mental development.

There is a clear relationship between diversity of surroundings and mental capacity. These relationships have been demonstrated under experimental conditions. All people try to avoid monotonous environments. For example, in a New York City study, social scientists found that pedestrians preferred streets with diversity to streets without diversity. Monotony has a pronounced effect on urban life, as well as on our perception of the environment.

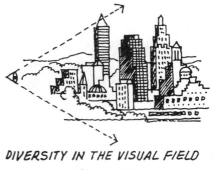

DIVERSITY IN THE VISUAL FIELD
Figure 7.4

People need and seek stimulation. On a monotonous stretch of open highway, we tend to drive faster. This is a way of compensating for a lack of variety in the visual field. We substitute diversity in time for diversity in space.

The pursuit of stimulation is especially evident in young people. The young have always explored their environments, at all stages of growth and development. We might keep in mind that delinquent behavior can be as much a manifestation of a need for adventure as an antisocial attitude. There is a great need for diversity in the urban environment, to provide visual stimulation and learning. Such diversity encourages healthy perceptual development and growth.

Knowledge of how people react to their physical environment and how they invest them with emotional qualities is an essential aspect of environmental design. It is particularly helpful to be aware of the permanent features in an environment, as well as the transitory. Environmental perception is discontinuous, partial, and fragmentary. It involves all the senses. Each person's environment comprises numerous connotations, memories, experiences, smells, feelings, hopes, and dramas, which affect that person according to his or her particular predilections. Each individual constructs a mental picture of his or her environment that may be stable in overall form, but is forever changing in detail. Thus they form a collective image, which Kevin Lynch has called the "image of the city."

Urban legibility refers to the ease with which parts of a city can be recognized and organized into a coherent pattern. Legibility in the environment is important because it is the basis of orientation. Maps, street signs, guide posts, and other such devices guide us around a modern city. Total disorientation can produce anxiety.

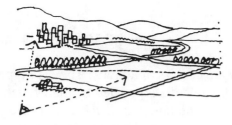

URBAN LEGIBILITY

Figure 7.5

Individual environmental images are a combination of both immediate sensation and memories of past experiences. They are also abetted by the array of commonplace informational artifacts: signs, directional information, house numbers, etc. All are used to interpret information, as well as guide action.

Our need to recognize and structure our environment has roots in the past. It is psychologically important, as well as practical, for each individual. A clear environmental image provides a sense of emotional security, which aids in maintaining a harmonious relationship between an individual and his environment.

The human mind is ingenious. With proper effort a person can find his or her way through the most disordered or featureless surroundings. However, everyone should be able to find one's way about a city readily. This is not to say that there should be no places of surprise

or complexity, but that even those should be within a context of a larger orienting clarity.

Imageability is the quality of a place that is clearly discernible and understandable as a physical environment. Many features contribute to imageability, producing a useful mental image of the environment. For example, San Francisco, New York, and Paris can be considered imageable cities. Kevin Lynch discerned the following five elements for structuring mental images of the environment:

PATH

Figure 7.6

Paths are the routes of circulation along which people move. Every area has a network of major and minor routes such as streets, foot paths, transit lines, railroads, and rivers. These are the predominant elements of most of our environmental images, since other elements are arranged along or related to paths.

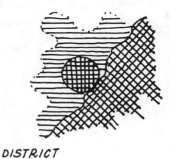

DISTRICT

Figure 7.7

Districts are sections of the environment having an identifying character. A district may be a residential neighborhood, a suburb, a college campus, or an industrial area. Many people "structure" their city by districts, which often become dominant elements of their mental images.

EDGE

Figure 7.8

Edges are the boundaries, terminations, or separations between districts. When two districts are joined at an edge, it forms a "seam." Edges may be railroad lines, shore lines, a wall of buildings, or a highway. A park or pedestrian boulevard may be thought of as a "seam" when it joins two districts.

LANDMARK

Figure 7.9

Landmarks are prominent visual features that act as points of reference. They may be large and visible at great distances, such as a skyscraper or even a mountain. Other landmarks may be small and meant to be viewed close-

up—a statue, a fountain, a sign, or a tree. Landmarks help to identify an area, and so serve to orient people.

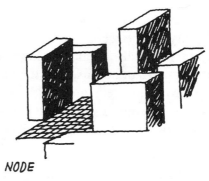

NODE

Figure 7.10

Nodes are centers of activity. They are types of landmarks, distinguished by their function. Nodes may be junctions, such as a square or a plaza. They may be the core of a district, such as a civic center, a financial district, or an entertainment area.

These elements of orientation and identity are not separate; they exist as mixtures and overlaps, such as an edge that is also a path or a node that is also a landmark. These elements are the basic material of environmental images. They are the structuring elements of city form, and they are quite important in any analysis of the environment.

The constituent elements of a "human city" are an organizing structure, together with a variety of complementary activities, juxtaposed so as to support each other.

A large city needs large, working, organizing systems, such as highways, public transit, or utility systems. The activities that such systems support are varied and juxtaposed. That is what makes a city workable yet complex.

As cities evolve, the public, with the help of designers (in the broadest sense), creates the structure. The variety of in-filling develops gradually, as the city becomes more mature (more complex) with time.

An example of this is recreational play. Play occurs in many places, even in vacant lots in the midst of a crowded city. No element exists in isolation, but rather overlaps with other elements of the city.

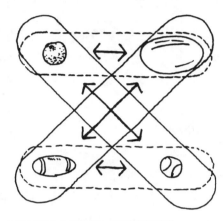

OVERLAPPING SYSTEMS
Figure 7.11

At the turn of the 20th century, French architect Tony Garnier, in his Cite Industrielle, suggested the separation of work from housing. Based on the nature of industry at that time, Garnier designed a model industrial city, in which such separation was appropriate. In our present era of "clean" industries, such as electronics, extreme separation may not be needed, or even desirable. For example, certain small businesses properly belong in residential, industrial, or commercial zones, if they complement the primary use in the zone.

Of note is another contribution of Kevin Lynch, in his writing about the early recollections of young adults. Lynch's purpose was to identify those elements of the early childhood environment that produced the deepest impressions. While it is obvious that cities cannot and should not be built exclusively for children, it is interesting to note how children perceived their

environments and what images were retained when those children became adults.

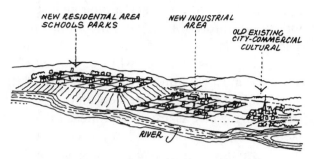

ORGANIZATION OF THE CITE INDUSTRIELLE OF TONY GARNIER
THE OLD CITY WAS INTEGRATED, THE NEW RESIDENTIAL AREA WAS ON THE HIGHEST GROUND, FOR FRESH AIR. NOTHING WOULD BE LOCATED "DOWNWIND" OF THE INDUSTRIAL AREA.'
Figure 7.12

FREQUENCY OF MENTION OF TOPICS	
Ground Surface	90%
Lawns	67%
Topography	60%
Trees	53%
Color	50%
Sense of Space	42%
Water	38%
Congestion	32%
Traffic	22%
Shopping	20%

Table 7.1

Although diverse social, economic, and ethnic backgrounds were represented among the respondents, many similarities were found to exist. Most subjects were keenly aware of ground surfaces. Lawns were particularly important. There was also a strong and pleasant memory of materials. Foliage, color, topography, and elements contributing to environmental orderliness were noted.

Children were found to have had an explicit perception of spatial qualities, with a preference for openness and spaciousness, and a dislike of crowding. Interestingly, there were no complaints expressed about too much space, nor of discomfort or loneliness in vast, open spaces. The majority preferred suburban living. Several expressed intense dislike of "the city." However, most admitted to the excitement of central urban areas. None perceived, or at least identified, the city as a source of pleasure in itself. There was no mention of an "enjoyable" city environment. Almost all were aware of play and, without exception, stated a preference for playing elsewhere than in conventional playgrounds.

It is clear that most responded favorably to variety, with the opportunity for adventure. The majority of respondents expressed the need to act upon their physical environment, and to be stimulated by it. A child's perceptions and memories, and his or her emotional responses to those experiences, may serve as a useful informational resource for design.

SOCIOPETAL

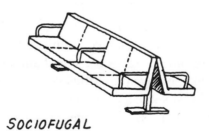

SOCIOFUGAL

Figure 7.13

DEMOGRAPHIC CONSIDERATIONS

The statistical study of human populations is called demography and includes statistics on birth, death, marriage, age, sex, educational level, length of schooling, family size, fertility, etc.

U.S. DEMOGRAPHIC PERSPECTIVE		
	1900	**1990**
Population	76 million	246 million
Life Expectancy	47 years	75 years
Median Age	23 years	33 years
Births per 1000	32	16.2
Deaths per 1000	17	8.7
Immigrants per 1000	8	3.1
Annual Growth	1.75 million	2.6 million
Growth Rate	2.3%	1.1%

Table 7.2

The study of population goes back to ancient times. Plato, for example, recommended a limited population for the ideal city that he proposed. Confucius, in a society which has often experienced overpopulation, favored the idea of an equilibrium between population and environment. In ancient Rome, the laws of Augustus were intended to prevent population decline.

During the 17th century, the Englishman John Graunt studied mortality bulletins, which led to the first life expectancy table. He further discovered that the ratio of sexes at birth was about equal, a fact that was far from evident in his time. His work marked the beginning of modern demography. About 100 years later, Malthus developed the first studies of the relationship between population growth and subsistence (i.e., people vs. food), a subject of great interest even today.

The means for gathering demographic information is the census, a periodic enumeration of the number of people, their conditions of living, and their resources.

The Romans undertook a census periodically throughout their colonies for purposes of registering adult males and their property for tax purposes, military obligations, and political status. In the United States, systematic census-taking began in 1790 and has continued ever since at ten-year intervals.

Current census information includes housing conditions, economic status, educational attainment, sex, and age. The information obtained serves to shape housing and other social legislation, as well as to guide government and industry.

Population growth cannot continue forever in a finite environment. Given the current growth rate of one percent annually, world population would multiply a thousandfold to 5,200 billion in 370 years. A population of this magnitude would occupy the entire land surface of the earth, including mountains and polar ice caps, at the density of Manhattan, 100,000 persons per square mile. Obviously, such an extreme is not possible.

Today, more and more people live in urbanized areas at densities far exceeding those in rural areas. But urban densities themselves are actually declining, because urbanized areas are becoming larger. It is important to distinguish between population density and population size.

Density is defined as the number of people per unit of area.

Population size refers to the actual number of people in a given location, without regard to density.

A small town may have a high density if building sites are small and buildings tall. Conversely, suburbs may have a low density but contain a large population, distributed over an extensive area.

High density does not necessarily imply crowding, since the type of activity a person is engaged in, its duration, and the person's attitude all contribute to one's perception of whether a particular place is crowded. For example, the high density of a movie theater does not cause a crowded feeling if each person has a seat. The same density in an office, however, would be perceived as crowded and unbearable. High density, therefore, is not in itself bad.

Jane Jacobs, for example, said that dense concentrations of people are necessary for diversity, and "densities are too low or too high only when they frustrate city diversity instead of abetting it."

SOCIOLOGICAL CONSIDERATIONS

Primary and Secondary Social Groups

The discipline of sociology furnishes numerous perspectives for understanding human society, many of them relevant to the work of environmental design. One perspective or framework is to describe two fundamental social groupings, the *primary social group* and the *secondary social group*.

The primary social group is that group of persons with whom one has the most intimate and hence greatest variety of social interactions. The family and one's immediate circle of friends constitute that group. It is also, by its nature, the group with which one has the longest association.

The secondary social group is that group with which one has less intimate and more specialized interactions, such as one's work or professional group. In the case of office or factory workers, it is one's fellow workers. In the case of school children, it is one's classmates. For many, it is one's church congregation.

Both groups are necessary for psychological health. The intimate circle of friends and family offers the opportunity to experience vital social and psychological interactions over long periods of time. This enables one to develop his or her emotional perspectives, and so helps to equip an individual to deal with the myriad of life's experiences.

Similarly, one's larger (but more specialized) circle offers the opportunity to contribute usefully to society generally, as well as to draw from it. At work as well as in school, at team play as well as spectator sports, one receives and gives in a manner that enhances personal development and capability.

The association with one's primary group helps a person develop as a full individual. The association with one's secondary group allows one to receive and to give to the larger society, which is equally essential to a sense of self worth.

Each individual lives, then, in two social worlds, which are interdependent. A developing child who is raised without an adequate primary social circle is inhibited from developing all of his or her necessary personal traits. Such a child is likely to be unable to participate usefully in his or her secondary social circle.

The primary social circle of poor and disadvantaged urban inhabitants sustains that group to a very large extent. Their physical relocation from an area of so-called "slum" or physically unhealthful urban surroundings may destroy that vital circle.

The military establishment, which often relocates its members and their families, has come to recognize the need to compensate for the stresses of relocation, through various social services.

In the creation of new communities, one method of creating a "sense of belonging" is to establish various clubs or associations, modeled around recreational interests, such as theater, cycling, hiking, art, woodcrafts, etc. These are secondary group activities, whose purpose is to provide a diversity of "primary groups" (i.e., families) with their vital "secondary group" associations.

Primary, Secondary, and Tertiary Work Groups

Not to be confused with the two main *social groups* described above is a three-part grouping whose distinctions are based on one's *work*, avocation, or profession.

In this classification the primary work group is that which deals with resources. It includes miners, lumbermen, fishermen, farmers, and cattlemen. The secondary work group takes the raw materials produced by the primary and converts them into usable products. It includes food processors, construction workers, and factory workers at all levels of skill. The third work group manages and services society and its industries. It includes professionals of all sorts, managers, salespeople, teachers, and a broad range of people who provide services of all kinds—repair, maintenance, delivery, communication, etc.

In both developed and underdeveloped nations today, the outstanding urban form is the metropolis, or regionalized city. In developed societies, like the United States and Europe, the reason is that production efficiency has resulted in fewer and fewer people being required to produce the food and products needed by society. At the same time, more and more people provide services. Thus, the large city is the result of fewer people needed on farms and factories, and more people free to pursue opportunities in the broad sector referred to as service industries. We are a society whose rising standard of living results in greater specialization in non-manufacturing service work.

In underdeveloped countries, large cities are also predominant, but for somewhat different reasons. The primary reason is the increase of population caused by improvements in public health and food supply, as primitive as they may seem by Western standards. But relatively few of those born in rural areas are able to remain there, because of the lack of opportunity. As crowded and even desperate as their large cities may be, they offer more opportunity than the rural areas. Within the extensive "favelas" (shantytowns) that they build and inhabit, some seemingly overnight, the primary-secondary-tertiary work structure can be found, but at a far lower overall level of development than in the developed countries.

What does any of this tell an architect or planner? The answer is very much, and at all economic and social levels.

When we design houses, or work places, or schools, or any type of building, we are designing places to accommodate the primary-secondary social needs of large numbers of people, whose individual needs must be acknowledged as the very basis of design. And this holds true even when the traditional primary social group-ing, the family, has undergone great change. The child still needs a traditional family, or a circle of people who serve that function. Thus, few work places should be without day-care facilities. The elderly, often alone and without their traditional family to care for them in old age, must be located within communities where they have daily association with a viable and stimulating "secondary group."

All individuals in a city, or indeed in rural areas, develop what might be thought of as a "use network," a physical pattern of places that they use for residence, for work, for recreation, for cultivation. For each of us this differs. Collectively it is provided by a well-designed city, one that has places of residence of many kinds, similarly varied places of work, of culture, of commerce, of services, of leisure, of learning— and all accessible by systems of convenient transportation.

The design of a city, and that of the buildings and places in it, is the key to the satisfaction of each individual's social and psychological needs. It cannot be achieved successfully without understanding these needs at their most fundamental level.

URBAN PATHOLOGIES

Much of the literature of cities has dwelt on the visible manifestations of its shortcomings, its failure to serve segments of society. Many studies have been done on such issues as public health, crime, and drug abuse. To recognize these failings is essential to society's improvement. But it is a great mistake to attribute these ills solely to excessive population density or substandard housing. These may be partly to blame, but they are certainly not the sole cause.

In the United States, we have an open society in which people are free to move about to seek greater opportunity. Those at the lower economic levels may endure great physical hardships in their quest for improvement. Those at that level who lack education or personal ambition, or who simply are victims of misfortune, may have no choice but to live under substandard conditions. But social pathologies, such as drug abuse and crime, are not strangers to low density, green-treed suburbs. Nor for that matter are they strangers to idyllic rural areas. The city, indeed the entire urban environment, reflects the well-being of the entire society, and it is not separate from it.

For the city to be successful in the social sense, there must be an equitable system to provide an adequate level of economic well-being, an open system for pursuing personal opportunity, and the provision of effective programs for aiding those who are socially destitute. Achieving these goals is no small task, but it is well within the capabilities of a society that wishes to achieve them. It is also, in the long run, the most economical approach.

HUMAN FACTORS: RESEARCH, DESIGN, AND BEHAVIOR

The most ancient and useful lessons for conducting human affairs are embodied in the many works of wisdom of the world's cultures. They are found, for many of us, in religious practices, and recorded in such works as the Old and New Testaments and the Koran. The Eastern world, too, has its codes: the Bhagavad Gita, the wisdom of Confucius, Zen philosophy, the principles of Buddha.

Such codes of interpersonal behavior were developed for agrarian societies, and their subject area was comprehensive, dealing with the relations between man and society, as well as man and nature.

Modern times have examined human behavior more systematically, and at the same time more narrowly. In all agricultural societies, it has been necessary to understand the composition of work forces, so as to organize them to be more productive. In our modern times, it has been necessary to study the work processes of factories in relation to human operations, again for reasons of efficiency.

The horrors of human exploitation of early factories aside, it was nevertheless vital to improve productivity. And this, in turn, led to a more healthful work place, if only to obtain the most from each worker.

The system of studying the factory environment in order to improve productivity of an individual's physical effort has been called "time and motion" studies. As a result of such studies, one recent innovation is to organize individuals as small teams, in which each person's task is conducted in view of all the others. Another has been to alternate tasks, to prevent boredom.

A whole field of behavioral information has grown up, and it has many applications. At the product design level, much has been gained by studying the relationship between vision, body motion, and response time. Perhaps the prime example of the results of this work are to be found in today's automobiles. No less a result is to be seen in useful tools and instruments, particularly the more complex ones. Such a design procedure is referred to as *ergonomics*, design based on the mechanics of the human body and its various senses.

Work place time and motion studies, combined with the techniques of ergonomic product design, have expanded into areas of architectural design, such as the design of the residential kitchen and bathroom.

Office design, and particularly the office workstation, has been another area greatly improved by design based on human factors. This work, based on human dimensions and mechanical capabilities, also draws on an understanding of color and its effects, as well as appropriate levels of lighting.

Sustainable design encourages the architect and engineer to appreciate not only the proper levels of artificial light but to include daylighting (natural light) in the design of the entire work space.

The design of large and complex places involving large volumes of human movement could not be done without a full understanding of human behavioral characteristics. Large airport terminals are the outstanding example. In them it is not only important to have logical and clear paths of movement, it is essential that the graphic information system be placed sequentially and with graphics that are clearly readable.

The "metro" rail and bus transit system of Washington, D.C., was designed by using a "palette" of design elements, all with the purpose of making the circulation system comprehensible to a passenger entering or leaving a station. A system of elements, logically deployed, is encountered by an entering passenger in such a way that movement to a transit vehicle is clear and free of confusion. Exit from a vehicle to the station exterior has a similar logic of arrangement.

The design "palette" was developed so that its elements could be utilized under a variety of station requirements. Indeed, each station, by virtue of its site and function, is unique. The

palette, applied to each situation, provides a familiar and always logical sequence of movement.

A similar approach was taken in a recent study of post office design, where complex handling operations must "interface" with the using public. In that case, as in all architectural design, the prime concern is the human being and his or her senses and physical mechanics.

A further example of this approach to design is found in modern research laboratories, at the forefront of technological inventiveness today. Through many years of study of the day to day operation of research laboratories, it has been found that a key to creativity on the part of individual and team researchers has been the phenomenon known as "chance encounter." The more spontaneous contacts a researcher has with fellow workers, the more he or she is stimulated mentally—by explaining the work being done, by posing questions, by expressing areas of doubt, etc. The same phenomenon occurs in a village square or a college campus, and produces the same results: the exchange of information and ideas.

But how does an architect make use of this phenomenon in designing a research laboratory? Some of the design principles, based on studies, include:

1. Movement and public places (corridors, corridor intersections, and small gathering places) are essential to chance encounters. A corridor should be thought of as a pedestrian street.

2. Horizontal (same floor) laboratory arrangement is preferable to multi-floor. The fewer floors, the more contact.

3. When horizontal distances exceed 200 to 300 feet, encounter tends to reduce markedly. A large laboratory should, thus,

be designed as a campus or incremental system, with the design connections between the increments being social links.

SUMMARY

The individual human being, whether alone or in groups, together with the sites occupied by our buildings and our cities, forms the basis for design.

Our habits, characteristics, and capabilities, developed over millennia, even tracing back to our animal origins, are a constant—they do not change. What does change are the levels of technology and thus the systems of organization society utilizes. These vary in complexity, size, locale, and function within an infinite range of possibility. To recognize that is to recognize that all designed systems must be based on the people they serve. Therefore, design derives from a thorough understanding of basic human characteristics, whose range is limited, but rich in complexity. Design serves this richness, allowing it to fulfill its many dimensions.

To approach all design with this understanding, this attitude of respect, is to begin on a very solid footing.

LESSON 7 QUIZ

1. Population size refers to the total number of people, whereas population density refers to the number of people

   A. at any specific time.

   B. relative to a specific area.

   C. that can be accommodated in a specific area.

   D. that is desirable for a specific area.

2. According to Kevin Lynch, a central city plaza would probably be classified as which of the following? Check all that apply.

   A. An edge

   B. A district

   C. A landmark

   D. A node

   E. A path

3. A partial failing of past low-income housing projects, in comparison to the substandard housing which they replaced, has been that they

   A. are excessively costly.

   B. tend to group an excessive number of people together.

   C. tend to lack variety and social support systems.

   D. are no more healthful.

4. Sociopetal space tends to

   A. discourage human contact.

   B. promote human contact.

   C. cause crowding.

   D. cause pathologies.

5. Environmental perception involves

   I. personal feelings.

   II. previous experience.

   III. individual memories.

   IV. human senses.

   A. IV only   C. I, II, and III

   B. I and II   D. I, II, III, and IV

6. When walking through a visually dull area, which also lacks functional variety, we tend to

   A. pause and look about.

   B. pass through as rapidly as possible.

   C. become wary and possibly alarmed.

   D. look for something interesting.

7. A "use network" is

   A. one's normal route to work.

   B. a system of places each person utilizes in his city or habitat.

   C. a communication system.

   D. a pattern of travel routes for all purposes.

8. Which of the following statements is correct?

   A. Rural environments are more healthful than urban.

   B. A uniform environment is better than a diverse one.

   C. People need great variety and have a broad capability of adaptation to places.

   D. Our adaptability means that any environment is potentially good.

9. Urban pathologies, including antisocial behavior, are often caused by

    I.   high density.

    II.   lack of opportunity, real and perceived.

    III. an oppressive and hostile neighborhood.

    IV.   poverty.

    V.   lack of hope and means to pursue one's personal aspirations.

    A. I and V   C. II, III, IV, and V

    B. III and IV   D. I, II, IV, and V

10. If the birth rate and death rate were equalized and immigration were eliminated, we would achieve

    A. a reduction in urban density.

    B. a reduction in total population.

    C. moderate population growth.

    D. zero population growth.

ENVIRONMENTAL FACTORS

CLIMATE

The Influence of Climate

Climate is one of the most important influences on site development. Climate analysis and its impact on site development can be examined at two levels: *macroclimate* and *microclimate*. Macroclimate is the general climate of a region and is defined by National Weather Service statistics, such as maximum and minimum temperatures, wind velocity and direction, precipi-

tation, cloudiness, hours and days of sunshine, etc. Microclimate is the local modification of the macroclimate by the features peculiar to a site: type of vegetation, elevation, slope, the presence or absence of water, wind velocity and direction, and manmade structures. While there is a general awareness of the effects of macroclimate, commonly referred to as "the weather," there is generally far less appreciation of microclimate and its effects on a particular site or building.

In site planning and design, information on both macro- and microclimate, for all seasons, should be obtained and analyzed. This information helps determine the orientation of buildings, their protection from (or exposure to) sun and wind, fenestration, building materials, heating and cooling systems, and the location and selection of plant materials. Aesthetics and appearance are also influenced, to a considerable degree, by the characteristics and quality of natural light and its daily and seasonal variations. Natural light establishes the conditions under which a building's mass, profile, colors, details, and materials are seen. For example, "warm" colors are best seen in bright sunlight, and "cool" colors in overcast light, or northern light, which contains more blue. However, we are primarily concerned with the practical considerations of climate and its influence on design.

Macroclimate

The macroclimate of an area depends primarily on its latitude, elevation, and proximity to bodies of water. All weather phenomena—indeed all life—depend on the sun. Thus, a primary determinant of the climate in a particular location is the amount of solar energy that it receives. That, in turn, depends on latitude, the distance from the equator. In the United States (excluding Alaska and Hawaii) the latitude varies from about 49° north at the northern tip of Minnesota to about 25° north in southern Florida.

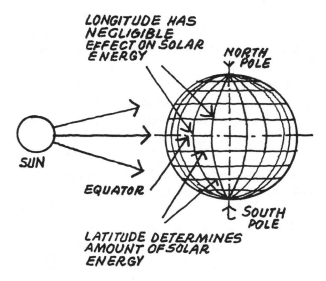

SOLAR ENERGY DETERMINED BY LATITUDE

Figure 8.1

Of course, there are several other factors which influence climate. As the elevation increases temperature decreases, about 1°F for each 300 feet. This is because the thinner air of the higher altitudes is not able to hold as much heat as the denser air of lower altitudes. Even near the equator, the climate at high altitudes may be very cold.

The proximity of bodies of water—rivers, bays, or lakes—also affects climate; water is much

slower to rise or fall in temperature than land, and does not reach the extreme high or low temperatures that are recorded on land. Consequently, the effect of bodies of water on nearby land areas is to reduce temperature extremes, both daily and seasonal.

This moderating influence increases as the size of the body of water increases. Thus, islands and coastal areas usually have a more constant and moderate climate than do inland areas at the same latitude. Compare the pleasant climate of Hawaii to that of central Africa, which is at about the same latitude; or the Pacific Northwest, with its mild winters and pleasantly warm summers, to Minnesota or North Dakota, where the extremes of temperature are far greater.

Even at a smaller geographical scale, a house located alongside a river or lake is apt to be more comfortable than one located far from water.

Prevailing winds also influence climate. The prevailing southerly winds (winds from the south) of the southeastern part of the country carry moisture and warm air from the Gulf of Mexico into the plains states, altering their climates considerably, particularly in the summer, when these areas are quite humid. Similarly, during the winter, cold Arctic air from the north makes the same central plains states quite cold. Such air is cold, dry, and clear.

Climate is also influenced by ocean currents. Areas warmed by the Gulf Stream (London, England) enjoy a warmer climate than those cooled by the Labrador Current (St. Johns, Newfoundland).

Mountain barriers influence climate by forcing prevailing winds to rise. The air cools as it rises, clouds form, and rain falls. This phenomenon has several interesting and important variations, depending on a number of factors, such as the strength and regularity of the winds, altitude, sunlight, soil and vegetation combinations, etc. For example, the western (windward) slopes of the Sierra Nevada and Coast Ranges are relatively humid, and the areas leeward of the mountains are hot, these being the dry regions of Nevada and Arizona. A somewhat different pattern is found in the Hawaiian Islands. The steady and uniformly flowing ocean breezes from the southwest, colliding with the mountain barriers of the islands, are forced to rise suddenly. The humid air, suddenly forced upwards and cooled, condenses into clouds and then rain. In this case, however, the rain generally occurs on the leeward side of the mountains.

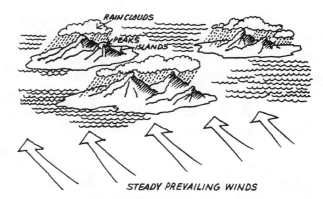

A VARIANT OF MOUNTAIN BARRIERS
Figure 8.3

Arid regions, with generally low humidity levels, experience great variation in temperature range, since humid air retains more heat energy than does dry air. Thus, desert areas and high mountainous areas, which also have dry air, experience great extremes of daytime and nighttime temperatures.

Microclimate

In analyzing a site, the designer should obtain data on the macroclimate of the area. This is available from the National Oceanic and Atmospheric Administration (NOAA). The data is available in many forms, from simple climatological summaries to detailed computerized information programs. Familiarity with an area comprises a useful source of information as well. To learn about the microclimate, a site designer should "walk the site," studying the indigenous plant material, as well as those features that are inherent to the particular site—elevation, land forms, slope, orientation, bodies of water, and structures. One of the best ways to survey a site is "through the soles of one's feet." But it is not an exclusive way. A designer may learn much about an area by studying the climate-influenced details of indigenous architecture, such as roof slopes and overhangs, window orientation, planting, etc. For example, the old farm houses located in the eastern United States are characteristically sited atop

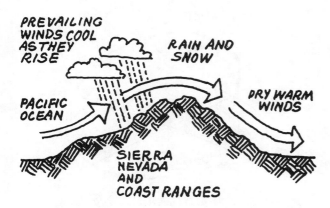

MOUNTAIN BARRIERS AFFECT CLIMATE
Figure 8.2

The range of daily and seasonal temperatures is also dependent on whether the sky is clear or cloudy. Clouds act as a blanket; less solar radiation is received during the day and less is lost at night than on clear days. As a result, there is a narrow temperature range on cloudy days. Similarly, clear winter nights are colder than cloudy winter nights and clear summer days are warmer than cloudy summer days.

hills, surrounded by trees. This simultaneously provides for positive drainage away from the house, exposes the house to summer breezes from all directions, and shades it from the hot summer sun. In winter, when the trees are bare of leaves, the southern sun warms the house through its south-facing windows.

The amount of solar radiation received on a site is a function of the angle between the ground surface and the direction of the sun's rays. The closer the rays are to being perpendicular to the surface, the greater the amount of solar radiation received. This is the reason for seasonal variations. The angle between the sun and the horizon, referred to as the altitude, is greater in the summer than in the winter. This also explains why the more southerly latitudes are warmer than those more northerly: the sun's angle with the horizon is higher in the south.

Added to this is the obvious factor of duration of exposure. In the northern hemisphere, the hours of sunlight are greater in the summer than in the winter. The day that has the maximum hours of sunlight exposure is referred to as the summer solstice. It occurs on June 21 or 22. The day with the minimum hours of sunlight exposure is referred to as the winter solstice; this occurs on December 21 or 22. Midway between these two extremes is a day when the hours of sunlight equal the hours of darkness. This is referred to as the equinox and occurs about March 21 (vernal equinox) and September 21 (autumnal equinox).

The slope of a site also affects the amount of solar energy that it receives. Since the sun's path is inclined southerly in the northern hemisphere, the angle between the ground surface and the direction of the sun's rays is greater if the ground slopes to the south than if it is level. Hence, south-sloping sites receive more solar radiation than level or north-sloping sites.

At the same latitude, the sprouting of plants in spring occurs earlier and more rapidly on south-facing slopes than on level or north-facing slopes. Indeed, the advantage of a south-facing slope for agriculture is great enough to justify modifying its topography, to accelerate and increase agricultural output.

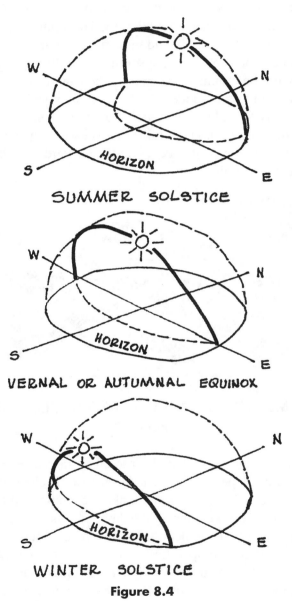

Figure 8.4

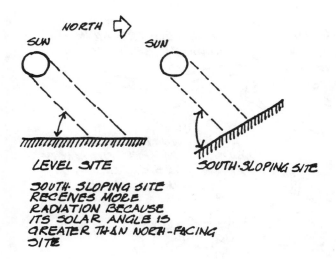

SOUTH-SLOPING SITE RECEIVES MORE RADIATION BECAUSE ITS SOLAR ANGLE IS GREATER THAN NORTH-FACING SITE

MICROCLIMATE AFFECTED BY SLOPE OF SITE

Figure 8.5

Topography affects the microclimate in a number of other ways. In hilly country, the wind velocity at the crest of a hill may be 20 percent greater than on the flat, while the wind velocity on the hill's surface is influenced by the steepness of the slope and the wind direction. At night, the layer of air along the ground is cooled by the ground. This cool air, being heavier, flows downhill and forms a pocket of stable, cold air in the valley. The midslope remains relatively warm, while the top of the hill is cold and windy.

On the windward side of hills, wind speeds are greater and more turbulent near the crest, while the leeward slope experiences less turbulent winds. On the leeward side of the hill, bottom wind velocity is minimal, in the so-called "wind shadow." Strong winds on the windward side of a hill may carry precipitation, either rain or snow, over the hill, where it falls on the leeward side, as previously described for the Hawaiian Islands.

Winds, whether an element of the macroclimate or the microclimate, are an important charac-

teristic of a site. Winter winds can make a site very unpleasant; a 30 mph wind with the air at 30°F has six times the cooling effect of still air at 10°F. This is referred to as the "wind chill factor."

This effect of wind chill on building energy consumption for heating is quite significant. The fuel consumption needed to heat an enclosed space in freezing temperatures will double as the wind increases in velocity from 3 to 12 miles per hour. In the summer, of course, the cooling effect of the wind is highly desirable. In developing a site plan, it is very important to study the direction of the prevailing winds during the different seasons. Since the wind direction often changes seasonally, it is wise to plan site developments to admit cooling summer breezes while blocking undesirable winter winds.

Before the advent of modern heating and cooling technology, buildings, entire villages, even cities, were oriented to the climate. An outstanding example is the ancient city of Peking, China, in which houses faced south, to receive the winter sun. Overhangs kept the sun out of rooms in summer, while courtyards admitted and directed cooling summer breezes into interior spaces. Northern exposures were blocked by blank northern facades. Similar examples were found in American Pueblo Indian settlements and other types of indigenous architecture, such as the ranch houses of the American Southwest.

Air movement also affects heat transfer. Turbulent air disperses heat, while a steady flow tends to contain it. Wind velocity and direction can vary significantly, depending on height. Wind speed generally increases with height because of the surface friction of the ground. At the ground surface, the wind speed decreases to almost zero.

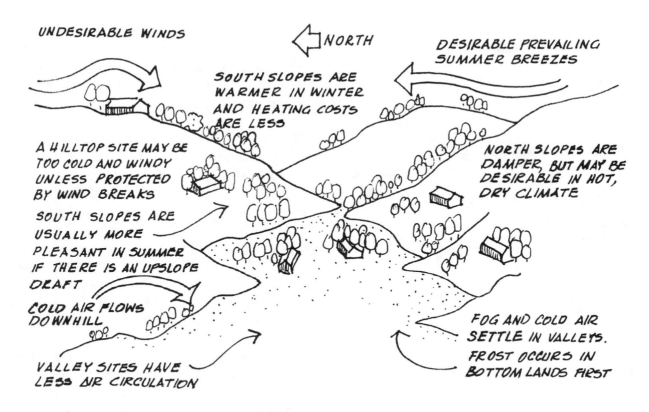

UNDESIRABLE WINDS

NORTH

DESIRABLE PREVAILING SUMMER BREEZES

SOUTH SLOPES ARE WARMER IN WINTER AND HEATING COSTS ARE LESS

A HILLTOP SITE MAY BE TOO COLD AND WINDY UNLESS PROTECTED BY WIND BREAKS

NORTH SLOPES ARE DAMPER, BUT MAY BE DESIRABLE IN HOT, DRY CLIMATE

SOUTH SLOPES ARE USUALLY MORE PLEASANT IN SUMMER IF THERE IS AN UPSLOPE DRAFT

COLD AIR FLOWS DOWNHILL

FOG AND COLD AIR SETTLE IN VALLEYS. FROST OCCURS IN BOTTOM LANDS FIRST

VALLEY SITES HAVE LESS AIR CIRCULATION

INLAND SITES

Figure 8.6

A body of water is usually warmer at night and cooler during the day than land adjacent to it. Similarly, it is normally cooler in summer and warmer in winter, than adjacent land. Thus, the effect of a water body on the land adjacent to it is to moderate the microclimate, just as oceans moderate the macroclimate.

Where land is adjacent to a large body of water, the difference in temperature between the two causes an almost constant breeze. Such locations generally have desirable climatic conditions. Other locations that enjoy desirable conditions include south and southeast slopes and upper or middle slopes, in contrast to those at the base or crest of a hill.

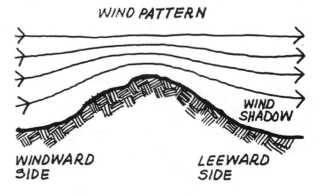

WIND PATTERN

WIND SHADOW

WINDWARD SIDE

LEEWARD SIDE

WIND PATTERN MODIFICATION

Figure 8.7

The microclimate is also affected by ground surface materials. To examine this phenomenon two terms should be identified. One is *albedo*, the other is *conductivity*. Albedo is that fraction of the radiant energy received on a surface that is reflected, expressed on a scale of zero to 1.0. Zero corresponds to a flat black surface that absorbs all the heat it receives and reflects none, while 1.0 corresponds to a perfectly reflecting surface, such as a mirror, which reflects all the energy directed to it, absorbing none. Materials such as grass and forest have low values of albedo, varying from about 0.05 to 0.30. Pavements have high albedo.

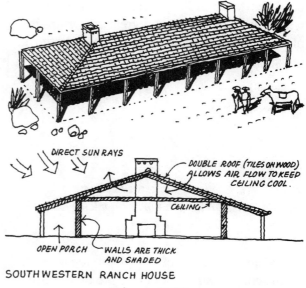

FARM HOUSE ON A HILLTOP – SUMMER

Figure 8.8

Conductivity refers to the speed with which heat passes through a material. Metals have high conductivity, while materials such as sand and soil have low conductivity.

SOUTHWESTERN RANCH HOUSE

Figure 8.10

Ground surfaces having low albedo and high conductivity moderate the microclimate considerably. Heat energy is absorbed and released later when the temperature drops. Consequently, grass surfaces are cooler in hot weather and warmer in cold weather than nearby paved surfaces. Grass areas are also less dusty, have less glare, and are more sound-absorbent than

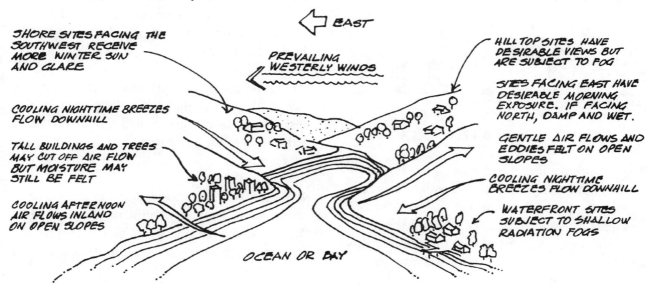

SHORELINE SITES

Figure 8.9

paved surfaces. It is apparent why urban areas, with few grassy areas and great concentrations of structures and pavements, become hotter in the summer than corresponding rural areas.

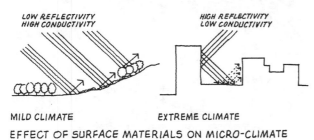

EFFECT OF SURFACE MATERIALS ON MICRO-CLIMATE
Figure 8.11

Trees have a variety of microclimatic effects, all of which tend to moderate the microclimate. Rows of trees act as effective windbreaks, reducing wind speeds within and downwind of the trees by at least one-half or more. The distance in which wind speeds are reduced is many times greater than the height of the trees, with certain configurations of trees being more effective than others. By carefully siting structures to take advantage of this reduction of wind in winter, the wind chill factor can be dramatically reduced, resulting in a more comfortable microclimate and less fuel consumption.

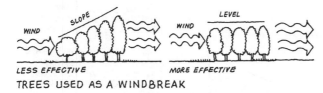

TREES USED AS A WINDBREAK
Figure 8.12

Trees block the direct radiation of the sun, as well as light and glare from secondary sources such as the sky and the ground surface. Deciduous trees provide an excellent example of nature's grand plan: they block the summer sun and glare, while allowing most of the winter sun and light to come through. Evergreens, on the other hand, have the same blocking effect all year round. A beneficial effect of evergreens in winter is that they help reduce snow glare.

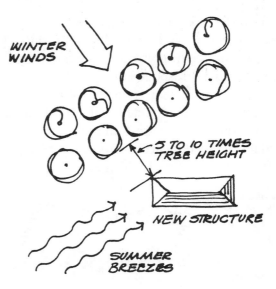

TREES ACT AS WINTER WIND BREAK
Figure 8.13

Another desirable effect that trees, as well as other plants, have on the microclimate is that they filter the air by absorbing dust, dirt, and other pollutants. In addition, all plants absorb carbon dioxide and release oxygen in photosynthesis. The air of the forest has a natural freshness that man cannot easily duplicate. Trees and other plants also evaporate water vapor into the air through transpiration, which cools and humidifies the air.

Trees, therefore, not only satisfy our instinctive desire for protection, but also help to maintain a stable, pleasant microclimate, clean air, and a naturally pleasing environment virtually free of maintenance.

If we think of "conditioned air" as air whose temperature, humidity, velocity, and freshness are within the parameters of human comfort, then trees are among nature's most effective air conditioners.

Thus far we have discussed the local modification of the macroclimate by natural features, such as topography, water, wind, and trees. Manmade structures also modify climate. In urban areas they may be the predominant microclimatic factor.

Structures alter air movement. They block, divert, and channel winds, sometimes in unpredictable ways. When wind strikes a large surface, the opposite face of the surface becomes a low pressure area, in which the air is relatively quiet but moves erratically, in a whirling flow. The thicker the surface in the direction of the air flow, the less significant is the leeward low pressure area. On large projects, scale models are sometimes tested in wind tunnels so that wind flow can be predicted more accurately.

We have mentioned how manmade structures and pavements in urban areas reflect solar radiation, elevating temperatures. Urban areas may be 10° warmer than comparable rural areas both day and night, winter and summer. In general, urban areas are not only warmer, but also noisier, drier, dustier, and more polluted than non-urban areas. They may also have more rain, clouds, fog, and glare. Urban wind velocities are generally lower, and the frequency and severity of flooding in urban areas is greater than in rural areas.

Climatic Considerations

The human comfort zone is that range of temperature and relative humidity in which the average person is comfortable wearing light clothing. The comfort zone ranges between 63° and 71°F in winter, and 66° and 75°F in summer, within a relative humidity range of 30 to 60 percent. As the humidity increases, discomfort is experienced at increasingly lower temperatures, until the relative humidity reaches 75 percent, at which point discomfort results regardless of the temperature.

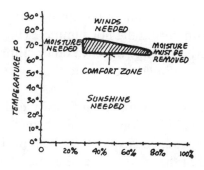

COMFORT ZONE DIAGRAM
Figure 8.14

At temperatures above the comfort zone, air movement makes people feel more comfortable. For example, if an individual is sitting in a light breeze of at least 200 feet per minute, temperatures of approximately 85°F may be quite comfortable in the 20 to 50 percent humidity range. When humidity levels are low, additional moisture must be introduced in order to maintain the sense of comfort. At temperature levels below the comfort zone, additional radiation from the sun is needed to maintain the sense of comfort. And when humidity levels are high, moisture must be removed to avoid discomfort.

Air movement causes a cooling sensation because of heat loss from the body by convection and evaporation. The greater the speed of air movement, the greater the cooling effect. Air movement less than 50 feet per minute is generally not noticed, 50 to 100 feet per minute is pleasant, 100 to 200 feet per minute is pleasant and noticeable, 200 to 300 feet per minute is felt to be drafty, and more than 300 feet per minute is uncomfortable.

Physical well-being as well as mental health are also related to climate. The closer the microclimate is to the comfort zone, the higher the level of health and energy. Consequently, in the temperate zone of the United States, this level is highest in autumn, drops to a low point in winter, rises again in the spring, dropping once again during the hot summer. The seasonal variation may differ in other climates, but it is always directly related to the comfort zone.

This does not mean that uniformity is desirable. Variation is conducive to change of mood and pace, and, consequently, a healthful stimulus. One of the tasks of the designer, then, is to try to temper the climate so it falls within the comfort zone, both indoors and outdoors. Obviously, this is not always possible. But if the designer is aware of the factors influencing human comfort—temperature, humidity, air movement, and solar radiation—as well as all the variables that make up the microclimate, he or she can produce a most effective design within a particular microclimate, and modify it where necessary. Winter winds can be intercepted and summer winds admitted. Summer sun can be shaded, but advantage can be taken of winter sun. Structures can be placed on desirable sites and optimally oriented.

Conversely, undesirable situations can be avoided, such as steep north-facing slopes with cold drafts, west slopes that face a body of water with uncomfortably strong glare, windy hilltops, frost pockets with low temperatures, bare dry ground subject to flash flooding, and areas with polluted air or noise. All such undesirable sites can simply be avoided for habitation, and used for activities serving few or no people, such as warehousing. Desirable microclimatic conditions, such as southeast to southwest slopes, locations close to water, and well-planted or forested sites, can be used to great advantage in site planning. By designing for sun, shade, breeze, and air quality we can improve the microclimate and hence the comfort of potential inhabitants.

Sustainable design planning is a design philosophy that tries to work with the virtues of the natural conditions, rather than forcing a solution that requires imported energy to overcome natural conditions. For example, by designing with minimal interference with the existing topography and existing drainage ways, the final design may be less costly, less homogenous, and have a unique quality reflective of local natural ecosystems.

Whenever the landscape is altered the microclimate is affected—sometimes improved, sometimes harmed. By changing the natural drainage flow, clearing forests, plowing, planting, or grading, we alter the environment. With the creation of the urban habitat, with its extensive paving, dense buildings, blocked air movement, noise and air pollution, we have also created a somewhat hostile environment in regard to climate. As a result, we have become more sensitive to the conditions of the urban climate and its sometimes deleterious effects upon the health and well-being of people. A sensitive and intelligent designer, however, may manipulate surfaces and structures, in addition to using modern mechanical means, to produce a climate as desirable as one found in nature.

Air Pollution

The envelope of air surrounding our planet sustains all life—plant, animal, and man. Therefore, air quality is of vital concern. Is air ever absolutely pure? By definition, being itself a mixture, it cannot be. The question of air quality is a question of the balance or imbalance of its constituent ingredients, and of the presence of undesirable, deleterious substances. These include certain dusts, particles, industrial gases, ozone, etc.

Man is not alone in harming air quality. Occasionally, acts of nature create air pollution. Sandstorms fill the air with whirling grit. Ash from erupting volcanoes and smoke from forest fires blanket huge areas. But such occurrences are relatively rare and, in any event, largely uncontrollable by man.

Of far greater concern is the air pollution caused by our own actions and practices. Over the years, the burning of coal, oil, and gas and the exhausts of millions of automobiles have discharged enormous quantities of gaseous and solid matter into the atmosphere. Noticeable and sometimes dangerous concentrations of air pollutants occur, principally in industrialized areas, such as the United States, Western Europe, and Japan. Under some circumstances, the extreme effects of air pollution are lessened by natural weather action such as wind, rain, and air currents.

But natural weather action can also magnify the effects of manmade pollution. Such an action is the temperature inversion phenomenon. This occurs because the air temperature at the ground level is lower than at some elevation above the ground. It becomes warmer as we go higher. At some point, this increase changes and the air then becomes cooler as we go still higher. The cooler air at the ground surface is heavier than the air above it and therefore cannot move upward. The air becomes trapped and any pollutants discharged into it cannot escape into the upper atmosphere. They linger over the city in the form of smog (smoke and gases) until a strong current of new air displaces the lingering layers, and the inversion disappears. Air pollution is damaging to plants, animals, and man.

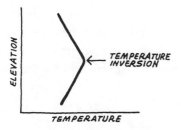

TEMPERATURE INVERSION
Figure 8.15

An increased public awareness of the effects of air pollution has resulted in the enactment of federal and state legislation designed to restrict noxious emissions from both vehicles and industry. Even with these measures air pollution will not disappear entirely. Therefore the process of site selection and design must take this modern problem of man and nature, and their coexistence, into consideration.

Noise

Noise is unwanted sound. The sound (sonic) environment within a building is a primary concern of design. Through careful acoustic design, absorptive insulation, and isolation devices, internal noise can be confined to its place of origin. External noise, however, is more difficult to control. Noise is created and aggravated by airplanes, automobiles, buses, rail systems, construction equipment, and the many activities of urban life. As cities and suburbs increase in area and population, more noise is generated. The increase in mechanization both indoors and outdoors results in an increase of noise. As you read this, you can probably hear vehicle noise in the street, ringing telephones, clacking typewriters, the sounds of radio or television. For some persons, noise-induced hearing loss can be an occupational hazard. Many workers are exposed each day to noise levels that are detrimental to their health.

Sound levels are measured in decibels, on a logarithmic scale that has a value of 1 at the threshold of hearing and 140 at the threshold of pain. One decibel is the smallest difference between two sounds that the human ear can detect. Each increase of 10 decibels represents a tenfold increase of sound energy, which the human ear perceives as approximately twice as loud. A noise 30 decibels higher than another has one thousand times the sound energy of the latter (10 × 10 × 10). Some typical sources and their approximate values are shown in Table 8.1.

Decibels	Source
10	Normal breathing
20 to 30	Soft whisper
40	Hum of small electric motor
50	Typical kitchen
60	Normal conversation
70	Normal office
90 to 100	Rock band
100	Subway train
160	Jet airplane

Table 8.1

A comfortable noise level for the average person is in the range of 50 to 60 decibels. No more than 30 decibels is recommended for sleep or study areas. 85 decibels is considered the safety threshold; exposure to higher noise levels over a prolonged period may cause hearing impairment.

Sound pitch is determined by frequency, which is the number of oscillations, or cycles, per second. Sound audible to humans generally ranges from 20 to about 20,000 cycles per second. The pitch of sound can be a major factor in causing discomfort: high-pitched sounds that contrast with background sounds can be irritating even if they are relatively soft.

Noise can contribute to stress, particularly when it disrupts sleep or rest. Apartment dwellers are especially subject to "noise invasion" from outside sources, such as traffic, as well as noises from nearby apartments and corridors.

Normal city noises can affect the heart and blood pressure, and severe noises may damage the auditory system permanently. Many sounds are attenuated (weakened) before they reach us. For example, doubling the distance between the source and receiver diminishes the sound level

six decibels. Since sound intensity decreases in proportion to the square of the distance from a point source, doubling the distance reduces the sound intensity to one-quarter. This does not apply to linear sources, such as freeways, where the sound level drops only three decibels for each doubling of distance, and the sound intensity drops to one-half.

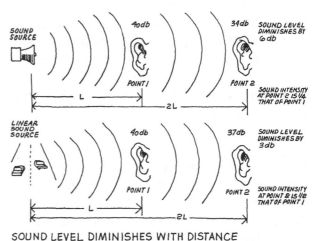

SOUND LEVEL DIMINISHES WITH DISTANCE
Figure 8.16

Gusty winds reduce the effect of sounds by adding a "white noise," a blend of all sound frequencies, which tends to blur a noise of a specific frequency. Thus, wind sound minimizes the effects of traffic noise.

Trees "thin out" high-frequency noises, but solid barriers, such as earth, walls, and structures, are more effective in reducing noise. A high wall close to the source of the sound reduces high-frequency noise. However, a low wall midway between source and receiver has little effect on low-frequency sound. Water movement, such as a fountain, helps to mask unpleasant sounds, while ground covers help to absorb noises. An example is the Freeway Park in Seattle, designed by landscape architect Lawrence Halprin. The "white noise" generated by its cascading fountain literally and figuratively drowns out the sound of the nearby interstate highway.

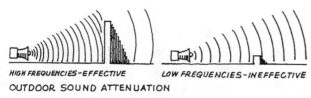

HIGH FREQUENCIES-EFFECTIVE   LOW FREQUENCIES-INEFFECTIVE
OUTDOOR SOUND ATTENUATION

Figure 8.17

Thus, noise may be controlled either by locating activities at some distance from the noise source, or by placing physical barriers between the noise source and the planned activity.

Glare

Glare is a common environmental problem that can be controlled by careful planning. Glare occurs when there are two sources of illumination of extremely different intensities, such as very light against very dark. Glare is not a result of too much light, but rather of too much contrast. In the natural landscape, glare can occur over water, snow, or sand. Glare can be eliminated from natural landscapes by such simple means as planting grass.

Some structures create problems of glare. Buildings that are located to take advantage of solar heating during wintertime may cause glare problems. Visual discomfort caused by glare can be severe. Looking out of a south-facing window into the low winter sun can be very uncomfortable. If the ground is covered with snow, or if windows face a lake, the glare problem can be even more severe. While consideration must be given to the desirable aspects of solar radiation, the objectionable problems of glare must also be dealt with.

Glare may be alleviated by certain wall treatments, such as blinds, drapes, and nonglare glass. In very warm climates, however, additional protection from the sun is needed. Such locations require buildings that continually shield windows from the sun. In tropical climates, sun screens can help reduce both construction and cooling costs.

Exterior sun control devices such as overhangs, fins, or louvers are very effective in reducing heat and glare. Natural landscape elements, such as trees, can also control glare.

ECOLOGY

Background

Although the term ecology is relatively new in environmental planning, an ecological approach to planning goes back well into history. The Old Testament, for example, contains admonishments that may be regarded as ecological principles, such as allowing land to rest periodically, not destroying trees in a conquered territory, and the consideration and care of animals.

In fact, all through history, societies have had to practice land and resource husbandry for their own survival. Present day ecology, as a science, was introduced in the late 19th century, by an American named George Perkins Marsh. His book, *Man in Nature*, published in 1875, is the landmark introduction to the study of ecology. It was the product of his reflections on mankind's historical experience in land settlement and development, some of which proved disastrous, and some highly responsible and consequently successful. Another pioneer in this field, who linked ecology to regional and urban planning, was the Scottish biologist Patrick Geddes. His work dates from World War I, and his influence was worldwide.

In the 1920s, a group of American environmentalists formed the Regional Planning Association of America to explore and expand the possibilities for large-scale comprehensive planning in the United States. That group included the American philosopher and environmental writer Lewis Mumford, as well as Benton Mackaye, a forester, who proposed the Appalachian Trail in 1922. Mackaye's writings include *The New Exploration: A Philosophy of Regional Planning* and *From Geography to Geotecture*. In 1926 two members of this group, Clarence Stein and Henry Wright, drafted a landmark ecologically-based plan for the entire state of New York. In essence, that plan identified the critical and vital natural resources of the state—water, forest, soil, and topography—and then determined the land uses or activities appropriate to those resources. From that derived a brilliant plan of appropriate uses. Natural and human activities were thus brought together in harmony. Larger applications of the same methods were made for the entire United States in the 1930s, many under the direction of a federal agency eventually known as the Natural Resources Planning Board (NRPB). Though operated under the federal government, much of its work was done by diverse and comprehensive groups of experts in various local regions. NRPB was a system of democratic planning, based on scientific knowledge and American values.

Among the notable regional planning efforts of the 1930s were the creation of the Tennessee Valley Authority and the development of the Columbia River. NRPB's work made it possible for the nation to mobilize rationally and rapidly for World War II. However, the war interrupted the nation's work in regional planning, and the post-war years were too occupied with rapid growth to pay much attention to it. In retrospect, that proved to be a tragic oversight, for regional planning, based on ecology, would have resulted in far more workable and livable metropolitan areas.

Our rapid growth, without sound regionally scaled ecological planning, resulted in many errors in urbanization. And that led to the realization that we had acted irresponsibly, giving rise to a renewal of interest in ecological planning. Landscape architects deserve the most credit for reformulating and, indeed, advancing ecologically based planning.

Two outstanding spokesmen in this field are Professor Ian McHarg, of the University of Pennsylvania, who authored *Design with Nature*, and Professor Philip H. Lewis, Jr., of the University of Wisconsin, whose plan, "Recreation in Wisconsin," is a landmark in method, wisdom, and common sense. The method is, simply, to survey a natural or man-transformed landscape, and to assess the possibilities or constraints for potential activities or uses according to the inherent capability of the landscape components. With that knowledge, it is possible to determine—in the words of the late American planner, S. B. Zisman—where to build, where not to build, and consequently to a large degree, what to build, and how much to build. Thus natural landscape and humankind's settlements become partners in a continuing enterprise, in ecological harmony. Among the most eloquent statements in this regard are the writings of the late Dr. Rene Dubos, a microbiologist. Particularly helpful is his insightful book, *So Human an Animal*. Ecological planning is the foundation of all successful design.

Ecological Considerations

Ecology is the science of the pattern of relations between a community of organisms and its environment, the community comprising all the living animals and plants occupying a given area. The community and its physical environment form an ecological system, or ecosystem. An ecosystem may be a forest, a desert, a pond, a laboratory culture, or a manned space vehicle. The organisms in an ecosystem compete as well as cooperate with each other to achieve a dynamic balance with the earth, air, and water that form their physical environment.

Ecosystems are constantly changing. As an ecosystem changes, it approaches a stable condition in which the diversity of its constituent species reaches a maximum. If a particular species in a complex ecosystem, such as a forest, is destroyed, the system itself will form new relationships.

SIMPLE ECOSYSTEM (UNSTABLE)   COMPLEX ECOSYSTEM (STABLE)

Figure 8.18

In contrast, simple, uniform ecosystems tend to be unstable. They are vulnerable to the destabilizing introduction of a single "foreign" element. The constituent elements of a fragile ecosystem are few in number. If, in such an ecosystem, one constituent element is destroyed, that entire ecosystem is likely to collapse.

In a broader sense, ecology refers to the interdependence of man, plants, animals, and the physical environment. The scale of the ecological approach to planning ranges from a single urban site to the entire planet. To the designer, it means understanding the complex web of relations existing on a site, and between the site and its surroundings.

In urban areas, the pre-existing natural ecology has been largely supplanted by a man-made ecology: an interdependence of people, institutions, circulation systems, etc. Site analysis must consider the effect of a given site development on the environment. Are existing circulation systems (streets, highways, public transportation) adequate? Are existing utilities, sewers, and storm drains adequate? How will the planned development affect the microclimate by modifying prevailing winds or creating glare? Will the development be harmonious with the neighborhood in appearance, use, and scale? Will the development produce noise, smoke, or other undesirable effects?

In rural areas, where the ecology may be such that the natural processes predominate, considerations may differ. In general, the environment should be altered as little as possible. Grading should be minimal, natural drainage patterns left intact, and points of interest, such as rock outcroppings, left undisturbed.

Obviously, whether the setting is rural or urban, a balance of objectives must be sought. Good judgment must be exercised in choosing alternatives, and in establishing priorities. With careful planning and continuing management, the development of a site can be accomplished while preserving its basic resources of air, water, and soil. At the same time it is possible to protect plant and animal life, while still solving the basic architectural problems.

AHWAHNEE PRINCIPLES

In 1991, in the Ahwahnee Hotel in Yosemite National Park, a group of architects, planners, and community leaders got together to present community principles that express new, sustainable planning ideas. These principles are summarized below:

Preamble:

Existing patterns of urban and suburban development seriously impair our quality of life. The symptoms are: more congestion and air pollution resulting from our increased dependence on automobiles, the loss of precious open space, the need for costly improvements to roads and public services, the inequitable distribution of economic resources, and the loss of a sense of community. By drawing upon the best from the past and the present, we can plan communities that will more successfully serve the needs of those who live and work within them. Such planning should adhere to certain fundamental principles.

Community Principles:

1. All planning should be in the form of complete and integrated communities containing housing, shops, workplaces, schools, parks, and civic facilities, essential to the daily life of the residents.

2. Community size should be designed so that housing, jobs, daily needs, and other activities are within easy walking distance of each other.

3. As many activities as possible should be located within easy walking distance of transit stops.

4. A community should contain a diversity of housing types to enable citizens from a wide range of economic levels and age groups to live within its boundaries.

5. Businesses within the community should provide a range of job types for the community's residents.

6. The location and character of the community should be consistent with a larger transit network.

7. The community should have a center focus that combines commercial, civic, cultural, and recreational uses.

8. The community should contain an ample supply of specialized open space in the form of squares, greens, and parks, whose frequent use is encouraged through placement and design.

9. Public spaces should be designed to encourage the attention and presence of people at all hours of the day and night.

10. Each community or cluster of communities should have a well-defined edge, such as agricultural greenbelts or wildlife corridors, permanently protected from development.

11. Streets, pedestrian paths, and bike paths should contribute to a system of fully-connected and interesting routes to all destinations. Their design should encourage pedestrian and bicycle use by being small and spatially defined by buildings, trees, and lighting, and by discouraging high speed traffic.

12. Wherever possible, the natural terrain, drainage, and vegetation of the community should be preserved with superior examples contained within parks or greenbelts.

13. The community design should help conserve resources and minimize waste.

14. Communities should provide for the efficient use of water through the use of natural drainage, drought tolerant landscaping, and recycling.

15. The street orientation, the placement of buildings, and the use of shading should contribute to the energy efficiency of the community.

Regional Principles:

1. The regional land-use planning structure should be integrated within a larger transportation network built around transit rather than freeways.

2. Regions should be bounded by and provide a continuous system of greenbelt/wildlife corridors to be determined by natural conditions.

3. Regional institutions and services (government, stadiums, museums, etc.) should be located in the urban core.

4. Materials and methods of construction should be specific to the region, exhibiting a continuity of history and culture and compatibility with the climate to encourage the development of local character and community identity.

Implementation Principles:

1. The general plan should be updated to incorporate the above principles.

2. Rather than allowing developer-initiated, piecemeal development, local governments should take charge of the planning process. General plans should designate where new growth, in-fill, or redevelopment will be allowed to occur.

3. Prior to any development, a specific plan should be prepared based on these planning principles.

4. Plans should be developed through an open process and participants in the process should be provided visual models of all planning principles.

Source: Local Government Commission's Center for Livable Communities, *http://lgc.org/center/*.

SUSTAINABLE DESIGN

History of Sustainable Design

What is sustainable design and how is it different from the ordinary process that architects have used for thousands of years?

In early human history, builders of human habitats used materials that occurred naturally in the earth, such as stone, wood, mud, adobe bricks, and grasses. With nomadic tribes and early civilizations, the built environment made little impact on the balance of natural elements. When abandoned, the grass roof, adobe brick, or timber beam would slowly disintegrate and return to the natural ecosystem. Small human populations and the use of natural materials had very little impact on a balanced natural ecosystem.

But as human populations expanded and settlements moved into more demanding climates, natural materials were altered to become more durable and less natural. In fact, it is the remnants of archeology that demonstrate some of the human creations that are not easily recycled into the earth; fired clay, smelted ore for jewelry, and tools are examples of designs that will not easily reintegrate into the natural ecosystem. These materials may be reprocessed (grinding, melting, or reworking) into other human creations, but they will never be natural materials again.

As human populations expanded, there is strong evidence that some civilizations outgrew their natural ecosystem. When overused, land became less fertile and less able to support crops, timber, and domesticated animals necessary for human life. The ancient solution was to move to a more desirable location and use new natural resources in the new location, abandoning the ecologically ruined home site.

The realization that global natural resources are limited is an age old concept. The term *conservation*, which came into existence in the late 19th century, referred to the economic management of natural resources such as fish, timber, topsoil, minerals, and game. In the United States, at the beginning of the 20th century, President Theodore Roosevelt and his chief forester, Gifford Pinchot, introduced the concept of conservation as a philosophy of natural resource management. The impetus of this movement created several pieces of natural legislation to promote conservation and increased appreciation of America's natural resources and monuments.

In the middle of the 1960s, Rachel Carson published *Silent Spring*, a literary alarm that revealed the reality of an emerging ecological disaster—the gross misunderstanding of the value and hazards of pesticides. The pesticide DDT and its impact on the entire natural ecosystem was dramatic; clearly, some human inventions were destructive and could spread harm throughout the ecosystem with alarming speed and virulence. Birds in North America died from DDT used to control malaria in Africa. Human creations were influenced by the necessities of the natural cycles of the ecosystem. Human toxic efforts could no longer be absorbed by the cycles of nature. Human activities became so pervasive and potentially intrusive that there needed to be a higher level of worldwide ecological understanding of the risk of disrupting the ecosystem.

Architects, as designers of the built environment, realize the ecological impact of their choices of architectural components, such as site selection, landscaping, infrastructure, building materials, and mechanical systems. The philosophy of sustainable design encourages a new, more environmentally sensitive, approach to architectural design and construction.

There are many credos for the approach to a new, sustainable design. Some architectural historians maintain that the best architects (Vitruvius, Ruskin, Wright, Alexander) have always discussed design in terms of empathy with nature and the natural systems. Now it is evident that all architects should include the principles of sustainable design as part of their palette of architectural best practices.

Principles of Sustainable Design

Why is sustainable design necessary?

Principles of the Scientific Laws of Nature

1.) In the earth's ecosystem (the area of the earth's crust and atmosphere approximately five miles high and five miles deep) there is a finite amount of natural resources. Mankind has become dependent on elements such as fresh water, timber, plants, soil, and ore, which we process into necessary pieces of our human environment.

2.) Given the laws of thermodynamics, matter cannot be created or destroyed. The resources that we have been allotted to manage our existence are contained in our ecosystem.

3.) All forms of energy tend to seek equilibrium and therefore disperse. For example, water falls from the sky, settles on plants, and then percolates into the soil to reach the subterranean aquifer. Toxic liquids, released by humans, and exposed to the soil, will equally disperse and eventually reach the same underground reservoir. The fresh water aquifer, now contaminated, is no longer a useful natural resource.

These laws of science indicate why it is necessary to maintain the delicate balance of natural ecosystems. There is a need to focus on the preservation of beneficial natural elements and diminish or extinguish natural resources contaminated with toxins and our destructive practices.

There are many credos for environmental responsibility. One, *The Natural Step*, was organized by scientists, designers, and environmentalists in 1996.

They were concerned with the preservation of the thin layer that supports human life in a small zone on the earth's surface: the ecosphere (five miles of the earth's crust) and the biosphere (five miles into the troposphere of the atmosphere).

Their principles are summarized as follows:

1.) Substance from the earth's crust must not systemically increase in the ecosphere. Elements from the earth such as fossil fuel, ores, timber, etc., must not be extracted from the earth at a greater rate than they can be replenished.

2.) Substances that are manmade must not systemically increase in the ecosphere. Manmade materials cannot be produced at a faster rate than they can be integrated back into nature.

3.) The productivity and diversity of nature must not be systemically diminished. This means that we must protect and preserve the variety of living organisms that now exist.

4.) In recognition of the first three conditions, there must be a fair and efficient use of resources to meet human needs. This means that human needs must be met in the most environmentally sensitive way possible.

5.) Buildings consume at least 40 percent of the world's energy. Thus they account for about a third of the world's emissions of heat-trapping carbon dioxide from fossil fuel burning, and two-fifths of acid rain-causing carbon dioxide and nitrogen oxides.[*]

---

[*] *Source:* David Malin Roodman and Nicholas Lessen, "*Building Revolution: How Ecology and Health Concerns are Transforming Construction.*" Worldwatch Paper 124 (Washington DC, Worldwatch Institute, 1995. Pg. 10). *The HOK Guidebook to Sustainable Design*, Sandra Mendler & William Odell, John Wiley & Sons, Inc., New York, 2000.

The built environment has a monumental impact on the use of materials and fuels to create shelter for human beings. The decisions about the amount and type of materials and systems that are employed in the building process have an enormous impact on the future use of natural resources. Architects can affect and guide those decisions of design to influence the needs of sustainability and environmental sensitivity.

It is not a quick process. Like moving a large boat in a new direction, it must be done gradually and with awareness of the many natural forces that are acting on it. But, the process has started and architects should be aware of the philosophy of sustainable design in order to influence the results.

Sustainable Materials and Products

As demonstrated in the previous section, sustainable design should be extended through the entire project, from conception to final construction details. Designers developing an environmentally responsible plan need to pay attention to these principles in every stage of the project. The materials and products specified carry an ecological responsibility, from the way they are manufactured to the manner in which they are transported to the job site. Materials and products should follow the same sustainable principles of waste reduction, increased use of recycled content, and maximized reuse of existing materials.

Most product manufacturers today are very familiar with the environmental concerns of the design community and have developed many alternatives to commonly used products. Most follow one or more of these guidelines:

1. Use a high percent of recycled content

2. Use local or regional materials that reduce environmental impact from transport

3. Use products containing rapidly renewable natural materials such as bamboo and cork

4. Use certified wood to ensure environmentally responsible forest management

5. Reuse existing materials

6. Use products free of toxic ingredients

7. Offer recycling or reuse programs

With increasing demand for more environmentally responsible product choices, designers today have a better selection than ever of materials that can be quite beautiful as well as more economically feasible.

Since this list is meant to be comprehensive for the purposes of this lesson only, candidates are encouraged to become familiar with Leadership in Energy and Environmental Design (LEED) and its green building rating system, the leading green building guidelines in the United States since their inception in 1995.

SUSTAINABLE SITE PLANNING AND DESIGN

Most architectural projects involve the understanding of the design within the context of the larger scale neighborhood, community, or urban context in which the project is placed.

If the building will be influenced by sustainable design principles, its context and site should be equally sensitive to environmental planning principles.

Sustainable design encourages a re-examination of the principles of planning to include a more environmentally sensitive approach. Whether it is called Smart Grow, sustainable design, or environmentally sensitive development practice, these planning approaches have several principles in common.

1.0 Site Selection

The architect and planner may assist the client in developing the criteria for site selection that reflects the proposed environmental goals of the complex of buildings.

The selection of a site is influenced by many factors including cost, adjacency to utilities, transportation, building type, zoning, and neighborhood compatibility. But, in addition to these factors, there are sustainable design standards that should be added to the matrix of site selection decisions:

■ *Adjacency to Public Transportation*
If possible, projects that allow residents or employees access to public transportation are preferred. Allowing the building occupants the option of traveling by public transit may decrease the parking requirements, increase the pool of potential employees and remove the stress and expense of commuting by car.

■ *Flood Plains*
In general, local and national governments hope to remove buildings from the level of the 100-year flood plain. This can be accomplished by either raising the building at least one foot above the 100-year elevation or locating the project entirely out of the 100-year flood plain. This approach reduces the possibility of damage from flood waters, and possible damage to downstream structures hit by the overfilled capacity of the floodplain.

■ *Erosion, Fire, and Landslides*
Some ecosystems are naturally prone to fire and erosion cycles. Areas such as high slope, chaparral ecologies are prone to fires and mud slides. Building in such zones is hazardous and damaging to the ecosystem and should be avoided.

■ *Sites with High Slope or Agricultural Use*
Sites with high slopes are difficult building sites and may disturb ecosystems,

which may lead to erosion and topsoil loss. Similarly, sites with fertile topsoil conditions—prime agricultural sites—should be preserved for crops, wildlife, and plant material, not building development.

■ *Solar Orientation, Wind Patterns*
Orienting the building with the long axis generally east west and fenestration primarily facing south may have a strong impact on solar harvesting potential. In addition, protecting the building with earth forms and tree lines may reduce the heat loss in the winter and diminish summer heat gain.

■ *Landscape Site Conditions*
The location of dense, coniferous trees on the elevation against the prevailing wind (usually west or northwest) may decrease heat loss due to infiltration and wind chill factor. Sites with deciduous shade trees can reduce summer solar gain if positioned properly on the south and west elevations of the buildings.

2.0 Alternative Transportation
Sites that are near facilities that allow several transportation options should be encouraged. Alternate transportation includes public transportation (trains, buses, and vans); bicycling amenities (bike paths, shelters, ramps, and overpasses); carpool opportunities that may also connect with mass transit; and provisions for alternate, more environmentally sensitive fuel options such as electricity or hydrogen.

3.0 Reduce Site Disturbance
Site selection should conserve natural areas, and restore wildlife habitat and ecologically damaged areas. In some areas of the United States, less than 2 percent of the original vegetation remains. Natural areas provide a visual and physical barrier between high activity zones. Additionally, these natural areas are aesthetic and psychological refuges for humans and wildlife.

4.0 Storm Water Management
Reduced disruption of natural water courses (rivers, streams and natural drainage swales) may be achieved by:

■ Providing on-site infiltration of contaminants (especially petrochemicals) from entering the main waterways. Drainage designs that use swales filled with wetland vegetation is a natural filtration technique especially useful in parking and large grass areas.

■ Reducing impermeable surface and allowing local aquifer recharge instead of runoff to waterways.

■ Encouraging groundwater recharge.

Ecologically Sensitive Landscaping

The selection of indigenous plant material, contouring the land, and proper positioning of shade trees may have a positive effect on the landscape appearance, maintenance cost, and ecological balance. The following are some basic sustainable landscape techniques:

■ Install indigenous plant material, which is usually less expensive, to ensure durability (being originally intended for that climate) and lower maintenance (usually less watering and fertilizer).

■ Locate shade trees and plants over dark surfaces to reduce the "heat island effect" of surfaces (such as parking lots, cars, walkways) that will otherwise absorb direct solar radiation and retransmit it to the atmosphere.

■ Replace lawns with natural grasses. Lawns require heavy maintenance including watering, fertilizer, and mowing. Sustainable design encourages indigenous plant material that is aesthetically compelling but far less ecologically disruptive.

■ In dry climates, encourage xeriscaping (plant materials adapted to dry and desert climates); encourage higher efficiency irrigation technologies including drip irrigation, rainwater recapture and gray water reuse. High efficiency irrigation uses less water because it supplies directly to the plant's root areas.

5.0 Reduce Light Pollution

Lighting of site conditions, either the buildings or landscaping, should not transgress the property and not shine into the atmosphere. Such practice is wasteful and irritating to the inhabitants of surrounding properties. All site lighting should be directed downward to avoid "light pollution."

6.0 Open Space Preservation

The quality of residential and commercial life benefits from opportunities to recreate and experience open-space areas. These parks, wild life refuges, easements, bike paths, wetlands, or play lots are amenities that are necessary for any development.

In addition to the aforementioned water management principles, the following are principles of design and planning that will help increase open-space preservation:

6.1) Promote in-fill development that is compact and contiguous to existing infrastructure and public transportation opportunities.

In-fill development may take advantage of already disturbed land without impinging on existing natural and agricultural land.

In certain cases, in-fill or redevelopment may take advantage of existing rather than new infrastructure.

6.2) Promote development that protects natural resources and provides buffers between natural and intensive use areas.

First, identify the natural areas (wetlands, wildlife habitats, water bodies, or flood plains) in the community in which the design is planned.

Second, the architect and planners should provide a design that protects and enhances the natural areas. The areas may be used partly for recreation, parks, natural habitats, and environmental education.

Third, the design should provide natural buffers (such as woodlands and grasslands) between sensitive natural areas and areas of intense use (factories, commercial districts, housing). These buffers may be both visual, olfactory, and auditory protection between areas of differing intensity.

Fourth, provide linkages between natural areas. Isolated islands of natural open space violate habitat boundaries and make the natural zones feel like captive preserves not a restoration or preservation of natural conditions.

Fifth, the links between natural areas may be used for walking, hiking, or biking, but should be constructed of permeable and biodegradable material. In addition, the links may augment natural systems such as water flow and drainage, habitat migration patterns, or flood plain conditions.

6.3) Establish procedures that ensure the ongoing management of the natural areas as part of a strategy of sustainable development.

Without human intervention, natural lands are completely sustainable. Cycles of growth and change including destruction by fire, wind, or flood have been occurring for millions of years. The plants and wildlife have adapted to these cycles to create a balanced ecosystem.

Human intervention has changed the balance of the ecosystem. With the relatively recent introduction of nearby human activities, the natural cycle of an ecosystem's growth, destruction, and rebirth is not possible.

Human settlement will not tolerate a fire that destroys thousands of acres only to liberate plant material that reblooms into another natural cycle.

The coexistence of human and natural ecosystems demands a different approach to design. This is the essence of sustainable design practices, a new approach that understands and reflects the needs of both natural and human communities.

SUMMARY

Each site has a unique combination of physical characteristics that distinguishes it from other sites. This lesson has dealt with the physical factors that the planner must evaluate in site planning and design: climate, air pollution, noise, glare, and ecology.

Although we have considerable control over the effects of climate and other natural factors, we must be fully respectful as well as understanding of nature as we analyze a site and design the structures to be placed upon it. Nature's patterns must be considered, along with man's, if we are to achieve harmonious and functional design.

LESSON 8   QUIZ

1. The ideal site for a residence is generally at

   A. the top of a hill.

   B. the bottom of a hill.

   C. halfway down a slope.

   D. between two hills.

2. Mountains influence climate by

   A. forcing prevailing winds to rise.

   B. creating shadow patterns.

   C. reducing temperature extremes.

   D. reducing relative humidity.

3. Indigenous architecture often comprises

   A. structures oriented to the south.

   B. courtyards facing north.

   C. multiple openings facing north.

   D. blank facades at the east and west.

4. Which of the following statements concerning ecology is NOT true?

   A. Ecology deals with the relationships of natural, rather than manmade, things.

   B. The organisms in an ecosystem are assumed to be in balance.

   C. The science of ecology is relatively new, being less than 100 years old.

   D. The size and scale of an ecosystem are theoretically unlimited.

5. Human comfort depends on which of the following? Check all that apply.

   A. Air temperature

   B. Air movement

   C. Relative humidity

   D. Longitude

   E. Solar radiation

6. One decibel is the

   A. sound level of normal breathing.

   B. sound level considered comfortable by the average person.

   C. lowest intensity of sound that can be produced.

   D. smallest difference in sound intensity that can be perceived by the human ear.

7. The wind velocities near a hill are generally greatest along the

   A. windward side.

   B. top of the hill.

   C. downward slope.

   D. northern slope.

8. Macroclimate differs from microclimate in its

   A. latitude.   C. elevation.

   B. extent.   D. location.

9. Which of the following are climatic effects of trees?

   I.   Modification of air flow

   II.   Obstruction of solar radiation

   III. Transpiration of water vapor into the air

   IV.   Reduction of wind chill factor

   V.   Filtration of air-borne pollutants

   A. I, II, and III   C. I, III, IV, and V

   B. II, IV, and V   D. I, II, III, IV, and V

10. Moderate climates, with few extremes of heat or cold, are most likely found in areas

   A. with strong prevailing breezes.

   B. with low relative humidity.

   C. that are close to large bodies of water.

   D. that are close to high mountain ranges.

LAND ANALYSIS

INTRODUCTION

Land has always been a precious resource, for the simple reason that it is limited in amount. Man has bartered his life and soul and waged war for possession of land. He has sometimes made it more beautiful and productive, through alteration and cultivation. But he has also damaged it, through poorly planned development.

To assure its proper use, numerous regulations have been adopted. The result is that we must now deal with a highly complex array of rules and procedures that were nonexistent until relatively recent times. In addition to complying with zoning ordinances, building codes, and height restrictions, we must also plan for the optimum use of the land. This requires a thorough knowledge of a site's topography, boundaries, soil, geography, and aesthetic qualities. The architect must seek ways to establish a relationship between a proposed development on a site and the existing character of the neighborhood around the site. And he must consider cost. Balancing these factors is a challenging task. A conscientious architect must be able to address these issues, considering a building and its site as a unity.

OWNERSHIP

The idea of ownership has ancient origins. Early man appropriated territory by occupying it. He chose to occupy areas plentiful in resources, such as water, game, and fertile soil. His choices were influenced by that which he could successfully defend.

Land was first owned communally, establishing the precedent for sovereign states to own land. With communal ownership, an individual might possess the right to use land. In medieval times, land ownership was in the hands of a few. Under the practice of primogeniture, land passed from father to eldest son, which limited the diffusion of land ownership. However, some societies divided land up among heirs, thereby creating a multitude of small and often inefficient farms.

In 1066, the Normans conquered England and introduced a system under which ownership of land was vested in the king, who granted parcels of land to nobles in return for loyalty, military support, and financial support. This feudal system of land tenure was gradually eliminated in England, and evolved into the system of "fee simple" ownership, under which land could be used or transferred by its owner as he pleased. However, land ownership today also carries the responsibility of payment of taxes, compliance with zoning ordinances, and other restrictions.

Some land in England, however, remains the property of the Crown, or the public, but its use can be obtained by leasing. Such leasehold property may be held by the lessee for a period of up to 99 years, after which time it reverts to the Crown.

Initially, land in America was controlled by colonizing companies, publicly franchised and privately financed. After the Revolution, the colonial lands were placed under the author-ity of the respective states. Individuals who had owned their lands under the Crown now owned it under the newly established states. The land gained from the British, and later the French, which had not been under the control of a colony became public domain, under the control of the federal government. The original public domain consisted of lands given up by several of the eastern states. This was known as the Northwest Territory, because it was northwest of the Ohio River. The land of the Louisiana Purchase was purchased from the French during the Napoleonic Wars. Land was also obtained from Spain and Mexico. Most of this public land, over 1 billion acres, has since been sold or deeded to individuals; some was transferred to states and municipalities for public use. Some land was given to veterans for their service, and a large amount of land was granted to universities and other educational institutions. Land grants were also made for the development of railroads and canals.

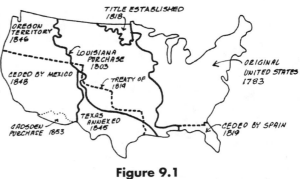

Figure 9.1

A large amount of public land was transferred to private ownership through the Homestead Act, passed by Congress in 1862. 160 acres of land were given, free, to anyone who built a house and lived on the land for five years. Thousands took advantage of this opportunity. About a third of a billion acres of land has been granted to homesteaders since the enactment of the Homestead Act. The only place in this country where homesteading is still practiced to any extent is Alaska.

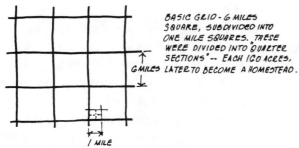

BASIC GRID - 6 MILES
SQUARE, SUBDIVIDED INTO
ONE MILE SQUARES. THESE
WERE DIVIDED INTO "QUARTER
SECTIONS" -- EACH 160 ACRES,
LATER TO BECOME A HOMESTEAD.

6 MILES

1 MILE

1787 LAND DIVISION SYSTEM OF THE U.S.A.

Figure 9.2

About 750 million acres, one third of the nation's area, still remains as public land. The policy of the federal government today, for the land in the public domain, is a combination of conservation and resource extraction.

As the nation grew in size and population, competition for land ownership intensified. Large estates, ranches, and land grants were subdivided and sold as parcels of varying sizes. Owning land and a home of one's own became the common goal of all. Building and development were synonymous with the 19th and 20th century American experience, at a scale and intensity not hitherto known.

With that eventually grew a consciousness that land is a scarce and easily damaged resource. And so we have developed a number of methods for the proper and responsible use of land, including planning, resource management, and land use regulation.

CATCHMENT AREAS

The term "catchment" means the geographic area from which the participants in an activity are drawn. For example, a catchment may comprise the area within which the patrons of a supermarket or shopping center reside.

Or, it may be the area within which the employees of an industrial plant reside. A given parcel of land may be located within numerous catchments simultaneously—some large, some small—each catchment containing a specific class of participants in a particular activity. Catchment areas may be distinctly defined by physical boundaries, or the boundaries may be indistinct. The size and shape of a catchment may be drawn with respect to a particular function or population.

Catchment boundaries may be determined by geographic features. Two neighborhoods, for example, may be separated by a physical feature such as a railroad or a waterway. A less definite boundary might be the demarcation between two ethnic neighborhoods. The boundary between two such areas may be set arbitrarily for purposes of analysis.

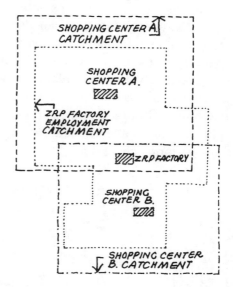

SHOPPING CENTER A
CATCHMENT

SHOPPING
CENTER A.

ZRP FACTORY
EMPLOYMENT
CATCHMENT

ZRP FACTORY

SHOPPING
CENTER B.

SHOPPING CENTER
B. CATCHMENT

OVERLAPPING CATCHMENT AREAS

Figure 9.3

Catchment areas may also be termed "market areas," "trade areas," or "tributary areas." The drawing shown in Figure 9.3 represents the employment catchment for a factory, along with the catchment areas for two nearby shopping centers. Note that some factory employees live in two separate but overlapping market catchments because they trade at both shopping centers. In this example, the market catchments are larger than the employment catchment area.

Catchments may increase or decrease in size. The employment catchment shown could easily increase if the ZRP Factory were to increase its business activity, or if a major connecting traffic artery were built, thus becoming more accessible to a greater number of workers by car. Conversely, if ZRP's activities were to decrease substantially, its employment catchment would shrink accordingly.

A catchment area can come into existence, or grow, as a result of population growth in an area or as a result of a municipal development program. School districts are catchments serving students residing within established boundaries. Recreation facilities can also form catchment areas. A catchment area may be local, regional, or national, and it can be all of these simultaneously. For example, Disneyland, in Anaheim, California, draws its visitors from Los Angeles and Orange Counties, along with visitors from out-of-state. The latter group constitutes the major catchment area.

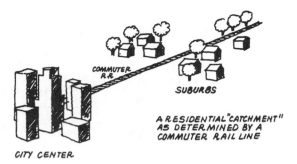

Figure 9.4

Residential catchments are determined by local transportation systems. Railroads or highways linking an urban center with an undeveloped area may encourage the formation and devel-

opment of that area, and the establishment of a new catchment. Under such conditions the commuting time, rather than the mileage, determines the maximum distance between home and place of work. For most people, a half-hour commute is the acceptable maximum for one-way travel by either automobile or rapid transit, although some people travel for up to one hour.

Zoning ordinances help to create and preserve catchment areas by specifying which land uses are permitted.

Existing catchments are subject to alteration from a number of sources. As new technologies are developed, their use may alter employment catchments. Retail stores selling new or innovative products may alter the shopping catchments.

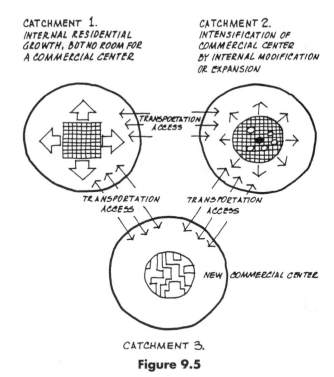

Figure 9.5

The improvement of underdeveloped land may alter catchments to a great extent. In Figure 9.5, the residential population of catchment 1 increases. This causes growth of the commercial area of catchment 2, by intensification or expansion. Or, commercial development may occur in catchment 3, hitherto undeveloped.

The point is that catchment areas change as a consequence of their interaction with each other. Thus, up-to-date information must be used in planning new or expanded uses which depend on their "catchment" or "user" areas.

LAND USE AND LAND VALUE

The use to which a parcel of land may be put depends on its potential role in a catchment area, its location, its topography, and its cost. Topography, access, zoning, utilities, and nearby uses are among the factors contributing to land value.

Land can be placed into eight basic categories of potential use, which determine value, as follows:

1. Natural resources (e.g., mining, forestry, etc.)

2. Agricultural

3. Residential

4. Commercial

5. Industrial

6. Governmental

7. Institutional

8. Open space/conservation

For the first five categories, there are four methods by which the value of land may be determined. It should be noted, however, that regional factors will cause variations in valuation.

Whether land is vacant or improved, it is valued in relation to the type of use which will yield the highest return. That use must, of course, be

warranted by prevailing market conditions, and its conformance to legal requirements of zoning and land use ordinances.

Note that the term "improvement" refers to any structure on a parcel of land which has value and "improves" the parcel's usefulness.

The first method is called the *comparison method or market data approach*. This method reflects the market value most closely. One of the requirements of this method, however, is the availability of sufficient data on comparable land being offered for sale at the time of valuation. Consequently, if industrial land in a given location, with all necessary access and utility services, sells for $20,000 per acre, a similar plot of ground with similar services in a similar location should also sell for about $20,000 per acre. Nevertheless, no two parcels of land are identical, and adjustments are often necessary to determine the value of a specific parcel of land.

THE COMPARISON METHOD
Figure 9.6

The second method is the *residual method* or *income approach method*. This is used in highly developed areas with no vacant land, where the appraiser is unable to obtain comparative data for land value. Value may then be determined by estimating the potential income from site improvements. The cost of site improvement must, of course, be taken into account when calculating the land value.

In order to make such calculations, the investor hypothesizes improvements which would provide the highest financial returns. This requires considerable knowledge, since variations in the investment rate of return as well as in the proposed improvements can result in substantial differences in value.

When calculating land value, the improvement must represent the *highest and best use* of the land. Highest and best use is defined as "that use which is most likely to produce the greatest net return over a given period of time."

The third method is the *allocation method*. It may be used to determine land value of improved properties. The value of the land can be estimated by deducting the value of the site improvements from the total value of the property. The reliability and accuracy of the allocation method depend on skill and knowledge.

Land that has a potential use for residential or industrial subdivision may be valued by the fourth method, called the *development method*. This method depends on estimated development costs. It should be used when sales prices of similar parcels are not available. The development method requires: determination of the ultimate selling prices of individual lots, the costs required to develop the subdivision (capital outlays, financing, carrying and sales costs), the period of time necessary to sell the developed lots, and possible discounting of the net sale price.

To summarize the four methods, the comparison method of determining land values is applicable to all classes of land. If proper data is available, it is the most accurate method. The residual, allocation, and development methods are used when data for comparable parcels is not available.

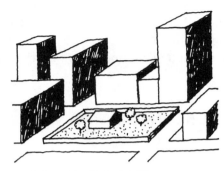

UNDERIMPROVEMENT

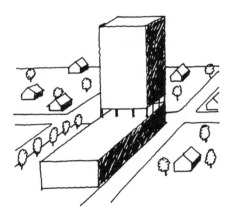

OVERIMPROVEMENT

Figure 9.7

OVERIMPROVEMENT AND UNDERIMPROVEMENT

The concept of overimprovement or underimprovement is related to highest and best use. The term underimprovement refers to a property that is not being used to its highest and best use. For example, an owner of land might erect a building on his property that produces substantially less income than could be obtained with a better, larger, or different building. Such an underimprovement will reduce the value of the property, because it is not being put to its "highest and best use."

Conversely, overimprovement means that the cost of the improvement exceeds potential revenue or income: more has been built on the site than is warranted. For example, someone may buy an old house and rehabilitate it. The cost of rehabilitation may be far greater than the market value of the house. This is an overimprovement.

In addition to determining the cost of land, other factors must be analyzed, as follows:

1. *Suitability.* Is the land suited for the intended purpose?

2. *Access.* Is the site sufficiently accessible?

3. *Circulation.* Can people, goods, and services comfortably circulate within the parcel?

4. *Variety.* Is it possible to accommodate a reasonable range of varied uses on the site?

5. *Cost.* Initial cost must be balanced against estimated operational and maintenance costs.

6. *Adaptability.* Successful development plans must possess flexibility to allow for modifications in the future, within the general form. Plans should permit future changes in use.

7. *Amenities.* What are the positive features of the site, such as views, landscaping, orientation, topography? Can these be utilized to advantage? Can they be augmented?

8. *Open Space.* How can the value of open space and wildlife habitats such as woodlands, prairies, wetlands, and waterways be maintained while considering development opportunities? Can open space preservation complement sustainable design techniques in the building architecture?

Through the process of analysis, an awareness of the special attributes of each site is revealed—its topography, drainage patterns, and plant life. Such elements constitute the intrinsic character of a site.

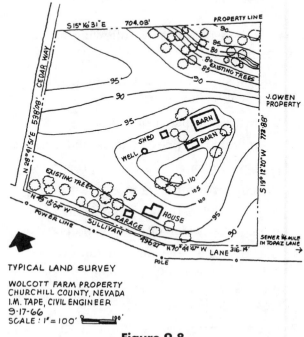

TYPICAL LAND SURVEY

WOLCOTT FARM PROPERTY
CHURCHILL COUNTY, NEVADA
I.M. TAPE, CIVIL ENGINEER
9-17-66
SCALE: 1" = 100'

Figure 9.8

SURVEYS

Surveys describe the location, form, and boundaries of land. They also describe all the special features of a site that are pertinent to site development and building design. Surveying for building construction is done at three levels of detail, commensurate with design needs.

These are:

1. *Preliminary survey*, which provides basic information to the architect for the preparation of building plans.

2. *Construction survey*, which describes the precise condition of the site and adjacent

structures, and establishes base lines, offsets, and bench marks.

3. *Possession survey*, made after the completion of construction to record the completed development, including site improvements and structures.

A land survey provides the following information:

1. Title of survey, property location, certification, and date

2. Scale and compass orientation

3. Tract boundary lines, courses, and distances

4. Names of owners of adjacent properties

5. Bench mark with reference elevation

6. Names and locations of all existing road rights-of-ways, on or near the property

7. Location of all existing structures on the site, including buildings, foundations, bridges, wells, cisterns, walls, fences, and rock outcroppings

8. Location, type, size, and flow of all existing storm and sanitary sewers on or contiguous to the tract; top and invert elevations of all manholes, inlet and invert elevations of other drainage structures

9. Location of roads, drives, curbs, gutters, steps, walks, and paved areas, indicating types of material or surfacing

10. Location, type, and size of all water and gas mains, meter boxes, hydrants, and other appurtenances

11. Location of utility poles, telephone lines, and power lines, with indication of nearest leads either on-site or off-site; pertinent information and ownership of all utilities

12. Location of all swamps, springs, streams, drainage ditches, lakes, and other bodies of water; elevation of maximum flood plain, if applicable

13. Outline of wooded areas, location of trees, identification of trees by type, and identification of trees with trunks over eight inches in diameter three feet above ground

14. Road elevations for all improved roads, on or adjacent to property; improved gutter elevations on property line side

15. Elevations through the site sufficient to develop a complete and thorough contour map or the topographic contour lines of the site, at an appropriate interval, depending on the steepness of the site

Land surveys are of two types: geodetic and plane. Geodetic surveys take into consideration the spherical shape of the earth. Thus they describe large land areas with great precision. Plane surveying assumes that the earth is a flat plane, and earth curvature is disregarded. Geodetic surveys are used for very large land areas, while plane surveying is sufficiently accurate for most site development work.

Among the various kinds of plane surveying are:

Land survey. This refers to the general measurement and description of land parcels or sites, where building development is contemplated.

Topographic survey. This refers to a map showing natural and manmade features and elevations, which are normally described by contour lines. For building projects the contours must be drawn very accurately.

Route survey. This is used by civil engineers when laying out a road or utility line.

Hydrographic survey. This describes and maps oceans, lakes, rivers, and other bodies of water for purposes of navigation, water supply, or water-related construction.

City survey. This is used to measure areas in and near cities, locate property lines and improvements, and determine the configuration and physical features of the land. Such surveys are essential to city planning.

Aerial survey. This is prepared through the use of aerial photography (photogrammetry), augmented with large scale land surveys to maintain accuracy.

Construction survey. This provides a system of markers to determine the precise location of a building on its site.

In all land surveying, distances between points are measured on a horizontal plane. Vertical distance, or elevation, is expressed with reference to distance above sea level or some other established point of reference. Such a point may be a U.S. Geological Survey monument, a bronze plate set in stone or concrete which shows the elevation above sea level.

Both horizontal and vertical distances are measured in feet and decimals.

SITE ANALYSIS

General Purpose

Site analysis is the process of investigating basic data that relates to a particular site, such as survey information, topographic data, geological information, zoning ordinances, existing character, microclimate, development patterns, social patterns, etc. The purpose of site analysis is to determine whether a parcel of land is suitable for a specific proposed use. It would be undesirable, for example, to situate a school adjacent to a major freeway. Similarly, a roadside cafe should not be located out of sight of the road, nor should a meat packing plant be

placed upwind of dwelling units. All of these are examples of inappropriate uses for a given site, or perhaps inappropriate sites for a given use. In theory, almost any site will support almost any use; however, the ideal situation is one that most fully satisfies the project criteria, while requiring the least modification or compromise.

Every site is as unique as an individual person, and even as identical twins have distinct personalities, so too, adjacent parcels of land possess distinguishable characteristics. Part of this uniqueness is reflected in a site's equilibrium. The flow of surface water creates a discrete drainage pattern, plant and animal life constitute an ecological system, and human use conforms to a workable social structure. Site factors such as these are interrelated, and at any given moment they are in balance, even if they are in the process of change. The recognition of a site's character reveals the practical limits imposed on a planner, as well as the potential damage that may be inflicted by development.

All development implies change, and occasionally this change produces undesirable effects. Excavation, for example, may alter drainage patterns, grading may cause erosion, and the construction of new facilities may destroy plants, pollute the air, or create traffic congestion. Environmental changes, therefore, are an inevitable result of the development process.

Relevant Data

The relevant site data that must be gathered and analyzed comprise those factors that determine the suitability of a site for its proposed use. Although no single set of factors applies to every situation, the following list includes data that is relevant in most circumstances.

Climate

Every site is affected by regional climate patterns, as well as the microclimate that applies to a small area. Climate is related to topography, slope orientation, vegetation, and the presence of water, and it is important because it bears directly on human comfort. Climatological data may be obtained from the National Weather Service, through talks with local inhabitants, and by personal observation of weathered structures and existing plant material. The following features may be analyzed:

1. Temperature averages and extremes
2. Precipitation averages and extremes
3. Snowfall averages and extremes
4. Wind intensity and directions
5. Humidity patterns
6. Solar angles
7. Days of sunlight
8. Frost data

Topography

Topography is the form of a site's surface features, and it is a factor that strongly influences land development. The gradient of roads, disposition of structures, and visual aspects of a site are all influenced by the character of the landform. Topographic data is available from the U.S. Geological Survey aerial photographs, or on-site surveys, and the features that may be analyzed are:

1. Elevations
2. Slope amount and direction
3. Unique landforms
4. Natural drainage patterns

Soils

Knowledge of the soil conditions on a site is important to determine the soil's capacity to support buildings and roads, as well as its ability to sustain plant material. Soils data is obtained from the U.S. Department of Agriculture Soil Conservation Service, test borings, visual inspection, and the experience of neighboring developers. The following features may be analyzed:

1. Soil types
2. Moisture content
3. Depth of organic topsoil
4. Depth to water table
5. Depth to bedrock
6. Drainage characteristics
7. Susceptibility to compaction
8. Soil fertility
9. Rock outcroppings

Hydrology

Hydrology refers to the occurrence, movement, and quality of water on a site. Surface water and drainage patterns affect vegetation, climate, and potential development, and this data is available from the U.S. Geological Survey, local hydrological studies, and on-site inspections. Hydrological considerations include:

1. The form of surface water (streams, lakes, etc.)
2. Drainage patterns
3. Runoff rates
4. Subsurface water characteristics
5. Aquifer (water-bearing) zones

Vegetation

Plant types and patterns represent a major site resource, and they contribute significantly to the unique character of an area. Native landscaping is closely related to climate, hydrology, and topography, and it often determines the form of development.

Data on vegetation is available from U.S. Geological Survey maps, aerial photos, and on-site observation. The factors that may be analyzed are:

1. Types and extent of vegetation
2. Density of vegetation
3. Heights of vegetation
4. Health of vegetation

Existing Land Use

As a site is developed, manmade features become more important than natural features. Structures, circulation systems, and activity patterns must be considered. Such data is obtained from land use maps, state highway maps, historical preservation societies, and personal inspections, and some of the factors that may be analyzed are:

1. Existing roads and paths
2. Existing utility lines
3. Existing air and rail facilities
4. Type and number of structures
5. Uses of open space
6. Human behavior patterns
7. Historical sites, structures, and trails

Sensory Qualities

The sensory qualities of a site are those intangible elements that affect people through the senses of sight, smell, touch, and hearing. The uniqueness of a site may be its view or its geometry, the smell of wildflowers or of the ocean, the feel of heat or of wind, or the sound of traffic, church bells, or singing birds. The perception of sensory qualities is as important to site analysis as any other relevant factor, and pertinent data of this sort is almost always obtained through first-hand on-site observation. The features to be analyzed may include:

1. Scenic vistas
2. Spatial illusions
3. Quality of light
4. Characteristic smells
5. Characteristic sounds (noises, echoes, etc.)
6. Sensation of natural forces
7. Perception of textures

Natural Hazards

There are several natural elements that are potentially hazardous to certain types of development, and others, such as earthquake faults, that may restrict almost all construction. Information on hazards is generally available from a variety of government agencies, local inhabitants, and sometimes (unfortunately) through personal experience. Analysis may include:

1. Earthquake fault zones
2. Hurricane zones
3. Tornado zones
4. Flood plains
5. Tidal inundation areas
6. Wet zones (peat bogs, quicksand, etc.)
7. Areas of poisonous plants
8. Areas of poisonous snakes or reptiles
9. Areas of annoying insects

The actual site analysis begins when all of the pertinent information is collected. At this point, a base map is prepared showing legal boundaries, contours, roads, buildings, utilities, and other natural or manmade key features. The base map is used as a background on which various overlays are produced, generally one for each area of concern. For example, a soils overlay may classify soils by type and depth, with locations and logs of known test borings. A visual survey overlay may consist of personal notes and observations regarding scenic views or unsightly features in need of modification or removal. When environmental concerns are explored, the resulting overlay may serve as a checklist for an environmental impact assessment.

A map on which all the overlaid information has been superimposed is known as a site analysis map, an example of which is shown in Figure 9.11. This map indicates the degree to which a site is suitable for a proposed function. At this point, the planner may discover that compromises may be necessary. For example, a site that appears optimum for a shopping center, based on population growth studies, topography, suitable soil, costs, etc., may be located too far from freeway access. For the shopping center and freeway access to be closer together, one may be forced to accept a lower quality site. Therefore, when a site is judged to be suitable for a proposed use, it is almost always a matter of striking a balance between what is ideal and what is reasonably possible.

NATURAL LANDFORMS

Landform refers to the shape of the earth's surface, which may include everything from mountain ranges to furrows in a field. Landform is important because it affects the aesthetic character of an area, as well as one's perception of space. Level land, for example, unifies the landscape, while hilly land tends to divide it. Landform types also have a direct impact on the development with which they are visually compatible. The natural shape of land, therefore, affects how it is perceived, modified, and used.

Landform may be classified by character, steepness, geology, etc., but where visual, functional, and perceptual qualities are concerned, the most significant factor is form. The landscape is a continuous composition of varying earth forms that blend into and rein-

force one another. Where a level stretch of desert ends, the concave slope of a mountain begins, but that precise point may be difficult to detect. Similarly, the merger of a slope and a valley may be nearly imperceptible. Following is a discussion of the most common landform configurations with some implications of their potential for site design.

Level Landforms

A level landform is any area that appears visually parallel to the horizon. Of course, there is no such thing as a perfectly level piece of land, because all ground has some amount of slope. Nevertheless, land perceived to be level is stable, static, and in equilibrium. Level land is comfortable because it requires little effort to stand, walk, or rest on a surface that is in balance with the earth's gravitational forces. For these same reasons, level areas are the most sought-after sites for buildings. In fact, when level sites are not available, they are often created by remodeling sloping terrain into flat pads.

Level landforms lack spatial definition; other than the horizon, no elements appear to enclose space. On the other hand, this openness permits extensive, uninterrupted views, which establishes a unifying force on the landscape. Level land induces a feeling of exposure; there is no protection against sun or wind, there is no defense against objectionable noises or views, and there is no privacy. In other words, there is no place to hide.

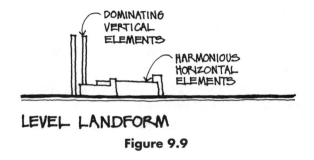

LEVEL LANDFORM
Figure 9.9

Development of level land is relatively unrestricted; structures may be built upward, outward, and in almost any direction. Horizontal forms appear harmonious when set on the level landscape, because they reflect the horizon and emphasize the earth's stability. Vertical elements, on the other hand, attract attention and tend to dominate the landform. Even the modest height of a farm silo on the Midwestern plain is clearly visible for miles.

Level ground offers little indication of the correct orientation for development. With no restrictions imposed by landform, all directions appear equally valid, and this has occasionally led to multidirectional developments that sprawl repetitiously across the landscape. A level landform provides a neutral, sometimes uninteresting setting that can be characterized as peaceful, calm, and quiet, although in reality it may be none of these. Nevertheless, level topography is flexible, practical, and highly desirable for the majority of human uses.

SITE DESIGN CHARACTERISTICS

We have stated that site design is the conscious rearrangement of the environment for human use. The environment comprises a number of components, or characteristics, including space, scale, mass, proportion, etc., all of which contribute to that elusive and subjective element known as aesthetics. The aim of all site design, therefore, is to produce a functional solution that is perceived as a visual whole, that is, aesthetically. And aesthetics is the consequence of a harmonious blend of design characteristics.

Space

Space is defined as the three-dimensional expanse that surrounds one, and it is perceived through all our senses. While architectural space is circumscribed by roof, walls, and

floor, outdoor space is defined by the variety of elements found in the open or urban landscape. This may include, for example, a group of university buildings around a quad, a narrow street lined with uniform structures, or an open park surrounded by trees. Some outdoor space is vast and limited only by sky, earth, and the distant horizon.

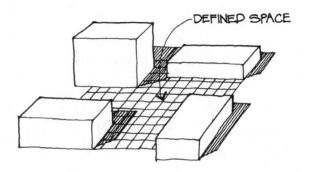

OUTDOOR SPACE DEFINED BY BUILDING PLACEMENT
Figure 9.10

Compared to architectural space, site space is generally larger in extent, more irregular, less geometric, and invariably perceived as being wider than it is high. People relate to exterior space differently from the way they relate to interior space. In a vast, open plain, some will feel threatened or overwhelmed, while others will experience a sense of freedom or a need for action. Large areas often encourage mass action, such as on a football field or a ski slope. Any tall object set on a large, unobstructed surface becomes an important element on which attention is focused, such as a solitary tree in a field or the Washington Monument.

Space is further defined by light, color, texture, and the scale of its elements, although perceptions may be modified through spatial illusions. It is difficult, for example, to accurately estimate outdoor distances, and actual gradients

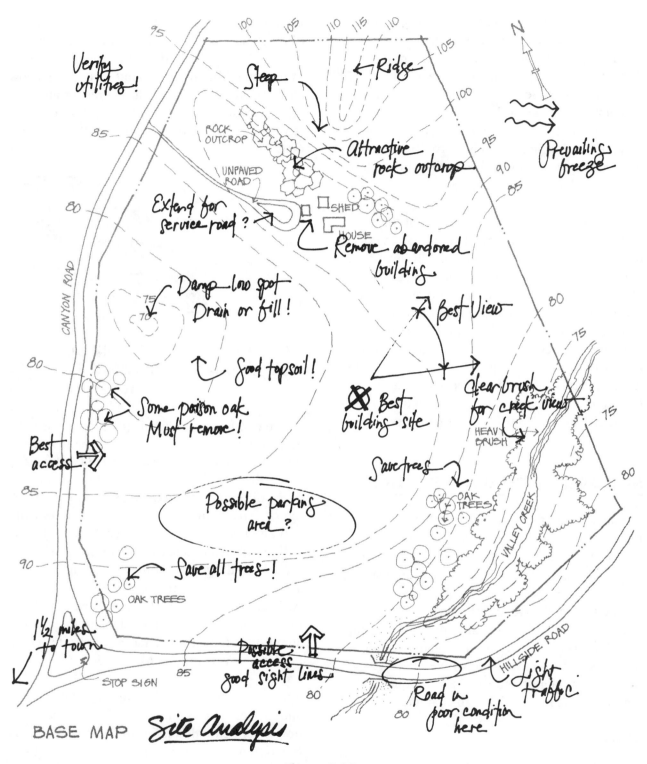

BASE MAP *Site Analysis*

Figure 9.11

may be considerably different from what they appear to be. And outdoor light is not constant, since the sun varies with the hour, the season, and the weather, all of which affect the form, color, and texture of the landscape.

OUTDOOR SPACE DEFINED BY ROWS OF TREES
Figure 9.12

Enclosure

People are aware when they are inside a building, regardless of how open it may be, but outdoor enclosure is perceived differently. Outdoor spaces can be enclosed by widely spaced trees, rolling foothills, or a change in ground texture. In other words, the definition of outdoor space may be a visual suggestion, rather than a visual obstruction. Even a low railing or a line of bollards defines outdoor space as effectively as a wall. In general, the amount of enclosure necessary to create a definable outdoor space is just enough so that one's attention is focused on the space, rather than beyond it.

Urban spaces are enclosed by the building masses of a city; they are the voids formed by the absence of solids. An urban square surrounded by tall buildings is easy to visualize, but the linear arrangement of houses is no less an enclosure for the corridor-like space it creates along the street. Unlike indoor spaces, outdoor volumes may be infinite in scope, limited perhaps only by the horizon. Site designers, therefore, are not nearly as restricted as build-

ing designers. Because outdoor space is loosely defined, the site designer has greater freedom, as well as responsibility, to create a clear, comprehensible volume.

Scale

Scale is a system of relative measurement based on anthropometric dimensions. For example, a stair riser is about seven inches high, because that is the height that people raise their feet comfortably when climbing steps. We say, therefore, that a seven-inch riser is in scale. The 20-inch risers of the Parthenon's stylobate, on the other hand, while in harmonious proportion to the structure, are clearly out of scale with human beings: people do not normally climb 20-inch high steps.

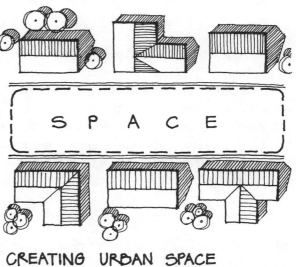

CREATING URBAN SPACE
Figure 9.13

Interior scale and exterior scale are quite different from each other. In general, outdoor spaces must be considerably larger, relative to interior spaces, in order to feel comfortable. A three-foot wide hallway in a house, for example, feels adequate, whereas a three-foot wide sidewalk will feel narrow. Similarly, a 10 by 12 foot bedroom is comfortable, while the same size patio will be undersized. This variation in perception between inside and outside scale is caused by differences in the fields of vision, as well as the physical behavior that is appropriate in each circumstance. One can run, shout, or throw a ball outside, while these same activities inside are considered inappropriate.

SCALE - PARTHENON STEPS
Figure 9.14

Outside activities can be visually distinguished up to about 450 feet, outdoor spaces appear intimate if they are between 40 to 80 feet in size, and people who stand three to ten feet away are considered to be in direct relationship. It is clear, therefore, that site planning requires an entirely different perception of scale than planning interior spaces.

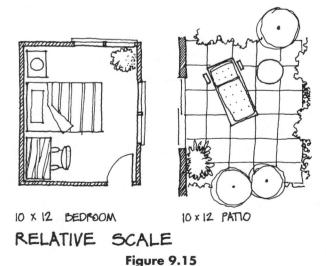

10 x 12 BEDROOM   10 x 12 PATIO

RELATIVE SCALE
Figure 9.15

Exterior scale is more than a matter of dimensions, however; it may also relate to speed, context, and custom. Walking speed, for example, which averages about 2-1/2 miles per hour, determines the size and scale of a city's elements. The willingness of people to walk only 10 to 15 minutes in performing routine tasks affects the arrangement of parking lots, shopping centers, commercial zones, and the size of neighborhoods. The relationship of scale to context means that neighboring spaces and buildings must be in scale with each other. A towering building in the midst of a community of single-family dwellings, for example, is out of context with the neighborhood, and consequently out of scale. All buildings in an area need not be the same mass or height, but when a structure changes one's perception of the local scale, the structure is likely to be disorienting.

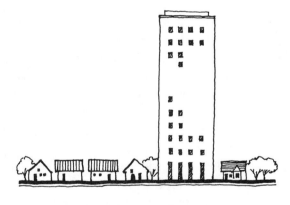

OUT OF CONTEXT / SCALE
Figure 9.16

Finally, scale is perceived in accordance with the customary way things have always been. If a coherent neighborhood has always consisted of 500 families who support a shopping center, recreational facilities, and an elementary school, then doubling the number of families would probably overwhelm the neighborhood and destroy the established scale. Similarly, a person who has spent his life on a farm will experience a dramatic disorientation in spatial scale if he were to move to a large metropolitan area.

Mass

The perception of mass is largely controlled by the way we see, as well as the prevailing light conditions. From a viewing distance equal to the building height, that is, a 45-degree angle from the eye to the roof line, one notices the details of the facade more than the entire building mass. From twice the viewing distance to the same roof line, that is, a 1 to 2 relationship, one can perceive the entire building mass together with its details. At a 1 to 3 relationship, the building mass is observed in relation to surrounding objects, and at 1 to 4, or a viewing distance of four times the building height, one sees the mass as an edge that frames a distant view.

Light conditions affect one's perception of mass: in bright sunlight, individual elements stand out, while on cloudy days, the mass is perceived in its entirety. Dark objects seen against a light background recede, such as a tree clump viewed against the sky. However, light objects seen against a dark background, such as a highway billboard set against dark hills, tend to advance visually. Depth perception is also affected by light conditions: distances are more difficult to discern on dull, grey days.

Aesthetics

Aesthetics refers to what is beautiful, and beauty, as we all know, can be quite subjective.

Most natural landscapes are beautiful, because the many factors of which they are composed have achieved an equilibrium. Beauty, therefore, must include a concept of order. A natural site may have existed for thousands of years,

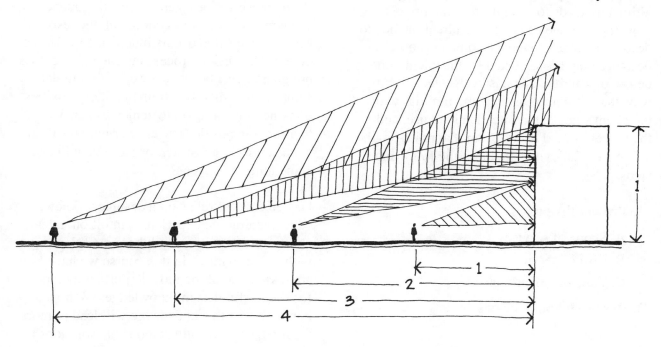

PERCEPTION OF MASS BASED ON VIEWING DISTANCE

Figure 9.17

but it only exists in relation to people through some positive development that establishes a permanent connection between people and site. Even a natural wilderness area has no relation to people unless there is access to the area, or at least vantage points from which the area can be observed. A structure introduced on a site will exist visually and spatially in relation to that site and the surrounding landscape. Building and site become one indivisible experience. Unity, therefore, is a goal of the design process and an essential element of beauty, because it confirms our idea of what is right, proper, and fit for human use.

SITE DESIGN PROCESS

The site design process is an exploration of possible solutions to a specific problem. This exploration involves a number of essential steps, generally performed in sequence, which ultimately leads to a solution of the project's objectives. In the usual case, a client intends to develop a piece of land for some purpose. The designer may be contacted by the client either before or after the site has been selected. Either way, the designer must become familiar with the client's goals, the intended land use, and the parcel of land itself. From that point on, the sequence of activities includes the following steps:

1. **Project Proposal**
    A. Scope of services
    B. Cost of services
    C. Time of performance

2. **Research and Analysis**
    A. Site inventory
    B. Data analysis
    C. Client objectives
    D. Program preparation

3. **Design Phase**
    A. Circulation pattern
    B. Functional pattern
    C. Form composition
    D. Diagrammatic plan
    E. Schematic plan
    F. Preliminary plan
    G. Master plan (design development)

4. **Construction Phase**
    A. Technical plan
    B. Grading plan
    C. Landscaping plan
    D. Construction details
    E. Contract documents

5. **Post Construction**
    A. Evaluation
    B. Maintenance

While these various steps occur in sequence, some may overlap or occur simultaneously. Moreover, no step occurs independently of the others. The design process outlined above does not guarantee a beautiful or even functional solution; it is merely a framework of activities that one must perform to achieve an answer to a specific puzzle. The answer may result in a masterpiece, a disaster, or more than likely, something in between.

Design success relies on a designer's knowledge, inspiration, experience, intuition, talent, ability, and creativity, and these qualities vary with the individual. In this course we have addressed one of the most important factors for successful design: knowledge. We hope, however, that this knowledge will lead to more inspired, creative, and responsible solutions to site problems.

SUMMARY

Site analysis must be undertaken with regard for the site's intended use. But the range of possible uses must be based on the site's intrinsic potential. While land should be used according to its suitability, its value is a function of its economic usefulness.

To be usable, the cost of a site must be commensurate with its potential uses. Determination of cost requires an appraisal of its value in relation to potential use, and an estimate of its operational costs.

Surveys describe location, form, and boundaries of the land. Topography describes the land's surface features. Slopes must be suitable for circulation, utilities, and special uses. Slopes should not be altered so as to cause water drainage problems or erosion. Other physical problems may derive from surface and subsurface soil, rock, and water.

Sites should be chosen, and their uses determined, according to the ease with which they can be developed, so that development costs will be commensurate with expected benefits. The role of landscaping is to achieve an artistic relationship between earth, rock, water, plants, and manmade details. It may also modulate climatic extremes, to assure comfort for the users.

LESSON 9 QUIZ

1. The principal purpose of site analysis is to determine if a site

   A. requires modification.

   B. is suitable for a proposed use.

   C. is capable of being developed.

   D. has a unique character.

2. Outdoor space is perceived differently from indoor space, EXCEPT in the matter of

   A. scale.

   B. enclosure.

   C. proportion.

   D. mass.

3. Development of a site always results in

   A. environmental modification.

   B. altered drainage patterns.

   C. increased pollution.

   D. damage to the ecological balance.

4. Which of the following site planning situations might be considered out of scale?

   A. A tall monument placed in an open area

   B. A small residential structure situated on top of a high summit

   C. An elevated freeway running through an area of small stores

   D. A high rise residential tower situated among commercial structures of equal height and mass

5. Which of the following statements regarding catchment areas are true? Check all that apply.

   A. Catchment areas are actually tributary areas.

   B. Catchment areas may be defined by specific functions.

   C. Catchment areas are generally fixed in size for an indefinite period of time.

   D. School districts may constitute catchment areas.

6. The term "highest and best use" is directly related to

   A. land value.

   B. land character.

   C. standard of living.

   D. population density.

7. Fee simple ownership of land is

   A. ownership of land for 99 years.

   B. ownership of land for a simple fee.

   C. absolute ownership of land without condition.

   D. absolute ownership of land by a governmental authority.

Lesson Five

1. **A** The system of architectural measurement is related not only to the natural world in general, but more specifically, to the human body. See page 72.

2. **A** Caryatids (B) are supporting members in the shape of human figures, dentils (C) are ornamental bands of small blocks resembling teeth, and pedestals (D) are vertical supports derived from the Latin term for "foot."

3. **Rhythm**   See page 78.

4. **A, B, and D** All visible objects have size, shape, scale, and texture, but not all have symmetry.

5. **D** See page 79.

6. **C** A designer may strive for a solution that is traditional, stylized, or indigenous, but function and beauty are generally considered to be more significant design goals.

7. **C** The other choices are either irregular or non-repetitive. See page 78.

8. **D** See page 78.

9. **D** All the choices are discussed on page 80.

10. **B** See page 77.

Lesson Six

1. **A, B, and D** Medieval towns were sometimes rectilinear, but more often circular or radiocentric. The other choices are all characteristics of medieval towns. See page 89.

2. **A** See page 91.

3. **C** Although dwelling units in cluster developments are more densely sited than in conventional developments, the overall densities in these two types are similar. See page 102.

4. **B** The term *megalopolis* was coined to describe an extensive linear arrangement of individual cities, such as the urbanized corridor between Philadelphia and Washington, D.C.

5. **C** Zoning ordinances regulate the use of property, including the type and density of improvements permitted. All such regulations aim for compatible development, which tends to protect and stabilize property values.

6. **A** See page 95.

7. **C** Choices A, B, and D may contain a grain of truth, but the preferred answer is C. See page 94.

8. **D** See page 101.

9. **B** Not only is 30 persons per acre typical in many European new towns, but that density may be found in some early American towns, as well. See page 101.

10. **A** Review Perry's principles on pages 98–99.

Lesson Seven

1. **B** See page 117.

2. **C and D** The plaza would be both a landmark and a node, since it would be a prominent point of reference, as well as a center of activity.

3. **C** See discussion on pages 109–110.

4. B   Sociopetal space promotes contact between people, such as chairs facing one another, while sociofugal space discourages human contact, such as chairs placed back to back.

5. D   See page 112.

6. B   One tends to walk faster through dull surroundings as a way of seeking stimulation.

7. B   See page 118.

8. C   See pages 110–111.

9. C   All of the choices may cause urban pathologies, except high density, which does not always mean crowding and, therefore, is not necessarily bad.

10. D   This is the definition of zero population growth.

Lesson Eight

1. C   The top of a hill is windy, and the bottom of a hill—whether or not between two hills—may have little air circulation and experience fog and cold air. Halfway down a slope, preferably one that is south-facing, is usually the best location.

2. A   See pages 126–127.

3. A   Before modern heating, structures were often oriented in a southerly direction to take advantage of the winter sun.

4. A   Ecology deals with the relationships between organisms and their environment, whether natural (a forest) or manmade (a city).

5. A, B, C, and E   All the choices except D affect human comfort. Choice D would be correct if it were latitude, rather than longitude.

6. D   Choice D is the definition of decibel. See page 135.

7. B   See page 130.

8. B   Macro means large, and micro means small, both terms coming from Greek roots.

9. D   See page 132.

10. C   See page 126.

Lesson Nine

1. B   See page 159.

2. C   Outdoor space is perceived differently from indoor space in scale, enclosure, and mass. Proportion, however, involves harmony between component elements and is perceived similarly indoors and outdoors.

3. A   The specific environmental changes in choices B, C, and D may or may not occur in any given site development. However, all site development results in some environmental modification.

4. C   An elevated freeway in an area of small stores is out of context with the neighborhood and consequently out of scale.

5. A, B, and D   C is the only statement that is incorrect. Catchments may vary in size whenever conditions affecting the catchment change. See page 153.

6. A   See page 155.

7. C   See page 152.

Part III

Codes and Regulations

LAND AND BUILDING REGULATION

INTRODUCTION

Ownership is the legal possession of property, such as land or buildings. Ownership by an individual, group, or other entity may be brief, long-lasting, or even permanent, as in the case of a government building or public park.

The ownership of property carries with it the right to use the property as one sees fit, subject to certain restrictions imposed by society. The uses to which property may be put are many and varied: housing, commerce, agriculture, manufacturing, education, etc.

Originally, the uses to which land and the buildings on the land were put were largely determined by nature. Agriculture developed in fertile lands, where permanent settlements were established; cattle raising, on the other hand, developed in marginal lands, where migratory settlement was the practice. Commercial towns developed at points of access to a hinterland region, at a major route crossing, or at a confluence of land and water transportation. Providing for defense against enemies was as much a determinant of land use as were the forces of nature. Such determinants were recognized through government, which gave or denied the rights of usage of property to its citizens. In time such rights were codified into laws. Thus, the laws and regulations governing property rights were both permissive and prohibitive. An occupant, temporary or permanent, could do certain things on his property, but was prohibited from doing others. One might be permitted to build a house within a town, but not to tan leather there; one might be permitted to tan leather outside of a town, but not to build a house there. Property rights and constraints have always gone hand in hand, and have always been conceived with regard to what is deemed the larger social interest.

The purpose of property rights and prohibitions is to serve the interest of society as a whole.

Uses of land and property that are appropriate and productive are permitted, but it is equally in society's interest to prohibit those uses that would be inimical. The two together, rights and prohibitions, are broadly called regulation.

Regulation of property usage has several forms. There is, first, the regulation of *ownership*, both of land and buildings. A corollary aspect of the rights of ownership involves transfer, by sale or rental. There is, second, regulation of *land* itself. Land use regulation is codified in several forms, varying from federal codes to privately conveyed covenants to publicly administered zoning laws. There is, third, regulation of the building of *structures*, including materials, fire safety, electrical and mechanical equipment, plumbing, etc. All of these, together, are quite complex. But their purpose is better understood when they are seen in the context of their origins and evolution, as well as their larger purpose.

The implications for architectural design are considerable. Regulations form a large part of the context within which land is planned and buildings designed. We will begin with the regulation of ownership and transfer, continue with the regulation of land, and conclude with a discussion of the regulation of the design of structures.

TYPES OF OWNERS

Land or buildings may be owned or leased by individuals (singly or in groups), corporations, churches, government entities, or such legal entities as trusts and estates.

A widespread form of ownership, often used by husband and wife, but not restricted to people related by marriage or blood, is *joint tenancy*. Two or more people may enter into this type

of ownership. Its distinguishing feature is that each of the joint tenants holds an undivided interest; that is, the land is not physically separated into individual portions, but rather each joint tenant has a share in the ownership of the whole. The interest of each joint tenant automatically passes to the survivor(s) upon his or her death. The advantage of this type of ownership to a husband and wife is that if one dies, the survivor becomes the sole owner of the deceased's share. If the property is sold, then both (or all) owners must sign the necessary legal papers. However, one owner may sell his or her undivided interest independently, in which case the purchaser assumes the place of the seller in the joint tenancy.

If the owner is a *partnership*, the situation is similar. The land is owned by the partnership as a group. Upon the death of one of the partners, however, the partnership may be dissolved and the assets distributed among the surviving partners and the estate of the deceased partner. The distribution is made according to the original agreement among the partners.

A *corporation* operates differently. A corporation is a legal entity with rights and liabilities independent of those of its shareholders. Thus, if a shareholder dies, his share of ownership of the corporation passes to his heirs, and the corporation itself continues unchanged. A corporation is treated by the law as if it were an individual; it may own or lease property, or enter into any arrangement which is available to an individual.

Another type of owner is a *trustee*, who holds property in his own name for the benefit of another person or group for whom he acts. Typically, this occurs when property ownership passes to someone who is unable to act in his own interest, such as a minor child or a person who is incompetent. The trustee is charged by law to act on behalf of this person or group and protect his or her interests. He may buy or sell property that he holds in trust, acting in good faith and in the best interest of the person or group for whom he is responsible.

All government entities may own property. These range from large areas, such as public lands, to small properties, such as a small post office.

Examples of the types of property owned by various governmental agencies include: fire and police stations, city halls, courthouses, legislative buildings, storage yards for state-owned vehicles, etc. The federal government owns millions of acres of public land, much of which was acquired in the course of westward expansion, and which it continues to own. Much of this land is administered by the U.S. Bureau of Land Management, and its uses are strictly controlled by that agency. In urban areas, the public may typically own a third or more of the land, in the form of public streets, as well as the sites of public buildings.

TYPES OF OWNERSHIP

The most common form of ownership of land is called *fee simple* or *fee absolute*. The owner has absolute title or ownership, which he can transfer by sale or bequest. Other, more restricted forms of ownership include the condominium, the cooperative, the leasehold, and sale-and-leaseback.

The *condominium* is an old, but recently revived form of ownership in which a buyer obtains fee simple ownership of a portion of a structure. Typically, this may be a residential apartment, but it may also be space in an industrial or office building.

Usually, one also owns a part of the shared service areas (hallways and garages), land and site improvements. Ownership of the land and public service areas, however, is an "undivided interest," or tenancy in common. The owner of a condominium has a marketable title to his property, which he may sell to another person, mortgage, lease, or bequeath to an heir. In some cases, the seller must give first "right of refusal" to the other owners through a tenants' or owners' council. This arrangement is intended to protect the other owners from an undesirable buyer. If the other owners decline to buy the condominium, then the owner is free to sell it on the open market. Each owner of a condominium pays his own property taxes and also a periodic fee for the maintenance of the service areas owned jointly. This fee may be nominal, but if the condominium has extensive grounds, a pool, clubhouse, tennis courts and the like, such fees may be quite substantial.

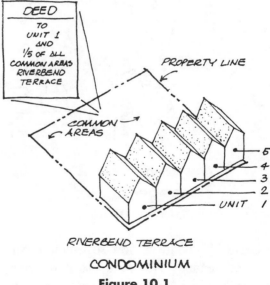

RIVERBEND TERRACE
CONDOMINIUM
Figure 10.1

A *cooperative* differs significantly from a condominium in that the owner of a cooperative does not legally own a specific piece of physical property. He owns, instead, a share of stock in a corporation that, in turn, owns the land and the structure. The owner of the share of stock is permitted to occupy some stated portion of the structure built upon the property. But the entire structure is still owned by the corporation. He can bequeath his share in the corporation to his heirs, but usually he must first obtain the approval of his fellow stockholders before he may sell his share.

In practice, therefore, a cooperative is less marketable than a condominium, because the "owner" cannot sell property directly. Hence, the condominium form of ownership has become much more common. A partial disadvantage of both, however, is that decisions relating to assessments for operating costs or repairs are not made by the individual, but by an owners' association.

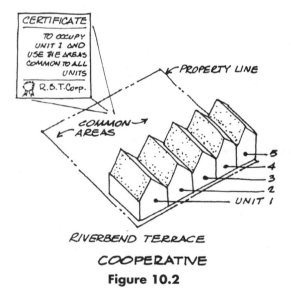

RIVERBEND TERRACE

COOPERATIVE

Figure 10.2

A *leasehold* is an even more restricted form of real estate tenancy. Here, the lessee, the person to whom the lease is granted, has the right to use a piece of property under certain conditions that are described in the lease. Lease rights do not include the right to sell the property, although it is possible, if not prohibited by the terms of the lease, to sell the right of use to another. This is termed a "sublease." A lease-

hold is usually paid for in cash, called rent. It may also be paid for in the form of a share of crops raised on or minerals extracted from the land. A leasehold, unlike the forms of ownership previously discussed, exists for a specific period of time. That time may be the life of the landlord (lessor) or tenant (lessee), or it may be at the pleasure of the parties, which means that either party can terminate the lease upon appropriate notice to the other. Usually, however, a lease is for a definite period of time, either with or without an option to renew. In some cases, the lease period is as long as 99 years. It is not unusual for the holder of a long-term lease to erect buildings on the land, even though the ownership of any structure erected on leased property reverts to the lessor upon expiration of the lease.

Sale-and-leaseback is a special form of leasehold, in which the owner of a piece of commercial or industrial property recovers the capital invested in the property, but at the same time retains the use of the property. The owner sells the property to a second party and enters into a leasehold agreement with that party, so that he may use the property for the specified life of the lease. The advantages to the seller are that he regains the use of his capital, and his lease payments (rent) become a tax-deductible expense. The buyer, in turn, has made an investment, from which he will derive a profit through rent receipts. If the property includes structures, the buyer also has a tax advantage in that he may depreciate the structures. When the lease period is over, the buyer may lease to another tenant, or occupy and use the property himself. Sale-and-leaseback agreements usually run for a number of years and may also have options for renewal and/or clauses to adjust the rent as some given index, such as the Consumer Price Index, fluctuates. Sale-and-leaseback arrangements are often made between a large industrial or service corporation and a large investment company. The corporation constructs the building to suit its needs, at the level of quality it desires, and under its complete control. The buyer is usually a large investor, such as an insurance company or a pension fund.

METHODS OF TRANSFERRING TITLE TO PROPERTY

When property is sold, the seller of the property gives the buyer a *deed*, which is a document conveying property from one owner to another. While the exact details vary from state to state, in general a deed must describe the property being transferred, it must be signed by the *grantor* (seller), and it must be delivered to the *grantee* (buyer). Even after it has been delivered, however, it is not legally recognized until it has been recorded in the office of the recorder in the city or county in which the property is located.

There are two methods generally used to finance the purchase of property: the *mortgage* and the *deed of trust*. The method used is determined by local practices and legal restrictions. Some areas, especially the eastern United States, utilize mortgages; others, especially in the West, use the deed of trust.

A mortgage is a contract by which a buyer of property (mortgagor) borrows money from a bank or other lender (mortgagee) with which to purchase the property, and pledges the property as security for the loan. The lender transfers the money to the seller, who then gives the buyer a deed to the property. The lender does not usually loan the full purchase price of the property, but only up to around 80 or 90 percent of it; the remaining 10 to 20 percent of the purchase price (the down payment) is paid by the buyer to the seller.

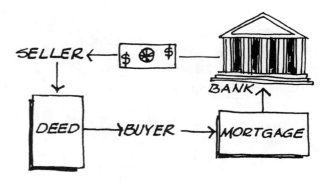

MORTGAGE
Figure 10.3

The mortgagor pays the principal and interest to the mortgagee over an extended period of time, generally 10 to 40 years. If the mortgagor fails to make a payment (defaults), the mortgagee has the right to take possession of the property (foreclose) and sell it to recover its investment. Any money from the sale in excess of the mortgagee's investment and costs is paid to the mortgagor. Foreclosure does not occur very often, except during a recession or when a development project is economically unsound.

In most cases, the borrower (mortgagor) continues to make payments to the lender (mortgagee) until the property is sold or the loan is paid off. When the loan is paid off, the lender cancels the mortgage, and the borrower then has clear title to the property: he owns it free of any debt.

The trust deed is similar to the mortgage, but differs in some respects. As in a mortgage, the buyer borrows money from a lender, who transfers it to the seller who, in turn, gives a deed to the buyer. The buyer, instead of giving a mortgage to the lender, transfers title to a fourth party, called the trustee, by means of the trust deed. The buyer makes principal and interest payments to the lender, and when the loan is completely repaid, the trustee transfers title back to the buyer.

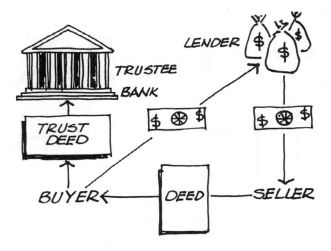

TRUST DEED
Figure 10.4

However, should the buyer default, foreclosure can be accomplished by trustee's sale under the power-of-sale clause, without any necessary court proceedings. The relative simplicity of foreclosure has made the trust deed popular with lenders in those states where it is permitted by law, generally in the West and South.

Property may have more than one debt against it. In addition to a first deed of trust or mortgage, it may carry a second trust deed or mortgage, which is subordinate to the first. The general rule is that "first in time is first in right." A second mortgage is generally at a higher interest rate, due to the greater difficulty the second lender will have in obtaining repayment, should the borrower default on one or both debts. A "default in prior mortgage" clause is commonly used in second mortgages, which states that if the mortgagor defaults in payment on a prior mortgage, the second mortgagee may pay the amount, add it to his loan, and immediately institute foreclosure. However, since the first mortgage is normally larger than the second, payment of such a sum may prove difficult for the holder of a second mortgage.

PROPERTY DESCRIPTIONS

The deed that an owner receives contains, among other things, a legal description of the property conveyed. A legal description may take any of several forms, including metes and bounds, subdivisions of public land, and lot and block. Rural land is often described by one of the first two methods, while urban land is usually described by lot and block. A statement of the calculated acreage is also generally included.

A description by metes and bounds is in the form of a narrative. The property is described by beginning at a specific point on the property boundary and then describing the length and direction of the boundaries of the property, until the entire property is encompassed.

A government survey authorized by Congress and begun in Ohio in 1785 is the basis for much of the legal description of areas outside the thirteen original states. This survey established a grid of north-south lines (called meridians) and east-west lines (called parallels). The lines are 24 miles apart in both directions. The grid thus delineated contains 24-mile-square areas sometimes called *checks*, which in turn are divided into 16 townships, each township being six miles square.

Further subdivisions are as follows: townships are divided into 36 square *sections*, each containing one square mile; sections may be divided into quarters and quarter-quarters, or sixteenths. Certain of the parallels are designated as *base lines*, and certain meridians are called *principal meridians*. Townships are numbered, and designated as north or south of the base line, and east or west of the principal meridian. Intermediate lines parallel to the meridians are *range lines*, and intermediate parallels are called *township lines*.

Land within a city is usually described as a specific numbered lot in a particular subdivision, for which there exists an official map of record.

DEED TERMS AND RESTRICTIONS

Covenants came into use in large scale residential land development prior to the advent of zoning. Their purpose was to maintain aesthetic harmony between buildings and prevent inimical land uses or structures, thus maintaining and even increasing the value of the development. Unfortunately, they sometimes also contained discriminatory covenants, under which persons of a specified race, religion, or ethnic identity were excluded. Such provisions have been determined to be illegal according to the Constitution and cannot be enforced. Covenants can be more effective than zoning in achieving and maintaining aesthetic harmony and overall quality. Legally, they are more difficult to alter than zoning.

Many deeds contain *restrictive covenants*. Covenants are normally used to limit the height, size, or appearance of a building. Restrictive covenants may require that a building have a certain minimum cost and floor area, and may specify the style, type of construction, and other such restrictions. Design approval by an architectural review board may also be required.

Covenants must be legal and enforceable. For example, if a property is subdivided and the deeds from the common grantor specify that all buildings must be located 25 feet back from the street, and if the restriction is commensurate with the quality and character of the land, then the restriction is enforceable. Anyone wishing to enforce the setback restriction could obtain a court injunction against any person violating the covenant.

Still another restriction on a property owner's right to utilize his land as he wishes is the *easement*. An easement is an acquired right of use, interest, or privilege by one party on the property of another, without the ownership of the portion of the property, and usually without compensation. There may be compensation paid for an easement, if it is newly established. Easements may also be temporary.

A common example of an easement is the right of a public utility or governmental entity to use private land to gain access for the placement and maintenance of utility services, such as sewers, electricity, water, gas, telephone, etc. Easements exist for other reasons, as well, such as to gain access through or across a parcel of land when there is no alternative method.

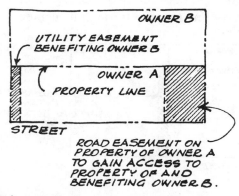

EASEMENT FOR INGRESS

Figure 10.5

A *party wall agreement* is another common type of easement. Such an easement is used in row housing, where a common or "party" wall is shared by two adjacent owners. A party wall straddles the property line, half on each side. Obviously, one owner owns the half of the wall on his side, and the other owns the half on his. However, each has an easement of support in the *other* half of the wall. If one owner wishes to build before the other, a party wall agreement is entered into under which the first owner builds and uses the wall. When the second owner builds, he makes use of the party wall and pays the first owner half of the cost of construction.

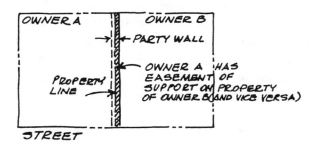

EASEMENT OF SUPPORT
Figure 10.6

Another common type of easement involves a driveway shared by two adjoining properties. Two private owners share in the joint use of a strip of land between two houses, which has a property line running through its center.

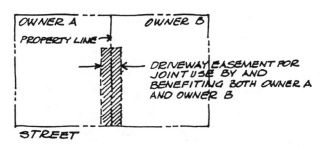

JOINT USE EASEMENT
Figure 10.7

Easements may be created by condemnation when, for example, land is taken by condemnation for a street, highway, or railroad right-of-way, or for a telephone or electric power line. The general practice is that the taker acquires only an easement, although some states require complete ownership of the land acquired.

An easement that allows one person to traverse the land of another in order to reach his own property creates a private right-of-way. A public right-of-way may come into existence simply by the long-established use of a pathway or roadway over private land whose owner fails to deter such use. If the practice continues for a long period of time without being contested by the owner, a public right-of-way is created.

AIR AND SUBSURFACE RIGHTS

As pressures to intensify land use have increased, the practice of utilizing the development rights above it and below it have also increased. Early common law held that "To whomsoever the soil belongs, he owns the sky and the depths." *Subsurface rights*, such as oil and mineral rights, are commonly leased or sold. This may have little effect on the usefulness of surface land if the terms of the conveyance (deed or lease) protect the surface use from interference. However, the ownership of mineral rights by another party may pose problems if that party has the right to enter the land at will. Subsurface rights may also involve pipe and cable lines, above or below ground.

Similarly, *air rights* can be sold or leased. Madison Square Garden and Grand Central Station, both in New York City, offer examples of such an arrangement. The leasing or sale of air rights is complicated and expensive and therefore feasible only in areas of extremely high land value.

OTHER RIGHTS AND RESTRICTIONS

There are several additional forms of rights and restrictions involving land use that have appeared in recent years. Among these are solar rights, historic facade easements, and developmental rights.

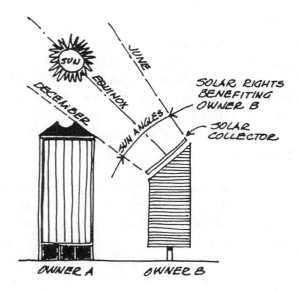

SOLAR RIGHTS
Figure 10.8

Solar rights refer to the right of a site or building to have access to solar radiation. Obviously, a tall neighboring building can block solar radiation from a site, if the neighboring building is located east, south, or west of the site. The problem is complicated by the fact that the solar radiation is needed in the winter months, when the sun is at a low angle. An effective solar access arrangement would require buildings to be spaced far apart, which is not economical in urban or even suburban locations. Or it might require, for rooftop solar collectors, that all buildings be the same height. Attempts to formulate protective legislation have not been too successful, since they require highly restrictive site usage and building design arrangements. Sustainable design planning encourages the architect to evaluate passive and active solar gains for all buildings. It makes sense that the sustainable approach would preserve solar rights for all nearby structures.

Such arrangements are more feasible in hot, dry climates where buildings are no more than two stories high.

A *historic facade easement* may be established by a municipality to protect a historically valuable architectural facade in an area where redevelopment is occurring, and where the existence of the facade is threatened. The municipality may declare the facade to be of historic value, and, consequently, be empowered to withhold a permit for its demolition or alteration. The municipality does not compensate the owner to preserve the facade. The owner may demolish the structure behind the facade, and build a new building in its place, while preserving or restoring the facade. The owner may, in some cases, benefit from special federal tax advantages.

EMINENT DOMAIN

An owner may sometimes be required to relinquish his property to a government entity if the property is needed for a public project, such as a highway or school. In such instances, the government may exercise its powers of *eminent domain*. The Fifth Amendment of the Constitution requires that the owner receive just compensation when property is appropriated in this way. Exercise of the power of eminent domain involves a condemnation proceeding, a legal process initiated by the public authority wishing to take the property in question. The "just compensation" to which the owner is entitled is the fair market value of the land. This value is determined by a jury, normally advised by an independent assessor. Public utilities also possess and exercise a limited power of eminent domain in the form of an easement for access, so that they may construct power lines and other distribution systems.

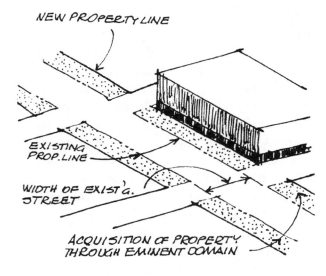

CONDEMNATION THROUGH
EMINENT DOMAIN

Figure 10.9

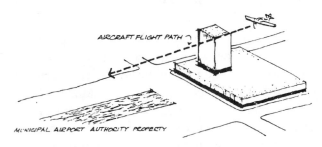

CONDEMNATION BECAUSE OF
AN OVERRIDING PUBLIC NEED

Figure 10.10

In practice, governmental entities are reluctant to exercise the power of eminent domain unless it is absolutely necessary, since the legal proceedings are complex, and the government is anxious to avoid the attendant publicity. Many projects, otherwise deemed necessary, have been abandoned for this reason.

DEVELOPMENT IMPACT FINANCING

In many municipalities, particularly those that have experienced rapid growth, the cost of providing and financing public services has outstripped their ability to pay for them. This situation has become particularly acute in recent years, as the federal government has curtailed many programs which provide financial support to cities and suburbs, such as grants for schools, utilities, open space acquisition, waste treatment, etc.

The response has taken several directions. Most severe have been "no growth" movements, in which a community attempts to prevent new development entirely. "Slow growth" is similar. The legality of such attempts is questionable, as is their advisability. Limiting the growth of the housing market serves to elevate real estate prices where housing is needed, preventing people who need adequate housing near their work from obtaining it, and to divert investment into building forms which may not be as critical as housing. Sustainable design planning encourages development called smart or sustainable growth. The principles of this approach are found in several areas including USGBC (U.S. Green Building Council, *usgbc.org*) and the Ahwahnee Principles (Local Government Commission's Center for Livable Communities, *http://lgc.org/clc/*). In general these sustainable developments encourage attention to mass transit, urban infill, higher density design, and a sensitivity to environmental issues.

In response to this, some municipalities have adopted a system whereby development rights are negotiated. The "exactions" from a developer typically include payments for the cost of schools, roads, utilities, etc. They may include the donation of open spaces, and possibly provide for a certain amount of "moderate" income housing in a development.

In fact, these "exactions" simply pass added costs on to the new homeowners of a development, further restricting the market being served. The traditional American method of community building and financing remains preferable: long term financing of shared facilities, paid for by all who benefit, that is, the whole community.

DEVELOPMENT RIGHTS TRANSFER

The community's interest in preserving historic buildings or sites in developing areas has led to the creation of still another type of public control of development. Let's say that a private owner of a historic building wishes to demolish it in order to free the site for a profit-making new structure. The community, on the other hand, may feel it has a right to assure that the historic structure or site is preserved as an asset to the community.

In response, the system of *development rights transfer* has been devised. The owner of a historic property may "sell" the development rights to his property to the owner of another nearby property, allowing that owner to develop his property at a higher intensity. Although considerable public examination is required, including public hearings, this method can serve to preserve historic property. It has limited applicability, however.

An alternative is to grant the owner of such a historically valuable property tax reduction or exemption, depending on the income-producing benefit of the property. Another alternative is for the public to acquire and maintain the property. Obviously, a community's limited financial resources are the chief obstacle to such a course.

In fact, tax exemption is already granted to schools, churches and other tax-exempt institutions, such as museums.

SUMMARY

Understanding of the concepts of land and building regulation provides the groundwork for communities to develop and for architects to begin to shape.

From the types of property ownership to land descriptions and limitations, all legal documentation and restrictions established for a piece of property begin to affect the direction the architect is going to take when laying out his or her solution for its development.

LESSON 10 QUIZ

1. Which form of real estate ownership exists for a limited period of time?

    A. Leasehold

    B. Fee simple

    C. Fee absolute

    D. Cooperative

2. Select the INCORRECT statement regarding mortgages.

    A. The security for a mortgage loan is real property.

    B. Mortgages are always provided by lending institutions.

    C. Second mortgages generally carry greater risk than first mortgages.

    D. When a mortgage loan is repaid, the mortgage is cancelled.

3. An owner wishes to construct a building that will provide substantial tax benefits while avoiding a long-term capital investment. Under these circumstances, the owner would probably choose to

    A. maximize the mortgage.

    B. arrange a sale-and-leaseback agreement.

    C. arrange a leasehold ownership.

    D. sell the trust deed to another party.

4. All of the following may require condemnation proceedings, EXCEPT the acquisition of a(n)

    A. access easement over one property to reach another.

    B. strip of land for road widening.

    C. permanent site for an elementary school.

    D. right-of-way for a rapid transit line.

11

ZONING ORDINANCES AND BUILDING CODES

INTRODUCTION

Zoning ordinances, building codes, and all other statutory restrictions that apply to a site or a structure must be identified and understood in the earliest design stages of a project. These restrictions may have significant effects on a project's feasibility, and at times they may be major determinants of form. Legal constraints on site use can also affect the program of a project. A particular deed restriction, for example, might have a critical and wholly unanticipated effect on how a project is permitted to function.

ZONING

Human societies have always regulated the use of land in order to serve the interests of society as a whole. The various European colonial powers, which settled what was to become the United States, all exercised various forms of land use control and, in some cases, regulated building construction. The Spanish "Law of the Indies" was the most elaborate colonial system of regulation, instituted shortly after Columbus's discovery and continuing in effect through the Spanish settlement of California.

The predominant system of American land use and building regulation is zoning. It was the product of the late 19th and early 20th century growth of American cities, in which the stability of development, particularly long-term investment, required protection.

The principal purpose of zoning is the protection of property rights. The first modern system of zoning was introduced in the United States in 1916 in New York City, where hitherto unregulated construction of tall buildings had created a perceived threat to property values. The 40-story Equitable Building cut off light and air from neighboring properties and thus threatened to undermine their value. This focused attention on the problem of overcrowding and overdevelopment. Zoning ordinances were adopted under the rationale of protecting the public's right of access to adequate light and air. In fact it was a building's access to light and air that was being protected.

The concept of zoning was legally validated in a landmark Supreme Court case, *Euclid v. Ambler*, in 1925. Euclid was a suburb of Cleveland that adopted zoning ordinances of a kind which have since become typical. Here again the underlying rationale was the protection of public health, welfare, and safety. Land use

districts, lot sizes and setbacks, and billboard restrictions were prescribed. In the 1920s such zoning ordinances were adopted by numerous municipalities throughout the country. The better residential suburbs, privately developed, had been protected through their use of covenants, which were used mostly for residential developments of fairly large scale.

Zoning was used for all types of land development: commercial, industrial, residential, institutional, etc. In comparison with covenants, zoning was less stringent in its requirements for residential development. Lots were often narrow, and side yards, and the separation between buildings, minimal.

Once established, zoning regulations became more complex, as provisions of a social and environmental nature were added. A landmark illustration was the Supreme Court case of *Berman v. Parker*, in 1954. In this case, the Court established aesthetics as a proper subject of public concern. The subject under consideration was an urban renewal project. The court ruled that "it was within the power of the legislature to determine that the community should be beautiful as well as healthy, spacious as well as clean, well-balanced as well as carefully patrolled."

Social, economic, and political events thus combined to establish systems of public regulation. A very important example of this began with the Depression of the 1930s. The government decided that one of the keys to economic recovery was the stimulation of the home building industry. This led to home loans guaranteed by the federal government. This, in turn, required that the housing thus built had to meet certain standards of land use and construction. So began the pervasive system of uniform standards of construction, the benefit of which was the safeguarding of investment funds and the improvement of quality, the disadvantage of which has been stultifying uniformity.

Public control through planning and construction regulations is now firmly established. The determination of applicable controls is a first step in the development of any piece of property. Starting with either the deed or similar documents pertaining to land ownership and use, and proceeding to municipal and even federal regulation, the most common types of controls and regulations will be discussed next.

Zoning in Operation

The buyer of a parcel of land must determine what he is allowed to do on his land, identifying possible deed restrictions but, more importantly, restrictions imposed by zoning. This is done by examining the applicable zoning ordinances in the specific area in which the property is located.

Land zoning is the division of the land of a city, county or other jurisdiction, into districts, or zones, and the allocation of different uses to these different zones. The primary purpose of zoning, as described earlier, is the protection of property values, and with that, investment stability. In support of that purpose, zoning exercises the following restrictions:

1. *Regulation of the use and intensity of use of a particular parcel of land.* A residentially zoned lot, for example, may only have a house built upon it. The house may have a maximum size, and there may be requirements related to lot coverage, setbacks, and height.

2. *Protection against discordant nuisances,* such as factories or commercial buildings.

3. *Protection against undesirable businesses.* Bars, poolrooms, and adult bookstores may be prohibited in certain areas.

4. *Protection against danger.* Hazardous industries, such as factories using explosive or toxic substances, may be prohibited from areas with dense populations.

5. *Protection of light, air, and open space.* Buildings are often regulated in accordance with the size of the lot they are to occupy.

Early zoning ordinances recognized three basic land uses: residential, commercial, and industrial. Within these broad categories, many sub-classifications have developed. Residential districts may be divided into single-family districts and multiple-family districts. Multiple-family zones may be divided into walk-up and high-rise. Commercial zones may be divided into retail and wholesale. Industrial zones may be designated as light or heavy manufacturing areas, etc.

The various uses defined in a zoning ordinance are usually ranked on a scale of priority, starting with single-family dwellings. Multiple-family dwellings usually rank lower on the list, with commercial and industrial uses ranking lower still. A piece of land in a particular zoning district may be used for the uses designated for that zone and usually for any use ranked above it, but not for a use ranked below it. For example, a single-family residence could theoretically be built in any zone, although economic and other considerations would probably make that unfeasible.

Zoning also regulates the size and location of a building on its site. Examples include required setbacks from the property lines, limits on maximum percentage coverage of the lot area, limits on the number of dwellings per acre, and off-street parking requirements as a ratio of cars to building floor area.

A zoning ordinance must provide for so-called *nonconforming uses*; that is, uses that do not comply with current zoning regulations, but that were permitted by the zoning ordinances in effect when the structure was built. In permitting a nonconforming use, zoning ordinances permit minor or nonstructural alterations, but they may prohibit structural alterations unless the building is also brought into conformance with current zoning regulations. If the owner abandons the nonconforming use for a certain period of time, often three years, he may lose the right to exercise the nonconforming use. If a nonconforming building is razed or destroyed by fire, rebuilding must be in compliance with existing zoning standards.

A *conditional use* is a use that is permitted by a zoning authority with certain restrictions attached, when the proposed use is not normally permitted in that location. A conditional use may be granted if it is found to be in the public interest. A school, for example, may be permitted in a residential zone, subject to such requirements as screening of playground noise and providing parking spaces. Such uses as airports, cemeteries, landfill projects, and public utility installations may be difficult to locate because local zoning ordinances make no provision for them. Under such circumstances, a zoning authority, working with other public authorities, may grant a conditional use for a site, subject to restrictions to protect the interests of nearby property owners.

Zoning ordinances may place unintended burdens on particular parcels of land, or make it difficult to develop a particular parcel. For that reason municipalities refer requests for a *variance* to a zoning board of review. In theory, a variance is granted only where exact and literal application of the ordinance would cause undue hardship or practical difficulties. For example, where a zoning ordinance requires a 60-foot frontage on residential lots, an irregular lot may have only 55 feet of frontage, but is otherwise in conformance. The zoning board would very

likely grant a variance for the reduced frontage to the owner so that he could build on the property.

A variance or conditional use does not change the basic zoning. A change in zoning is not easily accomplished. An owner seeking to bring about a change in zoning must institute a hearing procedure. He first submits a petition to the zoning board requesting a change. After this a notice is published in a local newspaper announcing a public hearing on the change. At the hearing, those favoring and opposing the change are heard. Finally, the board renders a decision. This might result in a change of zoning for the entire zoning district, if that was applied for, or it might result in a change of zoning for a specific parcel, if that was applied for. This is referred to as *spot zoning*. Spot zoning may be used to alleviate economic hardships that would adversely affect the owner of a particular parcel.

Zoning variances and spot zoning are obviously prone to manipulation by special interests. Hence, judicious public administration is vital to the proper exercise of zoning regulation.

Zoning as a Design Determinant

Although zoning was not originally intended to be a determinant of design, it has clearly become so. Since zoning ordinances specify setback, height, lot coverage, floor area in relation to lot size—even architectural character in some instances—zoning has become an important determining factor in design.

At its very best, even under well-intentioned management, zoning is an extremely crude determinant of design. By its nature it cannot operate at the level of subtlety or discernment which sensitive site and building design require. Zoning, as a design determinant, assures uniformity at the cost of subtlety, refinement, and variety, which are the basis of sensitive architecture. And, too often, such uniformity creates environmental sterility and monotony.

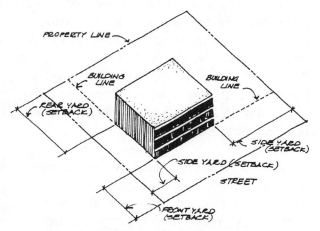

ZONING SETBACKS AS A DESIGN DETERMINANT
Figure 11.1

A more suitable system is a design plan in which land use and performance specifications are established, and for which a design review procedure is utilized. This system has long been in use in numerous European countries, and in urban renewal projects and "historic zones" in the United States. It is, in fact, the regulatory system for the physical development of American college and university campuses. It is also used in new town development and resort area development.

To avoid the uniformity of conventional zoning, a new type of zone, called the *planned unit development* (PUD) has been devised, which allows a mixture of uses not otherwise achievable in conventional zoning. In practice, however, it is still not widely used.

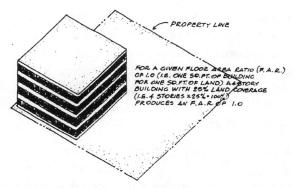

LOT COVERAGE SPECIFIED BY ZONING IS A DESIGN DETERMINANT
Figure 11.2

Zoning is no substitute for conscientious design. Unfortunately it has not only become a prime determinant of design, it actually prevents the highest level of design quality from being achieved. Nevertheless, it is the regulatory system within which most building is done.

Variance and Conditional Uses

A *variance* is a special authorization which grants an owner permission to deviate from the zoning requirements applicable to a land parcel. It may be granted in a case where the zoning requirements create a special or personal hardship, but only after a public hearing before an administrative authority, called a Board of Adjustment or a Board of Zoning Appeals.

A *conditional use* differs from a variance in that it is granted by a zoning board for a special purpose, such as a school, hospital, cemetery, or other such use.

Although a variance and a conditional use both permit deviation from the literal terms of the zoning code, the purpose of a variance is to avoid hardship to an individual owner, while a conditional use is for the welfare and convenience of the public. When a zoning variance or conditional use is sought, the advantages and disadvantages are discussed before the board, agency, or commission having authority. The important issues of the case are debated, and the final decision is made by the zoning authority.

Nonconforming Use

A nonconforming use is one that is no longer permitted by the zoning ordinance. The original development might have predated the adoption of a zoning ordinance, or it might have become nonconforming as a result of recent code revisions. Either way, it is referred to as a nonconforming use. Unless it is unsafe, such a use is generally allowed to continue. And although the building cannot be expanded or altered to any great extent, ordinary maintenance and repairs can be done.

Zoning ordinances and their interpretations vary from community to community, and therefore careful checking of the applicable ordinance is required. During site selection, a preliminary check of zoning must be made. In subsequent stages of preliminary design, a more detailed examination of zoning requirements and other possible restrictions must be made. In practice, zoning ordinances become modified over a period of time to suit local economic, political, geographic and environmental conditions. Thus, no two zoning ordinances are exactly alike, even though they may govern similar land uses.

Zoning Code Features

In the 1920s, the U.S. Department of Commerce published a standard zoning ordinance. Since then, however, many municipalities which adopted that model have been forced to modify it to suit their own special needs. For large municipalities, zoning ordinances have become extremely complex. Thus, there is no uniform zoning ordinance analogous to the Uniform Building Code, simply because zoning variations are too diverse to make one code practicable.

The application of zoning ordinances results in the segregation of permitted uses, control of population density, and provisions for parking and loading spaces. Zoning also influences building form—height, size, and setbacks—and thus, it is a determinant of form. Zoning stabilizes property values by preventing deleterious land uses, such as a noisy factory within a residential zone.

Permitted uses are regulated by zones established on a map, which is legally a part of a zoning ordinance. The prime intent of such maps is to segregate uses in order to prevent incompatibilities. In some cases, however, the practice of use segregation precludes compatible activities, such as a small convenience store in a residential neighborhood.

Zoning has also been used to attempt remedies for certain social problems; for example, to maintain low population density in the questionable belief that high density causes crime.

Zoning regulates the physical design of a building through such factors as height, number of stories, total bulk of building, setbacks at front, side and rear, minimum dimensions of lot, minimum lot area, minimum floor area of dwelling units, maximum coverage of the lot, number of dwelling units per acre, and number of off-street parking spaces. Other matters, such as control of advertising signs, driveway access to a site, loading dock requirements, etc., may also be controlled through zoning.

Building setbacks are justified by the demand for light, air, and spaciousness. Setbacks and height limitations may also be warranted on aesthetic grounds. For example, limitations on height and bulk in relation to street width may be established to prevent a sense of oppressiveness. A significant aspect of zoning designations is that they make it possible to forecast the kind and amount of utility services that an area will require in the future. Architects should also explore "infill" design, which explores the possibility of fitting additional buildings into an area that has low density. This sustainable design approach saves energy by designing buildings that reuse existing infrastructure (sewers, water supply lines, etc.).

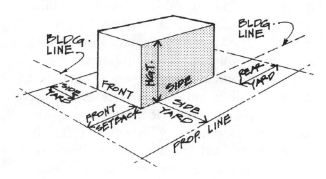

SETBACKS

Figure 11.3

Requiring setbacks of a building from the property lines is common practice in residential zones and sometimes in commercial and manufacturing zones. The term "building line" refers to a line beyond which a structure is not permitted to extend. In most cases, the building line is parallel to the property line and set back from it in accordance with the zoning ordinance.

In residential areas, setbacks provide increased privacy, encourage lawns and gardens for common enjoyment and general enhancement of a neighborhood, provide fire-fighting access to the sides and rear of buildings, and permit possible future street widening. In other zones, front setbacks may provide off-street parking, or the space may exist primarily for aesthetic reasons. Front setbacks are often related to

a structure's height, which is determined by means of a formula, the effect of which is to locate tall buildings back from the street, thus providing increased open space.

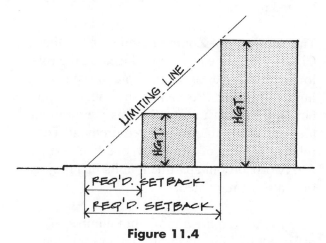

Figure 11.4

To encourage openness, some zoning codes limit the bulk of a building by means of a formula which restricts the total floor area to a multiple of the lot area. This is referred to as the *floor area ratio* (FAR). In addition, the ground area covered by a structure may be limited to a specified percentage of the lot area.

Height limitations are often established in residential areas. For single-family and duplex residences, three stories is a typical maximum, while the height of apartment buildings generally has no limitation, other than that applicable to all buildings.

Life safety is another consideration in establishing maximum building heights. The extended length of fire-fighting ladders was, historically, the basis for limiting height.

Building heights were also restricted by a structure's ability to resist earthquakes or lateral wind forces. Recent fire-fighting methods and modern structural engineering techniques have eliminated those earlier limitations.

Building components such as fan rooms, elevator penthouses, and skylights are usually allowed to exceed the established height limit, if they are set back from the parapet and limited in area.

The Summary of Zoning Regulations of the City of Los Angeles is reproduced on the following two pages as an example of typical zoning requirements. As can be seen, residential building lots must normally satisfy a minimum area and a minimum width requirement. The relative number of efficiency, one-bedroom, and two-bedroom apartment units in a project may also be regulated.

Many cities require a minimum number of off-street parking spaces for tenants and tenants' guests. This is related to the number of apartments in a project and, sometimes, to the number of bedrooms in each apartment. (Refer to Figure 11.5, the RD zones of the Los Angeles Zoning Regulations, as an example.)

The number of off-street parking spaces required for commercial buildings is often expressed in terms of the rentable floor space, which excludes equipment floors and similar non-rentable space.

To prevent the congestion of public streets, specified amounts of loading dock space are often required for commercial and manufacturing uses, as well as office buildings and hotels.

FEDERAL REGULATIONS

In addition to local regulatory controls, it is necessary to comply with any applicable state or federal regulations. This, of course, depends on the location and nature of the proposed construction. A state or federal building constructed within a city, such as a state univer-

sity building or a federal courthouse, need not comply with the city's building and zoning ordinances. However, as a matter of practice, the Federal or State Government may direct the designer to comply with city ordinances.

Because of widespread concern about environmental quality, the effects of certain projects on the environment must be assessed, through a procedure now quite familiar to architects and planners, namely, the *environmental impact statement*. The National Environmental Policy Act of 1969 requires that for every "major federal action" that may "significantly affect the quality of the human environment," the responsible official must prepare a "detailed statement" discussing the environmental impact of the proposed action. He must also prepare a statement describing any "adverse effects" that cannot be avoided, and any "irreversible and irretrievable commitments of resources" that would be involved.

This law has become quite far-reaching since it applies to federal construction projects as well as to any action in which there is a "major" federal involvement. This involvement includes technical or financial assistance, issuance of a license or permit, or other participation. In addition to the federal requirement, similar requirements have been established in many states and municipalities.

The general topics required in an environmental impact statement depend on the type of site, the building or development program, and the requirements of a particular agency. Such topics include:

A. A complete *resource inventory* of the existing conditions of the region and the project site, including the following general considerations:

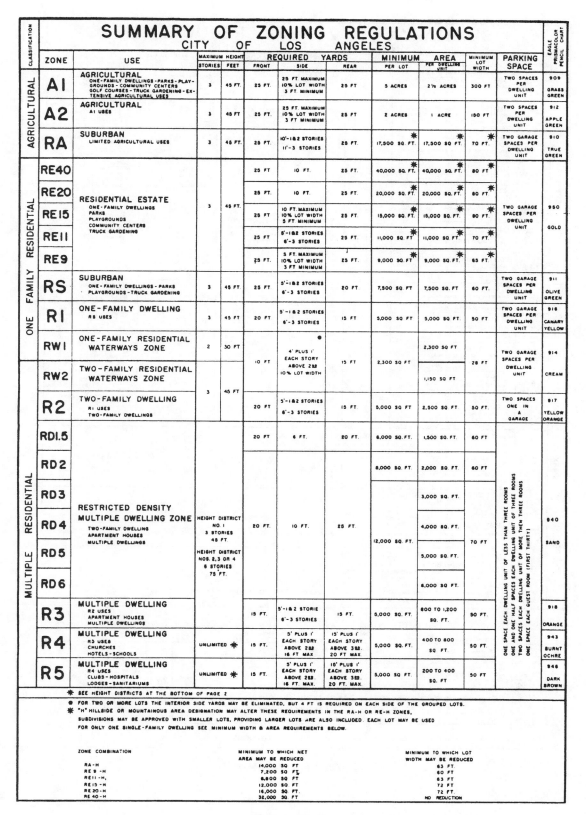

Figure 11.5

SUMMARY OF ZONING REGULATIONS
CITY OF LOS ANGELES

CLASSIFICATION	ZONE	USE	MAXIMUM HEIGHT STORIES	MAXIMUM HEIGHT FEET	REQUIRED YARDS FRONT	REQUIRED YARDS SIDE	REQUIRED YARDS REAR	MINIMUM AREA PER LOT AND UNIT	MINIMUM LOT WIDTH	LOADING SPACE	PARKING SPACE	EAGLE PRISMACOLOR PENCIL CHART
COMMERCIAL	CR	LIMITED COMMERCIAL — BANKS, CLUBS, HOTELS, CHURCHES, SCHOOLS, BUSINESS & PROFESSIONAL OFFICES, PARKING AREAS	6	75 FT.	10 FEET	5'-10' CORNER LOT, RESIDENTIAL USE OR ADJOINING AN "A" OR "R" ZONE SAME AS R4 ZONE	15' PLUS 1' EACH STORY ABOVE 3rd	SAME AS R4 FOR DWELLINGS OTHERWISE NONE	50 FEET FOR RESIDENCE USE OTHERWISE NONE	HOSPITALS, HOTELS INSTITUTIONS, AND WITH EVERY BUILDING WHERE LOT ABUTS ALLEY	ONE SPACE FOR EACH 500 SQ FT OF FLOOR AREA	939 FLESH
COMMERCIAL	CI	LIMITED COMMERCIAL — LOCAL RETAIL STORES, OFFICES OR BUSINESSES, HOTELS, LIMITED HOSPITALS AND/OR CLINICS, PARKING AREAS				3'-5' CORNER LOT OR ADJOINING AN "A" OR "R" ZONE RESIDENTIAL USE SAME AS R4 ZONE	5' PLUS 1' EACH STORY ABOVE 3rd	SAME AS R3 FOR DWELLINGS EXCEPT 5000 SQ FT PER UNIT IN CI-H ZONES — OTHERWISE NONE		MINIMUM LOADING SPACE 400 SQUARE FEET	ONE SPACE FOR EACH 500 SQUARE FEET OF FLOOR AREA IN ALL BUILDINGS ON ANY LOT	929 PINK
COMMERCIAL	CI.5	LIMITED COMMERCIAL — CI USES — DEPARTMENT STORES, THEATRES, BROADCASTING STUDIOS, PARKING BUILDINGS, PARKS & PLAYGROUNDS	UNLIMITED ✳					RESIDENTIAL USE OR ABUTTING AN "A" OR "R" ZONE OTHERWISE NONE		ADDITIONAL SPACE REQUIRED FOR BUILDINGS CONTAINING MORE THAN 50,000 SQUARE FEET OF FLOOR AREA	MUST BE LOCATED WITHIN 750 FEET OF BUILDING	928 BLUSH
COMMERCIAL	C2	COMMERCIAL — CI.5 USES — RETAIL BUSINESSES WITH LIMITED MANUFACTURING, AUTO SERVICE STATION & GARAGE, RETAIL CONTRACTORS BUSINESSES, CHURCHES, SCHOOLS			NONE	NONE FOR COMMERCIAL BUILDINGS RESIDENTIAL USES — SAME AS IN R4 ZONE	NONE FOR COMMERCIAL BUILDINGS RESIDENTIAL USES — SAME AS IN R4 ZONE	SAME AS R4 FOR DWELLINGS OTHERWISE NONE				922 SCARLET RED
COMMERCIAL	C4	COMMERCIAL — C2 USES — (WITH EXCEPTIONS, SUCH AS AUTO SERVICE STATIONS, AMUSEMENT ENTERPRISES, CONTRACTORS BUSINESSES, SECOND-HAND BUSINESSES)								NONE REQUIRED FOR APARTMENT BUILDINGS 20 UNITS OR LESS	SEE CODE FOR ASSEMBLY AREAS, HOSPITALS AND CLINICS	924 CRIMSON RED
COMMERCIAL	C5	COMMERCIAL — C2 USES — LIMITED FLOOR AREAS FOR LIGHT MANUFACTURING OF THE CM-ZONE TYPE										925 CRIMSON LAKE
COMMERCIAL	CM	COMM'L MANUFACTURING — WHOLESALE BUSINESSES, STORAGE BUILDINGS, CLINICS, LIMITED MANUFACTURING, C2 USES - EXCEPT HOSPITALS, SCHOOLS, CHURCHES						SAME AS R3 FOR DWELLINGS OTHERWISE NONE				905 AQUA-MARINE
INDUSTRIAL (RESIDENTIAL USES PROHIBITED IN ALL INDUSTRIAL ZONES)	MR1	RESTRICTED INDUSTRIAL — CM USES — LIMITED COMMERCIAL & MANUFACTURING USES, HOSPITALS, CLINICS, SANITARIUMS, LIMITED MACHINE SHOPS			15 FT.	NONE FOR INDUSTRIAL OR COMMERCIAL BUILDINGS RESIDENTIAL USES — SAME AS IN R4 ZONE	NONE FOR INDUSTRIAL OR COMMERCIAL BUILDINGS RESIDENTIAL USES — SAME AS IN R4 ZONE		50 FEET FOR RESIDENCE USE OTHERWISE NONE	HOSPITALS, HOTELS INSTITUTIONS, AND WITH EVERY BUILDING WHERE LOT ABUTS ALLEY	ONE SPACE FOR EACH 500 SQUARE FEET OF FLOOR AREA IN ALL BUILDINGS ON ANY LOT	901 INDIGO BLUE
	MR2	RESTRICTED LIGHT INDUSTRIAL — MR1 USES — ADDITION INDUSTRIAL USES, MORTUARIES, AGRICULTURE						NONE EXCEPT FOR DWELLINGS		MINIMUM LOADING SPACE 400 SQUARE FEET	MUST BE LOCATED WITHIN 750 FEET OF BUILDING	906 COPEN-HAGEN BLUE
	M1	LIMITED INDUSTRIAL — CM USES — LIMITED INDUSTRIAL & MANUFACTURING USES — NO "R" ZONE USES, NO HOSPITALS, SCHOOLS OR CHURCHES	UNLIMITED ✳		NONE					ADDITIONAL SPACE REQUIRED FOR BUILDINGS CONTAINING MORE THAN 50,000 SQUARE FEET OF FLOOR AREA	SEE CODE FOR ASSEMBLY AREAS, HOSPITALS AND CLINICS	904 LIGHT BLUE
	M2	LIGHT INDUSTRIAL — M1 USES — ADDITIONAL INDUSTRIAL USES, STORAGE YARDS OF ALL KINDS, ANIMAL KEEPING — NO "R" ZONE USES								NONE REQUIRED FOR APARTMENT BUILDINGS 20 UNITS OR LESS		902 ULTRA-MARINE
	M3	HEAVY INDUSTRIAL — M2 USES — ANY INDUSTRIAL USES — NUISANCE TYPE - 500 FT. FROM ANY OTHER ZONE — NO "R" ZONE USES				NONE	NONE	NONE — NOTE — "R" ZONE USES PROHIBITED	NONE			931 PURPLE
PARKING	P	AUTOMOBILE PARKING - SURFACE & UNDERGROUND — PROPERTY IN A "P" ZONE MAY ALSO BE IN AN "A" OR "R" ZONE PARKING PERMITTED IN LIEU OF AGRICULTURAL OR RESIDENTIAL USES						NONE UNLESS ALSO IN AN "A" OR "R" ZONE	NONE UNLESS ALSO IN AN "A" OR "R" ZONE	—	—	967 COLD GREY LIGHT
	PB	PARKING BUILDING — AUTOMOBILE PARKING WITHIN OR WITHOUT A BUILDING	✳✳	—	0', 5', OR 10' DEPENDING ON ZONING IN BLOCK AND ACROSS STREET	5' PLUS 1' EACH STORY ABOVE 2nd IF ABUTTING OR ACROSS STREET FROM "A" OR "R" ZONE	5' PLUS 1' EACH STORY ABOVE 2nd IF ABUTTING AN "A" OR "R" ZONE, TO A 16' MAXIMUM	NONE	NONE			936 SLATE GREY
SPECIAL	SL	SUBMERGED LAND ZONE — COMMERCIAL SHIPPING, NAVIGATION, FISHING, RECREATION										919 SKY BLUE
	(T)	TENTATIVE CLASSIFICATION — USED IN COMBINATION WITH ZONE CHANGE ONLY - DELAYS ISSUANCE OF BUILDING PERMIT UNTIL SUBDIVISION OR PARCEL MAP RECORDED										
	(F)	FUNDED IMPROVEMENT CLASSIFICATION — AN ALTERNATE MEANS OF EFFECTING ZONE CHANGES AND SECURING IMPROVEMENTS (WHEN NO SUBDIVISION OR DEDICATIONS ARE INVOLVED)										
	(Q)	QUALIFIED CLASSIFICATION — USED IN COMBINATION WITH ZONE CHANGES ONLY EXCEPT WITH RA, RE, RS OR RI ZONES - RESTRICTS USES OF PROPERTY AND ASSURES DEVELOPMENT COMPATIBLE WITH THE SURROUNDING PROPERTY										

SUPPLEMENTAL USE DISTRICTS: G ROCK AND GRAVEL • O OIL DRILLING • S ANIMAL SLAUGHTERING • RPD RESIDENTIAL PLANNED DEVELOPMENT
K HORSE-KEEPING • CA COMMERCIAL AND ARTCRAFT
(ESTABLISHED IN CONJUNCTION WITH ZONES)

HEIGHT DISTRICT		
✳	Nº 1	FLOOR AREA OF MAIN BUILDING MAY NOT EXCEED THREE TIMES THE BUILDING AREA OF THE LOT
	Nº 1L	SAME AS Nº 1 AND MAXIMUM HEIGHT - 6 STORIES OR 75 FT.
	Nº 1-VL	SAME AS Nº 1 AND MAXIMUM HEIGHT - 3 STORIES OR 45 FT
	Nº 1-XL	SAME AS Nº 1 AND MAXIMUM HEIGHT - 2 STORIES OR 30 FT
	Nº 2	FLOOR AREA OF MAIN BUILDING MAY NOT EXCEED SIX TIMES THE BUILDABLE AREA OF THE LOT
	Nº 3	FLOOR AREA OF MAIN BUILDING MAY NOT EXCEED TEN TIMES THE BUILDABLE AREA OF THE LOT
	Nº 4	FLOOR AREA OF MAIN BUILDING MAY NOT EXCEED THIRTEEN TIMES THE BUILDABLE AREA OF THE LOT

MAXIMUM PB ZONE HEIGHTS		
✳✳	Nº 1	2 STORIES AND ROOF
	Nº 2	6 STORIES
	Nº 3	10 STORIES
	Nº 4	13 STORIES

NOTE: ALL INFORMATION GENERAL - FOR SPECIFIC DETAILS CHECK WITH DEPARTMENT OF BUILDING AND SAFETY

Figure 11.5 (continued)

1. Landform, topography, location, and size.

2. Vegetation and land use.

3. Soils, geology, and groundwater.

4. Streams and water quality.

5. Wildlife.

6. Climatology.

7. Air quality.

8. Noise conditions.

9. Socioeconomics, demography, transportation, and utilities.

10. Archeology and historic attributes.

B. A complete *description of the proposed project*, emphasizing the way in which the project will affect the environment, including some of the following aspects:

1. Need, public benefit, and economic feasibility.

2. Facilities to be placed on the site.

3. Gaseous, liquid, and solid wastes to be generated from the project; project noise levels; ability to meet air and water quality standards, and noise limitations.

4. Energy and water requirements.

5. Transportation requirements, such as new material imports, product exports, employee traffic, and customer traffic.

6. Manpower requirements, such as expected local recruitment, expected transfer of employees from other areas, and the number of new employees to be attracted to the region.

C. The *environmental impact assessment* is the most important part of the process. It is unique to each project. It is an evaluation based on a comparative study of the proposed project in relation to the resource inventory of the site and region. The assessment determines the potential "fit" of the proposed project to its environment, identifies environmental and socioeconomic conflicts, and compares project requirements with available resources. Sustainable design planning also encourages the architect to make a complete assessment of environmental issues. But the focus of sustainable design is more affirmative—it attempts to find the virtue of environmental conditions (e.g., topographic slope for potential earth sheltered berming or ground water as a potential energy source). The sustainable design assessment in conjunction with an environment impact statement can allow the client and architect a good understanding of most of the environmental conditions that will affect the project.

Regarding air and water quality, the impact statement must address the direct and secondary impact of the proposed project during construction and during operation. The considerations must include both average and worst-case conditions of weather and facility performance. Such evaluations may result in revisions to a project's design. The most suitable solutions then determine the final plan. Less satisfactory designs may be described in a section on "alternatives."

D. *Alternatives* to the proposed project.

1. Alternative locations for project siting address such questions as: What are the determinants in the selection of a site? Why was the proposed site selected? What unique qualities does it provide for the project? What other sites were considered? Why were they rejected?

2. Alternative process or methods pose such questions as: In what other way can the goals of this project be achieved? Why was an alternative process or method not proposed? Can the proposed project be modified further to avoid or minimize some adverse impacts? If, for example, the project is an electric

generating station powered by coal, an explanation should be offered as to why an oil-fired generator was not proposed, or whether hydroelectric generation is possible. If once-through water is proposed for cooling, the applicant must explain why evaporative cooling towers or dry towers cannot be used. In the case of a road crossing a marshland, the alternatives of construction on fill, on piles, or on open structures should be discussed.

3. Alternative configurations within the site take into consideration certain sensitive areas within the site that can be preserved by careful arrangement. An alteration of ingress and egress locations may reduce potential traffic problems. The appearance of the proposed development from surrounding areas may be improved by adjusting the positions of certain components.

4. The "no-action" alternative examines the consequences of not implementing the proposed project at all. What public benefits would be lost? What alternative uses could be made of the site? What adverse impacts would be avoided?

5. Those adverse environmental and socioeconomic impacts of the proposed project which cannot be avoided are listed in their approximate order of magnitude, and each is described briefly.

These critical points, listed in the environmental impact statement, constitute a basis for regulatory agencies and other interested parties to review a proposed project. They also serve as a basis of suggestions for reducing the adverse effects of the proposed project.

Most state and local municipalities have authorized a designated official or agency to determine the acceptability of an environmental impact statement, based on its form, content, adequacy of analysis, and suitability of environmentally protective measures.

Public informational meetings and hearings are important components of the environmental assessment process. In publicly financed projects, public informational meetings are generally initiated in an early stage while the project is still amenable to modification.

In this lesson, we have only touched on the most common types of regulation encountered in the planning, design, and construction of buildings. In the case of a real project, of course, detailed knowledge of applicable regulations is required.

Lastly, the designer should be familiar with other federal laws that regulate the design of sites and buildings. Principal among these are the regulations that seek to make buildings and facilities accessible to the physically handicapped (persons of impaired or restricted mobility, the sight-impaired, or the hearing-impaired), and OSHA regulations, which govern the design of the workplace. Their purpose is to avoid any features that might pose a hazard to the life or limb of a worker.

The proper exercise of environmental regulations confers vital benefits on the public. Such regulations require constant review and improvement, and they constitute a large part of the design environment in which the architect works.

LEGAL RESTRICTIONS ON LAND USE

The previously described zoning codes represent limitations or restrictions on the use of private property. At the same time they are the basis for sustaining land values, or even increasing them, because unfavorable or possibly harmful land uses are prevented. There are a number of techniques, in addition to zoning, that protect public health, safety, and welfare. Architects should be familiar with those discussed in the following pages.

Easements

An easement is the legal right of a government or a landowner to make use of the property of another landowner for a particular purpose; for example, the right to traverse a neighbor's land to gain access to one's own, which is known as a *right-of-way*. To be legal and binding, such an agreement must be in the general form of a grant deed. It must describe the parcel of land subject to the easement, identify the land benefited by the easement, describe the purpose of the easement, and be signed and recorded in the public records.

An easement for a stated purpose may not be unilaterally modified for another purpose at a later date. If Mr. A has an easement for ingress and egress over Ms. B's land, A may not install a pipeline or water well on the easement. The land still belongs to B, and A can only use it in the manner originally agreed upon. Similarly, if the city has an easement over Mr. C's land for the installation and maintenance of an overhead power line, C can still use his land as long as he does not interfere with the power line.

An easement may be established by a municipality for any legitimately constituted public purpose. Private easements, on the other hand, are always the result of negotiations between private parties.

Normally, the taking of private property by a government for public use requires compensation to the deprived owner. But there are situations where development rights are taken

without compensation, such as the "scenic easement" concept, which has recently come into use. The purpose of such an easement is to prevent the development of land that is of scenic value to the public.

A similar situation exists where owners of old buildings with historical value have been deprived of the right to alter or raze them, but have not been compensated for the loss of their right to modify or dispose of their property. This apparent inequity is likely to be adjudicated in the courts in due time.

Deed Restrictions

Any clause in a deed which restricts the future use of a parcel of land by the buyer of the land is a *deed restriction*. Deed restrictions can be quite broad; for example, they may limit the type, the density, or even the use of buildings on a site. This type of agreement is enforceable between buyer and seller, and sometimes third parties.

A *covenant* is a legal agreement used to protect or uphold a condition of use in a parcel of land. Where a seller owns two adjoining parcels, restrictions on the one sold may benefit the parcel retained, and are legally enforceable. As an example, Ms. D owns two adjoining lots fronting on a street and backing on a public alley. She sells one lot to B with the covenant that B may not construct a driveway from the street to the garage, but may have access to the garage only from the alley.

If a developer establishes uniform restrictions on buyers of lots in a development for purely aesthetic reasons, the developer and other owners have a valid cause of action against an owner who violates the restrictions. When all the lots are sold, the developer will no longer have a legal standing for action against an owner who violates the restrictions. To provide for continuing enforcement, therefore, a developer may create a homeowners' association, whose members comprise all the original buyers. The association is empowered to enforce the restrictions for their mutual benefit. Such an association may include an architectural review board which is authorized to approve all proposed designs according to criteria established in the deed restrictions or covenants.

Affirmative covenants are those that legally commit a buyer to perform certain duties in the future, such as maintaining a fence or a roadway. Such covenants run with the land, so that future owners of record will always be responsible to perform the same duties. Affirmative covenants are also used to require buyers of planned unit developments and condominiums to make payments for the maintenance of common areas.

Still another form of restriction is a clause that imposes a restriction on a buyer and specifies that if the restriction is violated, the title to the land will revert to the original grantor or his heirs. Such an arrangement is known as a *conditional covenant* or *condition*.

Some deed restrictions expire after a definite time, but others may run indefinitely. In the latter case, a restriction can sometimes be eliminated by court action. Deed restrictions involving race or religion have been ruled invalid by the U.S. Supreme Court and are of no effect, even though they may still appear in recorded deeds.

The right to use the open space above land or above an existing structure is known as an *air right*; for example, the right to construct a building over a railroad track. An air right is a form of easement, and usually includes the right to construct foundations for and provide access to a structure built in the space. All such matters must be specified in detail in the agreement conveying the air right. Air right construction is costly, and therefore occurs infrequently and only where land is very expensive, as in the central areas of large cities.

A *party wall* is a wall located on an interior lot line that forms part of two adjacent buildings. A party wall is also a fire wall, and must be constructed accordingly; however, it is usually more economical than constructing two separate walls. Where adjoining buildings are under different ownership, an agreement must be reached by the respective owners prohibiting either owner from tearing down or significantly altering the party wall without the concurrence of the other owner. When the agreement is written and recorded, each owner has an easement on the other's land to the extent of one-half the thickness of the wall, and the agreement cannot be revoked unilaterally.

BUILDING CODES

Building codes and zoning ordinances have distinctly different purposes. As we have seen, zoning ordinances prescribe land usage and regulate the function, size, and certain exterior aspects of a building. In contrast, a building code deals with the structural and mechanical aspects of a building, as they affect public health, safety, and welfare. Building fires have caused countless deaths. The earliest building codes, therefore, were primarily fire-protection codes concerned with preventing fire, and allowing occupants to evacuate a building quickly and safely. In time, other hazards came to be recognized, such as earthquakes, wind storms, power supply failures, and the danger of panic that is likely to occur in crowded spaces. The concern for public health is manifested in codes which deal with plumbing, ventilation, electricity, and lighting.

There is a number of building codes that are being used as follows:

- The Uniform Building Code (UBC) is used as the model code throughout all ALS study material and it is published by the International Conference of Building Officials.

- The Standard Building Code (SBC) is published by the Southern Building Code Congress International and is used by some Southern states. Most have used it as the base code for their state specific building codes.

- The BOCA National Building Code published by the Building Official and Code Administrators is still being used in a few states, mostly in the northeast. This code was last published in 1999 and states that use this code are either changing to the International Building Code (IBC) or revising a model code to make it state specific.

All of these model building codes mentioned above are in use in some states, but in the last ten years the Southern Building Code Congress International and the Building Official and Code Administrators, in an effort to standardize Building codes, developed the International Code Council. They created the International Building Code (IBC), which has been adopted in most states to date.

The National Research Council of Canada published the National Building Code of Canada.

A building code is enforceable because the government having jurisdiction (city, county, etc.) has adopted the particular code by establishing it as law. It should also be noted that a municipality usually adopts a particular edition of the code, which remains in force even when a later edition of the code is published. In addition, the code may be adopted with specific additions, deletions, or alterations. Some large cities write and adopt their own building codes. And an increasing number of cities are adopting energy codes from a variety of models. One example used by large cities such as Chicago is the IECC (International Energy Conservation Code), a model energy code that can be modified to fit the needs of individual communities.

Types of Codes

There are two types of building codes: the first specifies construction techniques, methods, and materials in detail, while the other establishes the functional requirements that a structure must satisfy under specific conditions. The first, referred to as a *prescriptive code*, is simple to administer, but discourages innovation. The second, known as a *performance code*, promotes innovation in building design, but it may be difficult to administer. Of course, innovative or unconventional designs must be tested and proved to the satisfaction of code administrators. This may entail tests, which must be paid for by the owner.

Terminology may vary from one code to another. For example, one code may use the term "exit," while another may refer to "means of egress" and still another may speak of "exitway." Each code includes definitions of such terms, and these must be noted carefully.

Building Code Characteristics

An outline of the basic steps in determining code compliance for a building design follows:

1. **Construction documents:** Determine compliance with the requirements for construction documents.
2. **Use group:** Determine the appropriate use group classification of the building.
3. **Height and area:** Determine the type of construction required based on the building

use group and the height and area limitations.

4. **Type of construction:** Determine compliance with the required type of construction of the building by the building materials used and the fire resistance rating of the building elements.

5. **Siting:** Determine the location of the building on the site, including separation distances from lot lines and other buildings. Determine exterior wall and wall opening requirements based on proximity to lot lines and adjacent buildings.

6. **Fire performance:** Determine compliance with detailed requirements for fire resistance and fire protection systems.

7. **Interior environment and design:** Determine compliance with special use and occupancy requirements, *means of egress* requirements, accessibility requirements, and interior environment requirements.

8. **Exterior envelope:** Determine compliance with exterior envelope requirements, as well as energy conservation.

9. **Structural performance:** Determine compliance with structural requirements and building material requirements.

10. **Building service system:** Determine compliance with various building service system requirements.

These classifications establish requirements of the code that are applicable to a specific building.

Fire Zones

Some jurisdictions establish fire zones, which are geographic districts generally classified as high hazard, moderate hazard, or low hazard. The criteria for such classification include: population density, building height, street access and congestion which affect fire department response time, and the fire department's equipment and competence. Buildings in high hazard fire zones require greater fire resistance and other protective features than buildings located in less hazardous zones. In fact, certain forms of combustible construction are entirely prohibited in high hazard fire zones.

The fire zone of a particular site should be determined and considered during the process of site selection, so that its effects can be determined in the programming phase. Because certain uses are prohibited in specific fire zones, the investigation of this matter can be critical.

Occupancy Group

The number of occupants and the nature of their activity are important considerations in building codes. For example, night clubs and theaters have an inherently high risk of panic, and therefore warrant higher than normal levels of fire-resistive construction. Those who are not able to move easily, such as hospital patients and prison inmates, are in greater danger than more mobile people. Therefore, such people must be accorded the protection of greater fire resistance and other related safety features.

The occupancy classification (use-group) of a structure is determined by the activities for which the structure is intended; for example, public assembly, school, manufacturing, etc. The degree of hazard in an occupancy is determined by the amount and form of combustible materials normally present in a building. Code restrictions apply to potential fuels, such as flammable gases, explosive dusts, paints and varnishes, and waste paper.

Combustible materials that are stored, such as furniture, clothing, lumber, etc., pose less risk of fire than combustible materials that are processed. Inert materials such as glass, canned foods, metals, etc., are generally assigned a low hazard rating. Of course, certain materials can be atypical of their classification; for example, magnesium is a highly flammable metal when in powdered or shredded form.

When two or more occupancies are present in the same building, the code usually requires a fire-rated separation between them. The resulting additional construction costs must be considered in preparing budget and cost estimates.

The use of a building is legally designated by a so-called "occupancy" or "use" permit. That designation cannot be changed unless the building is altered to comply with the requirements of the proposed new use.

Type of Construction

All buildings must conform to specific types of construction which are classified according to the degree of their fire resistance. These classifications range from highly fire-resistant to wood frame construction, and they are usually designated by type numbers arranged progressively. A major effect of building codes is that the principal components of a structure, such as the structural frame, floors, and walls, are made fire-resistive. Certain elements of the building envelope, such as the roof and doors, may also be fire-resistive.

The type of building construction permitted on a particular site is determined in accordance with the applicable building code, the fire zone in which the structure is located, and the intended use of the building. Similarly, the type of construction specified has a great influence on the structure's height, floor area, and construction materials permitted.

Siting of Structure

The location of a structure on its site must take into account the possible spread of fire to or from an adjacent structure. In this regard, setbacks and alleys can serve as effective firebreaks. The fire resistance required of exterior walls is determined in part by the actual (or potential) nearness to structures on neighboring lots. Similarly, openings in exterior walls may be severely restricted or even prohibited, depending on their proximity to adjacent lots and structures.

Where two or more buildings on the same site are separated by a court, the court constitutes a firebreak. This influences the fire resistance of facing walls, as well as the permissible openings in those walls.

Floor Areas

Codes normally specify the maximum permitted floor area for a one-story building based on its use, construction type, and fire zone. These maximum allowable areas, however, may be increased in relation to the fire-resistive design of the structure, which is determined by the materials used as well as fire-fighting devices provided, such as sprinklers. Multistory buildings, as well, are usually permitted a significant increase in total floor area by the addition of an automatic fire extinguishing system.

If the permitted floor area of a building is inadequate, the building code may permit a larger building to be built if it is subdivided into discrete fire-resistive areas. These areas are established by constructing full-height, fire-resistive interior walls. When this is done, the area between separation walls is regarded as a separate building in order to satisfy the floor area requirements of the code. Separation walls must extend from the bottom to the top of the structure to provide the necessary legal division. Any openings through fire walls must be protected by automatic closure devices, as required and described by the building code.

Height

The height of a building permitted by code is generally determined by both its use and type of construction. The incorporation of an automatic fire extinguishing system usually allows an increase in building height. When the most fire-resistive type of construction is employed, the permitted height of a building is unlimited.

Occupant Load

The allowable number of occupants in a building is specified by the code on the basis of use, with a given number of square feet of floor area allocated to each occupant. These values range from approximately 7 to 500 square feet per occupant. The lower figure applies to assembly areas without fixed seating; the higher figure applies to warehouses, aircraft hangars, and other similar storage areas that are generally used by few people.

To summarize the preceding building code characteristics, let us consider the example of an eight-story department store of 320,000 square feet located in a downtown area and determine its classification under the Uniform Building Code (UBC).

1. Occupancy Group B, Division 2, based on occupancy description in Table No. 5-A of the UBC.

2. Type I Construction, because it has unlimited floor area, height, and number of stories. See Tables No. 5-C and 5-D of the UBC.

3. An Occupant Load of 6,000 persons, based on Table No. 33-A of the UBC, which specifies 30 square feet per occupant on the ground floor and 60 square feet per occupant on upper floors. ($40,000 \div 30 + 280,000 \div 60 = 1,333 + 4,667 = 6,000$.)

Since individual codes differ, one must always comply with the code applicable to the specific project being analyzed.

FIRE RESISTANCE

Fire resistance requirements serve several purposes. One is to permit the safe egress of the occupants in the event of fire. A second purpose is to maintain structural integrity and limit the spread of fire long enough for firefighters to extinguish the blaze. A third purpose is to provide sufficient protection to the structure to limit damage and avoid collapse. The major components of a building's structure are assigned minimum fire ratings by the code, depending on the fire zone, the building type, and the use of the building. Fire-resistance values are stated in terms of hours, and are required for the structural frame, the floors, walls, ceilings, roof, doors, and windows. Fire resistance is generally increased when automatic fire-extinguishing systems are incorporated. Required fire ratings range from 3/4 to 4 hours. The higher values apply to exterior walls, hazardous areas, and to elements that separate hazardous areas from adjacent areas with large occupancy loads.

It should be noted that a noncombustible structural material is not necessarily fire-resistant. Steel loses its strength and quickly distorts or collapses when subjected to high temperature. A fire-resistant building must have structural elements that are capable of withstanding heat for a definite period of time without collapse. Materials such as concrete, gypsum, or vermiculite plaster are used for this purpose. Their thickness is determined by the fire-resistive period required and the type and quality of insulating material employed. The use of asbestos for such insulation is now prohibited because it is carcinogenic.

Some codes specify in detail the construction of walls, ceilings, and other common building components, which satisfy various fire-resistive ratings.

Flame and Smoke Ratings

Flame-spread ratings and smoke-developed ratings are measures of the amount of flame and smoke generated by specific materials. Paint finishes and carpets are examples of rated materials. The ratings are established under standardized test conditions and are often used in specifying materials to be provided by contractors or vendors. Specifiers should be cautious of flame-spread ratings when materials are applied to large areas, since testing is performed on small samples. Caution should also be exercised with furnishings placed in buildings after completion, since they may greatly increase both smoke and flames in case of fire. Plastic and other similar materials now in use also contribute greatly to building fires, and they often generate highly toxic smoke as well.

Exits

A major aspect of all building codes is the provision of adequate exits from a building. Generally, the required number of exits is based on the number of occupants, with a minimum of two. Exits should always be separated in such a way that a single fire or other emergency cannot block all the exits simultaneously.

The total width of exits required for a building floor is determined by the total occupant load of that floor plus an additional allowance for occupants of floors above and below that floor, if those occupants must use the same exit routes. The width is usually calculated by dividing the total number of occupants to be served by a factor, such as 50, resulting in a total exit width expressed in feet. Another method found in some codes requires a "unit of exit width" for each 50 to 100 occupants,

the number of occupants being determined by a table in the code. Typically, a unit of exit width is 22 inches, with an additional half unit credited for each additional 12 inches of clear width.

Minimum widths of corridors, doorways, and stairways are specified by code, based on the use of the building. In some cases, the installation of a full sprinkler system permits a significant increase in the allowable number of occupants per unit of width, thus reducing the amount of circulation space required. The characteristics of required exit routes are usually specified by the code in some detail. These generally include: length, width, fire resistance of the enclosing surfaces, permitted length of dead-end corridors, lighting, directional signs, and ventilation.

Current practice also provides for an automatic ventilation control system which increases the air pressure in designated exit passages, thus preventing the flow of smoke into them.

The distance that an occupant must travel from any location in a building to a legal exit is usually limited to 150 feet in an unsprinklered building and 200 feet in a fully sprinklered building. Once the person has reached an enclosed exit passage, he or she is adequately protected from fire and may travel a lengthy route from there to a safe place outside the building.

Despite detailed exiting requirements, building codes cannot communicate to building occupants the critical evacuation procedures that may save lives. That must be done by periodic fire training and drills, which are often required by municipal law and fire insurance companies.

Stairways

Interior enclosed stairways must be protected by fire-resistant construction, the extent of which depends on the use of the building. Stairways that serve as required building exits must meet numerous detailed requirements described by the code. The width, handrail location, rise and run of the steps, size and location of landings, and headroom are all specified. The materials of construction and the fire ratings of the enclosing walls, ceilings, etc., are also specified, usually of one-hour rating.

In structures that are 75 feet high or greater, at least one of the required exits must be a smokeproof tower, which is also known as a "fire tower" or "smokeproof enclosure." A smokeproof tower consists of an enclosed stairway of noncombustible construction which is connected to interior areas of the building by balconies, open air vestibules, or mechanically ventilated vestibules. The intent is to prevent smoke from entering the tower, thereby creating a refuge through which occupants may exit a building. Not all codes permit mechanically ventilated vestibules, since their reliability depends on an uninterrupted electric power supply. Some codes require mechanical ventilation of smokeproof towers during an emergency, while others require a specified rate of air change by either gravity or mechanical circulation. If mechanical ventilation is used, the electrical power system must have emergency capability provided by an automatic and independently powered generator, or a reliable bank of charged batteries.

Ventilation systems should be designed to minimize circulation of smoke from a fire area to other parts of the building. This may be accomplished by isolating the circulation system of each fire area from that of every other. Another approach is to incorporate a circulation system which automatically shifts from normal operation to total exhaust when a fire is detected in the area. Some systems automatically increase the air pressure in corridors and vestibules, as previously mentioned, so as to prevent the flow of smoke and fumes into them. Thought should be given to the location of outside air intakes, in order to minimize drawing in smoke-laden air exhausted from a fire elsewhere in the building.

SMOKE PROOF TOWER

Figure 11.6

Panic

The possibility of panic during an emergency requires careful consideration, although it is not specifically detailed in the building code. A major factor in causing panic is the inability of a crowd of people to see escape routes clearly. The normally recognizable exits may be obscured by smoke, lack of light, or inadequate signage. Exit signs are particularly important and should be considered from the design stage through fixture specification. They should also be reviewed when partitions and doors are altered in the future, to ensure that escape routes remain accessible and clear.

In certain buildings, such as places of assembly, exit doors must be equipped with *panic hardware*, consisting of a horizontal bar on each door leaf, actuated by pressure in the direction of egress.

Exits and exit signs must be illuminated when a building is occupied and during emergencies. Their illumination power circuits must have greater reliability than general illumination lighting, but the means of providing this varies from one code to another. Special circuits connected ahead of the main breaker for the building may work well in some cases, but in others an independent source of supply may be necessary, such as batteries or an engine generator. The applicable electrical code will usually specify the requirements in detail.

In some situations, the building code may require public address equipment, called an "enunciator," to broadcast prerecorded or live messages to instruct occupants in the emergency evacuation process.

Vertical Transportation

Elevators are unacceptable as emergency egress from a building for the obvious reason that loss of electric power renders them useless and, worse, a trap for anyone caught inside. In addition, heat actuated elevator call buttons may direct elevators to the floor where a fire is located. In high-rise structures, many elevator shafts have no hall doors in the express portion of their travel. The occupants of a car stalled in this region, therefore, cannot escape, even through the elevator roof hatch. In addition, a car may be called to the fire floor, and it may stall there due to the panic-stricken crowd or because the door-closing photocells are obstructed by people or smoke.

Some codes require that an elevator must be available for use by firefighters during a fire.

The reason for this is that a fire floor in a skyscraper may be so high that it would be impractical for firefighters, burdened with hoses and other equipment, to reach the fire on foot. Such special elevators should have manual override controls and be free from the entrapment hazards of normal elevators.

Escalators penetrate floors and thereby provide a conduit for smoke and flame from one floor to another. Three methods are available for controlling this hazard. The first safeguard is an automatically operated rolling shutter door to seal the floor opening of an escalator. A second method consists of enclosing the escalator in a structure similar to a stairwell, with fire-rated enclosures and doors at each floor level. The third approach requires the installation of a sprinkler and automatic ventilation system to protect the escalator opening on each floor against smoke and flames.

Other Exitways

Ramps designed in accordance with the code may constitute a portion of the required legal exits from a building. However, escalators and moving sidewalks are not permissible as approved exits, since they may be operating in the wrong direction at the time of a fire. Revolving doors are sometimes permitted, depending upon the particular code, and in those cases the revolving doors must be collapsible. Pressure applied to opposite wings of such doors causes the wings to fold against each other in the direction of travel, opening both sides of the doorway as exits. However, a revolving doorway cannot always be counted as part of the required exit width due to uncertainty of use and limited effective width, even with the wings collapsed.

NORMAL POSITION

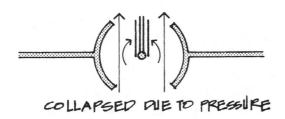

COLLAPSED DUE TO PRESSURE

COLLAPSIBLE
REVOLVING DOOR

Figure 11.7

Place of Refuge

The evolution of fire safety techniques in high-rise buildings has brought about the concept of a *place of refuge* during a fire. A floor space on the same level, but in a different part of a building or in an adjoining building, may serve as part of the required exit from a fire area. The place of refuge must be separated from the fire area by an adequately rated fire separation. In addition, there must be means of egress from the place of refuge; it cannot be a dead end. This method reduces the crowding of stairwells, which often occurs during the evacuation of large numbers of people to street level. It also provides quick access to a place of safety for the occupants; it lessens the need to descend many flights of stairs, which is tiring and time consuming; and it permits freer access by firefighters, there being fewer occupants in the stairwells. The floor area of the place of refuge must be adequate to accommodate both the normal occupants and those departing the fire area.

Standpipes

Codes may require several types of standpipes, depending upon building use, floor area, and building height. Standpipes are required for buildings of three or more stories.

Wet standpipes are continuously pressurized with water from a public source, a house tank, or other permanent water supply. They are connected to readily accessible hoses, in cabinets, so that they can be used easily by building occupants. There is usually a requirement for a fire department connection to a *siamese fitting*, which permits the fire department to increase water pressure and flow in the wet standpipe. Fire hose cabinets must be installed and provided with hoses of specified sizes and lengths. The location of the cabinets is determined by the requirement that at least one hose and nozzle must reach a specified distance to every point on its floor.

Dry standpipes, in contrast, are not connected to a constant source of supply, but have only a siamese fitting for the fire department connection. Being dry, they are not subject to freezing in cold weather. They are generally located in smokeproof stair towers and in enclosed stairways, for the exclusive use of the fire department. The requirements for dry standpipes vary widely from one code to another.

Combination standpipes are pressurized by a constant water supply and have a fire department siamese fitting. They serve both the occupants and the fire department, but are primarily used by the fire department. Not all codes allow combination standpipes.

Water supplied through wet or combination standpipe systems must flow at a specific rate, pressure, and time through a specified number of hoses, all of which constitutes the flow rate, expressed in minutes. A typical requirement for a wet standpipe is the ability to deliver 35 gpm (gallons per minute) from each of two outlets simultaneously for 30 minutes duration while maintaining 25 psi pressure at the outlets. This amounts to 2,100 gallons of water storage if a roof tank is used, but the required capacities vary widely from one code to another. Some codes require two sources of water supply under emergency conditions, and this may require the installation of a fire pump on the premises. If a fire pump is electrically driven, consideration must be given to the reliability of the electric power system. Engine-driven pumps are also available.

Building codes impose numerous safety requirements on projects during their construction phase, especially in the matter of fire protection. If standpipes are a part of the building design, they must be carried upwards, floor by floor, as construction progresses and kept in working order for immediate use at any time.

Sprinklers

Sprinkler systems are required by certain codes in specific situations, and may be optional in other situations. Automatic sprinklers are normally required in high hazard areas, such as high-rise hotels, vaults for storage of flammable film, paint spray booths, hazardous parts of theaters, some types of garages, and certain hazardous basements. But there is wide variation in the requirements of different codes. In general, installation of an automatic fire extinguishing system in areas where it is not mandatory increases the allowable floor area between fire-rated walls, or decreases the number of required exits. These economic incentives are often referred to as design "trade-offs." Sprinklers have a proven record of success in preserving life and property, but their high cost discourages their installation where not required by code.

An economic advantage of sprinklers is the reduced fire insurance rates applicable to a fully sprinklered building. The savings in insurance costs may well offset the initial costs of the full sprinkler system. A developer who plans on selling a building soon after completion, however, may decide to save money by omitting sprinklers and leave the increased fire insurance premiums to later owners. An institutional owner, on the other hand, may find it advantageous to do the opposite.

In light of recent fire deaths and injuries, it is clear that the public has a moral responsibility to insist that codes mandate the use of sprinklers in areas where their effectiveness in saving life and property has been clearly proven.

Fire-Rated Doors

Fire-rated doors are required to maintain the integrity of separation walls between fire areas. Windows are often provided in such doors to permit people approaching from opposite sides to see each other, and thus avoid collision. Such windows must be glazed with wire glass of restricted total area to avoid penetration by fire.

In areas of low or normal hazard, the code may permit fire doors to be held open under conditions of normal use, and closed automatically by springs or weights in the event of fire. Such doors may be held open by a fusible link which melts at a moderate temperature, or by an electro-mechanical device that is activated by a sensor responding to heat, smoke, or alarm system impulse.

As a general rule, whenever a separation between two fire areas is pierced by an air duct, an automatic fire damper (or fire assembly) must be installed. It is designed to close when activated by excessive temperature or smoke. The duct must be constructed so as to reduce the spread of fire through it.

Fire Alarms

Fire alarm systems are required in buildings such as hotels, schools, and other places of assembly. The systems are of two basic types: the first operates a local alarm on the premises only, while the second type additionally transmits a signal to the fire department. Such systems may be manually operated, or they may be equipped with automatic fire sensors. There are three basic types of sensing elements: fixed temperature sensors, which respond to ambient air temperature; smoke detectors, which respond to obstructing a light beam by smoke; and product-of-combustion detectors, which are activated by an interruption of a light beam or by ionization effects.

LOADS

Live Loads

Buildings must be designed to resist dead load (the weight of all the permanent parts of a building) plus live load.

Building codes specify the minimum live loads required for the design of floors and roofs. The design live loads on floors vary according to use, ranging from 40 to 250 pounds per square foot. The lower value is for occupancies such as dwellings, while the higher values are for heavy storage.

Roof live loads include those caused by people, equipment, materials, and objects, the design values of which are specified in the code. Snow loads are determined locally or regionally based on available snowfall records.

Lateral Loads

Lateral loads are of two types: seismic (earthquake) and wind.

The prevention of seismic damage to structures is considered by building codes in earthquake-prone areas. The underlying philosophy is as follows:

1. A structure whose foundation is situated on an earthquake fault is not expected to withstand the effects of an earthquake. However, every structure should be able to resist the effects of an earthquake occurring in a nearby fault.

2. A building should remain sufficiently intact to permit reasonably safe and rapid exit by its occupants.

3. Some components of a structure may fail, but the structure as a whole must not collapse.

A seismic zone map, such as that in the UBC, shows the degree of seismic risk in a given area. Design methods are also described in the code, based on research and the behavior of structures in past earthquakes.

Wind load design requirements are based on location, as shown on a map, and height above grade. For design purposes, building codes do not require that structures be able to withstand the effects of wind and earthquake simultaneously.

Other Code Requirements

Sanitation, ventilation, and illumination requirements are also covered by building codes, even though they are given less detailed attention than fire and other life safety hazards.

Toilet rooms and other sanitary plumbing facilities are covered in detail. In places of public assembly, separate water closets and lavatories must be provided for each sex. In addition, public water fountains are required. In larger work places, separate lavatory facilities are required for each sex. Food handling establishments are also subject to particular requirements, such as isolation of water closets from food preparation and storage areas.

The number of water closets, urinals, and lavatories in schools is normally based on the maximum student population expected. Codes also consider light and ventilation for spaces in general, while the ventilation requirements of toilet rooms are specified in greater detail. The required amount of ventilation is expressed in terms of cubic feet per minute (cfm) per occupant, minutes per air change, or air changes per hour. The air from toilet rooms, kitchens, and other odorous areas must be exhausted, and not recirculated.

Building codes often refer to specialized codes pertaining to individual trades such as electrical and plumbing. Where such references are made, performance, quality, and standards must meet the requirements of all governing codes. Sustainable design requires special attention to the type, quality, performance, and installation standards for design elements. (Sustainable design products often have unique performance standards governing the installation of products that need to be carefully specified.)

OTHER CODES

In 1970, a new set of federal standards came into existence, known as the Occupational Safety and Health Act or OSHA.

While its original purpose was to provide safe and healthy environments for employees, its practical effect was to create a whole new set of standards applicable to structures throughout the country. The standards are relevant to all projects during construction, and are predicated on the fact that construction work is inherently hazardous. It normally applies to work places such as factories, offices, and warehouses, but

residences are exempt after construction is completed.

Among the factors regulated by OSHA are: fire protection, scaffolding, electrical installations, ventilation, exposure to air contaminants, noise, and radiation hazards. In some instances existing codes were incorporated by reference into OSHA, such as the National Electrical Code, which makes it enforceable on a national scale. In other cases, new sections of code material were written. The requirements of OSHA are enforced by both state and federal officials, prompted in some cases by labor and employee groups.

Architects must learn how the OSHA code applies to their projects. Generally, the contractor is responsible for OSHA regulations during construction, but there are, inevitably, "gray areas" where responsibility is unclear.

The National Fire Protection Association (NFPA) develops more than 300 codes and standards adopted by different states and municipalities, in addition to their model codes. NFPA codes tend to be more restrictive than a standard code and in most instances, they govern.

Other standards that may concern the architect are those issued by the Federal Housing Administration (FHA), particularly "Minimum Property Standards for One and Two Living Units," FHA #300, and "Minimum Property Standards for Multi-Family Housing," FHA #2600. These cover many of the same areas as various building codes and are imposed upon residential construction financed by federally-guaranteed loans. Where building code and FHA standards differ, the more restrictive requirement is generally enforced. Sometimes a local code and FHA standard may conflict, in which case the difference is negotiated by the enforcing agencies, based on the practices of both.

SUMMARY

Building codes and other regulatory guides are in existence to maintain and constantly improve the safety and welfare of human life, and are to be used by architects as a minimum standard while reaching for a design objective. It is ultimately the responsibility of the architect to ensure that the project meets or exceeds the expectations prescribed by regulatory agencies and authorities possessing jurisdiction.

1. The total width of required exits in a building is determined by the

   A. degree of hazard of the building.

   B. flame-spread ratings of the building materials.

   C. number of occupants in the building.

   D. distance an occupant must travel to an exit.

2. The purposes of fire-resistance requirements in the building code include which of the following? Check all that apply.

   A. To permit safe evacuation of the occupants

   B. To prevent fire damage to the building

   C. To reduce the generation of toxic smoke

   D. To prevent structural failure for a specified period of time

3. Which of the following factors would NOT be regulated under the requirements of the Occupational Safety and Health Act?

   A. Exterior air quality

   B. Factory noise levels

   C. Warehouse fire protection

   D. Construction scaffolding

4. A building was constructed many years ago in compliance with the zoning ordinance in effect at that time. Since then, the zoning ordinance has been revised to be more restrictive. Therefore, the building would now be considered as

   A. restricted.

   B. conforming.

   C. conditionally acceptable.

   D. nonconforming.

5. If a private developer wished to develop a cemetery in an area currently zoned for light manufacturing, the developer should apply for a _____.

6. Which of the following are normally considered legal exits from a building?

   I.   Hydraulic elevator

   II. Reversible escalator

   III. Smokeproof tower

   IV. Revolving door

   V.   Open stairwell

   A. III only   C. II, III, and IV

   B. I and V   D. II, IV, and V

7. Among the advantages of a performance type building code is that it

   A. is easy to interpret.

   B. is simple to administer.

   C. promotes more imaginative design.

   D. results in lower construction costs.

8. Zoning ordinances normally regulate all of the following EXCEPT

    A. land use.

    B. emergency exits.

    C. building size.

    D. population density.

9. The difference between the terms "exit" and "means of egress" is that means of egress refers to

    A. all ways out of a building.

    B. all emergency ways out of a building.

    C. all legal ways out of a building.

    D. exactly the same thing as exit.

10. Proposed structures are classified by building codes according to which of the following characteristics?

    I.   Occupancy group

    II. Land use

    III. Fire hazard

    IV. Construction type

    A. I and IV   **C.** I, III, and IV

    B. II and III   **D.** I, II, III, and IV

11. Life safety codes

    A. are primarily intended to protect property from fire damage.

    B. are used in some jurisdictions instead of building codes.

    C. specify the location and number of exits in a building.

    D. consider all factors necessary to produce safe buildings.

12. Select the most correct statement. Building codes

    A. suggest ideal solutions to technical construction problems.

    B. are intended to insure that buildings will be structurally safe until the arrival of the fire department.

    C. are concerned only with assemblies of construction materials and systems, whereas zoning codes deal with the uses of a building.

    D. are concerned with containing fires so that a fire in one building will not damage other buildings.

13. A developer intends to construct an apartment project in a developed urban area that is adequately served by public transportation. Since the site is small and awkwardly shaped, the developer proposes providing one parking space per dwelling unit, rather than the 1-1/2 spaces required by ordinance. The developer should make application for a(n)

    A. easement.

    B. zoning variance.

    C. conditional use permit.

    D. nonconforming use permit.

14. Which of the following would NOT likely be a concern of an environmental impact statement for a new manufacturing facility?

    A. The socioeconomic level of employees

    B. The number of employees

    C. Employee traffic

    D. Employee working hours

15. On a 50,000-square-foot site with a FAR of 2, how many stories will a maximum-sized building be if half the site is set aside for parking?

A. 2   **C.** 4

B. 3   **D.** 5

16. Which of the following have an effect on a structure's ability to resist fire damage and protect occupants against fire hazard?

I.   Zoning ordinance

II. Building code

III. Building size

IV. Building location

V. Building covenants

A. I and II   **C.** II, III, and IV

B. II and III   **D.** I, IV, and V

17. If a local power company wished to gain access over private land to maintain their service poles, they would do so by means of

A. the zoning ordinance.

B. eminent domain.

C. a restrictive covenant.

D. an easement.

18. Neighborhood architectural review boards may have jurisdiction over a new dwelling's

I.   color.

II. cost.

III. size.

IV. style.

V. use.

VI. design compatibility.

A. I, IV, and V   **C.** II, IV, and V

B. II, III, and IV   **D.** I, III, IV, and VI

Lesson Ten

1. A See page 177.

2. B It should be obvious that a mortgage may be provided by anyone willing to lend money on a piece of property. See page 179.

3. B See page 178.

4. A The distinction here is that an access easement (A) merely permits passage over a piece of property, without any change of ownership of the property. Incorrect choices B, C, and D all require appropriating property for public use, and therefore, they may require condemnation proceedings. See page 182.

Lesson Eleven

1. C See page 205.

2. A and D Fire resistive requirements relate primarily to life safety, and only secondarily to structural damage.

3. A The purpose of OSHA is to regulate work places, not the exterior environment. Therefore, it applies to interior air quality, but not exterior. See page 211.

4. D See page 192.

5. Conditional use permit

6. A Legal exits are those that provide a protected path of escape from a building in the event of fire. Therefore, elevators and escalators are unacceptable, since loss of power would render them useless. Revolving doors are also generally unacceptable, as are open stairwells, which offer no fire protection.

7. C Since a performance code specifies desired results, rather than techniques, its use naturally encourages innovation. See page 201.

8. B The regulation of emergency exits is found in building codes, not zoning ordinances.

9. D The two terms are interchangeable.

10. C Land use is generally regulated by zoning ordinances, not building codes.

11. C Answer A is incorrect, since building and fire codes are intended to protect buildings from fire damage. In incorrect answer B, life safety codes are used in conjunction with, not instead of, building codes. Life safety codes primarily address egress (D is incorrect).

12. D Answer A is incorrect, since building codes are minimum, not ideal, standards. In incorrect answer B, the fire resistive requirements of building codes are intended to allow the evacuation of occupants within a specified period of time. Zoning ordinances regulate land use, while the type of construction required by building codes is a function of use as well as area, height, and fire resistive properties of materials and assemblies (C is incorrect).

13. B A zoning variance is granted when literal application of the zoning ordinance would cause undue hardship. See page 191.

14. A Choices B, C, and D all relate to the intrusion and impact of a large group of people on the existing environment. Correct answer A refers only to the economic level of those people, which would have little effect on the environment.

15. C FAR, or floor area ratio, is the ratio of the total allowable floor area to the area of the building site. Thus, a 50,000-square-foot site with an FAR of two allows a total floor area of 100,000 square feet on all floors. If half the site is set aside for parking, the remaining buildable site area is 25,000 square feet. Therefore, 100,000 allowable square feet of building divided by the buildable site area of 25,000 square feet results in a four-story building.

16. C   Among the choices, building codes (II) deal with fire-resistive standards, building size (III) is strictly limited by the type of fire-resistive construction, and building location (IV) may impose restrictions based on the fire district. Only zoning ordinances (I), which regulate land use, and building covenants (V), which limit the unrestricted use of a property, have little to do with fire hazard.

17. D

18. D   Architectural review boards operate by virtue of restrictive covenants, which are often incorporated with property ownership. Such covenants may control size (III) but not cost (II). They may also control exterior colors (I), style (IV), and general appearance (VI), but they may not control use (V), which is regulated by zoning ordinances.

Part IV

Project and Practice Management

SCHEDULING OF DESIGN AND CONSTRUCTION

12

ARCHITECTURAL PROCESS

After the planning process has been concluded, and the site has been selected, the architectural team will begin to focus on the project, including the project's buildings and related infrastructure.

Traditionally, the architect is faced with four components to every design decision:

1. Cost
2. Function
3. Aesthetics
4. Time

The new, sustainable ecological paradigm adds one additional component to form a pentagon of concerns.

5. Sustainability

The ingredients of the normal process have been discussed previously, but the new ingredient, sustainability, changes the meaning of all these pieces of this architectural process.

1. Cost

As architects put together budgets for their clients, they are always concerned with the first costs of the design components—the initial cost to purchase and install the design element.

Sustainable design has made the economic decision process more holistic. The decision to select a design element (such as a window, door, flooring, exterior cladding, or mechanical system) is now concerned with the "life-cycle" cost of the design.

1.1 *Life-Cycle Costing*

Life-cycle costing is concerned not only with the first cost, but the operating, maintenance, periodic replacement, and residual value of the design element.

For example, two light fixtures (A and B) might have different first cost: Fixture A has a 10 percent more expensive first cost than B. But when the cost of operation (the lamps use far less energy per lumen output) and the cost of replacement (the bulbs of A last 50 percent longer than the bulbs of Fixture B) is evaluated, Fixture A has a far better life-cycle cost and should be selected.

In this kind of comparison, the life-cycle cost may be persuasive; the extra cost of Fixture A may be recovered in less than two years due to more efficient operation and replacement savings.

In this situation the architect justified Fixture A to the owner, who benefits from more energy efficient lighting that continues to save the owner operating costs for the life of the building.

1.2 *Matrix Costing*

While designing a typical project, the architect faces numerous alternate decisions, a process that may be both intriguing and complex.

In nearly all projects, there is an established budget and program (including all the owner's functional requirements). The architect must balance the functional issues with the budgetary and aesthetic issues.

Sustainable design adds an ingredient to this matrix of decisions that may actually help the composition.

For example, decisions that allow the improved efficiency of the building envelope, light fixtures, and equipment may permit the architect to allow the engineer to reduce the size of the HVAC system, resulting in a budgetary trade-off. The extra cost of the improved envelope may be economically balanced by the diminished cost of the mechanical system.

This type of economic analysis, which evaluates cost elements in a broad matrix of interaction, is a very valuable architectural skill. The ability to understand the interaction between different building systems in a creative and organized fashion can differentiate an excellent architectural design from a simply adequate one.

2. Function

Functionality is one of the primary standards of architectural design. If the building doesn't perform according to the client's needs, then the building design has failed.

Sustainability adds a facet to functionality that even the owner may not initially appreciate.

As previously mentioned, life-cycle costing will affect the decisions in which elements are finally selected to form the final design. However, the search for sustainability may increase the dimensions of functionality.

Years ago, the design element could perform at the highest level regardless of its impact on the environment or energy use.

The fact that many industrial and residential buildings are operating much more efficiently now than in 1960 is evidence that the building design and construction profession is learning how to tune buildings to a higher degree of energy operation. But, with diminishing natural resources and increasing pollution of the environment, even more efficient design is necessary.

Today, architects will include sustainability in the selection of optimal functional design components.

For example, a roof system must be able to withstand a variety of weather conditions, be warranted to be durable a minimum of years, be able to be applied in a range of weather conditions, and have a surface with reflectivity that does not add to the urban heat effect.

3. Time

The schedule of a project is always a difficult reality of the design process. Time is a constraint that forces a systematic and progressive evaluation of the design components.

The sustainable component of the architectural process may add to the amount of time the architect will spend on the research for the project.

The architect may spend more time on a sustainable design with the result being a more integrated, sustainable project.

4. Aesthetics

The aesthetic of a project is the combination of the artistry of the architect and the requirements of the project.

Sustainable design has the reputation of emphasizing function and cost over beauty and appeal.

It is the architect's responsibility to keep all the design tools in balance. A project without aesthetic consideration will fail the client, its user, and the potential client that may be decid-

ing between the normal design process and one that considers a broader, integrated, sustainable approach.

5. Sustainability

The fifth point in the calculus of the architect is a new component that leads to a new, holistic evaluation of the design process. Because a piece of any living element must be part of the cycle of nature in order to survive, all manmade elements should now consider the mantra, "do no harm and be designed to be integrated within the cycle of all living things."

Architectural designs should create by-products, that can be recycled with other natural elements and not cause depletion of natural resources necessary for the health of future generations.

Sustainable designs should have four goals:

1. Designs that use less
2. Designs that recycle components
3. Designs that have components that are easily recyclable
4. Designs that have components that are fully biodegradable

DESIGN SCHEDULING

Establishing a Schedule

In furnishing professional services, an architect must prepare a time schedule that encompasses all phases of production, from initial conceptual planning to the start of construction. The architect must plan the judicious and efficient use of manpower and resources to achieve an economical, functional, and harmonious design, executed within a reasonable period of time, and with an efficient utilization of personnel. The managerial skills required for such planning and scheduling are based on experience and judgment.

To organize the schedule, the architect first separates the design effort into phases, which generally correspond to phases of the AIA standard owner-architect agreements as follows:

1. *Schematic design*, consisting of schematic drawings and other documents which describe the general relationships and space requirements of the project, along with a cost estimate.

2. *Design development*, consisting of preliminary drawings, outline specifications, and other documents which describe the form, size, and materials of a project, and the structural, mechanical, and electrical systems to be utilized. A preliminary cost estimate is also prepared during this phase.

3. *Construction documents*, consisting of working drawings, final specifications, and a final cost estimate.

4. *Bidding or negotiation*, which includes the receipt and evaluation of bids or negotiated proposals. It may also include preparing addenda to the contract.

5. *Construction administration*, consisting of the services rendered by the architect after bidding or negotiation to assure that the structure is built in accordance with the construction documents. In this phase the architect may issue change orders, approve shop drawings, choose or approve materials and colors, and issue payment approvals.

In complex projects, the five phases described may not be adequate. For example, schematic design may be divided into conceptual design and schematic design. Similarly, the construction documents phase may be organized into several subdivisions, so that work on one subdivision may be completed and bid before the next phase is begun.

The architect must estimate the time required for each phase of the work. The schematic design phase is the most difficult to estimate, since it has the greatest amount of variability. This phase of the work is usually done by a small design team, generally headed by a chief designer, and possibly including an engineer and other specialists. The design concept must be developed out of the skill and experience of the design team working closely with the client and each other. Among the factors affecting the time required for schematic design are:

1. *The size and complexity of the project,* complexity generally being more critical than size.

2. *The quality and completeness of the program information supplied by the client.* If the architect does not have an adequate statement of the client's requirements—a conclusive program—then it will be necessary to prepare one, or to improve what exists. In contrast, an experienced client will often furnish the architect with a thorough and reliable catalog of needs, thereby enabling the architect to begin work immediately. Such a client may provide the architect with information such as project goals, area requirements, functional relationships, zoning information, a site survey, and a budget.

3. *The decision-making ability of the client.* If the client has a decisive representative who has the authority to make decisions, schematic design can proceed at a rapid pace. On the other hand, if decisions require committee approval, or if they cannot be made expeditiously, schematic design time will be prolonged, with consequent loss of momentum. If the client and architect do not have an effective

communication system, the process is further delayed.

4. *The nature of the design team.* If the team is well balanced, if they work together harmoniously, if they are skilled and experienced, if they are able to work on the project without interruption, and if they can communicate readily with the client, then schematic design time will be kept to a minimum.

These factors illustrate why it is difficult to plan a time schedule for schematic design. For a simple, conventional project, schematic design can often be completed in one or two months. It is not unusual, however, for the schematic design of a complex project to require 12 months or more.

The design development and construction documents phases of the work are much more predictable than schematic design, assuming schematic design has been thorough and there are no program changes. A team of architects and drafters, headed by a project architect and/or job captain, develops the schematic design into preliminary design drawings, which are then developed into working drawings. If the project is large in scope, staffing must be increased commensurately. The length of time required to produce these drawings may not be directly proportional to the size of the project. A $10,000,000 project, for example, may require only 50 percent more time than a $2,000,000 project. The complexity of a project, rather than its size, determines scheduling and staffing requirements. During the preliminary design and design development phases, close coordination between consultants, client, and designers is vital.

Design development for a typical project takes from two to four months; the construction documents phase may typically require from three to seven months. The bidding or negotia-tion phase usually requires three to six weeks, regardless of the size of the project.

A less obvious factor that may influence the work schedule is project financing. Whether the client is an individual, a partnership, a corporation, or a public agency, money is required to convert a design into reality. Private clients may borrow money from a bank, while a public agency may have to obtain a bond issue. The client may use the time between work phases to obtain a financial commitment and may, in some cases, postpone authorization to the architect to proceed with a successive phase until financing is secured. This may take weeks or months for a private client and even longer for a public agency.

Client review and approval is customary between phases, and the time required for this will depend on the size and complexity of the project, as well as the ability of the client to make decisions.

Some projects require more than one cli-ent approval, which may lengthen the review period. For example, many public school projects require the approval of a state depart-ment of education as well as a local school district. Client review and approval usually takes between one week and one month, unless complications arise.

The time required for approval of plans by a building department or other public agency var-ies considerably, depending on the locality and type of project. For example, a state hospital project, which may require approval by a state agency as well as the local building depart-ment, may require up to three months for plan checking. In localities where the checking of plans is less critical, a building permit may be obtained within a week.

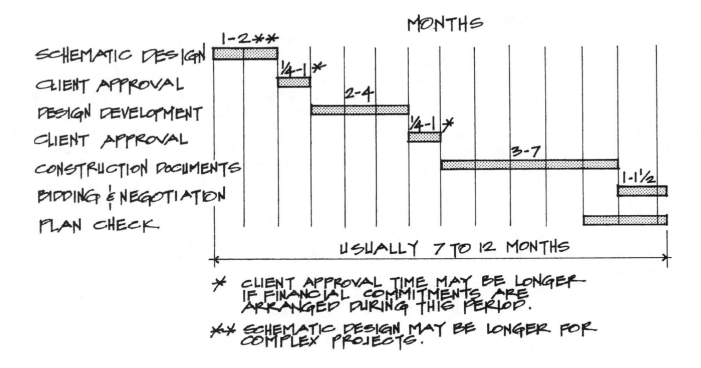

MONTHS

SCHEMATIC DESIGN 1-2**

CLIENT APPROVAL ¼-1*

DESIGN DEVELOPMENT 2-4

CLIENT APPROVAL ¼-1*

CONSTRUCTION DOCUMENTS 3-7

BIDDING & NEGOTIATION 1-1½

PLAN CHECK

USUALLY 7 TO 12 MONTHS

* CLIENT APPROVAL TIME MAY BE LONGER IF FINANCIAL COMMITMENTS ARE ARRANGED DURING THIS PERIOD.

** SCHEMATIC DESIGN MAY BE LONGER FOR COMPLEX PROJECTS.

BAR GRAPH FOR SCHEDULING OF DESIGN

Figure 12.1

Application for a building permit requires the filing of construction drawings and specifications and this is often done near the conclusion of the construction documents phase so that the building permit is obtained at about the same time the construction contract is let. This is not always the case, however. Sometimes the application for the building permit is not made until after the bidding period, while in other cases, the permit is obtained before the bidding phase. Whatever order is followed, the time required for plan approval should be considered by the architect in preparing the time schedule.

In completing the time schedule, the architect assembles all the time estimates into a bar graph, as shown in Figure 12.1. The bar graph indicates ranges of time for each phase. In an actual project, however, a specific period of time would be assigned for each phase.

Contingencies

In organizing the architectural production schedule, the architect must consider the possibility of unexpected problems that may arise. There may be delays with the building department, consultants may need additional time because of unique problems inherent in the project, there may be staffing problems in the architect's office if the work load changes suddenly, or the client may be less decisive than expected. For these and other reasons, it is wise to include a contingency factor in the schedule. If the architect estimates the total required time to be eight months, an additional allowance of at least two to four weeks seems prudent.

The schedule should be flexible and responsive to changing conditions. For example, if the schematic design phase extends beyond its scheduled completion date, it should be possible to reduce the time allotted to design development and construction documents.

Working with a Builder

The preceding discussion assumes a conventional sequence of events in which the construction documents are completed before bidding or negotiation begins. In recent years, however, closer methods of work coordination between the architect-engineer team and the builder have been developed. Many architects now work closely with a contractor from the conceptual phase through the completion of working drawings. A result of this cooperation is often a guarantee of maximum project cost, furnished to the owner by the contractor, upon completion of contract documents. This is referred to as a GMP—a "guaranteed maximum price."

Working closely with a builder has a significant effect on the architect's production schedule. More time must be given to schematic design if the architect is to produce a concept that the contractor considers economical. Design development, likewise, may take more time; however, construction documents will probably take the same time. Since the time during which the drawings are being prepared overlaps actual construction, overall project time is generally shortened. But there are risks in this procedure that the building design may not be fully developed or the components fully resolved.

Regardless of the procedure followed, the working drawings and specifications must be complete, clear, and correct. In some cases where the architect works closely with the contractor who will construct the project, the documents may be less specific, allowing the contractor leeway in procedures, details, and materials. But this practice can be risky for both, and hence, should be restricted to common or repetitive projects. With close architect/builder cooperation, the bidding and negotiation phase may be omitted entirely, since these activities become a continuous process.

The total scheduled production time is usually similar to what it would be if the project were done conventionally. The architect's staff hours, however, may be greater because of the time spent coordinating with the contractor and possible redesigning. There are no short cuts; architectural projects require attention to detail, and invariably that takes time.

Extending the Schedule

All creative activity requires time, which should be enough to absorb information and develop ideas, but not so much that momentum and interest lag. For architectural design, an optimum work schedule is one in which the necessary work can be accomplished comfortably without expanding or shortening the schedule.

On a project with an extended schedule, principal team members may retire or take other positions before completion of the work. A recent state college project was delayed four years, between design development and construction documents, because of lack of funding. When the project resumed, the original project architect, mechanical and structural engineers, and key client personnel had made career changes. The resumption of work entailed starting over. The groundwork had to be re-established, resulting in wasted time and effort.

One of the most significant effects of an extended design schedule is the increased cost due to inflation. In the recent past, inflation ran as high as 1 percent per month. At that rate, a $10,000,000 project that is delayed two months would cost the owner an additional $200,000. The additional cost resulting from the delay of a project may cause it to be terminated or reduced in scope. For example, in the case of the state college project mentioned above, the original project budget could not be increased during the four-year delay, and therefore the scope of the project had to be reduced by about one-third. The facility as finally built was smaller and of lower quality than it would have been without the four-year delay.

Shortening the Schedule

Clients often want their projects completed in as short a time as possible. During periods of inflation, there is additional pressure to shorten the design schedule. The purpose of any schedule, however, is to make optimum use of staff effort and resources. Therefore, to achieve significant reductions in time, one or more of the following methods must be employed:

1. The architectural team works overtime. While this saves time, it is costly and inefficient. A person working a ten-hour day over a long period of time cannot consistently produce 25 percent more work than someone working an eight-hour day.

2. Hire more people, bring in part-time or free lance staff, or subcontract work to another firm. All of these solutions are possible and will probably save time, but they are also costly and inefficient. New staff people will not be familiar with office procedures or the particular project, and their competence is unknown. Part-time people may be experienced and competent, but they are usually expensive. Subcontracting to another firm is feasible, but this is expensive, and coordination and supervision may be awkward.

3. Reduce the man-hours spent on the project. This generally results in a lower-quality job. Quality work requires adequate time to produce, and if that time is not available, an incomplete set of working drawings and specifications may result. Under these circumstances, one can expect documents which are incomplete, unclear, and likely to contain errors and inconsistencies. That, in turn, implies future problems, delays, and excessive change orders during construction.

Thus, the net effect of a reduced time schedule is likely to be a higher cost for design, a higher cost for construction, and a lower quality project. During periods of high inflation, an owner may be willing to tolerate a degree of increased costs with decreased quality, but this decision should be made only with the client's full appreciation of the consequences.

Methods of shortening both the design and construction schedule, simultaneously, will be described shortly.

CONSTRUCTION SCHEDULING

Establishing a Schedule

By their very nature, all construction projects are complicated, since they involve the work of numerous trades and subcontractors, all of which must be coordinated. Equipment must be utilized efficiently; materials must be ordered, stored, and used in a logical sequence; and accurate time schedules and costs must be recorded.

When a contractor prepares a construction schedule for a project, it is generally based on past experience. But no two projects are ever exactly alike, no two sites are the same, and therefore construction schedule estimates must be tempered with judgment. Contractors must consider a number of factors, including the following:

1. *The construction documents.* If these have been well prepared, relatively few problems or delays may be expected. Conversely, a poor set of working drawings or specifications will lead to disputes among the architect, contractor, and subcontractors. Such disputes consume considerable time and energy.

2. *The architect-engineer.* Some architects and engineers are extremely demanding regarding the interpretation of the contract documents. Others are less demanding and more amenable to changes.

3. *The subcontractors.* The contractor must evaluate their ability to perform the work properly and on time, and to coordinate their work with others.

4. *The contractor's organization.* The skills of the project manager, field superintendent, and the office and field staffs must be considered in relation to the specific project. Some managers and superintendents are more capable of expediting the work than others. Also, the particular work load of the contractor will influence his ability to divert staff and equipment to and from the project under consideration.

5. *Material dealers.* The contractor must assess their reliability in meeting delivery schedules on time and correctly.

6. *The size and complexity of the project.* Complexity is one of the most critical elements in planning a construction schedule.

7. *Site conditions.* The size and accessibility of a construction site work area are critical factors in schedule planning. So is the condition of the site itself—its drainage, vegetation, subsoil, etc.

8. *The weather.* This is important, especially in the colder areas of the country, where projects may have to be shut down during snowstorms, heavy rainstorms, or periods of extreme cold.

9. *The possibility of labor troubles.*

10. *The possibility of material shortages* or delay in obtaining critical equipment.

The contractor must estimate the time required for each construction operation and the sequence of these operations in order to establish the schedule.

CPM (Critical Path Method)

The first step in developing a "critical path" is the planning phase, in which a diagram is drawn indicating the order in which the various operations comprising the project are to be accomplished. The project is divided into concise tasks called "activities," and these are represented by arrows on the CPM chart.

Each activity has a definite start and finish represented by circles, and referred to as "events" or "nodes." An "event" is defined as that moment when a preceding activity has been completed and the following activity may begin. Important points in the construction process, such as the roofing of a new building, are referred to as "milestone events."

In CPM planning there is no indication of time; the arrows are not drawn to a time scale. The tail of an arrow indicates the start of an activity and the head of an arrow, the finish, and each arrow is associated with a start and finish event. No new activity can be started until activities represented by all the previous arrows have been completed.

The completed CPM diagram is known as a *network diagram.* The network must be continuous, with no gaps or discontinuities.

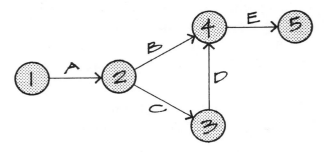

NETWORK DIAGRAM

Figure 12.2

In the network diagram shown in Figure 12.2, activity A starts at event 1 and terminates at event 2. Activities B and C cannot start until A is completed. Activities B and C can proceed simultaneously; however, activity D cannot start until C is completed. Activity E, starting with event 4 and finishing with event 5, cannot start until both activities B and D are completed. The construction of a footing supported on drilled cast-in-place concrete piers will now be considered.

Excavation of earth, construction of footing forms, and procurement of reinforcing steel can all proceed independently of each other. Drilling of piers follows excavation. Pier steel cannot be set until after *both* drilling of piers and procurement of pier steel have been completed. Pouring the piers follows setting of pier steel. Footing forms are set after *both* pouring of piers and construction of footing forms have been completed. Setting footing steel proceeds after *both* setting footing forms and procurement of footing reinforcing steel are completed. Finally, pouring footing follows setting footing steel.

The network diagram for the work described above is shown in Figure 12.4. Note that each

activity starts and finishes with an event, shown as a numbered circle, and that the end event always has a higher number than the starting event. Each event number occurs only once in the network.

While the pier-supported footing is a simple project, it serves to illustrate the value of CPM in job planning. The network is a model of the project, and its preparation requires the contractor to analyze the job logically from start to finish. The diagram communicates the job logic far better than any verbal description or bar graph.

Sometimes different portions of a project are planned separately, with separate network diagrams. For example, a project may consist of two buildings with connecting utilities. Events common to both networks are called *interface events*, and are usually shown as in Figure 12.3.

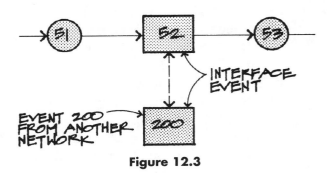

Figure 12.3

CPM Scheduling

After the project has been divided into concise activities and their logical sequence has been determined and charted in the network diagram, the time required for the project must be determined. Thus far, only the activities and their relationships have been considered; now the element of time is applied to the chart.

The contractor estimates the time required for each activity, based on past experience.

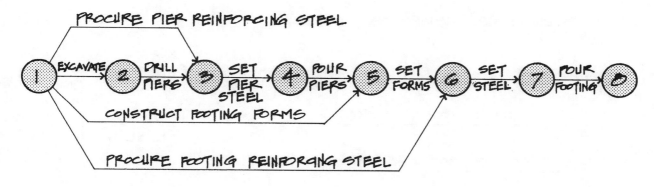

NETWORK DIAGRAM FOR PIER-SUPPORTED FOOTING

Figure 12.4

A normal working day is taken as the unit of time. The assumption is made that materials and labor will be readily available, and that a normal level of labor and equipment will be utilized. Where subcontractors are involved, the contractor may consult with them regarding the time required to perform their specific activities. The estimated activity times in working days are now noted on the network diagram below each arrow. (See the network diagram in Figure 12.5.)

In preparing an accurate time estimate, the reliability of the subcontractors is critical. A general contractor, therefore, should be familiar with the subcontractors and their work, and consider only those who are prequalified or otherwise highly dependable.

Critical Path

The simple project illustrated in the network diagram includes several paths, from start to finish, and each has a varying total time duration. For example, path 1-2-3-4-5-6-7-8 requires a total time of $1 + 1 + 1 + 1 + 2 + 1 + 1 = 8$ days. Path 1-5-6-7-8 requires $2 + 2 + 1 + 1 = 6$ days. Since *each* path must be traversed to complete the project, the total project time

is established by the path with the *longest* total required time. This is known as the critical path, and is generally shown as a heavy line. In the diagram in Figure 12.5, the critical path is 1-6-7-8, with a total time of $14 + 1 + 1 = 16$ days.

The activities along the critical path are called critical activities—in this case consisting of procuring reinforcing steel, setting footing steel, and pouring footings. If a critical activity is delayed, it will delay the completion of the project. These activities, therefore, must be carefully monitored during construction in order to keep the project on schedule.

Float

All paths in the network diagram, other than the critical path, are called *float paths*. The float is the difference in time duration between the critical path and any other path. Path 1-2-3-4-5-6-7-8, which requires 8 days, has a float value of 8, since it is 8 days shorter than the critical path time of 16 days. Similarly, Path 1-5-6-7-8, which requires 6 days, has a float value of 10. The float, then, is a measure of the extra time available for an activity or group of activities.

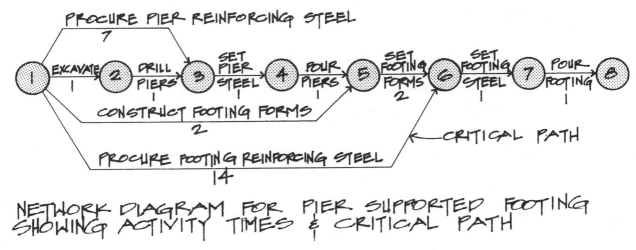

NETWORK DIAGRAM FOR PIER SUPPORTED FOOTING SHOWING ACTIVITY TIMES & CRITICAL PATH

Figure 12.5

As long as float time is not exceeded, no delay in project completion time will result. The path 1-2-3-4-5-6-7-8, for example, which we have determined to have a float value of 8, can be delayed up to 8 days without delaying project completion. This delay can occur in one or more activities along the path, providing the total delay does not exceed 8 days. The delay may occur only in activities from 1 through 6, since 6-7 and 7-8 form part of the critical path.

Project Calendar

The contractor, having determined that the finish date of the project is 16 working days after its start, now converts this to calendar days by multiplying by 7/5, since there are five working days in each seven-day week. ($16 \times 7/5 = 22.4$, say 23 calendar days.) Knowing the project starting date, the contractor can calculate the completion date, as well as the start and finish dates of all activities. He now establishes a project calendar, indicating the scheduled starting and completion dates of all the activities within the project. Critical activities are noted in color or boldface, since any delay in the schedule of these activities will delay completion of the project.

If the job schedule has been prepared carefully and realistically, the field work will proceed at an efficient pace. If excessive time has been allowed for certain activities, a more relaxed pace may result, leading to increased labor and overhead costs.

There can be great variation in the duration of construction projects, depending on the factors mentioned previously. However, most building construction projects require from 9 to 18 months.

Contingencies

A realistic schedule should incorporate an allowance for project delays caused by weather or other unforeseen events. A reasonable allowance can be made for the number of working days expected to be lost because of weather, depending on the season and the activity. Obviously, it is impossible to be precise regarding potential delaying factors such as accidents or labor strikes. Some contractors add a fixed percentage to the total estimated time to allow for such possibilities, or they may incorporate contingency provisions in the construction contracts.

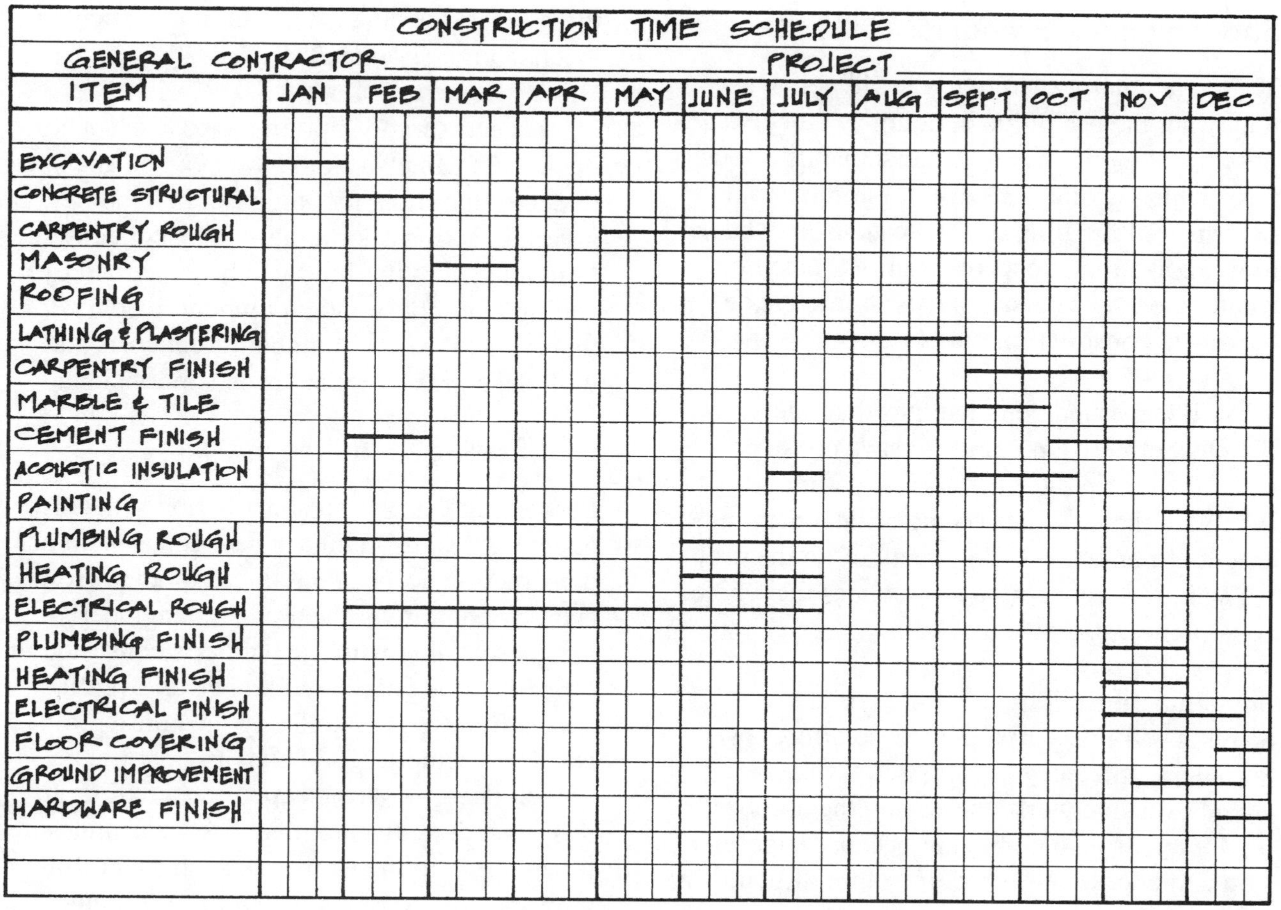

ITEM	JAN	FEB	MAR	APR	MAY	JUNE	JULY	AUG	SEPT	OCT	NOV	DEC
EXCAVATION	▭											
CONCRETE STRUCTURAL		▭		▭								
CARPENTRY ROUGH					▭							
MASONRY			▭									
ROOFING							▭					
LATHING & PLASTERING								▭				
CARPENTRY FINISH										▭		
MARBLE & TILE									▭			
CEMENT FINISH		▭									▭	
ACOUSTIC INSULATION							▭		▭			
PAINTING												
PLUMBING ROUGH		▭				▭						
HEATING ROUGH						▭						
ELECTRICAL ROUGH		▭					▭					
PLUMBING FINISH											▭	
HEATING FINISH											▭	
ELECTRICAL FINISH											▭	
FLOOR COVERING												▭
GROUND IMPROVEMENT											▭	
HARDWARE FINISH												

CONSTRUCTION TIME SCHEDULE
GENERAL CONTRACTOR_____ PROJECT_____

Figure 12.6

CPM Calculations

The example of a pier-supported footing describes a simple project; however, the same logic and scheduling technique is used on large and complex projects. CPM programming can be done at a simple level or a complex one. Computer programs designed for CPM have proven very useful, once the basic activity sequencing and activity times are known. CPM is an extremely helpful planning and management tool, and its use in construction planning and scheduling has become almost universal.

Bar Graphs

Bar graphs have long been used for planning and scheduling construction projects. They indicate the starting and finishing dates of major phases of the work and can be clearly understood by all concerned. Their main disadvantage is that they do not indicate the relationship between the sequence of activities, or the dependency of an activity on the completion of a previous activity. The bar graph therefore is inferior to CPM as a management tool, but superior to CPM as a means of visual communication. Bar graphs, such as the one shown in Figure 12.6, continue to be widely used in construction.

Shortening the Schedule

There are a number of reasons why an owner may want the use of his building as quickly as possible. Among these are the demands of business, which is often the case for commercial or industrial facilities. Other reasons may be to minimize the effects of inflation, inclement weather, or the persistent costs of interest on borrowed construction funds.

The CPM method demonstrates that one of the most effective methods to save construction time is to reduce the critical path time. Although the activities on the critical path may amount to only 25 or 30 percent of all the project activities, reducing them reduces the whole construction schedule.

Shortening the durations of the critical activities will very likely increase direct cost, because inefficiency is increased through added overtime work. Increasing the number of workers is also inefficient because supervision and coordination become more difficult. In general, the contractor's direct costs increase as the schedule is compressed into a shorter-than-normal time.

On the other hand, the contractor's overhead *decreases* as the schedule time is shortened. Since the total project cost is the sum of direct costs and overhead, and their effects by shortening the schedule are opposite, acontractor may find it worthwhile to analyze their effects and determine a balance which represents the lowest total project cost. A computer can be highly useful in doing this for a complex job.

Maintaining quality control becomes more difficult as the schedule time is shortened. Errors are more likely to occur because of the increased difficulty of proper supervision. The highest project quality is achieved when the project schedule is normal, that is, neither extended nor shortened.

If it is necessary to shorten the project schedule, the CPM network diagram can be analyzed to determine if the job logic can be modified, or if certain activity durations can be condensed. Individual activity times can be expedited by adding man-hours and equipment, recognizing that this will result in higher direct costs and will place greater demands on supervision.

Fast-Track Scheduling

Shortening design and construction schedules generally results in higher design costs, higher construction costs, and reduced quality. However, by combining the architect/engineer's design schedule with the builder's construction schedule, it is possible to realize an overall saving of time in completing the entire project. This technique is known as "fast-track," "accelerated," or "telescoped" scheduling. In this procedure, the architect first determines the major building elements, such as the column spacing, foundation system, mechanical systems, etc., before the detailed arrangements are worked out. The architect then produces detailed working drawings for a portion of the work on which the contractor may begin construction—site work, utilities, foundations, or possibly framing. Meanwhile, further detailed architectural design continues so that the architect produces his work just slightly ahead of the construction crews.

This approach requires close coordination among architect, engineers, client, and contractors. Since the design concept of building elements is established very early, oversights must be expected, and the correction of errors is generally an integral part of fast-track scheduling. However, major design revisions are all but precluded, except at very great cost.

Fast-track scheduling usually requires staged bidding, in which the project is organized into a number of separate stages or contracts—as many as 20 or 30—that are awarded to different contractors at different times. Thus, it may not be possible to obtain a fixed price for the entire project in advance of construction, as with conventional contracting that employs one general contractor. However, to assure some degree of cost and time control and establish responsibility, a construction manager (CM) may be used to supervise the construction process. Most contractors are able to function either as general contractors or construction managers.

Construction management may also be performed by architectural firms. But large and complex jobs are usually better served by those whose expertise is in the actual construction of buildings.

A comparison of conventional and fast-track scheduling for a $7,000,000 hospital is shown in Figure 12.7, indicating that the construction would be completed seven months earlier if fast-track scheduling were used. As design and construction become more complex and the use of building systems more widespread, we can expect that methods of design and construction scheduling will become more logical, increasing the use of computers for planning and management.

SUMMARY

Some architects may find their roles expanded to that of developer, builder, or manager. Whatever the role, it will be essential for the architect to become familiar with new management techniques, since they will have an increasing influence over how future construction work is done.

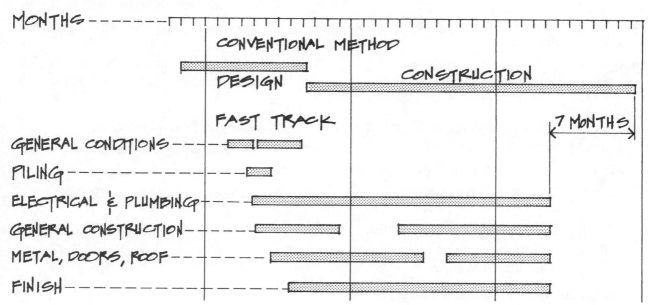

COMPARISON OF CONVENTIONAL METHOD (DESIGN·BID·BUILD) VS. FAST TRACK

Figure 12.7

LESSON 12 QUIZ

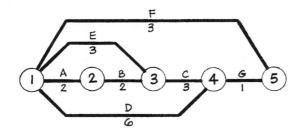

1. With reference to the CPM network diagram above, select the correct statement.

   A. Activity C cannot begin until both B and E are completed.

   B. Activity G cannot begin until F is completed.

   C. Activity F cannot begin until G is completed.

   D. Activity E cannot begin until A is completed.

2. Referring to the same diagram, what is the critical path?

   A. 1-5   C. 1-3-4-5

   B. 1-4-5   D. 1-2-3-4-5

3. Referring to the same diagram, what is the critical path time?

   A. 3 days   C. 8 days

   B. 7 days   D. 20 days

4. Which of the following would normally influence a contractor's construction schedule? Check all that apply.

   A. Quality of construction documents

   B. Reliability of material dealers

   C. Total construction cost

   D. Size of the project

   E. Anticipated weather conditions

5. Fast-track scheduling is appropriate in situations that require

   A. minimum construction costs.

   B. minimum construction time.

   C. strict adherence to the budget.

   D. strict adherence to the drawings.

6. An architect estimates that design and production for a project will take one year. The client, however, requests that the total time be reduced to nine months. By using the shorter time schedule, what would be the likely outcome?

   A. The general quality of design and production will be unaffected.

   B. The quality of the construction documents will be lower.

   C. The construction budget will be higher.

   D. The construction time will be greater.

7. By shortening an architect's time schedule for design and production of drawings, his or her

   A. labor costs would increase.

   B. overhead would increase.

   C. profit would increase.

   D. documents would be unaffected.

8. Arrange the following tasks for a typical project in ascending order of scheduled time, that is, from the task requiring the least time to the most.

I. Schematic design phase

II. Bidding phase

III. Client approval

IV. Design development phase

V. Construction documents phase

A. II, I, III, V, IV

B. I, III, II, V, IV

C. III, I, IV, II, V

D. III, II, I, IV, V

9. An architect's scheduling and staffing requirements for a specific project are dependent on the project's

A. size. **C.** complexity.

B. cost. **D.** quality.

10. Reducing the critical path time will very likely

A. increase the project cost.

B. extend the construction time.

C. have no effect on the float time.

D. have no effect on project quality.

BUDGET ANALYSIS AND COST ESTIMATING

13

THE IMPORTANCE OF BUDGETING

There are many ways to develop a project budget. Private developers, who build for profit, invariably begin with the idea that a certain type of building project in a certain location would be profitable. A more detailed feasibility study is then made that examines the costs of site acquisition, fees, financing, construction, etc. The study also examines the profitability of the project, including its likely income and its costs of operation, such as mortgage payments, taxes, utilities, and insurance.

On the basis of market studies, the developer begins to determine the feasibility of the proposed development. In the case of rental property, the developer studies comparable rental rates; in the case of properties for sale, he analyzes comparable recent sales. The developer then establishes a budget for the proposed building, and presents the architect with figures based on the economics of the venture. The architect, utilizing his or her professional skill and knowledge, then advises the developer of the limitations and possibilities of the project budget.

If the project requires a certain number of rentable square feet in order to be economically feasible, the gross size of the building will be determined. However, three basic components then come into play: construction cost, project size, and level of quality. These three components are variable and closely interrelated. For example, if the project size is increased, then the construction cost must also be increased or the level of quality will be reduced. Similarly, if the construction cost is decreased, then either the project size or quality will decrease as well.

Budgets must also be developed for institutional projects, those built to serve the public, rather than earn a profit. The budget may be based on a planning program prepared by the agency using the facility, or by a public building authority acting on the agency's behalf. Such a budget may become the basis for an appropriation by a legislative body, and therefore it must be reliable. Construction funds may have to be apportioned over a period of years, and should therefore allow for inflation.

When a project architect is hired, he or she must analyze the client's building program in relation to the construction budget. If a conflict between program and budget is found, an adjustment will have to be made in one factor or the other, otherwise the quality of work may suffer. Site conditions are among the most common sources of program or budget adjustment. Adverse geological conditions, for example, can result in added costs for excavation, grading, or utility installation. Unanticipated costs such as these can have a significant effect on the funds available for building construction. For projects with fixed budgets, adjustments in building size or quality may be necessary when high unanticipated costs occur. In such instances, it may be difficult for an architect to design to an acceptable quality level without reducing the size of the project.

These realities of the development process illustrate the importance of employing experienced professionals during the building project development in order to establish a workable balance among the variables of cost, size, and quality.

Inflation is another factor in project development planning, because a fixed budget in an inflationary period purchases less each day. An inflation factor should be included in the budget, and delays in project development should be reduced to a minimum. Good project planning will avoid, or at least lessen, the added costs of inflation.

It is important that project budgets be developed concurrently with building programs, that they be well planned, and that they convey a clear understanding of goals and priorities. Among the most critical budgetary decisions are those made during the earliest stages of development. Life-cycle costing, the economics of the full life of a building system, is a budgetary tool that the sustainable design approach encourages. It is a broader evaluation of the cost of architectural elements that consider more than the first cost of a component. Life-cycle costing considers also the maintenance and energy costs (operation) of the architectural system.

PROJECT DEVELOPMENT BUDGET

The total development cost of a project includes far more than the cost to construct the building; site costs, furnishings, professional services, and fees for permits, inspections, and financing must also be considered. In order to avoid unnecessary expense, a project budget should be prepared prior to committing large amounts of time, effort, and money. There are several ways to prepare a budget. Although no two projects are identical, and each situation involves somewhat different factors, certain similarities do exist between projects.

Therefore, it is possible to use standardized budget outline forms that apply to most situations. Some public institutions develop their own outlines, and it is common practice for an architect to follow such an established format. Since the basic items in a project budget are similar, although they may be expressed differently, it is not difficult to use modified formats.

An example of a typical project budget is illustrated in this lesson.

As previously mentioned, development budgets should consider the possible escalation of construction costs. Since these are projected at the time the budget is prepared, reliable historical figures must be applied and assumptions made regarding probable increases. It is normal practice to anticipate construction cost escalation on the basis of an annual increase, projected to the midpoint of construction. Care must be taken to use indexes that are applicable to the type of project, type of construction, and geographic location being considered.

Budget Composition of Example Project

In order to consider the various parts of a project budget, a hypothetical project will be examined, and the applicable categories discussed.

A division of a state university, specifically a research institute, plans to construct a laboratory of desert biology on a site donated by the state. The building program has been developed, and each function and space has been programmed in terms of function, area, and relationships.

The gross area of the building is 10,000 square feet, yielding approximately 6,400 net usable square feet. The site is gently sloping desert land without major improvements. It is bounded on one side by a paved secondary road; however, all utilities (water, gas, sewer, power, and communication) must be brought to the site from a point 3,000 feet to the north within existing easements along a road to be paved by the state. Site development will include parking for 25 cars, drives, curbs, gutters, concrete walks, landscaping, and irrigation.

Approximately 60 percent of the net usable area will be used for so-called "wet laboratories," which include water, gas, compressed air, distilled water, and sinks with chemical drains. The remaining net usable area will consist of office, library, cold storage and freezer rooms, animal rooms, aquatics rooms, plant rooms, data processing rooms, shop, and stock rooms. There will also be toilets, mechanical rooms, and circulation space, which constitute the remainder of the building's gross area.

The entire building will be air conditioned, and a special exhaust system for the laboratories is required. A uniform lighting system, achieving a minimum intensity of 75 foot-candles at the task level is specified. The building will be equipped with laboratory furniture, including acid resistant tops, sinks, and waste pipes. An internal communication system connected to the public telephone system is to be provided with instruments located in each laboratory and each office.

An architect has been asked to prepare a budget for the development of the entire project, from design through completion, which will be used as a capital outlay estimate to procure private funds for the development of the facility.

It is important to distinguish between the project budget and construction estimates, which will be developed later. The purpose of the project budget is to develop cost parameters within which the owner and architect will work. Construction estimates, on the other hand, generally require adjustments during the course of development. The project budget establishes development cost limits, which reflect all anticipated costs.

To assure inclusion of all possible expenditures, it is helpful to develop a budget outline form, as shown in Figure 13.1. Applying the budget outline form to our example project, it is now possible to prepare a project development budget, item by item, as follows:

1. Site Acquisition

Since the site has been donated to the institution, no major direct costs are incurred. To transfer title, both parties agreed to a sale price of one dollar. When land acquisition involves a conventional sale and purchase, such items as purchase price, commissions, legal fees, and other transfer costs must be included as part of the total project cost. Since our example site was donated, no amount is entered on this line.

2. Construction

A. Off-site work includes all improvements *outside* of the property lines of the project. This work may include basic utilities and all services required to make the development operable. In this project it is necessary to budget for the installation of water service, gas service, sewer line, power lines (underground or overhead), and communication lines from a point 3,000 feet to the north. These services are located in public easements along the road. Paving of the road, as well as installation of curbs, gutters, and storm drains will be paid for by the state. The size of each of these services will have to be determined and the costs estimated by the state or the architect's consulting engineers. Costs are determined on the basis of dollars per lineal foot for trenching, piping, conduit, and cable. These unit costs, multiplied by 3,000, will provide the budget figure for off-site development costs.

B. On-site work includes all improvements *within* the property lines, but excludes the building itself. This may include roads, walks, parking areas, landscaping, sprinklers, lighting, pools, fountains, walls, fences, etc. In preparing the budget for on-site work, the architect must be aware of any unusual site conditions that may require special work, such as blasting where rock is encountered. Here again, the architect's consulting engineers can furnish unit cost information for various elements of site work.

Experience may help the architect determine what percentage of the total construction cost is apportioned to site work. It is not unusual to allow between 10 and 20 percent of the construction cost for this. In the case of our example project, the budget must include installation of all utilities and services from the point of entry at the property line to the building, the installation of a paved parking lot for 25 cars (approximately 10,000 square feet), and all necessary driveways, service roads, curbs, gutters, storm drains, concrete walks, landscaping, and irrigation. Items such as works of art, special lighting, and signage should be included in a separate budget item provided for this purpose.

C. Building cost must include all work related to the structure and its systems. To estimate the cost of construction, the architect makes use of various cost data sources which are based on recent and relevant examples. One such data source is the *Dodge Building Cost Calculator and Valuation Guide*, published by McGraw-Hill. This provides unit cost figures for buildings of varying qualities in the following categories: 1) Residential, 2) Commercial/Industrial, 3) Public, 4) Medical, 5) Educational/ Religious, and 6) Miscellaneous. This source also includes cost multipliers, which adjust for varying geographic locations in the United States. Such cost tables provide accurate average unit costs.

BUDGET OUTLINE FORM

Name of Project: _____

Date of Budget: _____

Anticipated Construction Start: _____

Net Area: _____Square Feet

Gross Area:_____Square Feet

Efficiency Ratio: _____Percent

1. Site Acquisition

2. Construction

    a. Off-site work (roads, utilities, etc.)

    b. On-site work (roads, utilities, walks, paving, landscaping, irrigation, site lighting, etc.)

    c. Building (structure and all work to 5 feet outside exterior walls)

    d. Fixed equipment (built-in counters, cabinets, etc.)

    e. Furnishings and equipment (movable equipment)

3. Professional Services (surveys, soils analysis, planning, architecture and engineering, plan checking, special consultants, etc.)

4. Miscellaneous Costs (advertising, sewer connection fee, water connection fee, building permit fee, legal fees, etc.)

5. Inspection and Testing (job inspection, material testing, etc.)

6. Contingencies (bidding contingency, cost escalation and contingency, construction contingency, etc.)

7. Financing (loan fee, interim financing costs, permanent financing costs, bond legal fees, etc.)

Figure 13.1

Another method of calculating the building cost is to determine local unit costs, based on a certain quality of construction, and adjust this to the degree of complexity of the specific project. Our example building will be built of either masonry or concrete, it will contain a large number of spaces equipped with services and utilities, and it will have a number of special requirements, such as cold rooms. It will have above-average quality finishes to minimize maintenance and laboratory fixtures with special tops and storage cabinets. As a result, an above-average structure with a 20 to 50 percent premium can be assumed. The basic standards of quality should be established at this stage, including illumination, floor, wall and ceiling finishes, hardware, casework, etc. Based on these standards, the architect can establish a unit cost, which is multiplied by the gross area of the building to obtain the total construction cost.

3. Professional Services

This includes the cost of a topographic survey furnished by a licensed land surveyor; the preparation of a preliminary soil analysis and a soil report, including recommendations for bearing values to be used in the design of footings; any work involving site or master planning in excess of normal architectural services; the cost of all architectural and engineering services, from the inception of the project through the administration of the construction contract, which includes all work provided by civil, structural, electrical, and mechanical engineers, landscape architects, and interior designers; the cost of special consultants such as acoustical engineers; and, possibly, the cost of special consultants to check completed drawings for conformance to codes and safety orders.

These costs can be estimated by reviewing records of previous projects and are dependent on the complexity of the project. In general, they amount to about 10 to 15 percent of the cost of construction.

4. Miscellaneous Costs

Additional costs contained in the project budget include advertising for bids, fees for sewer and water connections to city services, building permits, fees for attorneys, etc. These costs vary according to the size of the project, and it is best to consult local authorities and the owner to establish an amount for these items.

5. Inspection and Testing

This category includes the salary of a full-time, on-site inspector engaged by the owner (if the project requires such services), as well as costs for testing soil compaction and strength of concrete, welding inspections, etc. The on-site inspector's monthly salary may be multiplied by the duration of construction.

6. Contingencies

Unforeseen developments prior to and during construction must be considered in the project budget. It is normal practice to allow a bidding contingency of between 5 and 10 percent. Inflation can be projected in several ways, for example, by projecting cost indexes as a straight line, based on cost escalations of the past year or two. Escalation of cost should be calculated to the midpoint of construction in order to arrive at an average.

A construction contingency of between 5 and 10 percent may be included to cover unavoidable change orders. These may occur as a result of the owner's need to include additional items, as well as costs resulting from unforeseen site conditions.

DESERT BIOLOGY LABORATORY BUDGET

Date of Budget:	December, 1998
Anticipated Construction Start:	July, 1999
Net Area:	6,400 square feet
Gross Area:	10,000 square feet
Efficiency Ratio:	64%

1. Site Acquisition $ -0-

2. Construction
   a. Off-site work 297,000
   b. On-site work 330,000
   c. Building 825,000
   Sub-Total: $ 1,452,000

3. Professional Services
   a. Surveys 4,950
   b. Soils Analysis 1,650
   c. Architecture/Engineering 115,500
   Sub-Total: 122,100

4. Miscellaneous
   a. Advertising 450
   b. Sewer Connection 3,300
   c. Water Connection 1,500
   d. Building Permit 1,800
   Sub-Total: 7,050

5. Inspection and Testing
   a. Inspector (12 months) 24,750
   b. Testing 4,950
   Sub-Total: 29,700

6. Contingencies
   a. Bidding Contingency 72,600
   b. Cost Escalation Contingency 145,200
   c. Construction Contingency 72,600
   Sub-Total: 290,400

7. Financing -0-
   Total: $ 1,901,250

Figure 13.2

7. Financing

These costs include loan origination fees, interim financing costs during construction, and permanent financing costs for "take-out" or permanent mortgages. If a public institution requires the sale of revenue bonds, the necessary legal fees must be included in the project budget.

The sum of all these items provides the total cost to develop the project. Interior furnishings, sometimes referred to as "fitting out," are usually treated separately. The project's design should not proceed until both owner and architect are satisfied that the project is feasible within the constraints of the budget.

Using this format, a budget for the aforementioned laboratory of desert biology is presented. It is interesting to note that nearly one quarter of the total project development costs may be budgeted for items other than construction.

COST ESTIMATING

Cost estimating is a highly developed technique with which architects should be fully familiar. Some architects are highly skilled estimators, while others employ expert cost estimators on their staffs. There are also independent cost consultants available to architects, owners, and contractors. When a professional estimator is consulted, an architect should become familiar with the methodology to be employed, the information needed by the estimator, and the critical periods during the development stages when estimates are appropriate. The reliability of cost estimates invariably depends on the accuracy of the base information and the conscientiousness with which the work is performed.

In order to avoid misusing design time and wasting energy, an architect should have an accurate idea of likely costs at each stage of the project development. The methods of preparing budget estimates at the pre-planning and proposal phase have already been discussed. These are often single unit costs based on such parameters as cost per student, cost per hospital bed, cost per square foot of floor area, or cost per cubic foot of building volume. The cost analysis methods commonly used at various stages of project development are as follows:

At the *programming phase*, the unit cost system, that is, cost per square foot, is quite appropriate. This is usually based on recent experience with similar types of buildings, adjusted by size, location, quality, etc. Costs may be related to the functional activities of each space, for example, square foot cost of wet laboratories versus square foot cost for offices and secretarial spaces. Distinguishable spaces that are calculated separately increase the accuracy of the estimate.

In the *schematic design phase*, it is helpful to employ cost information on the major elements of each building subsystem. This enables cost comparisons between different conceptual solutions and allows, for example, a comparison between steel and concrete structural framing systems. This holds true for all of the major subsystems: air conditioning, electrical distribution, lighting, plumbing, etc.

During the *design development phase*, detailed component costs are required, which permit a more precise selection of components and systems. With more accurate knowledge of probable costs, the architect may suggest changes, if estimates indicate that costs will exceed the project budget.

In the *construction contract documents phase*, when working drawings and specifications are prepared for bidding, it is necessary to use composite unit rates for construction components, assemblies, and systems. These unit rates are required for pre-bid estimates, final cost checks, and the contractor's cost breakdown. This information is also used during construction as a basis for verifying the contractor's payment requests.

General construction cost data is readily available and published in a wide variety of forms. Commercial publications or trade journals regularly furnish information on detailed unit prices, as well as the costs of common building types. Major construction companies also have current price information and will advise owners and architects on a professional basis.

Cost data furnished by contractors is usually categorized by building trades, similar to the way construction work is administered. However, these divisions, which parallel the format of specifications, may not provide a convenient framework for cost estimating during the programming or design phases. Effective cost control requires a framework based not on building trades, but on the component parts of a building, often referred to as subsystems, functional components, elements, or assemblies. Institutions or companies which do a great amount of building, such as government agencies, universities, large corporations, chain stores, etc., regularly use component cost estimating formats. Two examples are shown below.

Sample Cost Format A

The format is for construction cost only, without fees.

1. Structural
   A. Foundations
   B. Floors on grade (including columns)
   C. Floors above grade (including columns)
   D. Roof deck
2. Exterior walls
3. Interior walls and partitions
4. Finishes
5. Vertical circulation
   A. Stairs
   B. Elevators
6. Specialties
7. Equipment
8. Plumbing
9. HVAC (Heating, ventilating, and air conditioning)
10. Electrical
11. Site work

Sample Cost Format B

This format is considerably more detailed than format A. It reflects total project costs, including fees. Total costs are therefore greater than construction costs alone.

1. General conditions, fees, and permits
   A. Temporary services and roads
   B. Field office, temporary power, field toilets, etc.
   C. Head office overhead and profit
   D. Professional fees
   E. Permits
2. Substructure
   A. Normal foundations
   B. Basement excavations
   C. Roof construction
   D. Roof finish and insulation
3. Horizontal structural elements
   A. Slabs on grade
   B. Suspended floor slabs

C. Roof construction

D. Roof finish and insulation

4. Exterior cladding

   A. Walls below grade

   B. Walls above grade

   C. Windows

   D. Exterior doors, entrances, and screens

   E. Projections, balconies, etc.

5. Interior vertical elements

   A. Permanent partitions and doors

   B. Demountable partitions and doors

   C. Glazed partitions and doors

   D. Folding or sliding partitions

6. Multistory elements

   A. Stairs, steps, ladders

   B. Chutes

   C. Catwalks, gratings

   D. Elevators, escalators, hoists

7. Interior finishes

   A. Floors and base

   B. Ceilings

   C. Walls

   D. Special finishes

8. Fittings, furnishings, and building equipment

   A. Building equipment

   B. Special equipment

   C. Built-in furniture and fixtures

9. Cash allowances

   A. Hardware

   B. Graphics (signage)

   C. Miscellaneous

10. Alterations and renovations to existing structures

11. Site preparation and development

   A. Demolition, site preparation, drainage

B. Utilities (including mechanical and electrical site work)

C. Utility tunnels

D. Roads and parking areas

E. Pedestrian walks and steps

F. Exterior illumination

G. Site furniture

H. Ancillary structures, fences, etc.

I. Landscaping, planting

12. Plumbing and drains

   A. Plumbing and drains, roughing-in

   B. Plumbing fixtures and hardware

   C. Fire protection

   D. Special services systems

13. Heating, ventilating, air conditioning

   A. Mechanical equipment

   B. Heating system

   C. Air conditioning

   D. Ventilation system

   E. Controls

   F. Plant

   G. Special systems

   H. Testing and adjustment

14. Electrical

   A. Equipment

   B. Transformers and main distribution

   C. Power and lighting distribution

   D. Lighting fixtures

   E. Underfloor duct systems

   F. Communication systems

   G. Special services

   H. Safety and security systems

A useful listing of elemental categories for building cost analysis was prepared for the P/A Building Cost File. In addition to the elemental categories, this includes:

1. A description of elemental categories and units of measurement

2. Rules of measurement for areas and volumes of buildings

3. A building classification code

Construction trade costs are far more useful when converted into working indexes, such as described above. Once costs are redefined in this manner, the working relationship to programming and design is established. Each building cost analysis should be accompanied by information regarding the estimating basis or technique, so that it can be checked, modified, or corrected.

For comparative purposes, it is convenient to use a simple measure of cost which can be applied to a wide range of building types and building systems. The unit cost system best fits this need. Unit costs describe a specific element as a quantity, for example, curtain wall costs are expressed as "square feet of curtain wall area." This system enables estimators to apply cost data accumulated from one building to a different building type, provided the design and performance criteria are similar. Thus, a structural system for given spans, loads, and height may be transposed from an office building to a university classroom building.

Building cost analysis is useful to the extent that it considers the desirable performance criteria. For example, the cost analysis for partition systems should take into account height, frequency of doors and other openings, fire resistance, and sound transmission requirements.

An office file that documents building cost information on this basis is an excellent and reliable system; however, to be useful, it must be broadly based and reflect a wide range of recent experience. For that reason, it is diffi-cult for small architectural offices to establish extensive data systems and keep them current. Large architectural, contracting, and cost estimating firms often use computer-based data, but smaller offices more often rely on outside reference sources. Whatever the source, the most useful and reliable method invariably involves an expert estimator, a responsible contractor, and dependable information.

Collecting data for a building cost file requires the organization of information as follows:

Elemental categories and units of measurement comprise all the elements of a building, arranged in the usual sequential order of construction. Each element is described and related to its appropriate unit of measurement, such as square feet, linear feet, or cubic feet.

There are seven major cost areas:

100 *Foundations* include all those elements which support the structure.

200 *Building shell* includes the basic superstructure of the building, the exterior envelope, and the roofing.

300 *Interiors* include all architectural interior finishes, partitions, built-ins, specialties, and equipment. These costs are largely influenced by the functional requirements of the spaces.

400 *Conveying systems* include escalators, elevators, etc. Costs are closely related to building height.

500 *Mechanical and electrical* include all elements of the mechanical and electrical systems except exterior services (900).

600 *General conditions and profit* include the contractor's provisions for general conditions, site overhead, and profit.

900 *Site development* includes excavation, grading, utilities, roadways, landscaping, etc.

Each of the main categories is further divided into more detailed classifications. Items which are included and excluded in each category and the appropriate units of measurement are noted. This detailed listing relates trade costs to building component costs, which allows a practical comparison of values. Note that categories 700 and 800 are not assigned; they are reserved for special items.

Floor areas and volumes are calculated according to standard rules of measurement, which ensures that unit rates are consistent from one project to another. There are several rules of measurement, some of which apply to commercial buildings and others to institutional buildings. Large corporations that do a considerable amount of building may use their own particular rules.

Calculations should be made for both gross and net floor area. This allows one to compare the space efficiency of different designs, and to relate costs to a unit of net usable building area.

The building volume measurement permits one to translate costs into dollars per cubic foot. The ratio of gross floor area to building volume is also a useful measurement, since it takes into consideration the floor-to-floor height.

A *building classification code* establishes a convenient system to identify, classify, and store information on various projects.

The ultimate purpose of establishing a cost file is to enable one to analyze the costs of a proposed project.

Cost figures are based on bid prices, with no adjustments made for construction changes or geographic variations. This form of cost analysis saves time and effort, and it provides an efficient pricing system during the early programming and planning phases.

Parameter Costs

A second system of estimating costs, checking bids, and controlling costs was originally developed by Engineering News-Record (ENR) and is called *parameter costs of buildings*. The data derives from contractor-reported actual costs, which are published in detail for each project.

The parameter method bases the unit cost of each trade on the physical parameter (measure) of the building that is the main determining cost factor, among the 15 parameters used. For example, the "gross area supported" is used to calculate the unit cost of structural steel or whatever structural system is used. Items such as acoustical ceilings, resilient flooring, carpeting, sprinklers, plumbing, electrical fixtures, etc., are based on the "net finished area" parameter.

Using parameter costs is more accurate than basing the unit cost of each trade on total area or volume. ENR's parameter cost files are stated as unit cost ranges for each major trade. The range is based on 50 percent of projects centered about the median, using contract prices updated from construction start date to present, using the ENR Building Cost Index.

Parameter costs of buildings are useful in developing feasibility studies, determining preliminary budgets, aiding design decisions and cost-cutting procedures, determining and checking bids, and simplifying cost control. Given a building concept, architects can use building parameters to calculate preliminary costs quickly. Moreover, appropriate values of cost-saving alternatives may also be obtained.

A parameter estimate can be adapted for use in another location by applying ENR's 20 Cities Building Cost Index. It can also be updated by multiplying by an inflation factor. However, more reliable results are obtained when indexes in the same region are updated.

Table 13.1 illustrates a construction cost budgeting system that uses the ENR cost parameters. If a new hotel with a similar budget were being planned, an estimator could generate valid parameters and probable unit costs for the proposed hotel by expanding the given trades classifications and unit costs shown. The new tabulation would have the same form; however, the parameter unit costs would differ based on the judgment of the estimator and geographical factors.

During all phases of design, the budget of each component must be controlled to assure that cost targets are not exceeded. In the early stages of development, detailed estimates are impractical; however, general comparative costs can be projected.

Referring to the cost breakdown of a project in Table 13.2, let us examine an example of value engineering analysis. Note that the cost of structural steel is estimated at $270,000. Four structural alternatives were selected for comparative cost study:

1. Prefabricated reinforced concrete
2. Prefabricated prestressed concrete
3. Prefabricated steel with solid web beams
4. Timber

Studies of these four alternatives yielded the following costs:

1. Prefabricated reinforced concrete, $282,000
2. Prefabricated prestressed concrete, $288,000

3. Prefabricated steel, $270,000
4. Timber, $290,000

From this analysis it is clear that a prefabricated steel structure is the most economical. This type of analysis can be made for each of the major building components. Those items that exceed the parameter costs may have to be balanced by compensating reductions in other components, or the project budget may have to be adjusted.

Upon completion of preliminary design, the construction cost estimate should be reviewed with the owner for approval. The cost objectives established in preliminary design will determine the cost of the final design.

To examine another component, the budget for toilet partitions has been set at $3,080. According to the preliminary design, the project has a total of 17 toilet partitions. Shown below are the five partition types considered, with their unit costs and total costs:

Marble	$500 × 17 = $8,500
Metal	$200 × 17 = $3,400
Porcelain enamel	$300 × 17 = $5,100
Stainless steel	$430 × 17 = $7,310
Pressed wood	$140 × 17 = $2,380

The pressed wood partition would have the lowest cost and would realize an initial saving of $700, based on the original budget of $3,080. Since durability is essential, however, this partition material is unacceptable. Therefore, the next lowest cost partition, metal, is recommended. The anticipated partition cost overrun is $320, and this overrun must be absorbed in one of the other components.

This analysis illustrates the technique of value engineering; it also indicates that the parameter system is not entirely flawless. A budget must

		Parameter Cost:			Total Cost:
TRADE:		**CODE**	**Unit**	**Cost**	**Amount**
Type of building...............	Hotel	5	sf	$4.60	$296,000
Location........................	Anytown, U.S.A.	—		—	30,000
Construction start/comp....	January 1985/March 1986	—		—	30,000
Spec. site cond...............	Rock in basement	—		—	4,000
Type of owner.................	Private	—		—	—
Frame..........................	Structural steel	3	sf	11.24	70,000
Exterior walls.................	Masonry	3	sf	9.64	60,000
Fire rating....................	2-hr.				
	—	—		—	—
Precast concrete..............		—		—	—
Calssons, pilings.............		—		—	—
Con. arch.....................		5	sf	4.98	320,000
Ext. masonry..................		10	sf	300	300,000
Int. masonry..................		7	lf	8.00	80,000
Stone, granite, marble.......		—		—	—
Structural steel..............		5	sf	7.76	500,000
Misc. metal...................		2	flr	7,500	30,000
Ornamental metal.............		—		—	4,000
Carpentry.....................		7	lf	5.60	56,000
Curtain wall..................		8	sf	78.58	66,000
Waterproofing and dampproofing		8	sf	4.76	4,000
Roofing and flashing.........		15	sf	1.58	40,000
Metal doors and frames.......		—		—	—
Wood doors, windows..........		7	lf	0.36	3,600
Hardware......................		2	flr	5.000	20,000

PARAMETER MEASURES:

1 No. of floors, excluding basement	7
2 No. of Floors, including basement	8
3 Basement plan area	6,225 sf
4 Basement area, total	6,225 sf
No. of basement floors	1
5 Gross area supported (excl. slab on grade)	64,374 sf
6 Face brick area	31,300 sf
7 Interior partitions	10,000 lf; masonry, drywall
8 Curtain wall, incl. glass	840 sf
9 Net finished area	93,963 sf
10 Other exterior masonry wall	1,000 sf
11 Number of elevators	2
12 Store front perimeter	80 lf
13 No. fixtures (pl.) sinks, toilets	500
14 Parking area	250 cars
15 Roof area	25,458

Table 13.1

Glass & glazing	8	sf	28.10	23,600
Store front & lobby	—	—	—	23,600
OTHER MEASURES:	Metal windows	—	—	—	—
Area, typ. flr	10,729	Lath and plaster	—	—	—	—
Lobby area	2,640 sf	Drywall	9	sf	3.40	320,000
Air cond	Gas window	Tile	13	fixt.	73.60	36,800
No. of rooms	152	Terrazzo	—	—	—	—
No. of laboratories	—	Acoustical ceiling	9	sf	1.28	120,000
Story height	10 ft.	Resilient flooring	—	—	—	—
Swimming pools	—					
No. of apartments	—	Carpet	9	sf	1.86	120,000
		Painting	9	sf	2.02	130,000
		Toilet partitions	13	fixt	8.00	4,000
		Special equipment	—	—	—	270,000
		Elevators	11	ea	80,000	160,000
		Plumbing	9	sf	4.90	460,000
		Sprinklers	9	sf	0.10	10,000
		HVAC	9	sf	4.08	384,000
		Electrical: Contracts	9	sf	4.26	400,000
		Fixtures	9	sf	0.42	40,000
		Miscellaneous trades	—	—	—	120,000
		Parking	—	—	—	28,000
		TOTAL				4,620,000

Table 13.1 (continued)

be based on reality. The real conclusion of this analysis is that the original budget may have been flawed, and that an estimator's professional judgment is more reliable than any mechanical system.

Other Cost Variables

Project location is a major factor in influencing construction costs. This is particularly important when published cost indexes are used to convert cost data from one locality to another. Subdivided geographical areas of the country must consider labor rates, material prices, construction activity, and the availability of labor. Variations within geographical regions, particularly between urban and rural areas, must also be considered, as well as the possibility that certain regions may experience a change in cost patterns. Additional factors influencing costs include population densities, construction volume, wage levels, number of construction firms, etc.

From all of this the following conclusions can be drawn:

1. There is a direct correlation between labor rates, material prices, and construction costs.

2. Construction costs decrease as one moves away from heavily populated urban areas, until construction locations become remote and inaccessible, at which point costs rise rapidly.

3. Costs in rural or remote areas tend to be less predictable than in urban areas due to fluctuations in the construction market, lack of stable labor, and material delivery problems.

4. Rural and semi-urban areas are dependent on neighboring metropolitan areas, and they are influenced by distance and transportation access. The construction industry of a metropolitan area generally services the outlying areas.

Trade	Budget Amount
Civil	
Site work (clearing, drainage)	$ 110,000
Roads, walks	59,400
Civil Budget	169,400
Architectural	
Landscaping	24,700
Exterior masonry	92,500
Miscellaneous metal	9,725
Carpentry	94,185
A/C enclosures	21,490
Waterproofing & dampproofing	67,600
Roofing and flashing	8,230
Metal doors and frames	114,000
Hardware	22,440
Glass and glazing	20,000
Drywall	25,800
Tile work	10,250
Acoustic ceiling	7,350
Resilient flooring	5,700
Carpet	46,000
Painting	47,600
Toilet partitions	3,080
Special equipment	60,430
Architectural Budget	681,080
Structural	
Excavation	15,900
Conc. arch or formed concrete ...	112,060
Structural steel	270,000
Structural Budget	397,960
Mechanical	
Plumbing	99,000
HVAC	240,500
Mechanical Budget	339,500
Electrical	
Contracts	260,000
Fixtures	2,420
Electrical Budget	262,420
General Conditions Budget ..	205,540
TOTAL	$2,055,900

Table 13.2

The factors that contribute to construction cost differences, therefore, are: the availability of labor and materials, the resources to produce or fabricate materials, and the convenience of available transportation systems.

Construction costs are affected by a variety of influences; for example, when oil becomes scarce, fuel costs rise and construction costs increase. When construction activity exceeds what the local labor market can provide, labor costs rise. And when industrial wages are increased, the price of fabricated building components must rise as well.

Interest rates charged to developers have a substantial influence on construction volume, with resultant effects on labor and materials costs. High interest rates invariably cause a significant reduction in housing starts, which is normally followed by a decline in softwood lumber prices. This is illustrated by Figure 13.3, which shows that in the severe slump of 1973–74, lumber prices plunged some 20 percent.

The demand for wage increases and fringe benefits by building trade unions is the largest single influence on labor costs. These increases are more often based on cost-of-living increases than on an increase in productivity. Labor union pressures normally decrease as construction activity is reduced, when emphasis is placed on minimizing the loss of jobs.

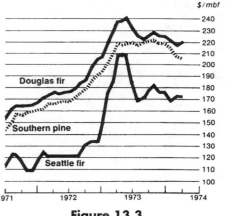

Figure 13.3

It is clear that any single influence, whether it is price control, credit control, shortage, demand, or supply can have a considerable effect on the overall cost of construction.

CONSTRUCTION OVERHEAD AND PROFIT

Overhead costs usually include all the general costs of operating and maintaining a contracting business plus all project expenses that are not included in material, labor, or equipment costs. Overhead costs can be assigned to either of two categories: general overhead costs or project overhead costs.

General Overhead Costs

Included in this category are all costs that cannot be charged to a specific project. Costs such as rent, for example, are continuous, although they may vary with the volume of construction and the number and size of projects being handled by the firm.

General overhead costs may range as high as 8 to 15 percent of the total value of business for a large firm. The following list illustrates the various items constituting general overhead costs. All projects will include some of these items, and a few projects will include them all.

General Overhead Costs:
Advertising
Automobile
Consulting fees
Entertainment
Furniture
Heat
Insurance
Interest
Legal expenses

Rent
Salaries
Stationery
Supplies
Taxes
Telephone
Travel
Utilities
Wages (staff)

Project Overhead Costs

These include all costs that can be charged to a specific project, but cannot be attributed to labor, materials, or equipment.

Project overhead costs depend on the type of project and the difficulties encountered during the work. These costs vary from 4 to 10 percent or more of the cost of construction, or from 10 to 20 percent of labor costs alone. The following list illustrates the various items that constitute project overhead costs. Each project normally includes several of these. (Note that payroll taxes are usually a part of labor costs, not project overhead.)

Project Overhead Costs:
Bonds
Equipment storage
Heat/air conditioning
Insurance
Interest
Light, power, water
Office maintenance
Permits
Project office
Project telephone
Sanitary facilities
Security

Stationery and supplies
Taxes
Temporary enclosures
Temporary walks and stairs
Transportation
Trash removal

Total overhead costs may vary from 5 to 20 percent of the total construction cost, or from 10 to 40 percent of the labor costs alone. The actual amount depends on the locality and type of project.

Other than the general building permit, contractors must often secure permits to cross a sidewalk, erect shelters over a sidewalk, store gasoline or other hazardous materials, construct temporary buildings, maintain sanitary facilities, obtain water or power, open streets for utilities, repair pavements, use dumps, and transport heavy or wide loads over city streets.

A contractor may also be required to secure surety or guarantee bonds, proposal or bid bonds, performance bonds, and labor and material payment bonds. Certain types of insurance may also be required by law or by the owner, as shown on the following lists.

General Insurance:
Fire
Owner's contingencies
Property damage
Public liability
Windstorm
Workers' compensation

Miscellaneous Insurance:
Automobile
Boiler
Earthquake
Flood

Forgery

Payroll

Plate glass

Rain

Theft

Vehicle

Wind

On most construction projects the contractor must make interest payments to finance the costs of labor and materials until progress payments are received. These interest payments are included in the project overhead. If the contractor, rather than the owner, is required to pay property taxes on a structure during construction, these taxes are also included as overhead.

There are several methods of apportioning overhead costs. The optimal way is to charge actual costs to each project, which requires, of course, that such costs can be determined accurately. The more common method is to apportion general overhead costs among all projects. In some instances, general overhead costs are divided equally among each of the projects; in others, according to the length of time required to complete each job.

The federal government and some states levy payroll taxes, which are normally a part of the contractor's labor costs. Included are Social Security Tax, Federal and State Unemployment Insurance Tax, and Disability Insurance Tax.

Profit

The amount of a contractor's profit is usually expressed as a percentage of the total estimated costs of materials, labor, equipment, and overhead. This percentage varies according to the type of project, size and amount of the contract, and the time required for completion. Smaller or more risky projects, for example, usually command a larger profit percentage. The profit

percentage also depends on how anxious a contractor is to build a particular project and the bidding climate created by the competition of other contractors interested in the same project.

The percentage allowed for profit varies from 5 to 25 percent. For smaller projects with many unknowns, the highest percentages are charged. 15 to 20 percent is typical for medium-size projects, 10 to 15 percent for larger projects when unknowns are limited, and from 5 to 10 percent for very large projects. Unknowns include such risk factors as local labor conditions, weather, and the owner's financial solvency.

CONSTRUCTION COST ESCALATION

The cost of construction is based on the cost of raw materials, manufactured materials, and labor, and therefore, it is directly affected by the vicissitudes of inflation. Thus, it is necessary to determine how construction costs relate to inflation, how they vary as a result of external influences, and how to use available information to predict future trends. This is vital for estimating costs of projects in the programming stage, often one or two years in advance of bidding.

One method is to chart historical curves, based on indexes of construction costs, and project these on a straight line basis. Thus, if a hypothetical index of 100 is set for a base year, such as 1986, and the index indicates 150 for 1991, the cost of construction for 1991 is one and a half times that of 1986. On the basis of this index, the cost of construction shows an increase of ten percent per year. In actual experience, however, inflationary cost increases are not uniformly linear, but rather they fluctuate.

For very large projects, even a minor fluctuation can involve a large amount of money.

COST INDEXES

There are numerous construction costs indexes published nationally, with price adjustment factors related to region. One group of such indexes is the ENR Construction Cost Index, which appears in *Engineering News-Record*, published by McGraw-Hill. Additional indexes for construction costs, common labor costs, skilled labor costs, and materials costs also appear in the same publication. All of these indexes are calculated by averaging costs in a number of major U.S. cities.

The ENR Construction Cost Index was created in 1921 to diagnose price changes that occurred during and immediately following World War I and to evaluate their effect on construction costs. The index was intended as a general purpose construction cost indicator. It is a weighted aggregate index of constant quantities of structural steel, portland cement, lumber, labor, etc., comprising a hypothetical block of construction, and for years it has indicated the basic underlying trends of construction costs throughout the country.

There are a number of other cost indexes published, based on varying criteria.

Major considerations in choosing an index for cost measuring purposes are:

1. Desired accuracy
2. Material and wage components and respective weightings that make up the index
3. Geographical area covered by the index

For approximate estimates in the early stages of development, a general purpose cost index is easiest and most economical to use. However, a check should be made to insure that various components in the index reasonably match those in the structures being estimated. Choosing a specialized index requires careful study of the components and their relative statistical weight, as well as the geographical area to which the index applies.

Calculations for forecasting cost escalation trends must be tempered by such factors as shortages, increased demand, credit availability, and government intervention, including economic incentives or restraints. Nevertheless, cost indexes must be considered an aid, not the final answer to the complex task of estimating project construction costs.

THE FINANCING OF BUILDING PROJECTS

Building projects, whether public or private, can be financed in a number of different ways, which we will examine.

Private Buildings

A private project may have an owner who develops it for his or her own use, whether it be a private residence or a corporate headquarters building. Most private building projects, however, are conceived by real estate developers, or entrepreneurs, as investments.

A developer may work at a very small scale, building houses or other small income producing projects, or at a very large scale, building skyscrapers, shopping centers, or whole communities. Because of the complexity of building, developers tend to specialize.

WAGE RATES, 20-City Average

	Jan. 1991	% Change From Dec. 1990	Jan. 1990
Common..	18.58	0	+2.8
Skilled (average three trades)	24.35	0	+3.5
Bricklayers	23.97	0	+3.4
Carpenters	23.29	0	+3.4
Structural ironworkers..	25.78	0	+3.6

MATERIALS PRICES, 20-City Average

	Jan. 1991	Dec. 1990	Jan. 1990
Asphalt paving, AC-20**	128.88	+5.0	+23.7
Cement, bulk, per ton, TL*	62.10	0	–0.7
Concrete blocks, sand/gravel, 8" × 8" × 16" per hundred*	84.08	–0.5	–6.7
Ready-mix concrete, 3,000 psi, per cu yd*	49.98	+0.7	+5.0
Ready-mix concrete, 5,000 psi, per cu yd*	56.97	+0.6	+6.0
Sand, per ton, CL**	6.92	+0.8	–1.5

	Dec. 1990	Nov. 1990	Dec. 1989
Conc sewer pipe, 24", prem joint, per ft, CL*†	17.50	–1.6	–2.2
Ductile iron pipe, push-on joint, 6", per ft, CL*	6.44	+2.5	+3.0
Lumber, 2" × 4" fir, per Mbf, CL*	325.99	+0.8	–3.2
Lumber, 2" × 4" pine, per Mbf, CL*	315.31	0	–2.9
Plyform, wood, 3/4", per Msf, CL*	592.22	–0.6	–3.2
Plywood, 5/8", per Msf, CL*	353.10	–2.4	–15.2
Reinforced bars, grade 60, per cwt.................................	17.85	–2.1	–2.7
Structural steel, base, per cwt††	24.97	–0.7	–4.2

* Delivered; **f.o.b. city; CL = carlots; TL = trucklots; † = revised; †† = average of fabricated channel beams, I-beams and wide-flange; na = not applicable because of revisions in quoting method.

Table 13.3

As previously discussed, the developer determines the feasibility of a certain kind of building in a certain place, and at a certain scale. He or she may also determine that a large project might be built in phases. With this vision of a project, the developer has to determine the likely acceptance for the project in a particular location. Is the zoning appropriate? Does the town plan, if it is specific, support the concept he has in mind? Is there likely to be commu-

ENR COST INDEXES IN 22 CITIES

Based on 1913 U.S. average = 100

City	CONSTRUCTION COST Jan. '91 Index	Percent Change From Last Month	Percent Change From Last Year	BUILDING COST Jan. '91 Index	Percent Change From Last Month	Percent Change From Last Year
Atlanta	3171.55	0	+1.0	2222.40	0	+0.9
Baltimore	3884.43	0	+4.8	2579.90	0	+6.1
Birmingham	3437.29	+0.3	+4.1	2160.84	+0.5	+1.3
Boston	5614.79	0	+4.5	3110.03	0	+0.6
Chicago	4993.36	−0.1	+1.3	2888.16	−0.2	+2.1
Cincinnati	4933.91	0	+1.2	2638.73	0	+1.9
Cleveland	5368.82	0	+4.0	2886.93	0	+4.6
Dallas	3190.69	−0.1	−0.9	2061.61	−0.2	−3.1
Denver	3541.20	0	+3.4	2321.28	0	+2.6
Detroit	5155.54	0	−0.3	2974.47	+0.1	+2.2
Kansas City	4763.94	0	+0.9	2645.28	0	+1.6
Los Angeles	5994.55	0	+3.5	3020.51	0	+5.6
Minneapolis	4798.61	0	+0.1	2648.43	0	+2.8
New Orleans	3602.41	0	+0.3	2220.20	0	+0.6
New York	6847.58	0	+6.1	3848.30	0	+3.7
Philadelphia	5433.52	0	+2.5	3043.10	+0.1	+2.5
Pittsburgh	4580.29	0	+3.3	2711.11	0	+0.8
St. Louis	5099.10	+0.2	−0.6	2610.32	+0.3	−0.4
San Francisco	6055.61	0	+2.1	3245.04	0	+4.0
Seattle	4933.39	0	+0.7	2552.58	0	−0.6
U.S. 20-city avg	**4770.03**	**0**	**+2.2**	**2719.46**	**0**	**+2.1**
Montreal	4977.06	0	+4.9	2803.10	0	+5.9
Toronto	6401.54	0	+6.3	3204.51	0	+3.1

Table 13.4

nity support, or opposition, to the envisioned development?

Some of these questions may not have simple answers, and further investigation may be required. When a developer feels that there is a real possibility for achieving his project, he proceeds, knowing that much still has to be investigated, and that the effort in terms of time and money may be considerable.

ENR WAGE, MATERIALS AND COST INDEXES 20 CITIES

Based on each city's 1967 average = 100

City	COMMON LABOR Jan. '91 Index	% Chg. fr. Jan. '90	SKILLED LABOR Jan. '91 Index	% Chg. fr. Jan. '90	MATLS. PRICES Jan. '91 Index	% Chg. fr. Jan. '90	Const. Cost Index	Bldg. Cost Index
Atlanta	397.42	+1.4	366.32	+1.7	375.37	0	389.83	370.34
Baltimore	505.02	+5.5	432.29	+8.5	368.44	+2.8	440.36	403.53
Birmingham	448.16	+6.2	374.98	+3.0	345.59	−0.7	411.98	359.94
Boston	580.36	+7.1	528.45	+3.9	353.83	−5.2	517.68	452.21
Chicago	450.57	+2.0	446.05	+4.1	320.28	−1.2	414.07	389.28
Cincinnati	489.49	+1.9	425.00	+4.4	380.86	−1.2	464.33	412.48
Cleveland	452.23	+2.9	435.57	+2.3	366.98	+8.5	428.46	406.12
Dallas	444.22	+2.3	347.73	+1.1	314.66	−7.5	403.77	341.28
Denver	381.52	+5.0	369.33	+5.2	345.08	−0.2	362.38	354.91
Detroit	441.18	0	462.28	+4.2	323.41	−1.2	411.58	402.38
Kansas City	501.11	+0.7	448.40	+1.5	365.95	+1.6	460.60	408.48
Los Angeles	550.00	1.6	482.96	+1.9	367.74	+13.4	508.42	438.76
Minneapolis	461.11	0	451.79	+4.4	341.06	−0.6	418.48	384.40
New Orleans	469.09	0	371.90	0	359.57	+1.2	430.73	366.10
New York	505.54	+7.5	516.45	+5.4	421.30	0	492.40	483.87
Philadelphia	582.00	+4.2	497.87	+6.1	386.98	−3.7	530.38	452.51
Pittsburgh	447.94	+4.7	401.87	+2.0	335.52	−1.0	411.54	368.11
St. Louis	452.16	+1.0	424.46	+3.6	324.61	−7.1	422.13	382.40
San Francisco	509.47	+0.4	478.85	+1.0	372.10	+10.5	478.42	436.14
Seattle	461.61	+2.6	438.78	+3.2	354.36	−6.6	437.01	403.81

Table 13.5

After investigating community acceptance with the appropriate public agencies—planning, zoning, public works, traffic and highways—the developer must investigate possible sources of financing. At this point, there is also the need for preliminary architectural and engineering concepts.

Let us focus on financing. Some developers have access to capital investment money, often in large amounts. Large developers often have long-standing relations with local banks. With that kind of financial backing, the task of such developers is to search for possible projects.

But most developers are not in that position. More often, they conceive of projects, and then search for capital. They may have some of their own money to invest, or for small projects, such as a medical clinic, they may be able to assemble a small investment partnership. More likely, they will go to a lender, such as a bank, to seek financing.

In order for a bank to lend money, it must be convinced that the investment project is sound. If it is a shopping center or office building, market studies, growth trends, and recent development experience may suffice to be convincing. If the project is very large, the lender may require a commitment on the part of major tenants, such as large firms seeking office space or chain department stores needing a new branch location.

If, as often happens, the lender is a pension fund or insurance company, the same evidence of either a market study or prime tenant, or both, is required.

The financial analysis of a building project, which involves cost and return on investment, is referred to as a "pro-forma." The cost of a building of a certain size and construction type can be reasonably estimated, as previously discussed. That same building can also be estimated to produce a certain annual rent. The "cost of money" (principal and interest payments, or "debt service") must also be considered. Other factors include vacancy rate, operating costs, repair allowance, taxes, inflation, etc., as well as depreciation. Depreciation is based on the idea that a building loses value as it ages, at least from a tax standpoint. In fact, however, the opposite is generally true: a viable building in a good location will probably appreciate in value.

Here enters the complex element of taxes and tax laws. The federal tax laws, particularly, greatly influence the type and volume of building construction in the nation. Depreciation is one of many factors that may make a project financially attractive, since depreciation is permitted to be deducted before calculating the taxable profit of a project.

All private investments in construction are made with the idea of making a profit. An individual developer, using his or her own finances, will only proceed with a project if he or she calculates that the return on investment is favorable, and an investment bank or pension fund investor will do the same. The return on investment must be equal to or greater than the return that the money would make in any other investment of comparable risk—stocks, raw land, a business venture, etc.

Most real estate investment is made for a long period of time, 10 to 20 or more years. In some cases, the actual cash return, or profit flow, may not begin for several years. Some projects may have to be carried for the first few years. The amount of real cash loss (carrying expenditure) or positive cash earnings is referred to as "cash flow."

Some investors invest in projects that have negative cash flow, offsetting the loss against current earnings, in the belief that their real profits will be made in the future.

Another important factor in determining the viability of an investment, also because of federal tax laws, is the capital gains tax, which is a tax on profit from the sale of tangible assets, such as a building.

In the past, capital gains were taxed at a lower rate than wages, interest, and other income. That tended to make the sale of buildings quite profitable after taxes, often soon after they were built, which stimulated construction. The capital gains tax advantage has been greatly reduced in recent years, and its partial restoration continues to be a matter of political debate.

We mention the capital gains tax and depreciation to point out that federal tax laws are a major determinant of building construction intensity. They have become, in many ways, an instrument for modifying economic activity, intensifying or reducing it.

All private for-profit building investment is done with a long-range view. But it should also be obvious that a developer, burdened willingly with a considerable entrepreneurial effort at the outset of a project, must control expenses. That puts architects who work for developers in the difficult but well-known position of having to do their work in a highly competitive market, under conditions in which a client seeks to minimize costs, particularly "front end" costs. Consequently, the architect's services are often poorly compensated in this sort of competitive and speculative environment. To improve this situation, some architects take an equity position or part ownership in a project, or even become developers themselves.

An exception is the developer who develops more elegant buildings in order to attract more prestigious tenants. Here a premium of 10 to 15 percent may be expected to produce a more attractive building. The architects for such projects are likely to be those who are recognized for their design quality and distinction and, on occasion, their ability to attract attention through their work. This has been called "signature architecture." Such architects may design those elements that affect the appearance of a building, the facade and lobby, with the rest done by a conventional architectural and engineering firm.

When a developer has assembled his entire project and secured financing for its construction, the financing is made available in the form of a construction loan. As the project is built, the loan funds are paid out to the contractor,

subcontractors, and suppliers. This provides the lender with the opportunity to determine that the work is proceeding properly. When the project is finished, the developer obtains a new loan for long-term financing, to be paid off during the financial life of the building through rental income.

One should also be aware of the term "FF & E"—furnishings, fixtures, and equipment. FF & E refers to the built-in furnishings (counters, cabinets, etc.), permanently installed fixtures (toilets, sinks, etc.) and equipment (lighting, etc.) needed for a building to operate. A moment's thought will reveal a quandary. How can a building be complete without FF & E? Such a building would be only partially built.

The reason for the term FF & E is to differentiate the real costs of a building, usually for budgetary convenience. A building without its FF & E is a structure and shell, including its main electrical and mechanical systems, which is obviously much cheaper than one fully equipped. But that equipment is paid for from another budget, which is why FF & E was devised.

Its origins trace back to British public health facilities. One budget provided for the building shell; the other, the FF & E, was the budget for completing the building so that it could be used, paying for much of the expensive finishing required in health facilities. Since then, FF & E has come to be used to reduce apparent building budgets by paying for finishing from a different budget or source.

It is customary in this country for a developer to build a basic building shell, ready to receive a tenant—a retail store operator or a law firm office. The tenant pays for the installation of "tenant improvements"—the finishing walls, floor, partitions, etc. This practice is more valid than FF & E, since the "tenant improvements" are just that, the interior construction unique to the tenant's needs, and subject to removal and replacement by a future tenant.

As for FF & E, it could be properly used in institutional buildings, such as hospitals, laboratories, and libraries, to describe the interior work that allows a building to serve its purpose.

Public Buildings

The financing of public buildings is no less complex than that of private projects.

A public building project starts when a public agency recognizes the need for a new school, county office, court house, etc. The agency itself may act as "owner." More likely, a department of government, often called a GSA or General Services Administration, or a Department of Buildings and Grounds, becomes the "owner" and proceeds much the same way as a private developer.

Studies are done, internally or by an outside consultant, to establish a facility program and cost estimate. A site is chosen, and a project schedule and budget are developed. This work is done to coordinate with the government's fiscal process, in which money for projects is requested and apportioned. If the project is approved in the budget allocation, it moves towards realization.

An architect-engineer firm or team is selected, either through an interview process or through a competitive selection based on design. The design work begins and is developed. When the design is approved, the project is put out to bid, a construction contract is awarded, and construction begins.

The entire process is carefully planned and scheduled, and each step is budgeted sepa-

rately. Public projects, then, often entail a considerable amount of time, due to the step-by-step approval and budgeting processes. Because of this, and as in private building, an inflation allowance is included in the budget.

The financing for public buildings and facilities is achieved through one or two general methods. The first is to pay for the project out of general tax revenues. Federal government buildings are generally paid for this way, with the government paying for the building as it is designed and built with operating funds derived from appropriations.

As the size of a government jurisdiction becomes smaller, so does its ability to raise the funds to pay for a building as it is designed and built. The design costs can be paid out of a specific appropriation. But often, the construction cost cannot be paid, simply because the municipality does not have sufficient money in hand. Instead, the municipality may issue a bond, to raise money from the investment community to pay for the building. In other words, the municipality borrows money, via a bond issue, to finance the building. The bond is paid back over a prescribed number of years.

Since municipal bonds are generally tax-free, interest costs to the municipality are reduced. Such bonds have a lower rate of return than other bonds, but the return to investors is not taxed.

There are two types of municipal bonds: *general obligation bonds* and *revenue bonds*. General obligation bonds are used to finance the construction of facilities that do not collect revenue, such as schools, roads, parks, etc. The principal and interest on such bonds are paid from tax revenues. Revenue bonds, on the other hand, are used to finance revenue-producing facilities, such as toll bridges, water treatment plants, etc., and the fees collected by such facilities are used to pay back the bonds.

The bonds are sold on the open market through brokers. Municipalities are rated according to their reliability in making bond payments, with a triple-A rating being the highest. A high rating allows a city or public agency to issue and sell bonds readily, and at a favorable rate.

The power of a city to plan and build projects and finance them through bond issues is strictly controlled, usually by the state government. These restrictions limit the types of projects a municipality can build (they must be for community services), as well as the total amount of indebtedness a municipality may incur, known as the debt ceiling. A municipality is, in effect, a regulated public corporation.

One should also be aware of special purpose government agencies which have the authority to build facilities. The federal government's General Services Administration is perhaps the largest building authority in the world. At the state, county, and municipal level, special authorities that have the power to finance and build include agencies which build water and sewer facilities, schools, hospitals, jails, public buildings of all sorts, highways, public transit facilities, port facilities, industrial parks, etc.

Similarly, utility companies, which supply electricity, gas, and telephone services, can be regarded as quasi-public authorities. In effect, they are private companies that provide public services. They are franchised to operate in certain areas, and are carefully regulated by public commissions.

Private companies whose purpose is to provide needed facilities for low income persons are another form of public authority. They operate on a non-profit basis, and are funded by low-interest tax-free obligations as well as private donations.

In some cases, a special tax may be levied to pay for specific public facilities. For example, a hotel tax can be earmarked to pay for a convention hall, on the theory that the convention hall attracts out-of-towners, who spend money and thereby enrich a city.

The financing and operation of private and public buildings requires skilled management and astute investment strategy. For public facilities, the primary responsibility is to provide an adequate public infrastructure.

The private sector requires skilled entrepreneurship as well as public scrutiny, particularly if investment funds come from government-backed institutions. (The ongoing problems involving savings and loan institutions illustrate all too clearly what can happen when such public scrutiny breaks down.)

Finally, there are projects that society needs and that are best realized by continuous long-term effort. Such projects, which include housing for the elderly and public acquisition of ecologically critical natural areas for preservation, are not financially feasible for the private sector and must therefore be financed through special programs. These essentially involve federal or state underwriting of financing, either through special issue bonds or direct financing. Projects of this kind provide long-term benefits to society and therefore represent an investment in the nation's future.

SUMMARY

Budgeting is an essential element of building design and project development. An architect must be aware of the probable cost of his or her design, from the earliest conceptual stages through design, with ever-increasing accuracy.

Several techniques are used in cost estimating—cost by building type, square footage cost in relation to quality of construction, and analysis by individual building elements.

In addition to the direct cost of construction, there are other costs such as professional fees, permit fees, contractor profits, contingency and inflation allowances, and financing costs.

Finally, it is also necessary to understand both the differences and similarities in funding private and public projects.

LESSON 13 QUIZ

1. An owner has established a fixed construction budget for a project. If the lowest project cost estimate exceeds the fixed budget, the architect should recommend that the owner do any of the following EXCEPT

   A. decrease the size or quality of the project.

   B. postpone construction until costs decline.

   C. rebid the project using other contractors.

   D. increase the construction budget.

2. If you were the architect for the project in the preceding question, your obligation would be to

   A. reduce the quality of construction so that the size and budget would remain unchanged.

   B. reduce the size of the project so that the quality and budget would remain unchanged.

   C. try to convince the owner to reduce the scope or increase the budget so the quality of the project would remain unchanged.

   D. advise the owner of the situation and allow him or her to determine whether cost, size, or quality should be modified.

3. During excavation of a site, it is discovered that unanticipated adverse geological conditions will add at least 10 percent to the total building cost. The architect should advise the owner to

   A. stop work until additional funds are secured.

   B. stop work and attempt to find an alternate site.

   C. make a change in the cost, scope, or quality of the project.

   D. reduce the project scope and quality in equal proportions.

4. Construction costs are significantly influenced by which of the following? Check all that apply.

   A. Project location

   B. Rate of inflation

   C. Skill of the estimator

   D. Availability of labor

   E. Availability of construction funds

5. An estimate indicates that an apartment project can be constructed for $80 per square foot at today's construction costs. The cost index used for the estimate is at 850. To determine the actual cost, you project the index to reach 1,020, at which point the actual construction cost will be _____ per square feet.

6. In a preliminary project budget, off-site development costs would include

   A. all access roads.

   B. all accessory buildings.

   C. fences placed on property lines.

   D. utilities outside of property lines.

7. The contractor's profit is computed by multiplying a fixed percentage by the

   A. cost of construction.

   B. cost of construction and professional fees.

   C. total project development cost.

   D. total project development budget.

8. Construction cost estimates prepared during the programming phase should be

   A. based on appropriate unit costs.

   B. based on a single lump-sum figure.

   C. disregarded, because there are so many unknowns.

   D. disregarded, because costs do not affect programming.

9. Which of the following statements, regarding the tendencies of labor costs, are true?

   I. Labor costs in rural areas tend to fluctuate more than in urban areas.

   II. When construction activity is high and labor is scarce, wage rates tend to increase.

   III. Wage demands tend to increase as interest rates rise.

   IV. Wage demands tend to increase as unemployment rises.

   A. I and IV

   B. I and II

   C. I, II, and III

   D. II, III, and IV

10. Which of the following construction costs would a contractor be UNLIKELY to pay?

   A. Topographic survey fee

   B. Building permit fee

   C. Workers' compensation insurance

   D. Labor and material bond

DELIVERY METHODS

14

OWNER REQUIREMENTS

The method of delivering design and construction services is typically based upon an owner's needs and capabilities. A small organization, a small firm, or an individual that wishes to develop a project would typically require full professional design services from an architect and a traditional design/award/build delivery process. An owner who desires to participate in the design process would likely select this traditional method, ensuring that the final project meets all of the owner's criteria. The design/award/build delivery method allows for all design decisions to be made before contracting with a builder.

A large organization or firm that wishes to develop a project may have an in-house staff that has capabilities for project programming, design, engineering, facilities management, construction management, or construction. Such a firm may not require the traditional

design/award/build delivery method. An owner also might have certain time frame and/or cost considerations that would require other types of delivery methods. An owner who has a commitment to deliver a project for occupancy in a short time frame may not be able to take the amount of time required of the traditional design/award/build process. Such firms may require other project delivery methods, which typically consist of either the construction management or design/build methods.

DESIGN/AWARD/BUILD DELIVERY METHOD

The design/award/build delivery method typically begins when an owner hires an architect to develop a project program and its subsequent design and construction documents. Bidding of the project to several contractors occurs after all construction documents and specifications have been completed. This allows for the establishment of the lowest reasonable cost for the project. The owner then awards a single prime construction contract to a general contractor to build the project based upon the completed design documents. The architect acts as the owner's agent, representing the owner's interests throughout the design and documentation phases. The architect's services typically include construction administration services. The architect then acts as an impartial interpreter of the construction documents during construction.

The benefits of the design/award/build delivery process include owner participation in the design of the project and well-established construction costs based upon relatively complete documents. The architect acts in the owner's best interests during design, and the architect acts as an impartial interpreter of the contract documents during construction. This process allows for clear separation of design and construction responsibilities, and allows for simplicity in project scheduling since each phase of the design and construction process is separate.

The design/award/build delivery process, however, requires an extended time period for design and documentation before final costs can be determined and construction can begin. This is a problem if an owner wishes to expedite a project. Also, pricing and constructability experience of the contractor who is to build the project is not available during the design and documentation phases of the project.

CONSTRUCTION MANAGEMENT DELIVERY METHOD

The construction management delivery method allows an owner to address constructability and cost issues during design. An owner can also address time issues by utilizing fast-track construction, in which multiple construction contracts are let for different parts of a project as soon as each part of the work is defined enough for a contractor to reasonably commit to a price. In this delivery method, the owner hires or utilizes his or her own construction manager to work with an architect to facilitate the process of design, bidding, and letting of the construction contracts. The construction

manager can act as either an advisor to the owner, or as a construction contractor. The construction manager typically has substantial expertise in construction technology, constructability issues, construction scheduling, and construction costs.

A construction manager who acts as an advisor administers the design contracts and works as the owner's representative with the design team. He or she also manages the various construction contracts, but does not have any financial responsibility for the construction of the project. A construction manager may, however, handle some of the typical nonconstruction activities at the site, such as arranging temporary site facilities, site and construction testing, engineering, building and site layout, and construction site cleaning. Some architecture firms offer construction management services, acting in an advisory role to the owner.

A construction manager who acts as a contractor assumes a vendor relationship with the owner. This person or firm will take on the financial responsibility for the construction of the project, typically utilizing a fixed-price, cost-plus, or guaranteed maximum price cost structure. The construction manager is brought onto the project before design work is complete so that he or she can help resolve constructability and cost issues.

A fixed-price structure allows the manager to establish a guaranteed cost of construction, including his or her own services, before the design is fully documented. The owner is not liable for bid-cost overruns. However, the owner does not obtain any of the savings that might occur from a positive bid climate. A cost-plus structure allows the construction manager to charge the owner the actual construction costs of the project plus a negotiated fee that is agreed to before construction begins. The actual costs are typically determined by the lowest bids received from the manager's subcontractors, plus the cost of any construction work performed by the construction manager's own forces. The guaranteed maximum price structure is a highest-probable-cost limitation for the construction of the project guaranteed by the construction manager. This price is established before design documents are completed, and anticipates the full scope of work and detailing needed to complete the project. Any cost savings from a positive bid climate go to the owner rather than the contractor. However, the contractor becomes responsible for any bid-costs over the guaranteed maximum price.

The advantage of using the construction management delivery method is the ability of the owner to determine the costs of a project before construction documents are complete. The ability to let portions of the work for bid before other portions of the design are complete allows for construction work to commence before all other project drawings are completed. This is a great advantage for an owner who has a short time frame to complete a project due to occupancy requirements or when an owner has to work with high interest rates, which can add substantially to the financing costs of a project. Another benefit of this method is the ability of the construction manager to resolve technological or constructability issues before construction begins, which helps reduce costs due to construction change orders.

The construction management delivery method, however, adds a cost for the construction manager that an owner would not have in the more common design/award/build process. The addition of a construction manager adds complexity to the design and construction team. This can be a benefit if the relationships are managed effectively, but can become problematic if these relationships are not adequately defined and handled. The use of the fast-track construction method also adds to the complexity of the project, requiring the management of multiple bidding periods and multiple prime construction contracts.

DESIGN/BUILD DELIVERY METHOD

The design/build delivery method allows an owner to utilize a single entity that is responsible for both the design and construction of a project. This is the single greatest distinction between this method and both the design/award/build and the construction management methods. A design/build firm can be a single company that has its own architectural and construction staffs, or a company that has its own construction staff that hires an architect to perform design services. A development firm can hire an architect for design services and a contractor for construction services. A design/build firm can also be a joint venture between an architect, construction, and/or a developer.

An owner who wishes to proceed with the design/build process typically issues a request for proposals to selected design/build firms that state the design and performance requirements for the project. The design/build entities submit proposals to the owner that provide a design for the project and the costs for the design development and construction of the project. The selected design/build firm then develops the design, provides construction documents, and builds the project based upon the proposal requirements.

An owner who wishes to have more control over the design of the building can have an architect develop the schematic concept for the project. This can then become part of the request for proposals, which makes the selected design/build firm responsible for the development of the design, the construction documents, and the building of the project.

The advantages to the design/build delivery method include a single source of responsibility for both design and construction of the project, allowing the owner to select from a number of submitted designs. A reliable cost for the project is determined early in the process, and conflicts between the designers and the builders are minimized. This process also facilitates fast-track construction, since the portions of the design work that can be built early can be released for construction before the balance of the design and documentation work is complete.

This delivery method, however, minimizes the ability of the owner to participate in the design of the project. The design/build firm acts solely as a vendor so that the owner does not have an independent agent working for his or her interests. This requires the owner to be adept

at managing the design/build contract through construction, or to hire an independent firm to act on his or her behalf. Any design changes would likely require a change order that the owner would have to pay. Since the submitted designs are likely based upon incomplete drawings, disputes may arise regarding the actual scope of work provided in the proposal. Also, a selection that is based solely on the lowest bid may have significant quality issues that would be difficult to address.

SUMMARY

Architects need to be well acquainted with different project delivery methods, from the possible liability issues they present to the extent to which the process may compromise the execution of the intended product. Candidates should be familiar with the different methods and their benefits and drawbacks as they apply to different types and sizes of projects.

LESSON 14 QUIZ

1. Which delivery method involves an owner hiring someone with constructability and cost expertise to work with the architect during the design phase?

    A. Design/build

    B. Design/award/build

    C. Joint venture

    D. Construction management

2. Which of the following is not an advantage of the typical design/build delivery method?

    A. Facilitates fast-track construction

    B. Provides a reliable project cost early in the process

    C. The owner participates fully in the design process

    D. The design/build firm provides a single source of responsibility for design and construction

3. An architect acts as an owner's agent in which of the following situations?

    I.   As a member of a joint venture with a construction company

    II. The design-award-build delivery method

    III. The construction management delivery method

    IV. The design/build delivery method

    A. I and III   C. II and III

    B. II and IV   D. I and IV

THE ARCHITECTURAL DESIGN TEAM

15

STRUCTURING THE ARCHITECTURAL DESIGN TEAM

The architect can act as the sole provider of design services if his or her firm has experienced and qualified in-house staff that can provide the necessary engineering and other specialty services that are required on a project. However, most architects typically form alliances with other firms to provide these services.

In a typical alliance, the architect has the prime contract with the owner and then subcontracts services to other professional firms that act as the architect's consultants for a project. Consultants can include structural, mechanical, electrical, plumbing, civil, or acoustical engineers; landscape design firms; kitchen design consultants; information technology/communications firms; and soil and construction testing services firms.

Architects may also create joint ventures with other firms, creating a single project-based entity with other architecture, engineering, or construction firms that have specific areas of expertise or geographical experience. An architect would typically form a joint-venture with a construction firm as part of a design/build delivery method, and would then act as a vendor rather than as an owner's agent. Acting as a vendor would then require the architect to act on behalf of the joint-venture and its best interests rather than for the owner.

An architect may also act as one of several independent design and engineering firms hired by an owner. In this situation, an owner would typically have some level of project and construction management capabilities to handle and coordinate the different contracts.

CONSTRUCTION DOCUMENTS OF CONSULTANTS

Compliance with Code Requirements and Regulations

A coordinated and detailed response to code requirements from the entire design team is essential to the success of a project.

Consider, for example, energy requirements. Siting, preliminary selection of materials, and schematic organization of programmatic elements are largely within an architect's control. These energy considerations must be balanced against other requirements more closely controlled by others, including structural requirements.

Fire protection also requires building team coordination. The incorporation of interior courtyards or atriums, for example, may require engineering for fire protection. Mechanical, electrical, and plumbing equipment are often critical elements in a fire protection plan. When there are no physical barriers to the spread of potential fires, protection depends upon sensing devices, sprinkler systems, and air handling equipment. These systems and building components are likely to be designed or selected by the engineering and fire protection consultants, rather than the architect.

The mechanical, plumbing, and electrical codes often have provisions that are the same as or that complement the building and life safety codes. These common provisions are generally understood by most design professionals. Architects, however, cannot always be certain that engineers and other consultants have complied with all code provisions. As a practical matter, architects of complex projects may simply inform consultants about which codes are applicable, and ask them to research the detailed requirements. This does not relieve architects, however, of responsibility to meet code requirements. As leader of the design team and the party contracting with the owner for professional design services, the architect has prime responsibility for code compliance. However, each engineering consultant must sign his or her drawings submitted for plan review by the code official and thereby also becomes responsible for compliance. Moreover, the AIA Architect-Consultant Agreement (Document C141) states that the consultant is responsible for code compliance in the same manner and extent that the architect is responsible to the owner.

Initially, architects should verify that each member of the project team is working from the same set of code requirements. Consultants should inform the architect about significant aspects of their work that are required by code. Although codes generally allow several responses to requirements, they occasionally require specific design features. Consequently, architects must know which design elements may change and which may not.

Architects are responsible to notify their consultants of design decisions that have code implications. For example, fire walls must be

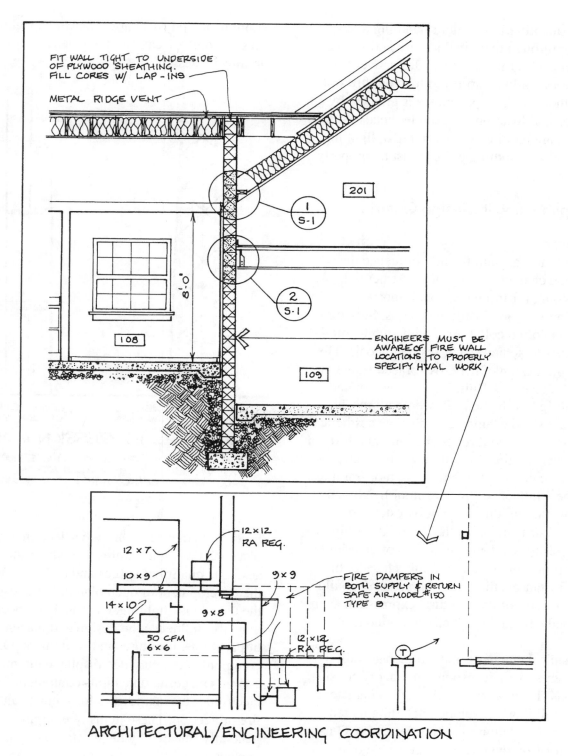

ARCHITECTURAL/ENGINEERING COORDINATION

Figure 15.1

clearly identified, so that air handling ducts passing through them include fire and smoke dampers. (See Figure 15.1.) Alternatively, the duct work could be arranged to avoid fire walls altogether. Ceiling appearance is affected by the type and location of sprinkler heads. If ceilings are required to be fire rated, light fixtures and air handling grilles must be properly accommodated.

Compliance with Design Criteria

Aesthetics

Consultants can significantly influence the aesthetic character of a project. Structural expression, for instance, is an important element in many architectural designs. Structural engineers often collaborate with architectural designers to achieve such aesthetic goals. The structural design of the cross-braced frame of the John Hancock Building and the bundled tube design of the Sears Tower, both in Chicago, are good examples of positive aesthetic qualities achieved through the mutual efforts of architects and their structural engineers. On a smaller scale, the structural design of framing members influences floor-to-floor height, and thus overall building height, by establishing the floor structure's depth. The relationship of spandrels to window openings is often critical to the proportions of a building's facade. In many instances, the basic character of a building is a result of its structural expression, as in a domed structure or an air-supported roof.

Mechanical engineers may influence wall treatments by their response to energy considerations. Their work can affect the character of the building's envelope, including its fenestration in relation to solar orientation. On a smaller scale, the location and design of air diffusers can affect the aesthetic appearance of interior spaces. Where mechanical equipment is exposed to view, architects normally ask to review and approve illustrations showing the

equipment's physical appearance. Unsightly fans on rooftops can seriously detract from an architect's design.

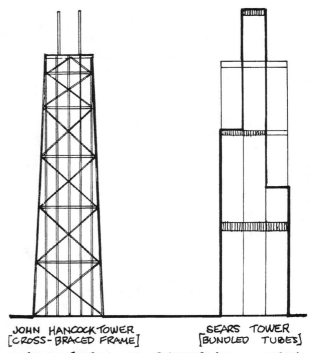

JOHN HANCOCK TOWER [CROSS-BRACED FRAME]   SEARS TOWER [BUNDLED TUBES]

STRUCTURAL EXPRESSION IN ARCHITECTURE   THE DESIGN OF THESE TWO WELL-KNOWN BUILDINGS HAS BEEN STRONGLY INFLUENCED BY CONSULTANTS TO THE ARCHITECT.

Figure 15.2

Electrical engineers, through selection and placement of light fixtures, can affect the aesthetic quality of spaces and ceilings. With the development of open plan office design and the use of task lighting, electrical engineers may also influence the design and placement of partitions, furniture, and equipment. Offices commonly contain video display equipment, computers, communications equipment, and electronic sensing devices for security and fire protection. These items of equipment are generally selected by the electrical engineer, in consultation with the architect.

Food service consultants, lighting consultants, acoustical consultants, and art advisors may also influence a building's aesthetic qualities. Architects must always inform their consultants of design criteria and the aesthetic effects they are trying to achieve. Product data, study models, and photographs may be used to assess intermediate design progress, and are subject to the architect's final approval. Architects must know enough about the details of their consultants' work to maintain design control. At times, they may suggest alternate approaches or solutions more compatible with the desired aesthetic character of the project.

Quality Control

Since many of the construction documents prepared by consultants are based on calculations, quality control is relatively easy to achieve. Parameters are well defined and solutions can easily be checked.

Details that are shown on the drawings must be in conformance with engineering design assumptions. If a structural engineer designs a moment-resisting frame, for example, the joint details must reflect that condition. Architects may review consultants' construction documents to confirm that designs, details, and specifications are compatible with the consultants' calculations and assumptions.

An architect can support a consultant's quality control by informing him or her of all relevant design criteria to which the consultant must adhere, and by requiring the consultant to schedule periodic reviews by experienced senior staff members or *peer review* by others in the consultant's profession.

Although architects can check for internal consistency and for apparent compliance with standards, consultants are primarily responsible for quality control of their own work.

Cost Control

Estimating *initial costs* is an essential part of a consultant's work. The percentage of the total budget allocated to each discipline varies with building type and project scope. Architects often establish budgets for the major elements of construction work for incorporation into an overall project budget. Once the budget is established, consultants are expected to design within its limits. Consultants must, therefore, be accurate in predicting initial costs so that the architect can prepare a reliable overall project estimate.

Because operating costs tend to vary inversely with initial costs, a relatively low construction budget may imply that life cycle costs will be relatively high. Consultants must evaluate conflicting considerations in order to produce optimum design solutions. Likewise, architects must review each alternative to be sure that a consultant's decision serves not only his or her particular discipline, but the project as a whole.

Operational costs may be difficult to calculate. Calculations involve more than the characteristics of specified equipment; they can involve the operating characteristics of the owner's organization and other factors affecting a facility, such as changing climatic conditions. Engineering calculations may, in some instances, be based on assumptions different from actual conditions. For example, a facility may be operated differently than anticipated by its program; calculations may be based on average conditions, in spite of the fact that extreme weather conditions may have been experienced in recent years; or fuel prices may have increased suddenly and unexpectedly.

It is important that basic design assumptions are realistic. Architects should understand the operating characteristics of facilities, and they must ensure that design assumptions are accurate and that designed elements and systems will be appropriate.

Maintenance is an important aspect in the selection of products and systems. Some mechanical and electrical systems are complicated, sophisticated, and sensitive. If properly balanced, they can be efficient and economical. But, they can also be troublesome and more difficult to maintain than simpler, less technically advanced systems. Equipment maintenance costs vary with the size and skill of maintenance staffs. Some design professionals have expanded their practices to include facilities management services, including the preparation of detailed operational and maintenance programs.

Specified systems must be properly installed, reliable, and receive scheduled maintenance to be successful. The architect should determine that such systems are appropriate to the contractor's and building manager's degree of sophistication.

Compatibility with Other Elements

The *size and weight* of equipment is another design consideration. Engineering drawings are largely diagrammatic, making it difficult to verify that design criteria have been met. For example, a large pipe or duct may be represented by a single line on a drawing, but its actual size determines the clearances which must be provided and maintained. Unfortunately, these considerations are sometimes ignored. Architects can create similar problems by providing insufficient space for equipment and services during design development phases. Allotted spaces might prove to be too small, and increasing the building's gross area may be difficult without disrupting the overall architectural solution and budget.

Operational characteristics of mechanical and electrical equipment must be considered by the design team before final selections and placement are made. In critical cases, a special consultant such as an acoustical engineer may be retained to advise the design team on the placement, isolation, and construction of large air handling equipment. Electrical distribution equipment can interfere with the operation of sensitive laboratory or hospital equipment. In this case, the architect may ask the owner to provide the services of a special consultant to advise the design team on the placement, selection, and isolation of certain equipment.

Ease of Construction

Labor and Equipment Requirements

Architects and their consultants should determine that the systems they design can actually be built, considering the space, equipment, and labor required. For example, if a floor system utilizes precast concrete T-beams, there must be sufficient room on the site to position the cranes required to erect these units. If construction access is available from one side of a site only, construction must be able to proceed in only one direction. Post-tensioned structures require accurate placement of tension cables and hydraulic jacks to stress tendons properly. The availability of the skilled and experienced labor necessary for these operations influences the decision to utilize such systems.

Large air-conditioning chillers and cooling towers are often placed on the upper stories or roofs of multistory buildings. If they cannot be disassembled and installed in sections, they must be lifted intact to their final locations. Once in place, equipment and systems may require sophisticated pneumatic and electrical controls and precise balance in order to operate properly. The installation of sensitive equipment requires the availability of skilled technicians.

In making design decisions, the architect's consultants must consider the limitations of local labor and the availability of special equipment. They must be aware of the implications of applicable union rules. Although contractors must determine the appropriate trade for each part of the work, both architects and consultants should follow established and generally accepted operating procedures, and understand their impact on design decisions.

Sequencing

Engineers and other consultants must see their drawings in terms of the construction sequence as well as the final product. Very large components of mechanical equipment must be brought up to, and placed into, equipment penthouses after they are manufactured. Buildings must remain structurally stable during construction. Once installed, equipment must be accessible for servicing or to remove and replace malfunctioning units.

Architects should review consultants' construction documents with the construction process in mind. The sequence of construction and workability of the scheme throughout the construction process must be considered. Major building elements must fit into place at the appropriate time and without disrupting other ongoing activities.

Scheduling

It may be desirable to order certain components of a building well in advance of their installation. Major HVAC components, large electrical transformers or switchgear, and curtain wall systems are frequently custom made for a particular project. These elements are not generally in a warehouse waiting to be purchased. Even standard catalog items are often manufactured only when specifically ordered and require a significant amount of lead time before delivery.

Architects' consultants must be involved in scheduling to enable major items to be available when needed. Contractors are often selected too late to order long-lead-time equipment in a timely manner. One solution is for the owner, on the advice of the architect and consultants, to order equipment directly. When a contractor is subsequently selected, purchase orders are assigned from owner to contractor. Upon delivery, the items are received and installed in the same way as if the contractor had been involved from the beginning.

Fast-track delivery procedures work generally the same way. A project is divided into packages or stages of work, each of which represents a separate prime contract. Starting construction and ordering items before all the construction drawings are completed helps to ensure the availability of products when needed, and tends to control costs during periods of rapid inflation.

Architects must be sure that consultants specify and package items according to proper criteria. Information about a project's ultimate character and configuration may be limited when ordering. Circumstances may change between the time orders are placed, or a construction package let, and the time an item is received, or final drawings completed. An architect must work with consultants to determine important features, while leaving other aspects open to inevitable change. This may result in excess capacity in equipment or the need to alter designs to integrate with equipment or items already ordered.

Consultants must also be aware of overall construction schedules and, within these schedules, pertinent installation periods. If a new chiller or cooling tower is required before summer, or a new boiler or heating plant before winter, engineering designs must allow equipment to be built and installed in time. Or, if construction must occur during winter months, structural engineers may want to avoid the use of reinforced masonry, which requires special measures to protect mortar from freezing.

These concerns are especially applicable to renovation projects. An old system may have to be changed to a new one, or an owner may require that a new wing or suite be ready before the old one is abandoned. Some considerations will be apparent from construction documents, while others will not. Architects must be certain that timing has been considered and is realistic.

An owner may rely upon the architect and the architect's consultants for pre-construction services such as cost estimating, scheduling and sequencing, and reviewing ease of construction.

Construction Management

With the advent of fast-track and other sophisticated methods of procurement, some owners have retained *construction managers (CMs)* to provide these pre-construction services.

Construction management may be defined as activities over and above normal architectural and engineering services, conducted during the pre-design, design, and construction phases, that contribute to the control of time and cost.

Despite this simple definition, the scope of the CM's functions vary widely from project to project. The CM often joins the project team during the design phases and either remains as an adviser or becomes the constructor as well.

If the CM is an adviser, it acts as the owner's agent and provides the owner with impartial technical advice. The appropriate AIA form is the Owner-Construction Manager Agreement (Document B801/CMa).

If the CM is the constructor, there are two appropriate AIA forms: either Document A121/CMc or A131/CMc.

Internal Coordination of Consultants' Documents

The architect is the prime professional under contract to the owner, and as such, liable for his or her consultants' work. Prudent architects, therefore, try to make certain that their consultants provide appropriate levels of professional service. There are some practical limits, however.

One limit is that architects cannot check each consultant's documents for internal consistency and coordination. That is the responsibility of each consultant. If an electrical engineer specifies one type of lighting fixture, the drawings should not show another. Dimensions should be accurate and drawings and specifications should be coordinated. The AIA Architect-Consultant Agreement (Document C141) specifically requires the consultant to be responsible for coordinating his or her own work.

When a consulting firm combines more than one engineering discipline, coordination becomes more complicated. For example, structural, HVAC, plumbing, and electrical work may all be done in different departments of the same consulting firm. Generally, a consultant's documents must be made internally consistent by that consultant. Structural and mechanical documents must be checked against each other for conflicts prior to being sent to the architect. Someone in the consulting firm must be responsible for this interdisciplinary checking.

Overall Coordination of Consultants' Documents

Format for Specifications

Specifications prepared by an architect and his or her consultants are bound together into a Project Manual. All the work of the individual parties must be coordinated to produce a unified document, not a collection of individual parts. To accomplish this, architects establish formats for consultants to follow.

Coordination extends from simple considerations, such as the color of the paper on which the specifications of different consultants is printed, to the format and numbering system used. The consultants' input to bid forms, including instructions to bidders, and to Division One, the general requirements of the specifications, must be established. Overall, each consultant's work must be coordinated with that of the architect and the other consultants.

The architect must require that his or her consultants participate in the preparation of the requirements of Division One, so that their individual specification sections are appropriately coordinated. The architect is the one professional on a project team with the required perspective to coordinate the many diverse elements of a Project Manual.

Diagrammatic Mechanical and Electrical Drawings

Most construction documents prepared by mechanical and electrical consultants are diagrams or schedules. HVAC drawings show dimensions of ducts. Major pieces of equipment are shown, but other physical conditions are not represented. Duct dimensions may not include the thickness of required insulation. Electrical documents are more diagrammatic. Typically, wiring is indicated in floors or in ceilings, as are home runs to panelboards.

Actual conduit locations, however, are usually determined by contractors in the field. Plumbing drawings are less diagrammatic than HVAC and electrical drawings, but pipes and fittings are not drawn to scale. The exact location of piping may be determined by the contractor in the field.

While these different methods of representation are logical, checking and coordination is difficult. Architects can overlay drawings of the various consultants to spot potential conflicts. Even where lines do not cross in such overlays, this does not guarantee adequate clearances, since the diagrams may not be precise enough. Overlay drafting and CAD make it easier for architects to identify and resolve conflicts before they become construction problems.

Serious construction problems may be caused by uncoordinated drawings. Contractors may have problems installing mechanical ducts and electrical conduits within the space actually provided. For example, walls may be framed without adequate space for plumbing lines. Architects must address such potential problems when checking the consultants' documents.

THE SUSTAINABLE PROJECT DESIGN TEAM

Is a sustainable design organized and implemented differently than a conventional design?

Design Team

What kind of design team is necessary for a sustainable project?

The scope of sustainable design invites an expanded team approach, which may include the following:

- Architects or engineers (structural, MEP) with energy modeling experience

- A landscape architect with a specialty in native plant material

- A commissioning expert (if LEED employed)

- An engineer/architect with building modeling experience

The design team for a sustainably designed project tends to have a larger pool of talent than a typical architectural project. Because the buildings will be more holistic, the sustainable design team will have additional consultants that bring a broader range of experience and innovation to the project. Wetlands, scientists, energy efficient lighting consultants, native plant experts, or commissioning engineers are examples of the additional talent that may be added to sustainable design project.

As with any architectural design, there is a hierarchy of design goals:

- *Initial imperatives* such as budget, timing, image, and program necessities.

- *Subjective goals* such as a functionality improved and more pleasing work environment, pleasing color schemes, and landscaping that complements the architecture.

- *Specific goals* such as more open space, more natural light, less water usage, and adjacency to public transportation.

And with the inclusion of sustainability there may be additional goals:

- *Initiatives that are specific to sustainability* such as fewer toxins brought into the space, daylighting in all spaces with people occupancies, less overall energy consumed, less water usage, adjacency to public transportation, and improved indoor air quality.

- Desire to exceed existing standards such as ASHRAE, USGBC, or American Planning Association (APA).

SUMMARY

The integration of the design team typically relies on the architect's ability to coordinate and manage the resources at hand. As challenging as the task may be, it is ultimately one of the most important steps towards the realization of a successful project. An overall understanding of the typical consultant's responsibilities and how they affect the scheduling and the execution of a project are expected from all candidates for the Programming, Planning & Practice exam.

LESSON 15 QUIZ

1. When selecting mechanical systems for a project, the architect and mechanical engineering consultant should consider which of the following factors?

   I. Skill of the owner's maintenance staff

   II. Weight of the equipment

   III. Noise characteristics of the equipment

   IV. Operating clearances

   A. II and IV   **C.** III only

   B. II, III, and IV   **D.** I, II, III, and IV

2. Plumbing drawings have all of the following characteristics EXCEPT

   A. they are diagrammatic.

   B. they are frequently superimposed on blank architectural floor plans.

   C. they graphically show the physical dimensions of pipes.

   D. they indicate connections between pipes.

Lesson Twelve

1. A Activities B and E both terminate at event 3, after which activity C may begin. See page 229.

2. D The critical path is the path with the longest total required time. See page 231.

3. C Critical path $1 - 2 - 3 - 4 - 5$ has a total time of $2 + 2 + 3 + 1 = 8$ days.

4. A, B, D, and E All choices impact construction schedule except choice C. Total construction cost has little to do with the construction schedule.

5. B See pages 234–235.

6. B Certain phases of design and production, such as client approval and project bidding, have fixed times. Therefore, the 25 percent reduction in time would probably come from the construction drawing phase. This would likely lower the overall quality of the construction documents. The construction budget and time would be unaffected.

7. A A shortened time schedule may reduce some fixed overhead expenses, such as rent, but it would undoubtedly lead to higher costs because of overtime work, additional hired help, and/or work that is subcontracted to others. Because of higher labor costs, profit would decrease, and the documents would be adversely affected. See page 224.

8. D See pages 223–226.

9. C Complexity is generally more critical than size, while cost and quality rarely affect scheduling.

10. A Project cost would be increased because of inefficiencies resulting from additional labor and overtime work. See page 234.

Lesson Thirteen

1. B Cost, size, and quality are directly interrelated. Therefore, if the construction budget is fixed, the project must be reduced in size or quality. The owner may also rebid the project or decide to spend more money, but a hoped-for decline in prices seems unrealistic. See page 239.

2. D It is not the function of the architect to reduce project cost, size, or quality; this is a prerogative of the owner.

3. C After advising the owner of the additional costs and reviewing the possible changes that would bring the budget back into line, the architect must allow the owner to choose one or more of the three variables (cost, scope, quality) that must be modified.

4. C The estimator's skill may affect the reliability of the cost estimate, but not the actual costs.

5. $96.00 per square foot The present cost of $80 per square foot will increase in the ratio $1,020/850 = 1.20$. Therefore, the actual construction cost will be $80 \times 1.20 = 96 per square foot.

6. D Off-site costs include costs of improvements outside project property lines, such as utilities. Access road costs are paid for either by the owner or a government agency, depending on the situation.

7. A See page 258.

8. A See page 246.

9. B Increased wage demands are generally a result of supply and demand, as well as inflation. See page 255.

10. A Topographic survey fees, as well as fees for other professional services such as soil investigations and architectural services, are always paid for by the owner.

Lesson Fourteen

1. D The construction management delivery method involves an owner who hires a construction manager to work with the architect to resolve constructabililty and cost issues during the design phase.

2. C The design/build entity is typically responsible for the design and construction of a project, based upon requirements established by the owner and issued in the request for proposal.

3. C An architect acts as an agent for the owner in the design/award/build and the construction management delivery methods (II and III are the correct answers). An architect acts as a vendor responsible for the cost and construction of a project in a joint venture with a contractor and in the design/build delivery method (I and IV are incorrect).

Lesson Fifteen

1. D All the factors shown influence the selection of a mechanical system.

2. C Plumbing drawings indicate the size of pipes by notation, not graphically. (C is the incorrect statement we are looking for.) Statements A, B, and D correctly describe plumbing drawings.

Part V

The Site Zoning Vignette

THE NCARB SOFTWARE

16

Introduction
Vignette Screen Layout
Computer Tools

INTRODUCTION

There is a wide variety of drafting programs used by candidates at the firms in which they work. Therefore, an essential part of every candidate's preparation is to practice using the exam software. Candidates may download this software from the NCARB Web site *(www. ncarb.org)*. This program contains tutorials and sample vignettes for all the graphic portions. You are encouraged to spend all the time necessary to become familiar with this material in order to develop the necessary technique and confidence. You must become thoroughly familiar with the software.

The drafting program for the graphic portions is by no means a sophisticated program. While this may be frustrating to a test taker used to advanced CAD software, it is important to keep in mind that the aim of NCARB in designing these tests was to develop an adequate drafting program that virtually anyone would be able to use—even candidates with no CAD background.

VIGNETTE SCREEN LAYOUT

Each vignette has a number of sections and screens with which the candidate must become familiar. The first screen that appears when the vignette is opened is called the Vignette Index and starts with the Task Information Screen. Listed on this screen are all the components particular to this vignette. Each component opens a new screen when the candidate clicks on it with the mouse. A menu button appears in the upper left-hand corner of any of these screens that returns you to the Index Screen. Also available from the Index Screen is a screen that opens the General Test Directions Screen, which gives the candidate an overview of the procedures for doing the vignettes. Here are the various screens found on the Index Screen:

- **Vignette Directions** (found on all vignettes) Describes the procedure for solving the problem

- **Program** (found on all vignettes) Describes the problem to be solved

- **Tips** (found on all vignettes) Gives advice for approaching the problem and hints about the most useful drafting tools

- **Tree Diagrams** A screen found on the Site Design vignette to show tree shading extents

The beginning of each vignette lesson in this study guide provides a more detailed description of each vignette screen.

To access the actual vignette problem, press the space bar. This screen displays the vignette problem and all the tools required to solve it. Toggle back and forth between the Vignette Screen and one of the screens from the Index Screen at any time by pressing the space bar. This is not as convenient as viewing both the drawing and, say, the printed program adjacent to each other at the same time. Thus it is a procedure that the candidate must become familiar with through practice. Also, some vignettes are too large to be displayed all at once on the screen. In this case, use the scroll bars to move the screen up and down or left and right as needed. The Zoom Tool is also helpful.

COMPUTER TOOLS

There are two categories of computer tools in the ARE graphic portions.

- Common Tools
- Tools specific to each vignette

The Common Tools, as the name implies, are generally present in all the tests and allow a candidate to draw lines, circles, and rectangles, adjust or move shapes, undo or erase a pre-

viously drawn object, and zoom to enlarge objects on the screen. There is also an on-screen calculator, and a tool that lets you erase an entire solution and begin again.

Vignette-specific tools include additional tools that enable the candidate to turn layers on and off or rotate objects. In addition, each vignette also includes specific items under the draw tool required for the vignette, such as property lines, deciduous trees, or grades. Become an expert in the use of each tool.

Each tool is dependent on the mouse. There are no "shortcut" keys on the keyboard. Press the computer tool first to activate it, then select the item or items on the drawing to be affected by the tool, and then re-click the computer tool to finish the operation. Spend as much time as required to become completely familiar with this drafting program. The Common Tools section of the practice vignettes available from NCARB is particularly useful for helping you become familiar with the computer tools. Two things to note: use the left mouse button to activate all tools. Also, there is no zoom wheel on the mouse, nor an associated tool on the program.

The standard computer tools and their functions are shown in Figure 16.1.

STANDARD COMPUTER TOOLS

BRINGS UP A MENU OF ITEMS, SUCH AS
BUILDING ELEMENTS, PARKING SPACES, ETC.
SOME MENU ITEMS MAY LEAD TO
SUB-MENUS ITEMS, SUCH AS *SPACING.*

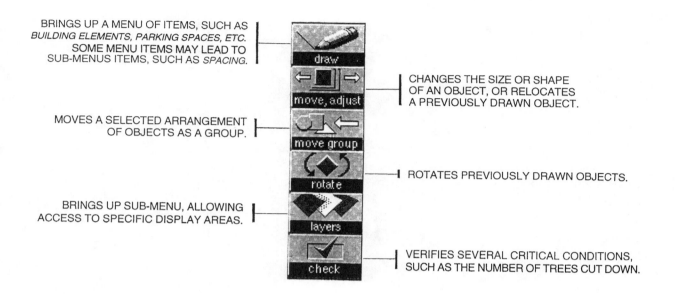

CHANGES THE SIZE OR SHAPE
OF AN OBJECT, OR RELOCATES
A PREVIOUSLY DRAWN OBJECT.

MOVES A SELECTED ARRANGEMENT
OF OBJECTS AS A GROUP.

ROTATES PREVIOUSLY DRAWN OBJECTS.

BRINGS UP SUB-MENU, ALLOWING
ACCESS TO SPECIFIC DISPLAY AREAS.

VERIFIES SEVERAL CRITICAL CONDITIONS,
SUCH AS THE NUMBER OF TREES CUT DOWN.

BRINGS UP A MENU OF HELPFUL TOOLS,
SUCH AS *A BACKGROUND GRID, LINES,
CIRCLES, RECTANGLES,* AND A MEANS
TO DETERMINE MEASUREMENTS.

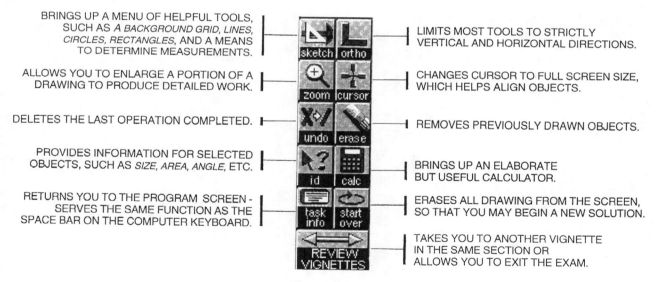

LIMITS MOST TOOLS TO STRICTLY
VERTICAL AND HORIZONTAL DIRECTIONS.

ALLOWS YOU TO ENLARGE A PORTION OF A
DRAWING TO PRODUCE DETAILED WORK.

CHANGES CURSOR TO FULL SCREEN SIZE,
WHICH HELPS ALIGN OBJECTS.

DELETES THE LAST OPERATION COMPLETED.

REMOVES PREVIOUSLY DRAWN OBJECTS.

PROVIDES INFORMATION FOR SELECTED
OBJECTS, SUCH AS *SIZE, AREA, ANGLE,* ETC.

BRINGS UP AN ELABORATE
BUT USEFUL CALCULATOR.

RETURNS YOU TO THE PROGRAM SCREEN -
SERVES THE SAME FUNCTION AS THE
SPACE BAR ON THE COMPUTER KEYBOARD.

ERASES ALL DRAWING FROM THE SCREEN,
SO THAT YOU MAY BEGIN A NEW SOLUTION.

TAKES YOU TO ANOTHER VIGNETTE
IN THE SAME SECTION OR
ALLOWS YOU TO EXIT THE EXAM.

Figure 16.1

TAKING THE EXAM

INTRODUCTION

Preparation for the ARE usually begins several months before taking the actual exam. The first step is to submit an application for registration with your state board or Canadian provincial association. Most, but not all, registration boards require a professional degree in architecture and completion of the Intern-Development Program (IDP) before a candidate is allowed to begin the exam process. Since the processing of educational transcripts and employment verifications may take several weeks, begin this process early. The registration board will review a candidate's application to determine whether he or she meets the eligibility requirements.

SCHEDULING THE EXAM

The exams are available to eligible candidates at virtually any time, since test centers are open nearly every day throughout the year. However, it is the responsibility of the candidate to contact a test center to schedule an appointment. This must be done at least three days prior to the desired appointment time, but it is probably more sensible to make an appointment a month or more in advance. It is not necessary to take the test in the same jurisdiction in which you intend to be registered. Someone in San Francisco, for example, could conceivably combine his or her test-taking with a family visit in Philadelphia.

FINAL PREPARATION

Candidates are advised to complete all preparations the day before their exam appointment, in order to be as relaxed as possible before the upcoming test. Avoid last-minute cramming, which in most cases does more harm than good. The graphic portions not only test design competence, but also physical and emotional endurance. You must be totally prepared for the strenuous day ahead, and that requires plenty of rest and composure.

One of the principal ingredients for success on this exam is confidence. If you have prepared in a reasonable and realistic way, and if you have devoted the necessary time to practice, you should approach the graphic portions with confidence.

EXAM DAY

Woody Allen once said that a large part of being successful was just showing up. That is certainly true of the licensing examination, where you must not only show up, but also be on time. Get an early start on exam day and arrive at the test center at least 30 minutes before the scheduled test time. Getting an early start enables you to remain in control and maintain a sense of confidence, while arriving late creates unnecessary anxiety. If you arrive 30 minutes late, you may lose your appointment and forfeit the testing fee. Most candidates will begin their test session within one-half hour of the appointment time. You will be asked to provide a picture identification with signature and a second form of identification. For security reasons, you may also have your picture taken.

THE EXAM ROOM

Candidates are not permitted to bring anything (except a calculator) with them into the exam room: no reference materials, no scratch paper, no drawing equipment, no food or drink, no extra sweater, no cell phones, no digital watches. You are permitted to use the restroom or retrieve a sweater from a small locker provided outside the exam room. Each testing center will have its own procedure to follow for such needs. The candidate is allowed to bring his or her own non-programmable, non-printing, non-communicating scientific calculator. The test center staff reserve the right not to permit a calculator if they deem it necessary. Some testing centers may have limited

function handheld calculators available. In addition, a calculator is provided as part of the computer drafting program. Scratch paper will be provided by the testing center. The candidate might wish to request graph paper, if available. Not all testing center staff will remember to offer graph paper to ARE candidates.

Once you are seated at an assigned computer workstation and the test begins, you must remain in your seat, except when authorized to leave by test center staff.

Exam room conditions vary considerably. Some rooms have comfortable seats, adequate lighting and ventilation, error-free computers, and a minimum of distractions. The conditions of other rooms, however, leave much to be desired. Unfortunately, there is little a candidate can do about this, unless, of course, his or her computer malfunctions. Staff members will try to rectify any problem within their control.

EXAM ROOM CONDUCT

NCARB has provided a lengthy list of offensive activities that may result in dismissal from a test center. Most candidates need not be concerned about these, but for those who may have entertained any of these fantasies, such conduct includes:

- Giving or receiving help on the test
- Using prohibited aids, such as reference material
- Failing to follow instructions of the test administrator
- Creating a disturbance
- Removing notes or scratch paper from the exam room
- Tampering with a computer
- Taking the test for someone else

BEGIN WITH THE PROGRAM

You can either solve the vignettes in the order they are presented or build confidence by starting with one that looks easier to you. Only you know what works best for you; the practice software should give you a sense of your preferred approach.

The vignette solution begins with the program. Read the entire program carefully and completely, and consider every requirement. During this review, identify the requirements, restrictions, limitations, code demands, and other critical clues that will influence your solution. Feel free to use scratch paper to jot down key points, data, and requirements. This will help confirm that you understand and meet all the requirements as you develop your solution.

The vignette problem has two components, the written program and a graphic base plan. Both components are complementary and equally important; together they completely define the problem. You should not rush through a review of the program and base drawing in an attempt to begin your design sooner. It is more important to understand every constraint and to be certain that you have not overlooked any significant detail. Until you completely understand the vignette, it is pointless to continue.

GENERAL STRATEGIES

The approach to all vignette solutions is similar: Work quickly and efficiently to produce a solution that satisfies every programmatic requirement. The most important requirements are those that involve compliance with the code, such as life safety, egress, and barrier-free access.

Another important matter is design quality. Strive for an adequate solution that merely solves the problem. Exceptional solutions are not expected, nor are they necessary. You can only pass or fail this test, not win a gold medal. Produce a workable, error-free solution that is good enough to pass.

During the test session, candidates will frequently return to the program to verify element sizes, relationships, and specific restrictions. Always confirm program requirements before completing the vignette, so that you may correct oversights or omissions while there is still time to do so. Candidates must always keep in mind the immutability of the program. That is, you must never—under any circumstances—modify, deviate from, or add anything to the program. Never try to *improve* the program. Only solve what the program asks you to solve, and don't use real world knowledge, such as specific building code requirements.

Candidates should have little trouble understanding a vignette's intent. However, the true meaning of certain details may be ambiguous and open to interpretation. Simply make a reasonable assumption and proceed with the solution.

THE TIME SCHEDULE

The most critical problem on the exam is *time*, and you must use that fact as the organizing element around which any strategy is based. The use of a schedule is essential. During the preparation period, and especially after taking a mock exam, you should note the approximate amount of time that should be spent on each vignette solution. This information must then become your performance guide, and by following it faithfully, you will automatically establish priorities regarding how your time will be spent.

It is important for a candidate to complete each vignette in approximately the time allotted. You cannot afford to dwell on a minor detail of one vignette while completely ignoring another vignette. Forget the details, do not strive for perfection, and be absolutely certain you finish the test. Even the smallest attempt at solving a vignette will add points to your total score.

Vignettes have been designed so that a reasonable solution for each of the problems can be achieved in approximately the amount of time shown in the *ARE Guidelines*. These time limits are estimates made by those who created this test. In any event, a 45-minute-long vignette may not necessarily take 45 minutes to complete. Some can be completed in 30 minutes, while others may take an hour or longer. The time required depends on the complexity of the problem and your familiarity with the subject matter. Some candidates are more familiar with certain problem types than others, and since candidates' training, experience, and ability vary considerably, adjustments may have to be made to suit individual needs.

Candidates who are aware of the time limit are more able to concentrate on the tasks to be performed and the sequence in which they take place. You may submit an imperfect solution, but you *will* complete the test. Lastly, taking time at the end of each section to review all the vignettes can help to eliminate small errors or omissions that could tip the balance between a passing and failing grade.

TIME SCHEDULING PROBLEMS

It is always possible that a candidate will be unable to complete a certain vignette in the time allotted. What to do in that event? First, avoid this kind of trouble by adhering to a rigid time schedule, regardless of problems that may arise with a particular aspect of the problem. Submit a solution for every vignette, even if some solutions still have problems or are not totally complete.

Candidates are generally able to develop some kind of workable solution in a relatively short time. If each decision is based on a valid assumption and relies on common sense, the major elements should be readily organized into an acceptable functional arrangement. It may not be perfect, and it will certainly not be refined, but it should be good enough to proceed to the next step.

MANAGING PROBLEMS

There are other serious problems that may arise, and while each is potentially fatal, they must be managed and resolved. Consider the following:

- You have inadvertently omitted a major programmed element.
- You have drawn a major element too large or too small.
- You have ignored a critical adjacency or other relationship.

The corrective action for each of these issues will depend on the seriousness of the error and when the mistake is discovered. If there is time, you should rectify the design by returning to the point at which the error occurred and begin again from there. If it is late in the exam and time is running out, there may simply be insufficient time to correct the problem. In that case, continue on with the remainder of the exam and attempt to provide the most accurate solutions for the remaining vignettes. The best strategy, of course, is to avoid critical mistakes in the first place, and those who concentrate and work carefully will do so.

WORKING UNDER PRESSURE

The inflexible time limit of the graphic portions creates subjective as well as real problems. This exam generates a unique psychological pressure that can be harmful to performance. While some designers thrive and do their best work under pressure, others become fearful or agitated under the same conditions. It is perfectly normal to be uneasy about this important event, and although anxiety may be a common reaction, it is still uncomfortable.

Candidates should be aware that pressure is not altogether a negative influence. It may actually heighten awareness and sharpen abilities. In addition, as important as this test may be, failure is not a career-ending event. Furthermore, failure is rarely an accurate measure of design ability; it simply means that you have not yet learned how to pass this difficult exam.

EXAMINATION ADVICE

Following is a short list of suggestions intended to help candidates develop their own strategies and priorities. Each item is important in achieving a passing score.

The *ARE Guidelines*, available from the NCARB Web site, also lists suggestions for examination preparedness.

- **Get an early start.** Begin your preparation early enough to develop a feeling of confidence by the time you take the exam. Arrive at the exam site early and be ready to go when the test begins.

- **Complete all vignettes.** Incomplete solutions risk failure. Complete every problem, even if every detail is not complete or perfect.

- **Don't modify the program.** Never add, change, improve, or omit anything from a program statement. Never assume that there is an error in the program. Verify all requirements to ensure complete compliance with every element of the program. If ambiguities exist in the program, make a reasonable assumption and complete your solution.

- **Develop a reasonable solution.** Since most vignettes generally have one preferred solution, solve the problem in the most direct and reasonable way. Never search for a unique or unconventional solution, because on this exam, creativity is not rewarded.

- **Be aware of time.** The strict time constraint compels you to be a clock-watcher. Never lose sight of how much time you are spending on any one vignette. When it is time to proceed to the next problem, quit and move on to the next vignette.

- **Remain calm.** This may be easier said than done, because this type of experience often creates stress in even the most self-assured candidate. Anxiety is generally related to fear of failure. However, if you are well prepared, this fear may be unrealistic. Furthermore, even if the worst comes to pass and you must repeat a division, all it means is that your architectural license will be delayed for a short period of time.

SITE ZONING VIGNETTE

In this vignette you are given a program, a site plan, and a cross-sectional grid on which the zoning solution is to be drawn. The site plan will indicate existing lot lines, streets, and other features. This parcel will need to be divided into two lots and labeled as to the buildable areas for structures and other site improvements, based on the programmatic requirements. On the zoning grid, you are to draw a schematic section that includes (1) the existing site grade and (2) the maximum building envelope above that grade allowed by the program's restrictions.

INTRODUCTION

This vignette combines two previous vignettes, Site Zoning and Site Analysis, into a single vignette. This problem evaluates a candidate's understanding of two important site-related issues:

1. Cross-sectional building area limitations imposed by zoning and other setback restrictions (site zoning)

2. Factors that influence the subdivision of land and determining suitable areas on a site for construction of buildings and other surface improvements, such as parking areas (site analysis)

VIGNETTE INFORMATION

The vignette begins with an index screen that lists other information screens, such as the following:

■ **Vignette Directions**—This screen describes the site plan and the grid in general terms. You are directed to accomplish four tasks:

  1. Outline the area on the site plan suitable for the construction of surface improvements

  2. Outline the area on the site plan suitable for the construction of buildings only

  3. Draw the profile of the existing grade line on the grid below the site plan

4. Draw the profile of the maximum building envelope, in accordance with program and site conditions

■ **Program**—This screen begins with a general description of the site plan and what you are expected to accomplish in the exercise. The screen continues with a detailed description of restrictions that will dictate the parameters of the design, including:

1. Location of property lines
2. Setback information for surface improvements
3. Setback information for the construction of buildings
4. Easements
5. Height limits
6. Solar access planes
7. Other site conditions

■ **Tips**—These are suggestions about procedures intended to make a candidate more efficient, such as using the *sketch* tools, and particularly the line tool, to plot the elevations of the section profile. Other helpful tools include the *full screen cursor* and the *ortho* tool, which insures that a line projected from a point on the plan to the grid will be perfectly vertical.

■ **General Test Directions**—These are the same directions that apply to all vignettes, and they may be reviewed at any time for any vignette. However, one reading is probably all that is necessary for most candidates.

The preprinted site plan and sectional grid on which candidates are required to present their solution are found on the work screen. The site plan generally includes property lines, an access street, topographic contours, a bench mark elevation, and a cross-sectional line that runs horizontally across the middle of the site

plan. The cross-sectional grid is graduated both vertically and horizontally so that one can visually measure height and length. Again, one can find the computer tool icons displayed along the left side of the screen.

DESIGN PROCEDURE

This is a straightforward and mechanical vignette, requiring not so much design skill as close attention to the restrictions and limitations and drawing the profiles and buildable areas as required. For each part of the exercise there is only one solution possible:

■ One area on the site plan suitable for the construction of surface improvements
■ One area on the site plan suitable for the construction of buildings only
■ One profile for the existing grade line on the grid
■ One profile for the maximum building envelope on the grid

Begin the site plan buildable areas by determining the setbacks for surface improvements and the construction of buildings. Determine the maximum area allowable for the construction of surface improvements first. Use the *sketch* tool or *sketch grid* tool to lay out the limits of the secondary construction area. Under the *draw* tool on the site plan screen you will find the necessary tool to outline the boundaries of the secondary construction area. Once you have established the secondary construction area, lay out the buildable area in the same fashion.

To draw the profile of the grade line and building envelope on the grid, project the elevations along the section cut line on the site plan to the cross-sectional grid.

KEY COMPUTER TOOLS

■ **Sketch Tool**   On the site plan, use this tool to measure the distances for setbacks. On the cross-sectional grid, this will be an indispensable tool for helping layout the elevations and building profile before using the draw tool to add the grade and buildable area profile.

■ **Ortho Tool**   Candidates will most likely find this tool of great assistance in laying out the site. On the section, this tool will be helpful for keeping elements in line with each other, the site plan, and the grid.

■ **Full Screen Cursor**   Similar to the ortho tool for working on the cross-sectional grid, the Full Screen Cursor aids in keeping components lined up.

VIGNETTE SITE ZONING

Introduction

The following Site Zoning vignette asks you to determine buildable areas on the site plan and to draw the existing grade and buildable profile on the cross-sectional grid. As with the other vignette examples, our solution is presented in a logical progression of steps in which each element of the problem is considered in sequence. Those who learn to solve vignette problems this way should have few difficulties.

The Exam Sheet

Shown are the Site Zoning program, site plan, and site section grid on which candidates were to present their solutions. You may notice that the plan and section grid have no scale, because all the dimensions one needs are indicated on the grid.

The program directs you to draw the following:

1. An outline of the area on the site plan suitable for the construction of surface improvements
2. An outline of the area on the site plan suitable for the construction of buildings only
3. The profile of the existing grade line on the grid
4. The profile of the maximum building envelope on the grid

The profile of the existing grade and the allowable building envelope will be drawn along the section cut line X-X shown on the site plan.

The site plan shows a narrow plot of land that runs basically east and west. At the front of the property is Sun Street, and at the center of the curb is noted a bench mark elevation of 50 feet. Along the length of the property we note randomly spaced contours, which are essentially vertical. Our only concern about these contours

is their elevation at the points where they cross the section cut line noted as X-X.

On this plot the candidate is to determine the limits for the construction of surface improvements and limits for the construction of buildings. A utility easement is indicated between the two lots.

The site section grid is a simple graph with horizontal and vertical dimensions shown along the bottom and right side. Although the horizontal and vertical dimensions are at the same scale, that is, one small square equals 10 feet in both length and height, the two scales could conceivably be different. It should matter little to you, since you are drawing an abstract diagram.

Drawing the Secondary Construction Area

The Site Zoning vignette requires the examinee to identify the secondary construction limits of the site—the area where surface improvements can be made, excluding buildings. The program defines the parameters for the secondary construction limits. The logical thing to do is draw these setbacks on the lots and infill the resulting space with a hatch and label it "Secondary Construction." The secondary construction area will in all likelihood be more generous in size that the buildable area on site. Conceivably, the secondary construction area might match the buildable area. At no time, however, may the buildable area be larger than the secondary construction area.

In this vignette the limits of the secondary construction zone is fairly straightforward to determine. It is simply 5 feet in from every property line, excluding the utility easement, as shown in Figure 18.1.

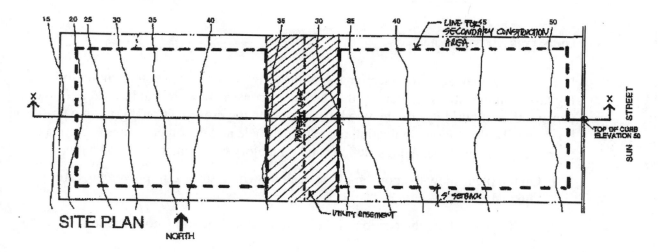

Figure 18.1

Drawing the Buildable Area

Once the secondary construction area has been established, it is easy to layout the area in which buildings can be constructed, or the "buildable area." The program will inform you of the setback requirements and other stipulations for determining this area. For this exercise, we discover that the setback from Sun Street is 15 feet. The candidate simply draws a line parallel 15 feet from Sun Street. The side-yard setbacks for the buildable area match the limits of the secondary construction zone, 5 feet from the side property lines. This will not always be the case.

The buildable area will often be more restrictive than the area allowed for surface improvements. Finally, we see that the rear setback is 10 feet from the property line. One thing to note in this problem is that there is a special condition for Lot A. The program informs us that the front and rear setback for this property is 10 feet. The candidate will also note that no building of any sort is allowed in the utility easement.

We now have the limits for buildable area. The examinee may wish to use a different hatch to indicate this area to differentiate it from the secondary construction area.

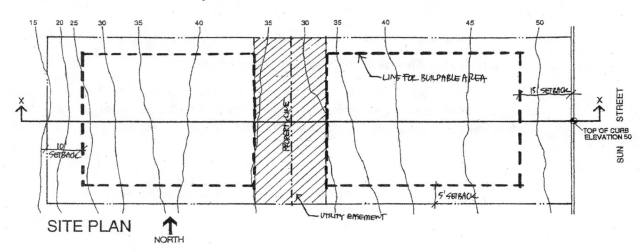

Figure 18.2

VIGNETTE SITE ZONING

Using the site plan and cross-sectional grid drawings you are to accomplish the following tasks: on the site plan, identify the secondary construction area and the area for the construction of buildings on the two lots shown. On the cross-sectional grid, two profile lines must be drawn: one indicating the existing grade and the other outlining the maximum building envelope. All restrictions and regulatory requirements are to be met.

1. On the plan, show the portion of the each lot where surface improvements are allowed.

2. On the plan, show the portion of the each lot where building construction is permitted.

3. On the grid, draw the profile of the existing grade at section X-X.

4. On the grid, draw the profile of the maximum building envelope for each lot at section X-X.

Observe all the following restrictions:

- Surface improvements are prohibited within 5 feet of any property line.

- Construction of building or surface improvements are prohibited within the utility easement.

- Construction of buildings is prohibited within the following setbacks:

  - Setbacks from Sun Street are 15 feet.

  - Rear yard setbacks are 10 feet.

  - Side yard setbacks are 5 feet.

  - Front and rear setbacks on Lot A are 10 feet.

- Maximum height limit within 75 feet of Sun Street is 30 feet above the curb elevation.

- Maximum building height is 45 feet above the curb elevation.

- The maximum building envelope is restricted to an elevation defined by a 45-degree line rising eastward from a point on the rear setback line on Lot A at an elevation equal to the curb elevation and ending at the maximum building height elevation.

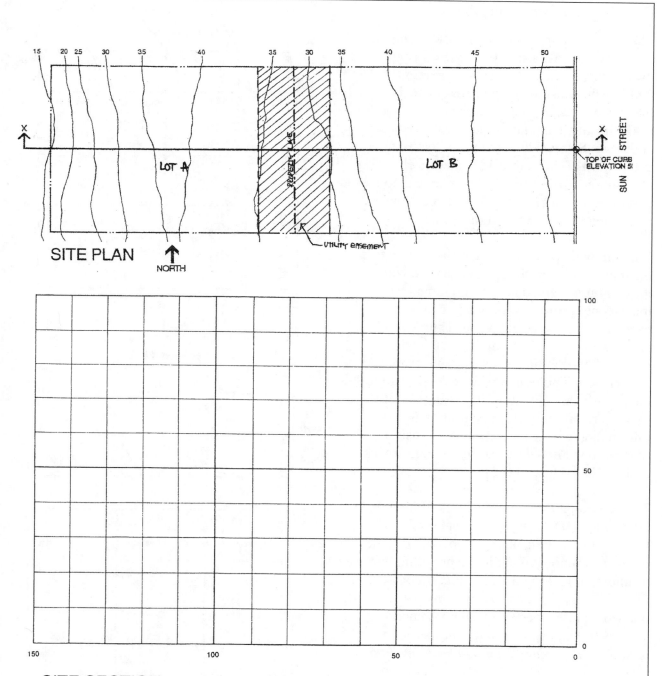

SITE PLAN

NORTH

LOT A

LOT B

PROPERTY LINE

UTILITY EASEMENT

TOP OF CURB
ELEVATION 5[

SUN STREET

X

X

15 20 25 30 35 40 35 30 35 40 45 50

SITE SECTION - VIEW TOWARD THE NORTH

150 100 50 0

100 50 0

Drawing the Grade Profile

The solution to the sectional profile of the Site Zoning vignette consists of two distinct parts, the existing grade profile and the maximum building envelope. You must always begin with the existing grade profile, and one may plot this profile from either end of the site. If we begin at the Sun Street side of the property, we note that the top of the curb is indicated as elevation 50. Without projecting any lines, we can immediately go to the grid and place a dot at the 50 level, along the far right vertical line.

The following points are determined by noting the intersections of the section cut line with the contours. Candidates should remember that a contour line is simply a line that connects points of equal elevation. Thus, every point along the 50 contour, including where it intersects the cut line, is exactly at elevation 50. When that point is projected downward to the grid, we already know its position relative to the vertical scale; it is at elevation 50. The information we are projecting is its position relative to the horizontal scale, the left-to-right scale at the bottom of the grid.

The second part of the problem is a bit more complicated. Drawing a sectional profile of the maximum buildable envelope will depend on the restrictions found in the program. For example, if the program stated: *the setback from the front property line is 10 feet*, then one would draw the front wall of the building section 10 feet away from that property line. And if *the maximum building elevation within 50 feet of the street is 40 feet* (measured on the graph's vertical scale), then the same front wall would be limited to that specific height.

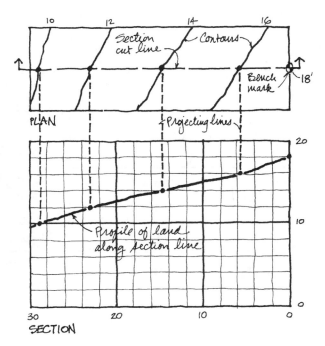

DRAWING A GRADE PROFILE

Figure 18.3

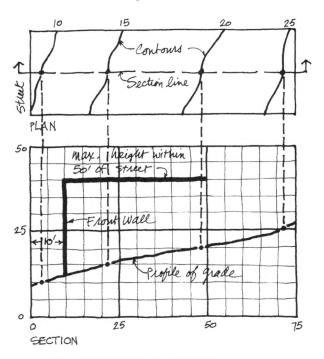

MAXIMUM BUILDING HEIGHT

Figure 18.4

Incidentally, height limits may be stated in a variety of ways. For example, the height limit may be a specific value, such as: *the maximum building elevation is 80 feet*. The building height may also be expressed as a certain number of feet above the property line, or above the bench mark elevation (wherever that mark is located), or a certain number of feet above the bench mark elevation within a certain distance of a property line or street. In other words, one must be prepared to decipher the convoluted language of this exercise and then follow the directions precisely.

The restrictions of the Site Zoning vignette generally include front and rear yard setbacks, height limitations, and possibly an easement restricting all development within its boundaries. As an example, the program might read as follows: *Construction is prohibited over a 20-foot-wide utility easement whose center line runs parallel to and 60 feet distant from the rear property line*. The delineation of this restriction is illustrated in Figure 18.5.

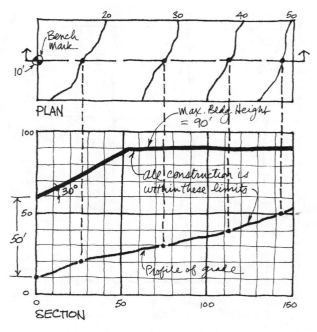

SOLAR ACCESS PLAN

Figure 18.6

There is one more restriction that one may find confusing. It is often known as a solar access plane, and an example of this restriction might be stated as follows: *The maximum building envelope is restricted to an elevation defined by a 30-degree line rising eastward from a point on the front property line that is 50 feet above the bench mark elevation and ending at the maximum building height elevation of 90 feet.*

The language of this restriction may take another reading or two and perhaps a diagram such as the one in Figure 18.6. It is not the design concept that is difficult to understand, it is the expression of the idea.

All programmatic restrictions must be considered and plotted one at a time until they form a complete building profile. You must remember that you are not designing a structure; you are simply following the directions and restrictions of the program until the structure's profile is completed.

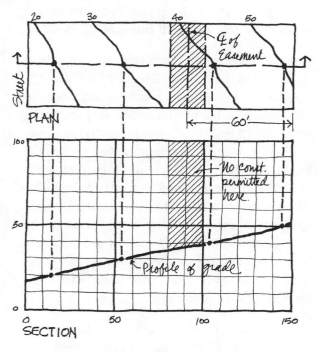

EASEMENT RESTRICTION

Figure 18.5

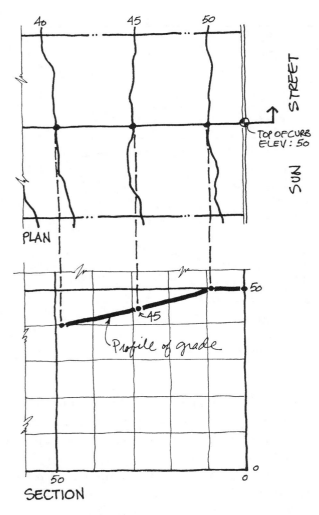

PLOTTING THE GRADE

Figure 18.7

We place a dot on the grid where indicated, and thus, we see the lot is level for the first 10 feet or so. The next contour to the west is the 45 contour, and again we project its intersection with the section cut line down to the 45 level of the grid, which is located midway between the 40 and 50 designations.

In a like manner, we proceed westward and find the intersections of the remaining contours with the section cut line. We project these points downward and place a dot at the appropriate spots on the grid. When we have completed this mechanical exercise, we will see a series of dots on the grid, which represent the elevations

of all the contours cut by the section cut line in plan. If we connect the dots, we will have an accurate profile of the land along the section line. One must be careful not to omit even a single contour intersection, because such an omission will alter the profile and lower your test score.

Drawing the Building Envelope

The term *building envelope* refers to the outline of a structure or the limits of its enclosure. In the case of the Site Zoning vignette, we are referring to the section cut through a structure that will enclose the maximum allowable space.

It is best to begin this process by following the order of the program's several restrictions. The first of these notes the setback from Sun Street as 15 feet. Thus, we can locate a vertical line that is 15 feet west of the zero on the bottom scale. Similarly, we note that the rear yard setback is 10 feet, and so we locate another vertical line 10 feet east of the left edge of the grid, which is at the 140-foot mark on the bottom scale. With these two vertical lines, we have defined the left and right limits of the building.

The third restriction states that the maximum building height within 75 feet of Sun Street is 30 feet above the curb elevation. Since the curb elevation is noted as 50 feet, 30 feet above this level would be 80 feet. Returning to the vertical line at the east, we find the 80-foot level and draw a horizontal line running westward. But how far west should this line be drawn? The requirement says the 30-foot height limit extends 75 feet from Sun Street. However, the utility easement starts 70 feet from Sun Street. Since the east building line is already 15 feet from Sun Street, we draw the horizontal line another 55 feet to the west.

At that point, the next restriction takes precedence: the utility easement. The program indicates that no building can occur within the utility easement, so the line will drop down to grade at the 70 foot mark. It will start from grade again at the 90 foot mark, which is the west side of the utility easement. At this point the maximum allowable building height changes. It is 45 feet above the curb elevation here, or 95 feet according to the grid lines. The vertical building line we start at the horizontal 90 foot mark will extend up to the 95 foot elevation. This new roof line will now continue westward.

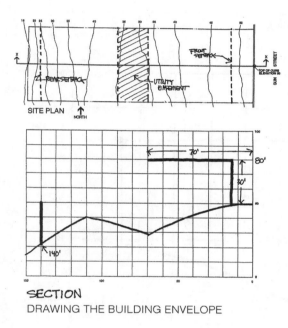

SECTION
DRAWING THE BUILDING ENVELOPE

Figure 18.8

Our final restriction should allow us to complete the diagram. However, this restriction is the most complicated. It states that *the maximum building envelope is restricted to an elevation defined by a 45-degree line rising eastward from a point on the rear setback line at an elevation equal to the curb elevation and ending at the maximum building height elevation.* To understand this wordy requirement, it is best to take it one step at a time. First, the limit line will be a line angled at 45 degrees. Thus, when the requirement says you are restricted to *an elevation*, it really means that

you are restricted to all elevations falling along this 45-degree line.

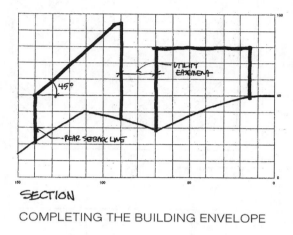

SECTION
COMPLETING THE BUILDING ENVELOPE

Figure 18.9

Next, the 45-degree line originates along the building's rear setback line, which is at the 140-foot mark measured along the lower grid scale. Its beginning elevation equals the curb elevation, which is 50 feet. With this information we can establish a point on the grid along the rear setback line, at an elevation of 50 feet. From this point we project a 45-degree angle eastward until it intersects the maximum building height of 95 feet. The geometric shape is closed, and our solution is complete.

CONCLUSION

The discussion of this solution is perhaps more lengthy and complicated than the actual problem. Success on the Site Zoning vignette is simply a matter of following every direction precisely. If one complies with every restriction, and avoids simple mistakes, there is no reason why he or she should not succeed on this vignette. Those who fail are those who lose their concentration, or ignore, misunderstand, or misinterpret a requirement.

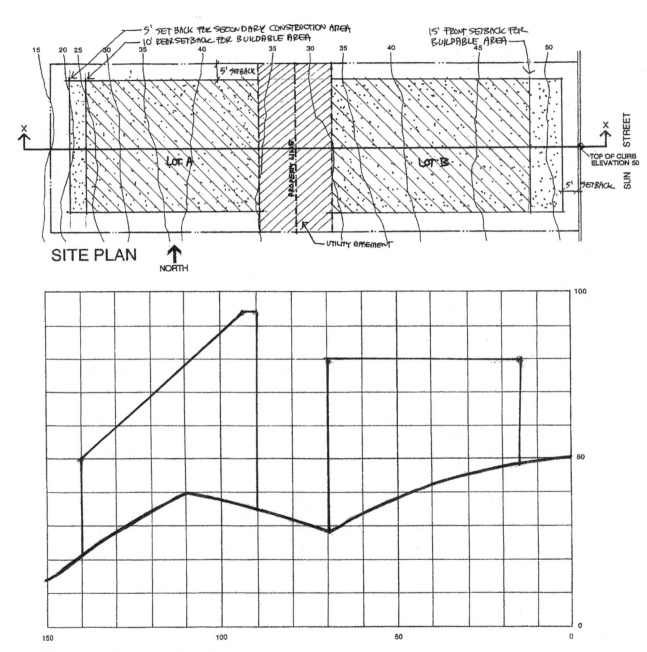

SITE PLAN

NORTH

SITE ZONING VIGNETTE - SUGGESTED SOLUTION

Figure 18.10

The following glossary defines a number of terms, many of which have appeared on past exams. While this list is by no means complete, it comprises much of the terminology with which candidates should be familiar. You are therefore encouraged to review these definitions as part of your preparation for the exam.

A

Abutment   A buttressing or supporting structure.

Acoustics   The branch of physics that deals with sound. In architectural application, the sound qualities of a room or space.

Acropolis   In an ancient Greek city, a citadel, usually on a high plateau.

Adobe   A sun-dried brick of earth, used in the American Southwest.

Aesthetics   The branch of philosophy that deals with the quality, aspects, and perception of beauty.

Air Rights   The rights to the use or control of space above a property, such as highways, railroad tracks or buildings.

Albedo   Reflectivity measured as the relative permeability of a surface to radiant energy flowing in either direction.

Alignment   Horizontal or vertical deviation from the straight or level centerline of the road.

Amphitheater   An arena encircled by tiers of seats.

Annunciator   An electromagnetic device that indicates the activation of certain circuits; a device to signal the existence and location of a fire in a building.

Apse   The eastern or altar end of a church, usually semi-circular in plan.

Ashlar   Masonry having a face of square or rectangular stones.

Azulejo   A glazed decorative tile with the color blue most prominent.

B

Backfill   Earth or other fill material placed between an outside foundation wall and the excavation.

Baffle   A partial obstruction against flow, in a duct or pipe.

Balance   The proportioning of components by offsetting or contrasting so as to produce an aesthetic equilibrium in the whole.

Baroque   A style of European architecture developed in the late Renaissance in reaction to classical forms, containing elaborate curves, scrolls, and ornament.

Base Lines   East-west lines from which townships are established on government surveys. They run perpendicular to meridian lines.

Bat   A part, usually half, of a broken brick; also a unit of flat insulation.

Batten   A cleat-like member placed across a series of boards to tie them together; also, a narrow strip covering the joint between two vertical boards.

Belvedere   Roofed structure or pavilion located to command a view.

Bench   An excavated level terrace in a slope used to collect running water.

Bench Mark   A relatively permanent surveyor's mark of known location and elevation.

Berm   A bank of earth, often piled up against a wall.

Bituminous   Describing cement, mastic, or roofing material which contains asphalt as a principal ingredient.

Blighted Area   An area, usually urban, that has deteriorated in quality and value, and which functions well below its economic and social potential.

Block   A division of urban land, normally private property, that is surrounded by public streets, and which is officially established and recorded.

Bollard   A stone guard to prevent damage to a wall; also, a free-standing stone or metal post to divert vehicular traffic.

Boring   Drilling into the earth to obtain soil samples in order to determine soil bearing capacity.

Brise-Soleil   A sun break, an architectural shading device for blocking unwanted sun rays.

BTU   British Thermal Unit, the amount of heat required to raise the temperature of one pound of water 1°F.

Building Line   A defined limit within a property line beyond which a structure may not protrude.

C

Caisson   An air chamber without a bottom, used in excavation through water or mud.

Campanile   A bell tower.

Cant   To set at a slant from the horizontal or vertical.

Carrel   A small room in a library.

Catch Basin   A sieve-like device at the entrance to a storm sewer to trap matter that could block up the sewer.

Catchment   A geographical area from which the participants in an activity are drawn, such as the customers of a shopping center, or the employees of a manufacturing plant.

Caulk (or Calk)   To fill a joint with mastic, usually done with a pressure gun.

Cella   The inner enclosed room of an ancient temple.

Channelization   The separation of traffic lanes by use of islands or dividers.

Check Valve   A valve in a pipe that permits water to flow only in one direction.

Circulation   The flow or movement of people, goods, vehicles, etc., from place to place.

Climate   The prevailing or average weather conditions of a place as determined over a number of years.

Clinker   A brick that has been overburned by being near the fire in a kiln.

Cloverleaf   A type of grade-separated interchange used in highway design. Named for its shape.

Cluster   A method of residential siting in which a series of housing units are grouped to form common interior spaces, as well as a unified peripheral space.

Collector Street   A street to which minor streets connect and that, itself, leads to a major arterial.

Color   The sensation resulting from stimulation of the retina of the eye by light waves of certain lengths; the property of reflecting light of a particular wavelength.

Concave   Hollow and curved inward (e.g., the inside surface of a hollow sphere).

Conductivity   The speed with which energy (normally heat energy) passes through a given material after penetrating its surface.

Coniferous   Pertaining to cone-bearing trees and shrubs, mostly evergreens, such as pine, spruce, fir, cedar, etc.

Constellation Pattern   A pattern of land use in which random clusters of development are connected to one another.

Construction Management   A procedure in which an owner contracts with a construction manager (CM), who is generally responsible for control of a project's time, cost, and quality.

Contingency Allowance   An amount included in a construction budget, normally 5 to 10 percent, to provide for unforeseen or unpredictable costs.

Contour   An imaginary line of constant elevation on the ground surface used to designate elevation and describe the form of land surface graphically.

Convection   The distribution of energy (normally heat) by fluid movement of air or water.

Convex   Curved outward (e.g., the surface of a sphere).

Covenant   A deed restriction that regulates land use, construction materials, appearance, and aesthetic qualities of an area.

Craze   To develop minute surface cracks in stucco, concrete, or glaze.

Critical Path Method   A system of planning and scheduling construction operations that analyzes sequences and durations of time using network diagrams and identifies construction tasks that have great impact in schedule.

Cul-De-Sac   A short road with no outlet, serving only those buildings or properties that front on it.

Culvert   A length of pipe, running under a road or other barrier, used to drain or carry water.

Curb   A raised margin running along the edge of a street pavement, usually of concrete.

Cut and Fill   Earth that is removed and earth that is added in grading.

D

Dais   A platform raised above floor level.

Datum   A horizontal plane elevation used as a reference for other elevations in surveying and mapping.

Deciduous   Shedding leaves annually, as contrasted with evergreen.

Deed   A written instrument that is used to transfer property title from one party to another.

Density   A measure of the number of people, families, etc., that occupy a specified area.

Design   The arrangement of parts, details, form, color, etc., so as to produce a complete entity.

Dew Point   The temperature at which air becomes saturated with moisture and condensation occurs.

Double Glazing   Two sheets of glass with an air space between, to insulate against the passage of heat or sound.

Drainage   The system by which excess water and wastes are controlled, collected, transported, and disposed.

Drain Tile   Clay pipe, usually with open joints, to convey water away from a footing or to disperse fluid in a septic tank field.

Dry Well   A pit, usually filled with coarse stone, into which water is conducted for leaching out into surrounding soil.

Duomo   A dome, hence often a cathedral.

Dwelling Unit   An independent living area that includes its own private cooking and bathing facilities.

E

Earthwork   The modifications involved in altering existing topography.

Easement   A legal right that an individual or the public may have to use or have access to a portion of another person's land.

Effective Temperature   Sensation produced by the combined effects of absolute temperature, relative humidity, and air movement.

Elevation   The height above a known point of reference, often taken as the height above sea level.

Eminent Domain   The right of a public agency to expropriate private property for public use.

Entasis   The slight convexity of a column, used to give an impression of vertical strength.

Erosion   The gradual wearing away or disintegration of land caused by water running over its surface, wind, etc.

Esquisse   A preliminary sketch or plan.

Evergreen   Having green leaves throughout the year, as opposed to deciduous.

Excavation   The digging or removal of earth or soil, as for a foundation.

Exedra   A semi-circular open area, with or without a roof, providing a continuous seat.

Expressway   See Freeway.

F

Facade   The exterior face of a building, usually the front.

Faience   Enameled clay products.

Fast Track   A construction technique in which construction on each phase of a project is begun when its design is completed, without waiting for overall project design completion.

Fault   The boundary between adjacent rock plates along which movement may take place during an earthquake.

FHA   Federal Housing Administration. Founded in 1934 to provide mortgage insurance.

Fire Brick   Brick composed of clay not containing any fusible material, which can resist high temperatures.

Fire Wall   A wall resistant to the spread of fire.

Floor Area Ratio   The ratio between the gross floor area of a building and its site area.

FNMA   Federal National Mortgage Association (Fannie Mae), an agency whose function is to stabilize the housing market by purchasing mortgages or providing mortgage money directly.

Form   The shape, outline, or configuration of a structure or the parts of a structure that gives it its distinctive appearance.

Freeway   A high speed, multiple-lane highway designed to move traffic smoothly and without interruption.

Frieze   A horizontal band on a vertical surface, located beneath a cornice, sometimes decorated with relief sculpture.

Frost Line   The limit of penetration of soil by frost.

Furring   Attaching wood or metal strips to a rough wall, to provide a flat plane for the finish or to provide an air space.

G

Gazebo   A belvedere or viewing place.

Ghetto   A specific residential area in which people of a particular ethnic identity are concentrated.

Glare   Extreme contrast between light and dark in the visual field, which can cause discomfort.

GNMA   Government National Mortgage Association (Ginnie Mae), an agency that functions in the secondary mortgage market.

Grade   The degree of rise or descent of a sloping surface. Also, the act of altering or finishing existing topography.

Granolith   Concrete used for paving, which uses crushed granite as the coarse aggregate.

Greenbelt   A belt-like area around a city, reserved for park land, farms, open space, etc.

Grid Pattern   A pattern of land division for development as well as circulation, so named for its shape.

Guaranteed Maximum Cost   An amount established in an agreement between an owner and a contractor as the maximum cost of performing specified work.

H

Harmony   Agreement or proportionate arrangement of parts in size, color, form, etc.

Hippodrome   A race course bordered by tiered seating.

Housing   The type, arrangement, and quality of dwelling units distributed over a given area.

HUD   Department of Housing and Urban Development. Federal agency concerned with all phases of housing activities.

Humidity   The amount or degree of moisture in an area expressed as a percentage, a determining element of weather.

I

Icon   A sacred picture or object.

Impost   The cap of a pier or pilaster that supports the spring of an arch.

Ingress   An entrance.

Inner City   The sections of a large city in or near its center, especially when crowded or blighted.

Intaglio   A surface decoration formed by a slightly depressed plane of lines and patterns.

Interchange   An access and egress point on a freeway that permits traffic to enter, exit, or change direction.

Intersection   The point at which two streets come together or cross.

Inversion   A situation, generally the reverse of normal, in which cold air is close to the ground and a layer of warm air is above it.

Invert Elevation   The elevation of the lowest inside surface of a pipe or sewer.

J

Jalousie   A window or door blind made of movable horizontal slats.

K

Keystone   The wedge-shaped top member of an arch.

Kiosk   A small pavilion, usually in a public place.

L

Lanai   A Hawaiian terrace or veranda.

Landscaping   The design and arrangement of natural elements on a site.

Lantern   A superstructure on a roof, dome, or tower, glazed along its sides, that admits light to the area below.

Lien   A legal claim on property, as security for money owed.

Light   Radiant energy that is perceived by the human eye.

Linear Pattern   A pattern of land use that develops along a line, such as a highway or river.

Lintel   A structural member placed over an opening and supporting construction above.

Loop Street   A street that starts at a major street, extends in curvilinear fashion for a short distance, and then returns to the major street.

Louver   One of several horizontal slats, slanted to exclude rain but allow the passage of air.

M

Macadam   Paving using crushed stone.

Macroclimate   The general climate over a large geographical area.

Manhole   A hole through which a person can enter a sewer, pipe, conduit, etc., in order to inspect, repair, or service a utility.

Master Plan   Long range, overall concept of an area's development.

Mastic   Caulking that remains elastic.

Megalith   A stone of great size.

Megalopolis   A term referring to a group of large cities or metropolitan areas that merge.

Metes and Bounds   A description of property boundaries expressed by directions (bearings) and distances.

Metropolitan Area (or Region)   The characteristic form of large scale American urbanization; a city form with an operating radius of 30 miles or more.

Microclimate   The general climatic characteristics that are peculiar to a very small area.

Module   A repetitive dimension used in architectural design and planning.

Mortgage   An agreement to pay for the cost of a property over a long period of time, in which the property is pledged as security.

Mullion   The vertical division member between windows or doors.

Muntin   A wood or metal member used to hold the panes within a window.

N

Naos   An inner chamber of a classical temple.

Narthex   The entrance vestibule of a church.

Nave   The main longitudinal portion of a church interior.

Neighborhood   A community of people living in a general area. The area can generally support an elementary school.

Network   A system of circulation channels that covers a large area.

O

Obelisk   A commemorative shaft, square in section, with a small pyramid on top.

O.C.   An abbreviation for "on-center," used in dimensioning.

Orientation   The positioning of an object in relation to certain directions; the sense of direction as disclosed by an object in a particular position.

P

Pagoda   In Far Eastern architecture, a tower-like structure.

Palazzo   A palace.

Panopticon   A building planned so that a person at the center can observe converging corridors.

Parterre   A level and patterned garden.

Parti   The general scheme of a design.

Party Wall   A wall built astride a property line.

Patio   An open court enclosed by the walls of a building.

Pediment   The triangular face of a roof gable.

Planting Strip   A landscaped strip of ground dividing a pedestrian walk from a street.

Plat   A plan of a land area, lots, streets, etc.

Plot   A parcel of land.

Prefabricated   Constructed off-site in standardized sections for shipment and quick assembly, such as a prefabricated house.

Proportion   A system of sizing and division to establish harmonious relationships between component elements.

PUD   Planned Unit Development, a zoning designation that allows greater freedom in site planning, while usually maintaining the same density. Similar to cluster developments but larger in scale, including commercial and industrial developments, in addition to housing.

R

Radial Pattern   A circulation pattern in which channels spread out from a central point.

Rake   A slope or incline, as on a roof.

Rhythm   The recurrence of design elements in space.

Right-of-Way   A path of circulation conveying persons, vehicles, services, etc.

Ring Pattern   A land use pattern that is developed in a circular or doughnut form, the center being relatively unused.

Ring Road   A circumferential or loop roadway around an urban area or development.

Rotary   A device used at an intersection of streets in which all vehicles merge and then diverge at relatively low speeds.

Rotunda   A circular space covered by a dome.

Runoff Coefficient   The fraction of total rainfall that is not absorbed in the ground and, hence, runs off. It must be collected in a system of surface and sub-surface drains.

S

Satellite   In urban planning, an outlying community of secondary importance, dependent on a larger city.

Scale   The relative measurement of an object, with reference to the dimensions of the human body.

Setback   A legally defined distance from the property line into which a structure may not project.

Sewer   An underground pipe or drain used to carry off rain water (storm sewer) or waste matter (sanitary sewer).

Site Planning   Designing the external physical environment in which buildings and structures are placed.

Slope   The amount of deviation from the horizontal or vertical.

Slum   An urban area that is overcrowded and whose buildings may be unsafe and unhealthful to inhabit.

Spot Zoning   Zoning of a parcel of land that is different from that of the surrounding area.

Star Pattern   A pattern of land use developed in the shape of a star.

Stoa   A portico used in Greek architecture, often as a covered shopping way.

Storm Sewer   A sewer for carrying away surface rain water, as opposed to sanitary sewage.

Style   Specific or characteristic manner of expression, execution, construction, or design, in any art, period, work, etc.

Subdivision   The division of vacant land into smaller parcels to be used as sites for individual buildings, together with public rights-of-way affecting these sites.

Subsoil   The soil layer beneath the topsoil.

Suburb   An outlying portion of a city, which is largely residential.

Superblock   A very large area of land in which all through traffic is eliminated, but which may be penetrated by cul-de-sacs or minor loop roads.

Survey   The process of determining location, form, and boundaries of a parcel of land by measurement, computation, and drawing.

Symmetry   A mirror image arrangement of elements on either side of a dividing line or plane.

T

Tar   A dark sticky oil, dry distilled from resinous woods, coal, or peat; used in roofing and road surfaces.

Texture   The arrangement of particles of a material that affects the appearance or feel of the surface.

Topography   The configuration of the surface features of an area of ground.

U

Underpass   A road that crosses under another road.

Urban Renewal   A process of public intervention in the development of an existing urban area, in which the public acquires ownership of property and administers its resale and development to mainly private owners.

Utility   A public service, such as telephone, water, gas, or electricity.

V

Viaduct   A bridge across a valley.

Vomitorium   An entrance (or exit) passage in a large amphitheater.

W

Water Table   The level below ground at which water is found flowing.

Windbreak   Structures or plants that, because of their form and location, reduce wind velocities.

Y

Yard   An area of land not built upon, which may be used for exterior activities.

Z

Zoning   The legal means whereby land use is regulated and controlled for the welfare of the community.

The examination on the following pages should be taken when you have completed your study of all the lessons in this course. It is designed to simulate the Programming, Planning & Practice division of the Architect Registration Examination. Many questions are intentionally difficult in order to reflect the pattern of questions you may expect to encounter on the actual examination.

You will also notice that the subject matter for several questions has not been covered in the course material. This situation is inevitable and, thus, should provide you with practice in making an educated guess. Other questions may appear ambiguous, trivial, or simply unfair. This too, unfortunately, reflects the actual experience of the exam and should prepare you for the worst you may encounter.

Answers and complete explanations will be found on the pages following the examination, to permit self-grading. **Do not look at these answers until you have completed the entire exam.** Once the examination is completed and graded, your weaknesses will be revealed, and you are urged to do further study in those areas.

Please observe the following directions:

1. The examination is closed book; please do not use any reference material.

2. Allow about 60 minutes to answer all questions. Time is definitely a factor to be seriously considered.

3. Read all questions *carefully* and mark the appropriate answer on the answer sheet provided.

4. Answer all questions, even if you must guess. Do not leave any questions unanswered.

5. If time allows, review your answers, but do not arbitrarily change any answer.

6. Turn to the answers only after you have completed the entire examination.

GOOD LUCK!

EXAMINATION ANSWER SHEET

Directions: Read each question and its lettered answers. When you have decided which answer is correct, blacken the corresponding space on this sheet. After completing the exam, you may grade yourself; complete answers and explanations will be found on the pages following the examination.

1. Ⓐ Ⓑ Ⓒ Ⓓ
2. Ⓐ Ⓑ Ⓒ Ⓓ
3. Ⓐ Ⓑ Ⓒ Ⓓ
4. Ⓐ Ⓑ Ⓒ Ⓓ
5. Ⓐ Ⓑ Ⓒ Ⓓ
6. Ⓐ Ⓑ Ⓒ Ⓓ
7. Ⓐ Ⓑ Ⓒ Ⓓ
8. Ⓐ Ⓑ Ⓒ Ⓓ
9. Ⓐ Ⓑ Ⓒ Ⓓ
10. Ⓐ Ⓑ Ⓒ Ⓓ
11. Ⓐ Ⓑ Ⓒ Ⓓ
12. Ⓐ Ⓑ Ⓒ Ⓓ
13. Ⓐ Ⓑ Ⓒ Ⓓ
14. Ⓐ Ⓑ Ⓒ Ⓓ
15. Ⓐ Ⓑ Ⓒ Ⓓ
16. Ⓐ Ⓑ Ⓒ Ⓓ
17. Ⓐ Ⓑ Ⓒ Ⓓ
18. Ⓐ Ⓑ Ⓒ Ⓓ
19. Ⓐ Ⓑ Ⓒ Ⓓ
20. Ⓐ Ⓑ Ⓒ Ⓓ
21. Ⓐ Ⓑ Ⓒ Ⓓ
22. Ⓐ Ⓑ Ⓒ Ⓓ
23. Ⓐ Ⓑ Ⓒ Ⓓ
24. Ⓐ Ⓑ Ⓒ Ⓓ
25. Ⓐ Ⓑ Ⓒ Ⓓ
26. Ⓐ Ⓑ Ⓒ Ⓓ
27. Ⓐ Ⓑ Ⓒ Ⓓ
28. Ⓐ Ⓑ Ⓒ Ⓓ
29. Ⓐ Ⓑ Ⓒ Ⓓ
30. Ⓐ Ⓑ Ⓒ Ⓓ

31. Ⓐ Ⓑ Ⓒ Ⓓ
32. Ⓐ Ⓑ Ⓒ Ⓓ
33. Ⓐ Ⓑ Ⓒ Ⓓ
34. Ⓐ Ⓑ Ⓒ Ⓓ
35. Ⓐ Ⓑ Ⓒ Ⓓ
36. Ⓐ Ⓑ Ⓒ Ⓓ
37. Ⓐ Ⓑ Ⓒ Ⓓ
38. Ⓐ Ⓑ Ⓒ Ⓓ
39. Ⓐ Ⓑ Ⓒ Ⓓ
40. Ⓐ Ⓑ Ⓒ Ⓓ
41. Ⓐ Ⓑ Ⓒ Ⓓ
42. Ⓐ Ⓑ Ⓒ Ⓓ
43. Ⓐ Ⓑ Ⓒ Ⓓ
44. Ⓐ Ⓑ Ⓒ Ⓓ
45. Ⓐ Ⓑ Ⓒ Ⓓ
46. Ⓐ Ⓑ Ⓒ Ⓓ
47. Ⓐ Ⓑ Ⓒ Ⓓ
48. Ⓐ Ⓑ Ⓒ Ⓓ
49. Ⓐ Ⓑ Ⓒ Ⓓ
50. Ⓐ Ⓑ Ⓒ Ⓓ
51. Ⓐ Ⓑ Ⓒ Ⓓ
52. Ⓐ Ⓑ Ⓒ Ⓓ
53. Ⓐ Ⓑ Ⓒ Ⓓ
54. Ⓐ Ⓑ Ⓒ Ⓓ
55. Ⓐ Ⓑ Ⓒ Ⓓ
56. Ⓐ Ⓑ Ⓒ Ⓓ
57. Ⓐ Ⓑ Ⓒ Ⓓ
58. Ⓐ Ⓑ Ⓒ Ⓓ
59. Ⓐ Ⓑ Ⓒ Ⓓ
60. Ⓐ Ⓑ Ⓒ Ⓓ

61. Ⓐ Ⓑ Ⓒ Ⓓ
62. Ⓐ Ⓑ Ⓒ Ⓓ
63. Ⓐ Ⓑ Ⓒ Ⓓ
64. Ⓐ Ⓑ Ⓒ Ⓓ
65. Ⓐ Ⓑ Ⓒ Ⓓ
66. Ⓐ Ⓑ Ⓒ Ⓓ
67. Ⓐ Ⓑ Ⓒ Ⓓ
68. Ⓐ Ⓑ Ⓒ Ⓓ
69. Ⓐ Ⓑ Ⓒ Ⓓ
70. Ⓐ Ⓑ Ⓒ Ⓓ
71. Ⓐ Ⓑ Ⓒ Ⓓ
72. Ⓐ Ⓑ Ⓒ Ⓓ
73. Ⓐ Ⓑ Ⓒ Ⓓ
74. Ⓐ Ⓑ Ⓒ Ⓓ
75. Ⓐ Ⓑ Ⓒ Ⓓ
76. Ⓐ Ⓑ Ⓒ Ⓓ
77. Ⓐ Ⓑ Ⓒ Ⓓ
78. Ⓐ Ⓑ Ⓒ Ⓓ
79. Ⓐ Ⓑ Ⓒ Ⓓ
80. Ⓐ Ⓑ Ⓒ Ⓓ

81. Ⓐ Ⓑ Ⓒ Ⓓ
82. Ⓐ Ⓑ Ⓒ Ⓓ
83. Ⓐ Ⓑ Ⓒ Ⓓ
84. Ⓐ Ⓑ Ⓒ Ⓓ
85. Ⓐ Ⓑ Ⓒ Ⓓ
86. Ⓐ Ⓑ Ⓒ Ⓓ
87. Ⓐ Ⓑ Ⓒ Ⓓ
88. Ⓐ Ⓑ Ⓒ Ⓓ
89. Ⓐ Ⓑ Ⓒ Ⓓ
90. Ⓐ Ⓑ Ⓒ Ⓓ
91. Ⓐ Ⓑ Ⓒ Ⓓ
92. Ⓐ Ⓑ Ⓒ Ⓓ
93. Ⓐ Ⓑ Ⓒ Ⓓ
94. Ⓐ Ⓑ Ⓒ Ⓓ
95. Ⓐ Ⓑ Ⓒ Ⓓ
96. Ⓐ Ⓑ Ⓒ Ⓓ
97. Ⓐ Ⓑ Ⓒ Ⓓ
98. Ⓐ Ⓑ Ⓒ Ⓓ
99. Ⓐ Ⓑ Ⓒ Ⓓ
100. Ⓐ Ⓑ Ⓒ Ⓓ
101. Ⓐ Ⓑ Ⓒ Ⓓ

1. Performance specifications deal with

   A. generic products.

   B. specific dimensions.

   C. methods of fabrication.

   D. final results.

2. Concerning the subject of construction time, select the INCORRECT statement.

   A. Construction time estimates are generally a matter of educated guess-work.

   B. Construction time is almost always longer than drawing-production time.

   C. Construction time is calculated using five-day work weeks.

   D. Construction time may be shortened by using the critical path method.

3. _____ warning devices are principally used on doors to hazardous areas.

4. If a total project budget is $4.2 million, and $1.4 million has already been spent on site acquisition, what is the approximate amount of money available for the actual construction contract?

   A. $1.8 million   C. $2.8 million

   B. $2.4 million   D. $5.6 million

5. A wall assembly that has a high U-factor should be used in areas that

   I. have small daily temperature variations.

   II. have a consistently hot climate.

   III. lie below the 40th parallel.

   IV. enjoy a moderate climate throughout the year.

   V. enjoy low energy costs.

   A. IV only   C. II, III, and V

   B. I and V   D. I, III, and V

6. The requirement for a smokeproof enclosure is determined by a building's

   A. total height.

   B. total floor area.

   C. type of construction.

   D. type of occupancy.

7. If you were commissioned to restore and enlarge a 19th-century building that was originally designed in the Greek Revival style, you might have to consider the

   A. groins of cross vaults.

   B. angle of flying buttresses.

   C. radii of pendentives.

   D. entasis of columns.

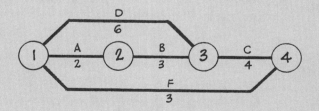

8. In the critical path network diagram shown above, what is the critical path?

   A. 1-4   C. 1-3-4

   B. 1-2-3   D. 1-2-3-4

9. The number of test borings that should be drilled on a particular site is determined by all of the following, EXCEPT the

    A. uniformity of the subsurface conditions.

    B. complexity of the building foot-print.

    C. ground floor area of the proposed building.

    D. depth at which firm strata are encountered.

10. The construction of a federal courthouse must comply with which of the following requirements? Check all that apply.

    A. ANSI standards

    B. OSHA requirements

    C. Local municipal regulations

    D. Filing of an environmental impact statement

11. Which of the following facts would be immaterial during the information analysis phase of the programming process?

    A. The site is zoned to permit light manufacturing.

    B. The production department will employ 125 people.

    C. The facility will utilize a prefabricated shelving system.

    D. The sitework may cost 5 percent of the total project budget.

12. A high-rise apartment structure with exterior balconies is planned for a site that is subject to occasionally strong winds. Solid balcony railings on the higher floors should be designed to withstand forces that are

    A. greater than those on the lower floors.

    B. different at each of the four building faces.

    C. somewhat less than those on the lower floors.

    D. about the same magnitude as on all other floors.

13. If an open entrance plaza is on the windward side of a high-rise building, the plaza may be sheltered from the wind by

    A. planting a row of closely spaced deciduous trees adjacent to the plaza.

    B. planting a row of closely spaced evergreen trees adjacent to the plaza.

    C. building a six-foot-high masonry wall adjacent to the plaza.

    D. relocating the entrance plaza to the leeward side of the building.

14. In order to comply with ANSI standards, elevator cars should have which of the following features? Check all that apply.

    A. 36-inch-wide door

    B. 60-inch turnaround space

    C. 54-inch-high control buttons

    D. Tactile control indicators

    E. Hard finish flooring surface

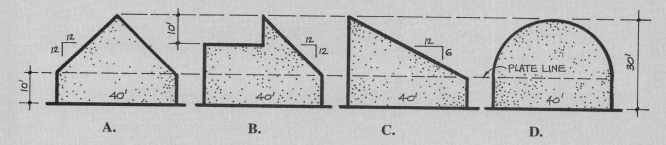

A.   **B.**   **C.**   **D.**

15. The most effective way to reduce the consequences of vandalism would be to employ

A. exterior floodlighting.

B. trained guard dogs.

C. impact-resistant materials.

D. burglar alarm systems.

16. An aquifer is

A. a surface soil that experiences heavy runoff.

B. an underground permeable material through that water flows.

C. the boundary between the zone of aeration and the zone of saturation.

D. the boundary between soil layers, along which sliding may occur.

17. The preliminary plans for a 75,000 gross square-foot office building indicate an efficiency of 72 percent. The developer insists that the net rentable area is insufficient to produce a viable project, and therefore, requests that the efficiency be increased to 78 percent. How much additional rentable area must be provided to satisfy the developer?

A. 1,650 square feet

B. 4,500 square feet

C. 5,850 square feet

D. 6,000 square feet

18. Which roof shape would add the greatest volume to the buildings shown at the top of the page, all of which have the same floor area and plate height?

19. Materials with high heat-storage values would be most appropriate to use in

A. Phoenix, Arizona.

B. Honolulu, Hawaii.

C. Miami, Florida.

D. Houston, Texas.

20. A primary reason for using fast-track scheduling is to

A. guarantee project costs prior to construction.

B. decrease the cost of construction.

C. minimize cost increases caused by inflation.

D. reduce the cost of professional services.

21. Compared to conventional foundations, pile foundations

I.   are more costly.

II.   are more permanent.

III. employ a wider range of materials.

IV.   support greater building loads.

V.   can be constructed more quickly.

A. I and IV   C. II, III, and V

B. I and III   D. I, III, and IV

22. The indoor temperature for which a facility should be designed

    A. is always approximately the same.

    B. is generally higher in summer than in winter.

    C. varies among different regions of the country.

    D. varies according to the cultural backgrounds of the occupants.

23. In establishing a building program, which of the following factors should be considered?

    I. Client's objectives

    II. Users' requirements

    III. Users' organization

    IV. Client's method of financing

    V. Builders' qualifications

    A. I and II   **C.** I, II, and III

    B. I, II, and IV   **D.** III, IV, and V

24. A building with a high efficiency ratio might possibly have

    I. many small spaces.

    II. an absence of vertical shafts.

    III. substantial circulation.

    IV. a small mechanical room.

    V. few toilets.

    A. I and III   **C.** I, II, and V

    B. II, IV, and V   **D.** III, IV, and V

25. Which of the diagrams below illustrates the most serious security problem in the space relationships of a supermarket?

A.
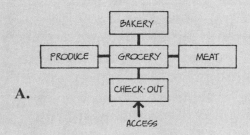

B.
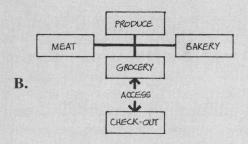

C.
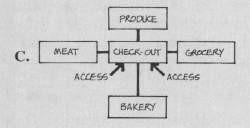

D.
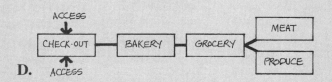

26. Legal restrictions imposed on land by private parties are known as _____.

27. If the critical path time equals 121 days, what is the value of the "float" for a path requiring 54 days?

    A. 0.45
    B. 2.2
    C. 67
    D. 175

28. Which of the following is the LEAST important consideration during the preparation of a program for a new building?

    A. Soil bearing values
    B. Zoning ordinances
    C. Net-to-gross floor area ratio
    D. Costs of project financing

29. Architectural programming is the process of

    A. interpreting the problem.
    B. acknowledging the problem.
    C. discovering the problem.
    D. resolving the problem.

30. Among the following building elements, the one for which flexibility is LEAST important is

    A. church social halls.
    B. shopping center tenant spaces.
    C. hospital patient rooms.
    D. school instructional areas.

31. In the northern hemisphere the use of horizontal "brise-soleil" would be most effective on the _____ face of a building.

32. Which of the following building elements are important considerations in the event of panic?

    I.   Illuminated exit signs
    II. Panic hardware
    III. Reversible escalators
    IV. Collapsible revolving doors
    V.   Elevators with emergency power

    A. I and II
    B. I, II, and IV
    C. III, IV, and V
    D. I, II, III, and IV

33. All of the following might serve as a standard basis for preliminary cost estimating, with the exception of

    A. cost per student.
    B. cost per pedestrian.
    C. cost per inmate.
    D. cost per bed.

34. Which of the following is NOT a consequence of zoning ordinances?

    A. Limited population density
    B. Segregated permitted uses
    C. Restricted lot coverage
    D. Diminished fire danger

35. Referring to the plan shown below, what are the are the correct values of dimensions 1, 2, and 3?

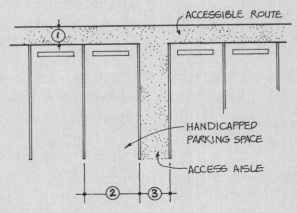

ACCESSIBLE ROUTE

HANDICAPPED PARKING SPACE

ACCESS AISLE

② ③

A. 3' - 0", 8' - 0", 3' - 0"

B. 3' - 0", 8' - 0", 5' - 0"

C. 3' - 6", 8' - 6", 5' - 6"

D. 4' - 0", 9' - 0", 4' - 0"

36. The type and size of a shopping center is primarily determined by its catchment area, which is defined as the area

A. from which it derives its user population.

B. within a 30-minute driving radius of the shopping center.

C. housing a sufficient user population to make the facility viable.

D. necessary to situate a major department store and its required parking.

37. If the cost index, used for estimating construction costs, stands at 920, and the estimate indicates that a commercial project can be constructed for $72 per square foot, what will be its cost of construction when the index reaches 1,150?

A. $90.00 per square foot

B. $115.00 per square foot

C. $129.60 per square foot

D. $165.60 per square foot

38. The sun chart for a specific latitude reveals which of the following?

I. The sun's altitude

II. The sun's azimuth

III. The amount of sunshine

IV. The number of degree days

V. The time of sunrise

A. I and III   **C.** I, II, and V

B. II and V   **D.** I, IV, and V

39. On a moderate hillside that rises behind a housing development, one could reduce the need for a complex drainage system by

A. paving the hillside area with an impervious material.

B. grading level areas into the hillside.

C. providing a thick ground cover of plant material.

D. creating earth berms at the foot of the slope.

40. Which of the following might be considered project overhead costs? Check all that apply.

A. Job-site telephone

B. Sidewalk barricade

C. Temporary power

D. Performance bond

E. Workers' compensation insurance

For questions 41 to 44, refer to the Planning Relationship Matrix shown below.

41. Which of the following elements has the greatest flexibility in its location?

A. Dietary

B. Surgery

C. Maintenance

D. Laboratory

42. The Stores element should be located near

A. Radiology.

B. Labor and Delivery.

C. Student Health Services.

D. Med./Surg. Nursing Unit.

43. Labor and Delivery has approximately the same functional relationship to the Central Sterile Supply as it does to

A. Dietary.

B. Nursery.

C. Med./Surg. Nursing Unit.

D. Post Partum Nursing Unit.

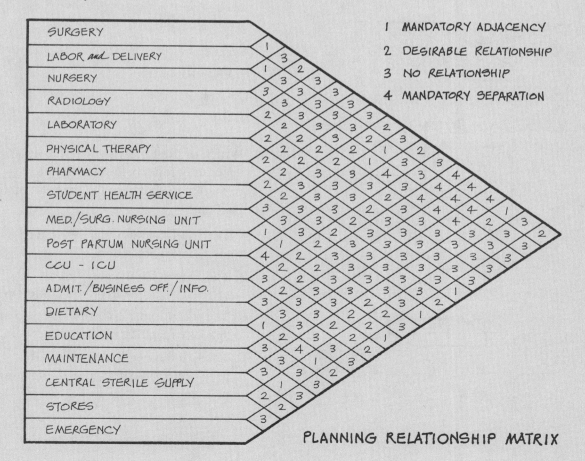

PLANNING RELATIONSHIP MATRIX

44. Among the following elements, which requires the greatest isolation from other elements?

A. Stores

B. Nursery

C. Surgery

D. CCU-ICU

45. During the programming phase, space needs should be expressed by means of _____.

46. Which of the schematic diagrams shown below would be the most suitable for expanding an acute care hospital?

A.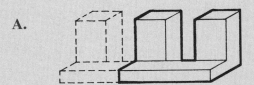

B.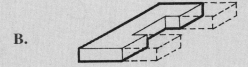

C.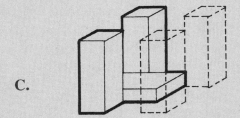

D.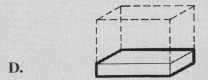

47. Which of the following organizational forms would be best suited to a large, low-cost housing development if the primary concern were cost?

A. Linear

B. Radial

C. Compact

D. Decentralized

48. Which organizational pattern best describes the configuration of a conventional suburban shopping mall?

A. Axial

B. Linear

C. Grid

D. Radial

49. Which organizational pattern formed the basis of development in ancient, classical Rome?

A. Linear

B. Precinctual

C. Grid

D. Ring

50. Which of the following statements accurately reflects the functional relationship shown in the diagram on the next page?

A. The Administrator has direct access to the Conference Room.

B. The Director must pass through his secretary's office to attend conferences.

C. The receptionist controls access to all spaces except the Conference Room.

D. The Conference Room is equally accessible to visitors and administrative personnel.

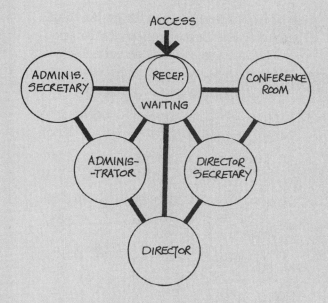

51. In a large corporate office building, the concept of territoriality is best expressed in a(n)

A. reception/waiting room.

B. corporate conference room.

C. secretarial cubicle.

D. employee lunch room.

52. Which of the following directly impose(s) legal constraints on proposed land developments? Check all that apply.

A. Deed restrictions

B. Zoning ordinances

C. Easements

D. Environmental impact statements

53. Which of the following building types would have the most severe negative impact on the environment of an existing residential neighborhood?

I.   Bus terminal   III. Fire station
II. High school   IV. Recreation center

A. I only   C. II and IV
B. III only   D. I and III

54. The predominant design motif or layout of most American cities is based on the

A. cluster concept.

B. grid concept.

C. radial concept.

D. linear concept.

55. The collective mental picture of what people extract from the physical reality of a city is referred to as the "urban image." Among the basic elements that people use to construct this image are "edges," which are defined as

A. the legal boundaries of a city.

B. the physical boundaries of a city.

C. the boundaries that separate city districts.

D. major circulation routes that divide a city.

56. What is the floor area ratio (FAR) of a three-story building on a one-acre parcel of land, if each floor contains 14,520 square feet?

A. One   C. Three
B. Two   D. Ten

57. Within the greater metropolitan area, where would an urban campus for higher education best be located?

A. Close to a major expressway off-ramp

B. Accessible to the urban student population

C. Distant from a manufacturing district

D. Adjacent to a central public library

58. The amount of solar radiation received by a site is influenced by which of the following? Check all that apply.

A. Slope   C. Wind patterns

B. Latitude   D. Longitude

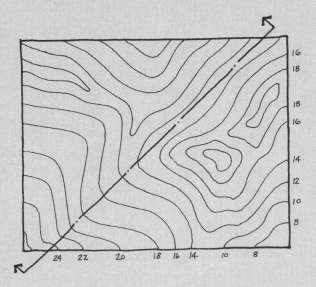

59. Which of the topographic profiles shown below correctly represents the section cut through the plan above?

A.

B.

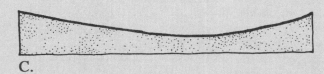
C.

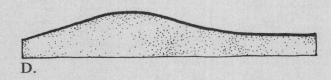
D.

60. The owner of an unoccupied building refuses to sell his property at the price offered by the urban renewal agency. Which of the following statements concerning this situation is true?

A. The owner is required by law to accept the price.

B. The owner must be paid what he feels the property is worth.

C. The owner must be paid fair market value for the land, but only salvage value for the unoccupied building.

D. The property could be taken from the owner before a final price is determined.

61. Which of the following facts is NOT relevant for analyzing the orientation of a new building on a particular site?

A. Neighboring buildings to the west are supported on piers drilled into bedrock.

B. Prevailing winds are from the southwest.

C. The greatest source of noise is an expressway to the east.

D. The new building is to be heated partially by solar energy.

62. A site slopes up from the street five feet for every 20 feet of horizontal distance. In order to use this site for parking cars, the site

A. may be used as is.

B. must be regraded to 1.5 in 10.

C. must be regraded to 1 in 10.

D. must be regraded to 0.5 in 10.

63. Compared to a site containing a large amount of loose silt, a site with a similar amount of organic soil would be

A. more costly to develop.

B. less costly to develop.

C. similar in cost to develop.

D. too costly to develop.

64. If an architect is presented with a sloping site with large areas of loose fill, and the client wishes to develop this site for an elementary school, the architect should

A. reject the site because schools require level land.

B. reject the site because of inadequate soil-bearing value.

C. reject the site because development costs will be excessive.

D. attempt to find a solution using the site's unique properties.

65. Which of the following measures would help reduce automobile usage, and hence congestion, in the development of an office building in a central city area?

I. Provide low-rate parking in the building, with free parking for all tenants and their staffs.

II. Provide only market-rate monthly parking.

III. Provide no parking (or limited parking) with a tax system in which a portion of the real estate tax on the building is earmarked for public transit.

IV. Provide incentive rates for tenants and their staffs who car pool.

A. I and II **C.** I and IV

B. II, III, and IV **D.** II and IV

66. For the graded bank shown below, the grade of the slope is

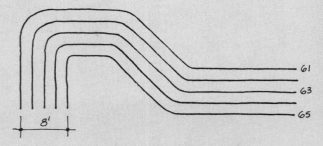

A. 20 percent **C.** 40 percent.

B. 25 percent **D.** 50 percent.

67. To produce a formal design, which of the following design qualities should be used?

A. Balance **C.** Harmony

B. Symmetry **D.** Style

68. A two-dimensional form is unable to possess

I. mass. **III.** texture.

II. space. **IV.** volume.

A. I only **C.** III and IV

B. II only **D.** I and IV

69. The quality of space may be perceived by one's sense of

I. vision. **III.** sound.

II. smell. **IV.** touch.

A. I only **C.** I, II, and III

B. II and III **D.** All of the above

70. The predominant design quality of the Great Pyramid at Gizeh is

A. harmony. **C.** repose.

B. balance. **D.** rhythm.

71. Which of the following locations is the most desirable in selecting a site for a performing arts center?

A. Adjacent to busy pedestrian routes

B. Convenient to public bus and subway routes

C. Near a municipal airport

D. On an island offshore from an urban center

Questions 72 and 73 utilize the following data:

Building Site: 100′ × 180′

Proposed Open Space: 80′ × 100′

Floor Area Ratio: 3

Efficiency Ratio: 70 percent

Floor Area Bonus: 2 square feet for every square foot of open space

Setbacks/Height Limit: None

72. What is the maximum number of stories that can be built above grade if the building is developed to its maximum allowable floor area?

A. 3   C. 7

B. 5   D. 8

73. If the project is developed without any open site space, what will be the maximum net floor area of the building?

A. 12,600 square feet

B. 37,800 square feet

C. 54,000 square feet

D. 66,600 square feet

74. In analyzing a building site, which of the following conditions would indicate the probability of poor drainage?

I. Existing dense ground cover

II. Existing flowing stream

III. Existing high water table

IV. Relatively flat site

V. No storm drainage system

A. I and II   C. II, III, and IV

B. III, IV, and V   D. I, III, and V

75. Compared to a town located at the base of a mountain, the summer temperature of a mountain resort 3,000 feet above the town would be

A. cooler at all times.

B. cooler in the higher latitudes.

C. warmer by day and cooler by night.

D. generally the same.

76. According to ANSI Standards, accessible routes must meet which of the following criteria? Check all that apply.

A. Continuous

B. Unobstructed

C. Designed for all disabilities

D. Designed for exterior circulation only

E. Free of all protruding objects

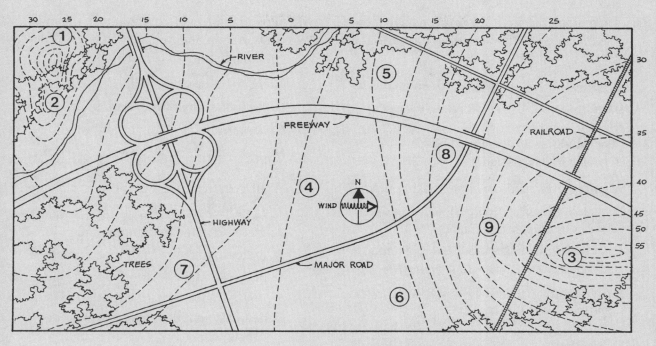

77. The drawing in question 76 illustrates inappropriate

   A. proportion. **C.** balance.
   B. scale. **D.** harmony.

78. On the map illustrated above, the best location for a shopping center would probably be at point

   A. 4. **C.** 8.
   B. 7. **D.** 6.

79. Referring to the same map, the windiest area would probably be at point

   A. 5. **C.** 9.
   B. 1. **D.** 3.

80. The coldest area on the same map would probably be at point

   A. 4. **C.** 1.
   B. 2. **D.** 3.

81. In planning the outdoor seating area of a new restaurant in an urban area, which of the following factors could LEAST be controlled through design?

   A. Traffic noises
   B. Afternoon breezes
   C. Air pollution
   D. Solar radiation

82. A community in the Rocky Mountains has a climate that is mild, sunny, and semi-arid. Extremes of hot and cold weather are rare and of short duration, and prevailing winds are southerly at about 10 miles per hour year round. With low relative humidity, low average precipitation, and considerable sunshine, one may conclude that

   A. air conditioning is not a necessity.
   B. heating costs will be below those in the Gulf Coast area.
   C. fenestration should be minimal.
   D. sloping roofs are inappropriate.

83. Using the criteria of the previous question, the most appropriate building form in such an area would be one that is

    A. compact.   C. earth-sheltered.
    B. multistoried.   D. relatively open.

84. The Modulor as developed by Le Corbusier was a system

    A. of prefabricated concrete housing units.

    B. that employed predetermined, standard-sized building components.

    C. in which the basic module was fixed at 10 centimeters or about 4 inches.

    D. that employed a related series of proportional dimensions.

85. Under normal conditions, a steady slope of 10 percent is a desirable limit for which of the following?

    I.   Storm drainage flow
    II.   Pedestrian walks
    III. Planted banks
    IV.   Unretained earth cuts
    V.   Drainage ditches
    A. II and V   C. I, II, and V
    B. II and III   D. I, III, and IV

86. Compared to a developed urban area, a planted rural area will

    A. reduce the normal amount of rainfall.
    B. reduce wind velocities.
    C. purify the air of harmful pollutants.
    D. stabilize the microclimate.

87. For a majority of communities, the most important planning factor to be considered in the planning of cemeteries is

    A. the location of the land.
    B. the suitability of the terrain.
    C. accessibility to a major highway.
    D. proximity to known sources of noise.

88. With regard to highway design, increased vehicular speed requires a(n)

    A. increase in the maximum road grade.
    B. increase in the radii of road curves.
    C. decrease in the forward sight distance of roads.
    D. decrease in the length of expressway off-ramps.

89. A major metropolis has a great diversity of social, ethnic, cultural, and economic groups in the population. As an urban planner, which of the following would you recommend?

    I.   Develop zoning ordinances that favor diversity, including development bonuses.

    II.   Improve and increase public transit on a metropolitan scale.

    III. Encourage festivals and gatherings which promote inter-group familiarization.

    IV.   Assure that public policies do not place lower income families at a disadvantage with respect to housing.
    A. I and II   C. I, II, III, and IV
    B. II and IV   D. I and IV

90. Compared to a conventional development, a cluster development generally has

I. higher site development costs.

II. lower site development costs.

III. greater overall density.

IV. lower overall density.

V. similar density.

A. I and III

C. II and IV

B. I and IV

D. II and V

91. The space required for a parking lot to accommodate 325 cars, parked at 90 degrees, is approximately _____ acres.

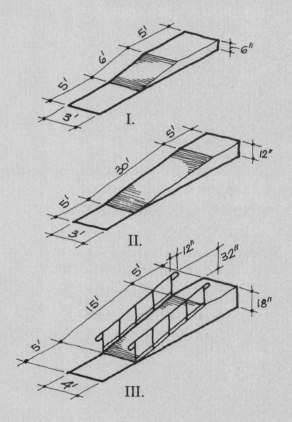

92. Which of the exterior sloping walks shown below left conforms to the ANSI handicapped standards for new construction?

A. I only

C. II and III

B. I and II

D. III only

93. The most effective way to diminish the effects of urban noise is by

A. increasing the distance between the noise source and the receiver.

B. providing a physical barrier of plant material.

C. creating water movement, such as a fountain.

D. eliminating private vehicular traffic.

94. Air which is moving at a speed of 100 feet per minute may be described as

A. pleasant.

C. unnoticeable.

B. drafty.

D. unbearable.

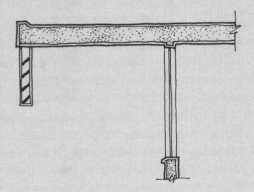

95. The shading device illustrated in the section above would be most effective to

A. reduce the solar radiation on a south elevation.

B. reduce the solar radiation at low sun angles.

C. permit maximum sun control with air circulation.

D. permit maximum sun control with optimum view.

96. In response to the congestion of the industrialized urban environment, most planners advocated low-rise, low-density residential development, with the notable exception of

A. Clarence Stein.

B. Frank Lloyd Wright.

C. Le Corbusier.

D. Ebenezer Howard.

97. Baron Haussmann had the greatest effect on the city of _____.

98. Who designed the early 20th-century community of Radburn, which utilized the superblock concept for the first time?

A. Patrick Geddes

B. Daniel Burnham

C. Clarence Stein

D. Frederick Olmstead

99. An architect wishes to establish the value of a site for a proposed manufacturing building in a suburban location. There is no comparable facility in the area, and in fact, the site is surrounded by completely undeveloped land. Under these circumstances, what method of land evaluation should be used?

A. Comparison method

B. Residual method

C. Allocation method

D. Development method

100. Front yard setback requirements are often expressed as

I.   the distance between the front lot line and the building front.

II. the distance between the street centerline and the building.

III. the distance between the front sidewalk and the building front.

IV. a percentage of the lot depth.

V.   a multiple of the lot width.

A. I, II, and IV   C. II, III, and IV

B. I, III, and V   D. I, II, and III

101. The Ahwahnee Principles include which of the following ideas?

   I. Communities with only residential use should be relegated to areas outside the central business district.

   II. Preserved open spaces should be either wildlife habitats or recreational areas.

   III. Transportation planning should include roads, pedestrian paths, bike paths, and mass transit systems.

   IV. Job creation and economic diversity is a desired goal.

   A. I

   B. II, III, IV

   C. III, IV

   D. None of the above

The examination answers and explanations will be found on the following pages.

Do not look at the answers until you have completed the exam.

EXAMINATION ANSWERS

1. **D** Performance specifications describe a desired final result, rather than the means used to achieve that result. For example, an HVAC system may specify desirable temperature limits, humidity range, and air f low levels, without naming a particular product. The specific components and methods are then left to the HVAC contractor, and the system must achieve the standards established by the specifications.

2. **D** Construction scheduling is invariably based on past experience, and thus, it involves good judgment, as well as some educated guesswork. Construction time is generally longer than drawing-production time and is computed using five-day work weeks, which are then converted to calender days. However, it is unaffected by using the critical path method. CPM is a system of logical planning and scheduling that establishes the optimum sequence of construction operations.

3. **Tactile** Tactile warning devices employ surface textures that are perceived through the sense of touch. They may be located on the interior or exterior of a building and may be applied to walking surfaces, door handles, stair treads, or the edges of reflecting pools. Their purpose is to warn visually-impaired people of existing hazards in the path of travel.

4. **B** From the total project budget of 4.2 million dollars must be subtracted the 1.4 million cost of land, leaving 2.8 million dollars. This amount must cover not only the actual cost of construction, but also professional fees, costs of surveys, soil tests, inspections, material testing, furnishings, etc. These costs average about 15 percent of the net budget of 2.8 million dollars, or 2.8 × .15 = $420,000,

leaving 2.38 million dollars available for the actual construction contract, which is closest to the correct answer of 2.4 million dollars.

5. **A** The U-factor is a measure of heat transmission through a material or assembly of materials. Low values indicate a slow rate of heat loss or gain, while high values indicate a rapid loss or gain of heat. Materials with high U-factors should therefore be used in areas that enjoy a moderate climate all year long (IV). Areas with small daily temperature variations (I) might be very hot or cold all day long, and consistently hot climates (II) would necessitate low U-values. Since about half of the country lies below the 40th parallel (III), this criterion is too inexact to be applicable. Finally, the cost of energy should have no effect on the insulation properties of materials used; materials should be chosen for their ability to provide optimum insulation.

6. **A** The purpose of a smokeproof enclosure is to allow building occupants to exit safely without encountering the hazard of rising smoke from a building fire. Such enclosures are required by building codes in structures that exceed a specific height, regardless of area, construction type, or occupancy.

7. **D** Groins, which are the joints created where two barrel vaults intersect at right angles, were developed by the ancient Romans. Flying buttresses were conceived to transfer the lateral thrust of Gothic vaults and roofs. The pendentive was a Byzantine solution to building a circular dome over a square space. Finally, entasis describes the tapering of Greek column shafts for the purpose of visually correcting an optical illusion. Most likely,

the Greek Revival building would contain columns built in one of the three classical Greek orders.

8. **C**   The critical path is the one in the network diagram that requires the greatest amount of total time to complete the activities. In this case, path 1-3-4 requires 10 days, whereas 1-4 requires 3 days, and 1-2-3-4, 9 days. Path 1-2-3 is not actually a critical path, since it does not include activity 4.

9. **D**   Soil test borings are drilled in order to investigate the subsoil conditions existing on a particular site. When subsurface conditions are relatively uniform, borings may be spaced further apart. Conversely, more borings are required as the shape of the ground floor plan becomes more complex, and as the floor area increases in size. The number of borings, however, is unaffected by the depth of firm strata. Regardless of where these strata are encountered, borings should extend at least 20 feet into such strata, if possible, unless the material cannot be penetrated, such as rock.

10. **A, B, and D**   State or federal projects, which have the government as client, are subject to federal regulations, but are usually exempt from municipal regulations. Regardless of their location, however, they may not disregard ANSI handicapped standards, Occupational Safety and Health Act requirements, or the requirement to file an environmental impact statement.

11. **C**   Collecting, organizing, and analyzing facts is an essential step in the programming process. The architect must discriminate between pertinent facts and unimportant details in order to avoid confusion. Among the pertinent facts are those concerning site zoning, number of employees, and project budget, but excluding special interior equipment, such as shelving. This kind of information is considered at a later stage of project development.

12. **A**   According to the Uniform Building Code, the higher the building, the greater the horizontal wind forces for which it must be designed. Since wind loads increase with height, the highest balcony rails should be designed for forces that are greater than those on the lowest floors.

13. **D**   Using a tree windbreak or masonry barrier will be only moderately successful in blocking uncomfortable winds, since the greatest wind force flows down the face of the building and creates a high-velocity vortex at ground level. The best solution, if possible, is to locate the entrance plaza on the leeward, rather than the windward, side.

14. **A, C, and D**   The handicapped standards that apply to elevator cars include a 36-inch-wide door (A) and 54-inch-high control buttons (C) with tactile control indicators (D). A turnaround space (B) is not required, and the car dimensions are generally less than 60 inches square in any event. Finally, almost any finish flooring material (E) can be used in an elevator car, providing it is securely attached. If carpet is used, however, the maximum pile height is restricted to one-half inch.

15. **C**   Vandalism, which is the willful destruction of property, may be controlled to somedegree with the use of floodlighting, guard dogs, or burglar alarms. However, the results of vandalism can be reduced by using impact-resistant materials or those that are difficult to damage and easy to repair or clean.

16. **B**   An aquifer is the permeable underground rock or earth through which water flows. Definition C refers to the ground water table, while definitions A and D are irrelevant.

17. **B**   The efficiency of a building is the ratio of net to gross area. To determine the original rentable area, multiply 75,000 gross square feet by .72, which equals 54,000 net square feet. Similarly, the desirable rentable area is 75,000 × .78 = 58,500 square feet. The difference between the two net areas is 58,500 – 54,000 = 4,500 square feet. Alternatively, you might have figured the difference in efficiency ratios, 78 – 72 = 6 percent × 75,000 = 4,500 square feet.

18. **D**   This question is a simple geometric problem requiring the computation of cross-sectional areas. If one recalls that the area of a triangle is bd/2 and the area of a circle πr^2, then the calculations of the areas above the plate lines should result in the following amounts: A, B, and C = 400 square feet, and D = 628 square feet.

19. **A**   Materials with high heat-storage values (thermal inertia) are most appropriately used in areas with high daily temperature variations, such as Phoenix. In such hot and arid locations, concrete or masonry walls store heat during the day and later release this heat when the temperature drops, which tends to balance the extremes of day and night. There is little benefit to using high heat-storage materials in hot and humid areas with little temperature variation, such as the other cities listed.

20. **C**   Fast-track scheduling is the best means available to shorten the time between the inception and completion of a construction project. Using this scheduling method, separate bid packages are prepared, which makes it impossible to know the final cost until well into the construction phase. Separate bid packages also generally increase the cost of professional services. Although fast-track scheduling cannot reduce construction costs, it can reduce construction time, which is a way of minimizing inflationary cost increases.

21. **B**   Pile foundations are used where the soil strata beneath a structure are incapable of supporting the imposed building loads using conventional spread footings. They may be constructed from timber, concrete, or steel (III), unlike conventional footings that are invariably made of concrete. Compared to conventional spread footings, pile foundations are generally more costly (I), but they do not outlast spread footings (II). Pile foundations do not normally support greater building loads (IV), nor are they generally constructed more quickly (V).

22. **B**   Indoor design temperatures are predicated on the range of conditions under which most people feel comfortable—a temperature of about 65 to 75°F. with a relative humidity between 30 and 60 percent. Normally, this comfort range is higher in summer than in winter, because indoor temperatures bear some relation to outdoor temperatures. In addition to seasonal variations, design temperatures vary with the activity, being lowest in high-activity areas, and highest in low-activity areas, such as hospitals. Design temperatures and human comfort, however, vary only slightly by region or cultural background.

23. **C**   All of the factors listed are necessary to consider in establishing a building program, with the exception of the financing method (IV) and builders'

qualifications (V). Although both of these considerations are important, they are not relevant to establishing a building program.

24. **B**   The efficiency ratio, that is, net to gross area, is high when the area devoted to circulation and general service is relatively small. For example, a building with many small spaces (I) is less efficient than one that has large open spaces, because the circulation would probably be substantially greater (III). Conversely, a building with few vertical shafts (II), mechanical spaces (IV), and toilets (V) would be more efficient than one in which the services use a higher proportion of the gross building area.

25. **B**   Diagram B is the only arrangement that places the access between the checkout area and the various supermarket departments. Customers, therefore, can theoretically exit the market before passing through the check-out area, which serves as the control point of the entire operation. Any of the other arrangements would solve this security problem.

26. **Deed restrictions**   Deed restrictions are clauses in a deed that place conditions, limitations, or restrictions on the use of property. Private developers often impose such restrictions on buyers for the purpose of maintaining the consistency or integrity of a development.

27. **C**   The float is the difference in time between the critical path and any other path in a critical path network. Because the critical path time is 121 days, and the alternate time path is 54 days, the difference is $121 - 54 = 67$ days. This means that there are 67 days of extra time available for activities along the alternate path, without delaying the project completion.

28. **A**   All of the considerations listed are related to the programming process, except soil bearing values. Although essential for the design of the building foundation, soil bearing values have no effect on the statement of the owner's architectural, functional, or budget criteria.

29. **C**   Architectural programming is the process of problem seeking, whereas design is the process of problem solving. Programming clarifies the intentions of owner and user so that the problem can be discovered and defined. In this discovery process, goals are established, facts are analyzed, and needs are determined, so that the final problem may be revealed and expressed.

30. **C**   Flexibility is an important functional asset in all the building elements listed, except hospital patient rooms. Because a private toilet for every patient room is now regarded as a necessity, the location of plumbing facilities precludes flexibility. In other words, the fixed location of toilet rooms makes it reasonably certain that the original arrangement will remain unchanged for a long time.

31. **A**   The term "brise-soleil" is French for sunscreen, and it is often used to describe the horizontal or vertical fins placed on the face of a building to screen unwanted sunlight. The term was popularized by Le Corbusier, who with Lucio Costa and Oscar Niemeyer, used these elements on the Ministry of Education Building in Rio de Janeiro in 1937. In the northern hemisphere, horizontal elements are effective on southern exposures, while vertical fins are more suitable for east and west building faces.

32. **B**   In the event of panic, which is generally caused by fire, building

occupants must be able to exit a building as quickly and safely as possible. In this regard, all of the building elements listed would be important considerations, with the exception of escalators and elevators. Escalators may be operating in the wrong direction at the time of panic, and elevators are never acceptable as part of a required escape route. They can stall, stop at floors where fire is raging, or become overcrowded due to panic.

33. **B** Among the standard bases for preliminary cost estimating are those expressed as cost per use unit. Schools, for example, are often priced on a per student basis. Similarly, detention facilities are sometimes priced on a per inmate basis, and hospitals on a per bed basis. Pedestrians, however, since they are rarely considered a user class, are the exception in this question. Estimating costs on the use unit basis is quick and effective, but subject to considerable error if the facility being planned is not conventional.

34. **D** Zoning ordinances are laws established by local governmental agencies to regulate and control land use for the general welfare of people living or working in the area. They may achieve any of the results listed, with the exception of diminished fire danger, which is more properly the concern of building codes.

35. **B** According to the ANSI Standards, handicapped parking spaces must be at least 8'-0" wide and have an adjacent access aisle that is a minimum of 5'-0" wide. In addition, the access aisle must be part of a 3'-0" wide access route leading to the building entrance.

36. **A** A catchment area, also known as a market area or trade area, is the tributary area from which a facility derives its user population. Depending on the type and size of the shopping center, the catchment area fluctuates in size on the basis of travel time and convenience in reaching the facility.

37. **A** Historical price indexes are often projected on a straight line basis to estimate current or future costs. In this case, construction costs are expected to escalate over a period of time from an index figure of 920 to 1,150, which is one and one-quarter times ($1,150 \div 920 = 1.25$). Therefore, the cost of construction when the index reaches 1,150 will be $1.25 \times 72 = 90$ dollars per square foot.

38. **C** A sun chart shows the path of the sun, by means of altitude (I) and azimuth (II), usually on the 21st day of each month, from sunrise (V) to sunset. The amount of sunshine (III) is based on the cloudiness at a particular location, and this cannot be determined from a sun chart. Finally, degree days (IV) is a unit used to estimate the heating requirements of a building at a particular locality, and it too is unobtainable from a sun chart.

39. **C** The purpose of drainage systems is to collect, conduct, and dispose of excess rain water. Complex drainage systems are required when any of these three purposes cannot be accomplished in a natural way. Paving or grading the hillside might help collect and conduct water, but neither would dispose of the water. Therefore, one would be better off to provide a thick ground cover, which would slow down the rate of runoff. This would allow greater water absorption and percolation into the soil, as well as reduce erosion. Finally, an earth berm at the toe of the slope would do little more than dam or divert the surface flow, again without solving the problem of water disposal.

40. **A, B, C, D, and E**   Project overhead costs include all expenses attributable to a specific project that are not included in labor, materials, or equipment. These costs can vary considerably from one job to another, but they generally include all of the items listed. Project over-head costs normally amount to between 5 and 10 percent of the project construction cost.

41. **C**   In tracing the Maintenance column, we see a large number of 3's and 4's, indicating that Maintenance has either no relationship to or mandatory separation from every other element in the project, except the Dietary element. Since it has little relation to other project elements, one would have considerable flexibility in locating this element.

42. **D**   The answer may be read directly from the matrix, which shows a 2 where it intersects Med./Surg. Nursing Unit and 3's at the intersection of all other choices in this question. Since 2 represents a desirable relationship, these two elements must be located near one another.

43. **C**   The functional relationship between Labor and Delivery and Central Sterile Supply is noted on the matrix as 2, which is a desirable relationship. A quick review of the other Labor and Delivery relationships reveals only one other 2, and that is the Med./Surg. Nursing Unit.

44. **B**   With four 4's in the matrix, Nursery has more mandatory separations from other elements than the other choices listed. Therefore, we can assume it requires the greatest isolation.

45. **Area or square footage**   The final program, which is the result of the programming process, includes space requirements expressed as net usable floor area. It is the amount of space or area, therefore, which defines the client's needs and objectives. Dimensions, proportions, and configurations all deal with the shape of spaces, which is determined during the later design phases.

46. **A**   Both diagrams A and C represent acceptable patterns for growth; however the radial arrangement (C) is relatively inflexible and limited in scope. Therefore, the axial pattern (A) is the preferred arrangement for expansion. Both diagrams B and D represent traditionally poor approaches to enlarging a hospital. Extending existing wings (B) places new beds or patient services too far from existing ancillary facilities, and vertical growth (D) generally lacks adequate vertical circulation, in addition to creating noisy and complicated construction conditions.

47. **C**   Large housing projects devote much of their total cost to site work, such as grading, road construction, utility layouts, etc. Therefore, the most efficient organizational form would be a centralized or compact arrangement that would group these costly elements in the smallest possible area.

48. **A**   Suburban shopping malls are generally planned with *anchor tenants*, which are major department stores located at both ends of a shopping street. The street may be crossed by secondary paths perpendicular to the primary axis. Although this arrangement is similar to a linear pattern, axial patterns are distinguished by their orientation to fixed objects at the ends, while linear patterns are more open-ended.

49. **B**   The development of classical Rome was based on the gradual accumulation of self-contained building complexes. Each

served a distinct activity and interrelated with its neighbors. Thus, Rome achieved a rational order through a precinctual arrangement of separate, balanced components. Precinctual patterns allow growth in any direction and are generally flexible, compact, and efficient.

50. **D** The Administrator must circulate through the Waiting Area to reach the Conference Room, whereas the Director has the choice of passing though either the Waiting Area or his secretary's office to attend conferences. The receptionist, located within the Waiting Area, controls access to all spaces including the Conference Room. Therefore, answers A, B, and C are incorrect. The Conference Room is accessible through the Waiting Area, making it equally accessible to visitors and staff.

51. **C** Territoriality is the behavior by which an animal lays claim to an area and defends it against all others. People, too, behave in accordance with the concept of territoriality and defend what they consider to be their "place." In a large office, a secretarial cubicle would be considered a private, individual space, in contrast to the other choices, which are spaces that belong to many people. A mail clerk in the corporate conference room or a board chairman in the employees' lunchroom might feel "out of place," but for one secretary to sit at another secretary's desk could be considered an invasion of personal space.

52. **A, B, and C** Deed restrictions, zoning ordinances, and easements all represent legal restrictions that prescribe and enforce limitations on the use of property. Environmental impact statements (EIS), however, provide a basis for regulatory agencies to review a project's effect on the environment. Impact statements do not determine a project's approval; they are simply a means of studying a project's potential negative impact and possible alternatives.

53. **A** Schools, recreation centers, and fire stations all provide necessary and desirable services for residential neighborhoods. Although each of these generates a certain amount of traffic, noise, and air pollution, these negative effects are considerably less than those of a bus terminal.

54. **B** Most American cities were developed around the grid layout, which was as suitable for colonial settlers as it was for subsequent developers across the country. It originated as a practical method for the organization of urban land to facilitate new development, surveying, and recording of land parcels. Many early towns were developed in large square blocks, with the middle square devoted to a central "common" or village green, which remains the pattern of many American cities today.

55. **C** As originally conceived by planning theorist Kevin Lynch, edges are linear elements that form boundaries or separations for districts of a city. They separate neighborhoods, surround industrial areas, or define suburbs by means of streets, parks, rivers, shorelines, etc. When two districts are joined at an edge, they form a seam. Aside from edges and districts, other elements used to construct mental images are paths, landmarks, and nodes.

56. **A** To solve this problem one must know two facts: the meaning of FAR and the number of square feet in an acre. FAR (floor area ratio) is the ratio of the gross

floor area of a building to the ground area of its site. The ground area in this case is one acre, which is 43,560 square feet. The gross floor area = 3 floors × 14,520 square feet per floor = 43,560 square feet. The FAR is therefore 43,560 ÷ 43,560 = 1.

57. **B**   Although there are advantages in each of the choices, the most desirable location for an urban campus is where the student population has easy access. That is, in fact, the fundamental reason for locating a college campus in an urban area.

58. **A and B**   The amount of solar radiation received by a site is determined by its latitude (distance from the equator) and its slope. The closer the rays are to being perpendicular to the ground surface, the greater the amount of solar radiation. Wind patterns and longitude do not affect solar radiation.

59. **A**   A clue to the topographic profile can be found by proceeding from either end of the section line in order to determine whether the land rises or falls. Since the section cut line parallels the contours on the right, we know that the right side of the section must be represented by a level line, and therefore we can immediately rule out choices B and C. As we follow the section cut line from right to left, it is apparent that the land rises steadily. Thus, there is little doubt that section A is the correct topographic profile.

60. **D**   Under eminent domain, the owner is compelled to sell his property at an equitable price; however, if the parties cannot agree on a price, it is established by a court, not the renewal agency or the owner. The final price represents the fair market value of both the land and improvements. Sometimes, this price is

determined after the land is lawfully taken and the building razed.

61. **A**   Building orientation is determined largely by external influences, such as climate, noise, and views. Orientation plays a major role in sheltering outdoor spaces from strong winds, in shielding spaces from airborne noise sources, and in receiving solar energy. The building's foundation system, however, is unrelated to orientation on the site.

62. **D**   The existing slope of 5 in 20 translates to a 25 percent grade (5 ÷ 20 × 100 = 25%), which is far too steep for parking cars. Regrading the site is necessary, and the finish grade should not exceed 0.5 in 10, which represents a 5 percent grade. Paved driveways, however, may be as steep as 10 percent.

63. **A**   Organic soil, such as peat, is elastic, weak, and has little cohesion. For these reasons, it is normally removed and replaced in areas to be developed. Since loose silt may be compacted or, in some cases, used as is, a site with organic soil would be more costly to develop.

64. **D**   An architect is obliged to make a reasonable attempt to solve a client's problem. The fact that a site slopes and has some loose fill is not reason enough to reject the site. Sloping areas with loose fill may be leveled and used for outdoor play, or they may inspire a more imaginative plan.

65. **B**   Choice I would encourage automobile usage, and is therefore an incorrect choice. The other three choices would all help to reduce automobile usage to some extent. Monthly market-rate parking (II) would be partly effective since only building occupants (or occupants of other buildings nearby) would use the parking. III would

be most effective, although such a system is not in common use. IV is practical and in common use, but the incentive rates might be eliminated if the owner of the building were not making a sufficient profit, rendering its continued usage uncertain.

66. **D**   The grade of any slope can be determined by using the formula G = V/H and multiplying by 100 to convert it to a percentage. In this case, the vertical rise (V) is 65 – 61 = 4 feet. Dividing by the horizontal distance (H) of 8 feet, we have 4 ÷ 8 = .50 × 100 = 50 percent.

67. **B**   Symmetry is the arrangement of elements which are identical on both sides of a central axis. Over the centuries, symmetry has become closely associated with formality and authority, from an avenue of sphinxes in ancient Egypt to the Capitol in Washington, D.C.

68. **D**   A two-dimensional form is a plane, which has no thickness. Therefore, a plane cannot have mass or volume, which are qualities found in three-dimensional forms. Two-dimensional forms may have space, or two-dimensional area, but not the kind of space defined as three-dimensional volume.

69. **C**   Visual perception is the most obvious way to sense space; it converts perspective lines to distance and light and shade to form. However, spatial information may also be perceived through the smell of a space's activities, and the sound and echo within a space help define its dimensions. Although touch can reveal texture and possibly shape, it does not help to perceive space.

70. **C**   The Pyramid of Cheops at Gizeh is a perfectly regular geometric form that is harmonious, balanced, and symmetrical.

However, its predominant quality is one of repose, which gives the impression of stability, permanence, and immobility. It also has a strong quality of mass, appearing to be a large, solid volume.

71. **B**   One of the primary considerations in locating a facility that serves large numbers of people is accessibility by car or public transportation. It is not particularly important to be near pedestrian routes. Adjacency to an airport is also unimportant and may create acoustic problems. A site surrounded by water would be picturesque, but it would create problems in transporting spectators to the facility. Public transportation, however, is virtually mandatory if the center is to draw a sufficient number of people to make it economically viable.

72. **C**   The solution to this problem requires a number of sequential steps. First, the building site area is 100 × 180 = 18,000 square feet, and the open space is 80 × 100 = 8,000 square feet. Since the FAR (floor area ratio) is 3, the allowable floor area of the building is 3 × 18,000 = 54,000 square feet. To this total must be added the floor area bonus of 2 square feet for each of the 8,000 square feet of open space, or 16,000 square feet. Thus, 54,000 + 16,000 = 70,000 gross square feet of building. This figure is then divided by the buildable site area, which is 18,000 less 8,000 for the open space, or 10,000 square feet per floor. In conclusion, 70,000 ÷ 10,000 = 7 stories, which is the maximum that can be built.

73. **B**   If the project is developed without any open space, the buildable site area will be 18,000 square feet. With a FAR of 3, the maximum allowable floor area of the building will be 3 × 18,000 = 54,000 gross square feet. If this figure is multiplied

by the efficiency ratio of 70 percent, the maximum net area becomes 54,000 × .70 = 37,800 square feet.

74. **B** Poor drainage is indicated by a high water table (III), since relatively little water could seep into the ground before it would reach a point of saturation. A relatively flat site (IV) would also drain poorly, since the water would tend to pond, rather than flow. Finally, with no storm drainage system (V), all surface water would drain haphazardly, rather than be conducted effectively away from the site. The other two choices would actually indicate good drainage. Dense groundcover (I) would impede the water flow and allow the earth to absorb the moisture, and a flowing stream (II) would act as an efficient surface drainage system.

75. **A** As the elevation increases, the temperature decreases by about one degree for every 300 feet or so, because the thinner air of higher altitudes is unable to hold as much heat. Therefore, the mountain resort would always be cooler than a town located 3,000 feet below it.

76. **A, B, and C** According to ANSI A117.1, an accessible route is a continuous unobstructed path connecting all accessible elements of a building that can be negotiated by people having any type of physical, mental, or sensory disability (A, B, and C are correct). Accessible routes must be provided at both the exterior and interior of buildings (D is incorrect), and objects are permitted to protrude into such routes, depending on the height of the protruding object (E is incorrect).

77. **B** Scale is the relative measurement of an object using the human body as the measuring device. When an element does not conform to its expected size, such as the door height in this case, we say the door is out of scale, unless of course the doorway is not intended for the use of normal adults. Nevertheless, we have no reason to believe the structure is poorly proportioned, or lacks balance or harmony.

78. **A** The location of a shopping center depends on many factors, some of which are not revealed by the map shown. For example, one should know something about population distribution, economic level and buying power of nearby residents, location of competing centers, traditional routes of travel, etc. Therefore, our decision must based only on the following criteria: shopping centers should be located along major arteries but accessible from more than one direction. They should be easily visible from main lines of travel, but located some distance from the congestion of freeway ramps or busy intersections. The area to be developed should be ample in size and fairly level in topography. Finally, shopping centers should provide easy service access, sufficient public parking, and ideally, be tied into a system of public transportation. In consideration of the above, the best location would be at point 4. Point 7 fails in two major respects. First, it is too close to a major intersection and would therefore create additional congestion; and second, it is hidden from the view of eastbound freeway traffic because of the intervening trees. Point 8 is too distant from the highway as well as freeway access, and the land slopes more than at the preferred point 4. Point 6 is desirable in several respects. Its major disadvantage is its distance from the freeway and freeway ramps.

79. D The prevailing wind blows from west to east. In addition, one should be aware that air movement is strongly affected by topography. Wind speeds at the crest of a ridge are greater than those on the flat, while wind is generally weaker on the lee side than on the weather side of a hill. Thick belts of trees also affect air movement by diverting winds and reducing velocities. With these criteria in mind, it appears that point 3 will be the windiest spot on the map. Point 1 runs a close second, but it would not be as windy since it lies just below the crest. Point 5 lies in a somewhat protected area and would probably be the least windy area, while point 9 falls in an open, exposed area and would therefore be neither more nor less windy than average.

80. C In northern latitudes, the coldest areas are generally found on unprotected north-facing slopes, such as point 1 on our map. Both points 2 and 3 are located just off the ridge on a slight, south-facing slope. These two points will actually be warmer than average because of their orientation. In addition, point 2 is well protected from the wind by a clump of trees. Point 4 will probably be a cold spot, but not as cold as point 1, because cold air flows down open slopes at night and tends to gather at low elevations. During the day, however, the ground is warmed and the cold air dissipates. It should also be noted that both points 1 and 4 are completely exposed to the prevailing winds. This, too, creates a much colder condition.

81. C All of the urban discomforts listed can be controlled to some degree, with the exception of air pollution, which is beyond the control of a designer. Traffic noises can be blocked by solid barriers or masked by running water or recorded music; breezes, as well, can be diverted by solid fences or landscaping; and solar radiation can be controlled with overhangs, trees, or patio umbrellas.

82. A In an area with relatively moderate weather throughout the year, one may conclude that air conditioning, while appealing, would not be necessary for human comfort. None of the other choices can be inferred from the information given.

83. D Compact, multistoried, and earth-sheltered building forms are desirable where extremes of temperature or long periods of inclement weather prevail. For the benign conditions described, a relatively open plan form would be most appropriate.

84. D To begin with, Modulor, a system of proportions, has nothing to do with modular, which refers to standardization. Le Corbusier's Modulor was a measuring system based upon the Golden Section and related to the human figure. The initial dimension was 7 feet 5 inches, which represented the height of a 6-foot-tall man with his hand raised. According to Le Corbusier, the 6-foot height represented the ideal man. The Modulor system was designed to replace meter and foot dimensions. In addition, the standardized proportions increased geometrically, rather than arithmetically.

85. A In questions such as this, one must not confuse percentage of slope with degree of slope. For example, a 10 percent slope, which means a vertical rise of 1 foot for a horizontal length of 10 feet, corresponds to a slope of about 6 degrees. With that in mind, the following grades are generally accepted standards. Storm drains slope between 0.3 percent and 1 percent, pedestrian walks should not exceed a slope of 10 percent or up to 15 percent for very short ramps, and planted banks should not exceed a slope of 50 percent. The maximum slope of unretained earth cuts varies from 50 percent to 100 percent, depending on the type of soil. Finally, drainage ditches vary in slope from a minimum of 2 percent to a maximum of 10 percent.

86. **D** The microclimate of an area is affected by its ability to absorb radiant energy. A planted area will absorb and store the heat it receives during the day and release this same heat when the temperature drops. Structures and paving, on the other hand, produce extremes of heat and cold in direct relation to the sun during the day and the cold at night. The planted area, therefore, tends to stabilize the microclimate. Plants also increase the area for transpiration, thereby making it more likely that rainfall will increase, not decrease. Both plants and structures affect air movement, and in this respect, there is little difference between the two. Although plants may purify the air around them, the small amounts of smoke and dust that they trap are relatively insignificant.

87. **A** All of the factors mentioned are important in planning a facility that not only uses a considerable area of land, but will probably occupy that land forever. However, the prime consideration is the location of the land. Most people prefer not to be reminded of death, which is reflected in a disinclination to live or even work in the vicinity of a cemetery. Cemeteries have been planned in conjunction with parks, recreational facilities, and even airports. Suitability of terrain and proximity to major highways are important considerations,

but the location of the land is of greater significance.

88. **B** Increased vehicular speed tends to compress the experiences encountered on a road. Therefore, more time and distance are required to make driving judgments, and the minimum radii of road curves must be increased. For the same reason, forward sight distance and expressway ramp lengths should also be increased, not decreased. With regard to road grades, as vehicular speed is increased, the grade of the road should be decreased to maintain the same speed.

89. **C** All of the actions described are in the domain of public planning policy, and all contribute to the health of a socially diverse metropolitan area.

90. **D** In a cluster development, the dwelling units are densely grouped, allowing the remaining land to be developed as common open space for the benefit of the development residents. Site development costs are reduced, because there is less length of utility lines and paved streets. Although the density of the land on which the units are built is high, the overall density is about the same as in a conventional development.

91. **3.0 acres** To solve this problem, one must know the number of square feet to allow per car for parking areas, as well as the number of square feet in an acre. Using the usual estimate of 400 square feet per car, the total area required is 400 × 325 = 130,000 square feet. If this total is divided by the number of square feet in an acre (43,560), the result is 130,000 ÷ 43,560 = 2.98.

92. **B** The ANSI handicapped standards for ramps clearly define the requirements for new construction. For example, ramp

I conforms to these requirements, since it has the minimum required width of 3 feet and an acceptable slope of 1:12. Furthermore, since its rise does not exceed six inches and its run does not exceed 72 inches, it does not require handrails. Ramp II also conforms, since a ramp according to the ANSI definition has a slope exceeding 1:20. Since the slope of ramp II is 1:30, it is technically not a ramp, and therefore, does not need handrails. Finally, ramp III conforms to the ANSI standards in every way except its maximum slope. The slope shown is 1:10 (18 ÷ 180), while the maximum permissible slope is 1:12. Therefore, the correct conforming ramps are I and II, as noted in correct answer B.

93. **A**   Noise pollution is a fact of life in every major city, and its control continues to be a source of concern. Each of the choices listed would help reduce the effects of urban noise to some extent. The most effective of these, however, is to increase the distance between the noise source and receiver, since sound decreases as the square of the distance from a point source. Plant material helps to disperse sound, and moving water masks sound. Finally, even if it were possible to eliminate private cars (which is unlikely), there would still be noise from buses, trucks, and other vehicles.

94. **A**   Air movement is only one factor that determines the degree of comfort. Other factors are temperature, humidity, and radiation. At an average temperature of 75 degrees with about 30 percent relative humidity, air moving at 100 fpm is quite pleasant. At less than 50 fpm, air is generally unnoticeable; while at 250 fpm or more, breezes can be drafty and annoying.

95. **B**   The shading device shown offers effective protection from low sun angles, where it is important to place an obstruction between the sun and glass. This protection is most effective on the east and west, but not as useful on a south elevation, where the sun is at its highest angle. Although the device shown would permit sun control and air circulation, it would certainly not be the maximum amount possible. Nor would it provide the optimum view, unless it were located several stories high and the predominant view were downward.

96. **C**   As a remedy to the pollution, congestion, and unhealthful conditions accompanying the industrial revolution, most planning theorists advocated smaller and less dense residential developments. The exception was Le Corbusier, whose proposals embraced high-density residential towers surrounded by large areas of open green space, as in his Voisin Plan for Paris and Ville Radieuse.

97. **Paris**   In an effort to facilitate urban circulation and create more open space, Baron Haussmann created a bold plan during the mid-19th century. Haussmann's plan resulted in many broad, tree-lined boulevards, spacious gardens, and classic vistas that distinguish Paris today.

98. **C**   Clarence Stein and Henry Wright created the new community of Radburn, New Jersey. Their aim was to organize a town into cohesive neighborhoods in which pedestrian and vehicular traffic were completely separated. The super-block concept consisted of dwellings arranged in an island of green surrounded by roads and parking. Radburn became enormously influential, bringing distinction to both the community and the designers.

99. D The comparison method can only be used when there is sufficient data about comparable land being offered for sale, which is not the case in this question. The residual method is used in highly developed areas where no vacant land remains. The allocation method is used to determine the land value of existing improved property, and finally, the development method depends solely on estimated development costs and is appropriately used when sales prices of similar parcels are unavailable, as is the case in our problem.

100. A Setbacks, which are regulated by zoning ordinances, are prescribed to insure adequate light, air, and privacy, and to reduce the hazards of fire and vehicular traffic. Setbacks are generally stated as fixed measurements or as relationships, as described in correct choices I, II, and IV. Measurements are never calculated from sidewalks, since one is never certain how the sidewalk relates to the property boundary, and lot widths have no relationship at all to front yard setbacks.

101. C I is not correct. Communities that are only residential are not encouraged. Mixed-use development (combining housing, retail, open space, and commercial) is a preferred sustainable design.

II is not correct. Open space should not be designed only for recreation and wildlife habitat. Additional uses such as environmental education, storm water retention, flood control, wetlands drainage, etc., should be considered in sustainable planning.

III is correct. The Ahwahnee Principles encourage a wide range of interconnected transportation to encourage many options for travel.

IV is also correct. Development that permits opportunities for a diverse number of jobs is a key goal of the Ahwahnee Principles.

INDEX

A

Activity center, 29–30

Adaptive aspects, 12

Aerial survey, 159

Aesthetics, 167, 278, 279

Affirmative covenants, 200

Air pollution, 134

Air right, 200

Air rights, 182

Albedo, 130

Allocation method, 156

American colonial planning, 90

American standard of living, 92

Anthropomorphic design, 71, 85

Applying for the test, 293

Approval of plans, 225

Architectural design, 3, 83

Architectural design considerations, 5–9

Autumnal equinox, 128

Axial pattern, 15

B

Balance, 79

Bar graphs, 233

Baroque town planning, 90

Beauty, 83

Behavioral interests, 12

Bench mark, 304

Bidding or negotiation, 224

Biological considerations, 110

Budgeting, 239, 246

Building codes, 200, 204

Building envelope, 309–310

Building permit, 226

C

Caryatid, 71

Catchment areas, 153

Churches, 58–59

Circular land pattern, 87

Circulation aspects, 12

City survey, 159

Classrooms, space needs, 34–35

Client review and approval, 225

Climate, 16, 18, 125–127, 129, 133–134, 137, 160

Cluster developments, 102

Cluster form, 96

Code compliance, 201, 276

Code requirements, other, 210

Color, 75, 80

Combination standpipes, 208

Comfort zone, 133

Community shopping center, 38

Comparison method, 155

Component building, 29

Concentric zone pattern, 94

Condemnation, 182

Conditional covenant, 200

Conditional use, 190–191

Condominium, 177

Conductivity, 130

Constellation, 98

Construction administration, 224

Construction cost escalation, 257

Construction documents, 224

Construction manager (CM), 282

Construction overhead and profit, 255, 257

Construction scheduling, 228, 235

Construction survey, 157, 159